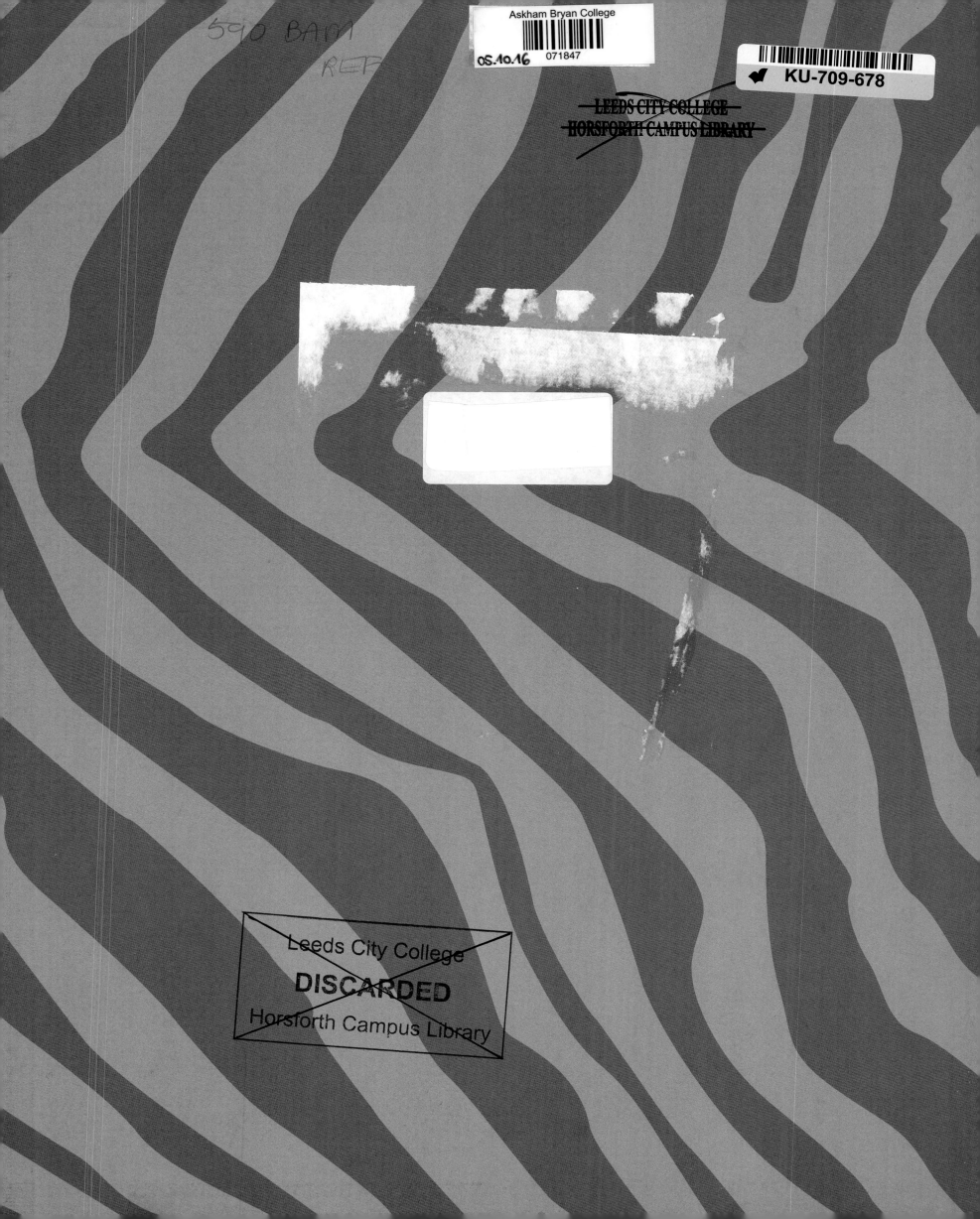

590 BAM
REF

Askham Bryan College
05.10.16   071847

KU-709-678

~~LEEDS CITY COLLEGE~~
~~HORSFORTH CAMPUS LIBRARY~~

Leeds City College
DISCARDED
Horsforth Campus Library

the illustrated
ATLAS OF
WILDLIFE

ASKHAM BRYAN
COLLEGE
LEARNING RESOURCES

LEEDS CITY COLLEGE
HORSFORTH CAMPUS LIBRARY

the illustrated
ATLAS OF WILDLIFE

WELDON OWEN

Conceived and produced by Weldon Owen Pty Ltd
59–61 Victoria Street, McMahons Point
Sydney NSW 2060, Australia
Copyright © 2009 Weldon Owen Pty Ltd

BONNIER PUBLISHING LIMITED
Group Publisher John Owen

WELDON OWEN PTY LTD
Chief Executive Officer Sheena Coupe
Creative Director Sue Burk
Art Manager Trucie Henderson
Senior Vice President, International Sales Stuart Laurence
Vice President Sales: United States and Canada Amy Kaneko
Vice President Sales: Asia and Latin America Dawn Low
Administration Manager, International Sales Kristine Ravn
Publishing Coordinator Gina Belle

Managing Editor Jennifer Taylor
Project Editors Jenni Bruce, Averil Moffat
Copy Editor Amanda Burdon
Editorial Assistant Hunnah Jessup
Designers Michelle Cutler, Gabrielle Green
Jacket Designer Michelle Cutler
Picture Research Joanna Collard
Cartographers Will Pringle, Laurie Whiddon/Map Illustrations
Illustrators The Art Agency: Robin Carter, Dan Cole, Fiammetta
Dogi, Mike Donnelly, Sandra Doyle, Jane Durston, Brin Edwards,
Ian Jackson, Stuart Jackson-Carter, Sandra Pond, Myke Taylor;
Peter Bull Art Studio; Bob Hynes; David Kirshner; Iain McKellar;
James McKinnon; Edwina Riddell; Guy Troughton
Information Graphics Andrew Davies/Creative Communication
Index Jo Rudd

Production Manager Todd Rechner
Production Coordinators Lisa Conway, Mike Crowton

All rights reserved. No part of this publication may be reproduced,
stored in a retrieval system or transmitted in any form or by any
means, electronic, mechanical, photocopying, recording, or otherwise,
without the permission of the copyright holder and publisher.

ISBN 13: 978-1-921530-00-5

10 9 8 7 6 5 4 3 2 1

Colour reproduction by Chroma Graphics (Overseas) Pte Ltd
Printed by Tien Wah Press
Manufactured in Singapore

A WELDON OWEN PRODUCTION

Authors and Consultants

Dr. Channa Bambaradeniya
Coordinator of the Asia Regional Species
 and Biodiversity Program
International Union for Conservation of Nature
Sri Lanka

Cinthya Flores
International Communications Consultant and Journalist
Former Communications Officer of WWF Central America
Costa Rica

Dr. Joshua Ginsberg
Vice President for Global Programs
Wildlife Conservation Society
Washington DC, USA

Dwight Holing
Natural History and Environmental Author
Orinda CA, USA

Dr. Susan Lumpkin
Research Associate
Smithsonian Institution's National Zoological Park
Washington DC, USA

George McKay
Consultant in Conservation Biology
Chair, NSW National Parks and Wildlife Advisory Council
Sydney NSW, Australia

Dr. John Musick
Marshall Acuff Professor Emeritus in Marine Science
Virginia Institute of Marine Science
College of William and Mary
Virginia, USA

Dr. Patrick Quilty
Honorary Research Professor
School of Earth Sciences
University of Tasmania, Australia

Dr. Bernard Stonehouse
Emeritus Associate
Scott Polar Research Institute
University of Cambridge, UK

Dr. Eric J Woehler
Honorary Research Associate
School of Zoology
University of Tasmania, Australia

Dr. David Woodruff
Professor of Biological Sciences
Ecology, Behavior and Evolution Section
Division of Biological Sciences
University of California, San Diego, USA

ASKHAM BRYAN
COLLEGE
LEARNING RESOURCES

The distinctive humphead wrasse is a common inhabitant of coral reefs but is also found in cooler waters. Easily recognized by the prominent bulge on its head, it is among the largest reef fish.

Red-spotted purple butterfly (below)
The red-spotted purple butterfly is common in the eastern United States on aspen and poplar trees. It avoids predation by birds by mimicking the pipevine swallowtail, which is poisonous.

Burchell's sandgrouse (above)
A Burchell's sandgrouse takes flight from a waterhole after drinking and soaking its belly feathers. This desert-dwelling bird flies long distances, returning with water held in its feathers for its chicks to "drink."

Ring-tailed lemur (left)
Ring-tailed lemurs, natives of Madagascar, spend much of their time on the ground, but early in the day they are likely to be found in the treetops, warming themselves in the sun.

Bobcat (far left)
The secretive, solitary bobcat, an inhabitant of eastern forests in the United States, is an efficient hunter. It remains out of sight by day but seeks its prey—cottontail rabbits and small rodents—at night.

FOREWORD

What always surprises me is not the richness of the world's biological heritage, but just how little we know about it. In recent years we have sequenced the human genome, rapidly advanced our understanding of atomic structure, and continued to explore and advance our understanding of the universe. In contrast, our best estimates suggest that there are 10 to 50 million species on Earth. Whatever the error in this number, we have only described 1.5 million species, at best 10 percent of the world's diversity. Our understanding of ecological communities is, at best, rudimentary.

Study of biodiversity is, increasingly, a time limited endeavor. Humans are growing in number and in their individual demands for resources. Habitats such as the Amazon, Borneo, and the Congo forests, once thought to be vast, wild, and infinitely resilient, are either highly fragmented and degraded, or under increasing threat from conversion. Some ecosystems, such as the North American sagebrush and grasslands, are represented by a small percentage of their original extent. Europe, dominated by humans for thousands of years, still harbors a remarkable diversity of wildlife, but many species are confined to small islands of their former range, a pattern likely soon to be seen globally. Australia and Oceania have some of the most unusual and unique biological diversity on Earth, but the islands and reefs of the Pacific, initially threatened by habitat conversion, pollution, and a phalanx of introduced species, now face the new threats of climate change, warming oceans, and rising seas. It is not surprising that island species show the highest rate of extinction across all taxa.

However, conservation efforts, while always an uphill battle, show that we can reverse some of the threats to the world's biological heritage, and mitigate others. While recent data suggest that perhaps 50 percent of the world's primates are threatened with extinction, a recent discovery of 125,000 western lowland gorillas by staff and colleagues of the Wildlife Conservation Society expanded the options for conservation of this species. The discovery may lead to new protected areas in northern Congo that will aid the conservation of not just gorillas, but dozens of primates, and thousands of species. In the last two decades, the proportion of Earth's surface under formal protection has continued to expand, and efforts now focus on extending protection of coastal and high seas. And because protected areas, while necessary, are not sufficient, new conservation initiatives work with industry, local and indigenous communities, and private landowners to expand conservation beyond park boundaries, to ensure connectivity and freedom for animals to roam.

The Illustrated Atlas of Wildlife helps us better understand both the diversity of life, and the threats that face wildlife and wildlands around the world. In a day and age where seemingly limitless information is on the web, why buy a book? For many of us, the physical act of holding a book, especially one this beautiful and well designed, will never be replaced by a web page and laptop. More importantly, this book is written by experts in their fields and the quality and accuracy of information is remarkable, drawing not just on information widely available, but on some of the most recent scientific research and unpublished studies that are not yet "popular" and hence not yet online. Finally, this book allows you to learn about the ecoregional structure of the entire world, and of the wildlife that inhabits these diverse environments. Hold it in your hands, and enjoy your global tour.

Joshua Ginsberg
Vice President, Global Conservation, Wildlife Conservation Society

HOW TO USE THIS ATLAS

This atlas is arranged in three main sections. The first, "Living Earth," provides an overview of how and where natural life occurs on Earth, including pages devoted to different kinds of habitats, the relationship between animals and their environment, and the impact of one animal species on another. The second section, which is the core of the book, is a chapter-by-chapter survey of the world's main continents and oceans, and the animal life they support. The third, reference, section consists of a detailed factfile on the animals presented in the book, a glossary, and an index.

Wildlife regions of the world
Each continent is divided into key wildlife regions. A double page is dedicated to a survey of the habitats and resident animal life found in each region, accompanied by an introductory overview and a locator and regional map.

Regional map
Regional maps are shaded to show the area within the continent that is being described for its animal life.

Conservation watch
At-risk animals are described under this heading. Symbols flag species that are either critically endangered or endangered.

Lavish photographs
Taken by leading wildlife photographers, these portray the habits and habitats of different species.

Feature box
Special-interest subjects are shown in a feature box, with their own introduction and selected photographs or illustrations.

Locator
These small maps locate the region within its continent.

Climate chart
Accompanying each map is a climate chart, showing average temperature and rainfall in the region.

Stunning illustrations
Individual species are beautifully illustrated. Habitat scenes show animals in context with each other and their surrounds.

Main map
Geographical and political maps of the continent show borders, topography, and key physical features.

Introduction
Each chapter opens with an overview of the featured continent and its natural life.

Regional overview
Each region covered in the chapter is identified with a map and a captioned wildlife photograph.

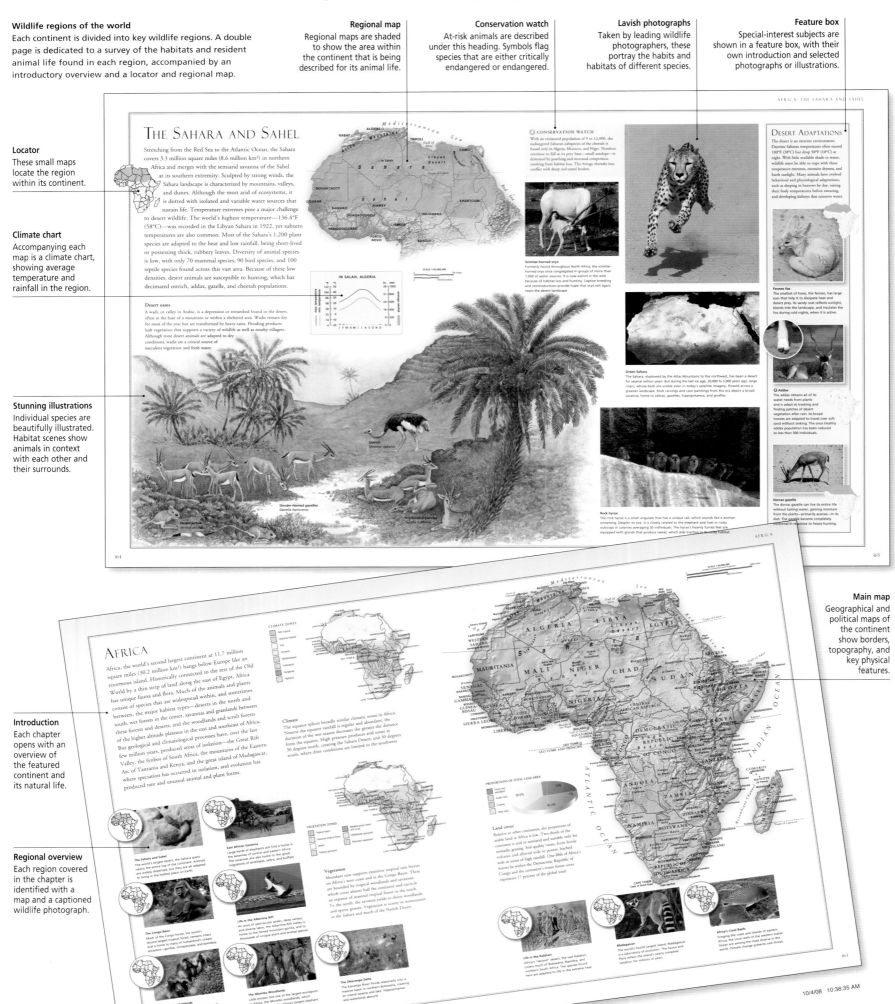

10/4/08 10:38:35 AM

Living Earth

Introductory pages provide an overview of a range of wildlife subjects, including the origins and ecology of animals, the variety of Earth's habitats—from polar to desert and forest to sea—the threats facing many wildlife species, ecological balance, and conservation measures for endangered animals.

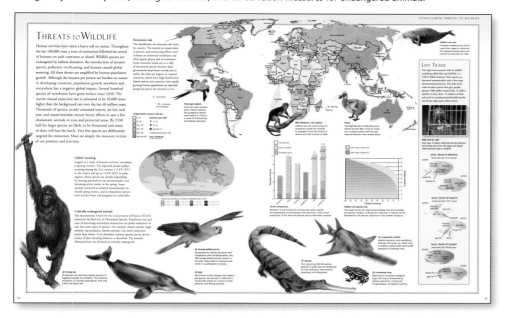

Special Subject

Throughout the chapters special-interest pages take a closer look at a particular animal, or group of animals. In the example below the cockatoos and parrots of Australia are displayed to show their variety and color, as well as the differences between them in nesting and feeding.

Animal Factfile

This detailed factfile profiles the common and scientific name, distribution, habitat, size, weight, diet, and conservation status of each captioned species in the atlas. The factfile is arranged by class and includes maps that show each order's global range. Refer to the index for a quick link to entries in the factfile.

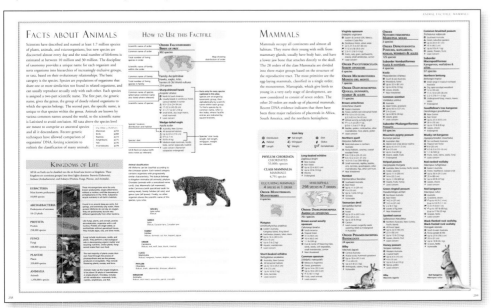

VISUAL KEYS

Map legend

The maps in this atlas contain a variety of labels, symbols, and other graphic devices to provide detailed information such as altitude and ocean floor topography, and the location of mountains, rivers, cities, and country borders.

TOPOGRAPHY

ELEVATION

Feet	Meters
6562	2000
4921	1500
3281	1000
2461	750
1640	500
1312	400
984	300
656	200
328	100
0	0

Ice cap

Ice shelf

PHYSICAL FEATURES

- *Lake*
- ~~ *Major river*
- —— International border
- —— State/territory border (Australia, Canada, U.S.A.)
- ▲ Mountain peak/volcano *Height, feet (meters)*
- + *Pole*
- △ *Geomagnetic Pole*
- ▲ Seamount
- ▼ Sea trench *Depth, feet (meters)*

CAPITAL CITIES OR TOWNS

- ○ **CAPITAL CITY**
- ○ **Major city or town**

Conservation icons

The conservation status of endangered and critically endangered animals, as determined by the IUCN Red List of Threated Species, is indicated by a red or yellow icon.

- 🔴 Critically endangered
- 🟡 Endangered

Charts, tables, and graphs

Additional details about regions, or the animal life found there, is provided in the form of tables, charts, or graphs. This at-a-glance information adds to captions and photographs.

LEOPARD SEAL DIET

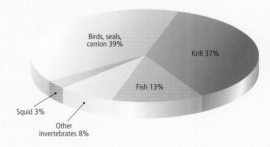

- Birds, seals, carrion 39%
- Krill 37%
- Fish 13%
- Squid 3%
- Other invertebrates 8%

THE FACTS	
Area	More than 1.3 million sq miles (+3.4 million km²)
Number of countries	6
Length of Congo River	2,900 miles (4,700 km)
Habitat	Rain forest, woodland, swamp, savanna, freshwater
Estimate of mammal species	More than 400
Estimate of fish species	More than 700
Estimate of bird species	More than 1,000

Range maps

Individual range maps accompanying some captions show the current (and former) range of selected species.

Each year at the end of the rainy season, millions of zebra, gazelles, and wildebeest migrate to Kenya from the grassy plains of the Serengeti National Park, Tanzania. In one of Earth's most impressive migrations, masses of wildebeest cross the Mara River into the Masai-Mara Reserve, Kenya—many drown in the crush to cross.

LIVING EARTH

LIVING EARTH

Life as we know it occurs only on Earth, where it assumes a fascinating diversity of forms. Of the millions of animal species, humans are the only one to appreciate the role of living organisms in creating a habitable planet. Without life, without plants and microorganisms releasing oxygen into the atmosphere, our planet would be a very different and inhospitable place. The world's wildlife depends on plants and phytoplankton and the billions of little things—bacteria, single-celled protists, and decomposing fungi—that make the biosphere work. Animal species are broadly distributed into eight biogeographic realms. Although many species are shared between realms, a good naturalist, blindfolded and put down anywhere on Earth, could quickly work out the location by observing the local assemblage of animals.

The effect of life

The Gaia hypothesis proposes that all life, working together as a superorganism, maintains the planet's atmosphere and temperature.

CONDITION	WITHOUT LIFE	WITH LIFE
Carbon dioxide	98%	0.03%
Nitrogen	1.9%	78%
Oxygen	Trace	21%
Temperature	419°F (215°C)	59°F (15°C)

SPECIES TALLY

Individual organisms are grouped into populations of interbreeding or genetically similar individuals called species. The total number of living species is estimated to be between 10 million and 30 million, with most of these being microscopic lifeforms. Vertebrates amount to only 5 percent of all known animal species. There are at least twice as many species of fungi and six times as many species of plants.

Estimated number of animal species 10 million

Known animal species 1.3 million (13%)

Invertebrates 95%

Vertebrates 5%

Fish 48%

Amphibians 9%

Mammals 9%

Reptiles 15%

Birds 19%

Animal groups

At least 30 animal groups and about 1.3 million living animal species are known. The vast majority are invertebrates and include marine sponges, flatworms, corals, segmented worms, mollusks, sea stars, and arthropods such as crustaceans, spiders, and insects. The vertebrates are a minority group that share 400 million years of evolutionary history. These conspicuous consumers of plants and microorganisms dominate most habitats.

Mammals

The giraffe is one of about 4,800 living mammal species, all of which have milk glands. Mammals comprise a few egg-laying monotremes, 298 pouched marsupials, and diverse placentals, including 291 species of primates.

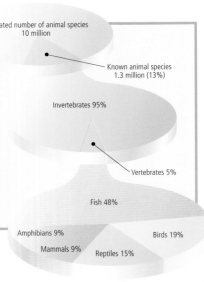

Biogeographic realms

Recognizable clusters of species characterize the eight biogeographic realms and tell us much about the geological history of continents and islands and the evolutionary history of different groups of animals. Life in the oceans is less clearly partitioned because of the homogenizing effects of global currents and the ancient connections of the ocean basins, but there are clear regional differences in the nutrient-based richness of coastal faunas.

Nearctic Realm
The species of the Nearctic and Palearctic are so alike that they form a super-realm, the Holarctic. Bald eagles typify North America but related eagles occur in the Palearctic.

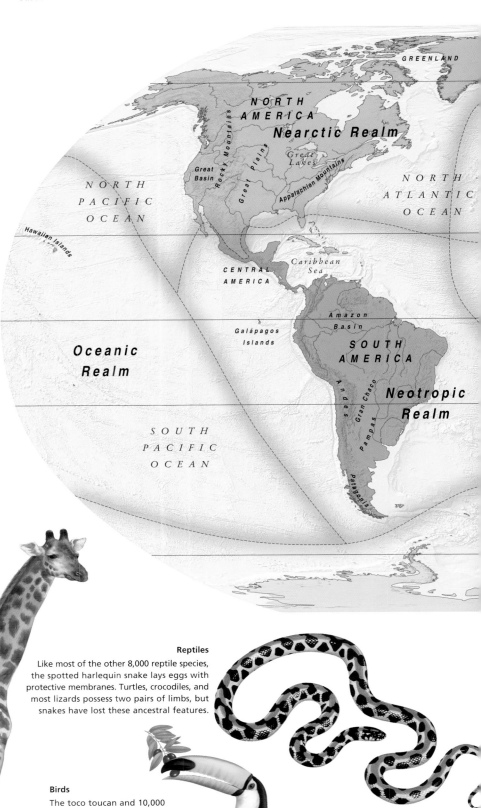

GREENLAND

NORTH AMERICA
Nearctic Realm

Rocky Mountains
Great Plains
Great Lakes
Appalachian Mountains

Great Basin

NORTH PACIFIC OCEAN

NORTH ATLANTIC OCEAN

Hawaiian Islands

CENTRAL AMERICA

Caribbean Sea

Galápagos Islands

Amazon Basin

Oceanic Realm

SOUTH AMERICA

Andes
Gran Chaco
Pampas
Patagonia

Neotropic Realm

SOUTH PACIFIC OCEAN

Reptiles

Like most of the other 8,000 reptile species, the spotted harlequin snake lays eggs with protective membranes. Turtles, crocodiles, and most lizards possess two pairs of limbs, but snakes have lost these ancestral features.

Birds

The toco toucan and 10,000 other species of living birds share ancestry with the dinosaurs. Defined by their feathered forelimbs (wings), most are superbly adapted for flight.

Palearctic Realm

The Palearctic includes Eurasia and northern Africa. Now hunted to near extinction, wild goats such as the alpine ibex once ranged from Spain to the Himalayas.

Neotropic Realm

Encompassing Central and South America, the Neotropic Realm includes more tropical rain forest than any other realm. The rich fauna includes the vivid blue poison-dart frog.

Afrotropic Realm

The Afrotropic covers all of sub-Saharan Africa and is almost entirely tropical. Its distinctive wildlife includes lions, elephants, giraffes, and baboons and other primates.

Indomalay Realm

Extending across most of South and Southeast Asia, the Indomalay contains forests that still harbor a few hundred tigers. Habitat loss and hunting have devastated tiger numbers.

Australasian Realm

This realm comprises Australia, New Zealand, New Guinea, and part of Indonesia. On isolated Australia marsupials such as kangaroos filled niches occupied by placental mammals elsewhere.

Oceanic Realm

Islands colonized by species that could swim, float, or fly make up the Oceanic Realm. In the absence of competitors, colonists evolved into unique species such as the Fiji banded iguana.

Antarctic Realm

Comprising Antarctica and some southern islands, this realm presents great challenges to wildlife. The emperor penguin is one of the few species that survives on the ice cap.

SCALE 1:108,000,000
Robinson Projection

Ray-finned fish

Yellowtail scad are among the 25,000 species of ray-finned fish. Found in both freshwater and marine habitats, ray-finned fish share their ancestry and bony skeletons with lobe-finned fish such as lungfish.

Amphibians

The 5,500 living amphibian species include frogs, legless burrowing caecilians, and salamanders such as this European fire salamander. Most depend on water for the embryonic and larval phases of life.

Cartilaginous fish

The skeletons of sharks and rays are primarily cartilage. The 960 species include carnivores such as this long-tailed thresher shark, and enormous plankton feeders such as the whale shark.

Invertebrates

Beetles, such as this seven-spotted ladybug, comprise more than 370,000 of the 1 million known species of insects and are the most species-rich animal group.

EVOLUTION

Evolution is life's little secret: a suite of processes that enable populations to change over time. Without the ability to evolve, no species could survive Earth's constant environmental changes. The fundamental process, natural selection, ensures that the individuals best adapted to their environment survive and pass on their genes to the next generation. Other processes, such as mutations and sexual reproduction, ensure the creation of the new genetic variation upon which evolution works. Animal evolution over the past 600 million years is a story of adaptation leading to solutions to life's challenges, played out in an ever-changing ecological theater. Occasional catastrophic change can eliminate even the most apparently successful species. Today's animal species, including our own, are here as much by sheer luck as by adaptive success. Time, process, and chance are responsible for the incredible diversity of species alive today and all their amazing fossil ancestors.

Continental drift

The slow movement of Earth's surface plates has reconfigured its continents and islands over time, a process known as continental drift. About 200 million years ago, the supercontinent Pangaea started splitting into the northern Laurasia and southern Gondwana landmasses. By 90 million years ago, these, in turn, had begun separating into today's continents. The continents continue to slowly change their positions.

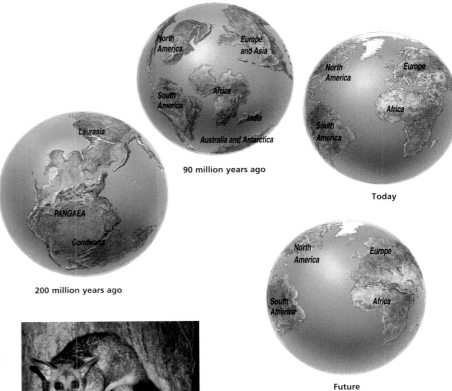

90 million years ago

Today

200 million years ago

Future

African vulture
The lappet-faced and other African vultures share looks and behavior with American vultures, but they are unrelated. African vultures are related to eagles.

American vulture
The turkey vulture is an American scavenger related to storks. Although unrelated to African vultures, it developed similar adaptations, a process called convergent evolution.

Parallel evolution
The brushtail possum of Australia (above left) and the common opossum of South America (left) are both marsupials. Once globally distributed, marsupials were replaced by placental mammals in most places. They survived only on the two southern landmasses of Australia and South America, where they became isolated by continental drift and evolved separately for more than 65 million years.

Rate of extinction

Extinctions are not distributed evenly through time. In the past 450 million years, there were at least five mass extinction events, when more than 50 percent of animal species and a high proportion of genera died out. Each event had different causes. The ongoing biodiversity crisis may soon qualify as the sixth mass extinction.

KEY
mya Million years ago
● Mass extinction

444 mya
Ordovician extinction
The possible causes of this mass extinction include prolonged global glaciation and irradiation from an exploding star.

359 mya
Devonian extinction
A long series of smaller extinctions destroyed 70 percent of all species.

251 mya
Permian extinction
The "great dying" of 96 percent of marine species followed global warming caused by volcanism and changes in ocean chemistry.

208 mya
Triassic extinction
About 20 percent of marine families and the last large amphibians vanished at this time.

Early mass extinctions

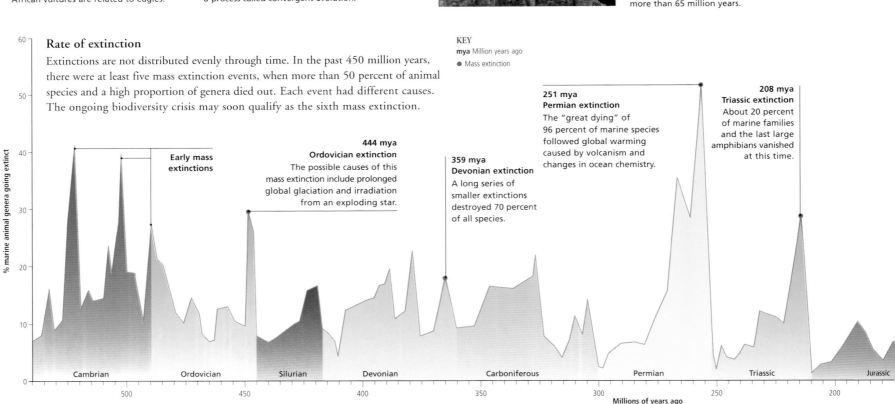

% marine animal genera going extinct

Cambrian | Ordovician | Silurian | Devonian | Carboniferous | Permian | Triassic | Jurassic

500 | 450 | 400 | 350 | 300 | 250 | 200

Millions of years ago

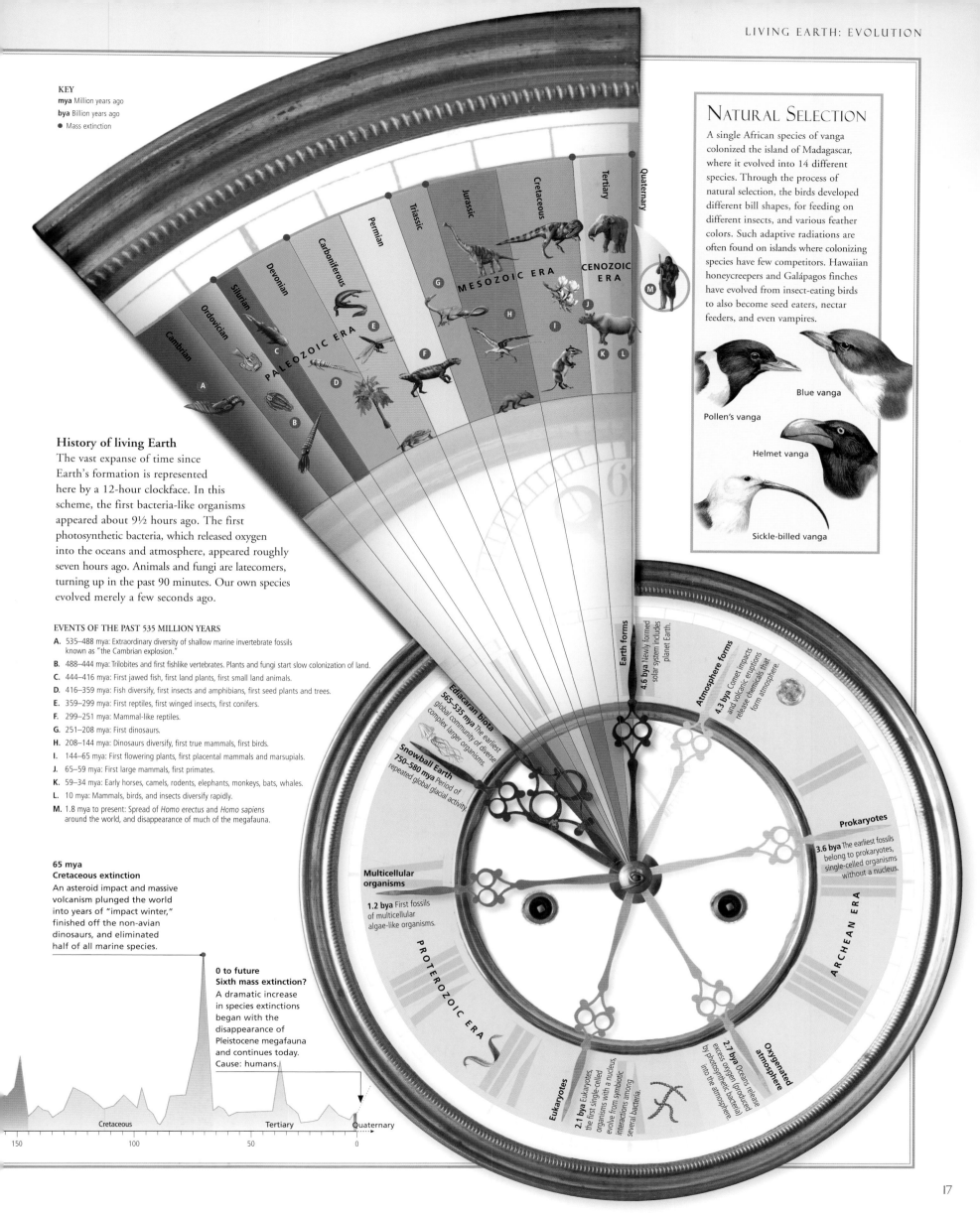

KEY
mya Million years ago
bya Billion years ago
● Mass extinction

NATURAL SELECTION

A single African species of vanga colonized the island of Madagascar, where it evolved into 14 different species. Through the process of natural selection, the birds developed different bill shapes, for feeding on different insects, and various feather colors. Such adaptive radiations are often found on islands where colonizing species have few competitors. Hawaiian honeycreepers and Galápagos finches have evolved from insect-eating birds to also become seed eaters, nectar feeders, and even vampires.

Blue vanga

Pollen's vanga

Helmet vanga

Sickle-billed vanga

History of living Earth

The vast expanse of time since Earth's formation is represented here by a 12-hour clockface. In this scheme, the first bacteria-like organisms appeared about 9½ hours ago. The first photosynthetic bacteria, which released oxygen into the oceans and atmosphere, appeared roughly seven hours ago. Animals and fungi are latecomers, turning up in the past 90 minutes. Our own species evolved merely a few seconds ago.

EVENTS OF THE PAST 535 MILLION YEARS

A. 535–488 mya: Extraordinary diversity of shallow marine invertebrate fossils known as "the Cambrian explosion."

B. 488–444 mya: Trilobites and first fishlike vertebrates. Plants and fungi start slow colonization of land.

C. 444–416 mya: First jawed fish, first land plants, first small land animals.

D. 416–359 mya: Fish diversify, first insects and amphibians, first seed plants and trees.

E. 359–299 mya: First reptiles, first winged insects, first conifers.

F. 299–251 mya: Mammal-like reptiles.

G. 251–208 mya: First dinosaurs.

H. 208–144 mya: Dinosaurs diversify, first true mammals, first birds.

I. 144–65 mya: First flowering plants, first placental mammals and marsupials.

J. 65–59 mya: First large mammals, first primates.

K. 59–34 mya: Early horses, camels, rodents, elephants, monkeys, bats, whales.

L. 10 mya: Mammals, birds, and insects diversify rapidly.

M. 1.8 mya to present: Spread of *Homo erectus* and *Homo sapiens* around the world, and disappearance of much of the megafauna.

65 mya
Cretaceous extinction
An asteroid impact and massive volcanism plunged the world into years of "impact winter," finished off the non-avian dinosaurs, and eliminated half of all marine species.

0 to future
Sixth mass extinction?
A dramatic increase in species extinctions began with the disappearance of Pleistocene megafauna and continues today. Cause: humans.

Cambrian · Ordovician · Silurian · Devonian · Carboniferous · Permian · Triassic · Jurassic · Cretaceous · Tertiary · Quaternary

PALEOZOIC ERA · MESOZOIC ERA · CENOZOIC ERA

Earth forms
4.6 bya Newly formed solar system includes planet Earth.

Atmosphere forms
4.3 bya Comet impacts and volcanic eruptions release chemicals that form atmosphere.

Prokaryotes
3.6 bya The earliest fossils belong to prokaryotes, single-celled organisms without a nucleus.

Oxygenated atmosphere
2.7 bya Oceans release excess oxygen (produced by photosynthetic bacteria) into the atmosphere.

Eukaryotes
2.1 bya Eukaryotes, the first single-celled organisms with a nucleus, evolve from symbiotic interactions among several bacteria.

Multicellular organisms
1.2 bya First fossils of multicellular algae-like organisms.

Snowball Earth
750–580 mya Period of repeated global glacial activity.

Ediacaran biota
565–535 mya The earliest global community of diverse complex larger organisms.

ARCHEAN ERA · PROTEROZOIC ERA

Cretaceous · Tertiary · Quaternary

150 · 100 · 50 · 0

WHERE ANIMALS LIVE

Biogeographers study where animals live today and how climate, vegetation, and competition affect their distribution. Species numbers tend to be highest in tropical rain forests and coral reefs, and lowest in hot deserts and polar regions. Some places, such as Madagascar, have a high number of endemics—species found nowhere else—and are of special interest to conservationists. Each species has a preferred habitat, its surroundings, and niche, what it does there, which determine the extent of its range. Although most animals are found in only one area, a few, such as rats and house sparrows, have worldwide distributions. Humans move such invasive species accidentally or intentionally, and they often become major pests in areas where they have no natural enemies. The ranges of species change over time. During the last glacial period, much of northern Europe was covered in ice, forcing animals to move south. Once the ice caps melted 18,000 years ago, the animals moved back north. Many species are now shifting their ranges because of global warming.

Feral rabbits
In 1859 European rabbits were introduced into Australia. Their populations exploded in the absence of native predators and competitors. They spread rapidly across the continent, destroying vegetation, soils, and grazing lands. Controlling introduced species that become pests is an expensive challenge.

Endemic lemur
Isolated on the island of Madagascar, lemurs radiated into 40 or so endemic species, including the ring-tailed lemur (right), and ranging from mouse-size lemurs to recently extinct species larger than gorillas. These unique primates are found nowhere else.

Vanished mammoth
Ice age woolly mammoths ranged across the northern continents. By 10,000 years ago, they had all but disappeared as a result of climate and vegetation changes and overhunting.

Biodiversity around the world

Biodiversity varies dramatically across the continents and islands. This map shows the number of vascular plant and vertebrate species—species richness—in each country, as well as which countries have high numbers of endemic vertebrates. Two-thirds of all animal species live in tropical forests, so conservationists are especially active in such biodiversity hotspots.

BIODIVERSITY LEVELS

Highest	**Countries with more than 100 endemic species**	
Medium high	Mammals	
Medium	Birds	
Medium low	Reptiles	
Lowest	Amphibians	

SCALE 1:92,000,000
Robinson Projection

Today's climate zones

Animals are sensitive to both local day-to-day weather and regional year-round climate. Climates vary by latitude, altitude, and distance from the sea, and are characterized by temperature, rainfall, and seasonality. Human activities, such as the burning of fossil fuels and the clearing of forests, are changing weather and climate on a global scale.

Wet tropical	Mediterranean	Cold temperate
Seasonal tropical	Subtropical	Subpolar
Arid	Continental	Polar
Semiarid	Temperate	Highland

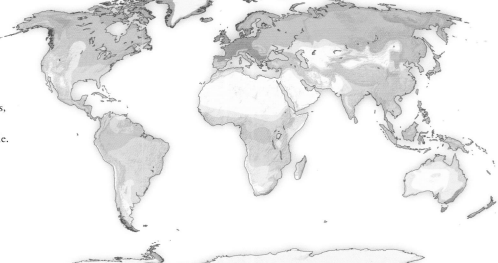

Vegetation zones

This map shows the distribution of major biomes—plant communities and their associated animals—before humans began dramatically changing the planet's surface. Widespread ecological communities can also be recognized in marine and freshwater habitats. Human actions have altered about half of these natural communities, threatening the vital ecological services that they provide.

Tropical forest

Seasonal tropical forest

Desert

Tropical grassland and savanna

Mediterranean forest and scrub

Midlatitude grassland

Midlatitude forest

Boreal forest

Tundra

Ice sheet

Mountain vegetation

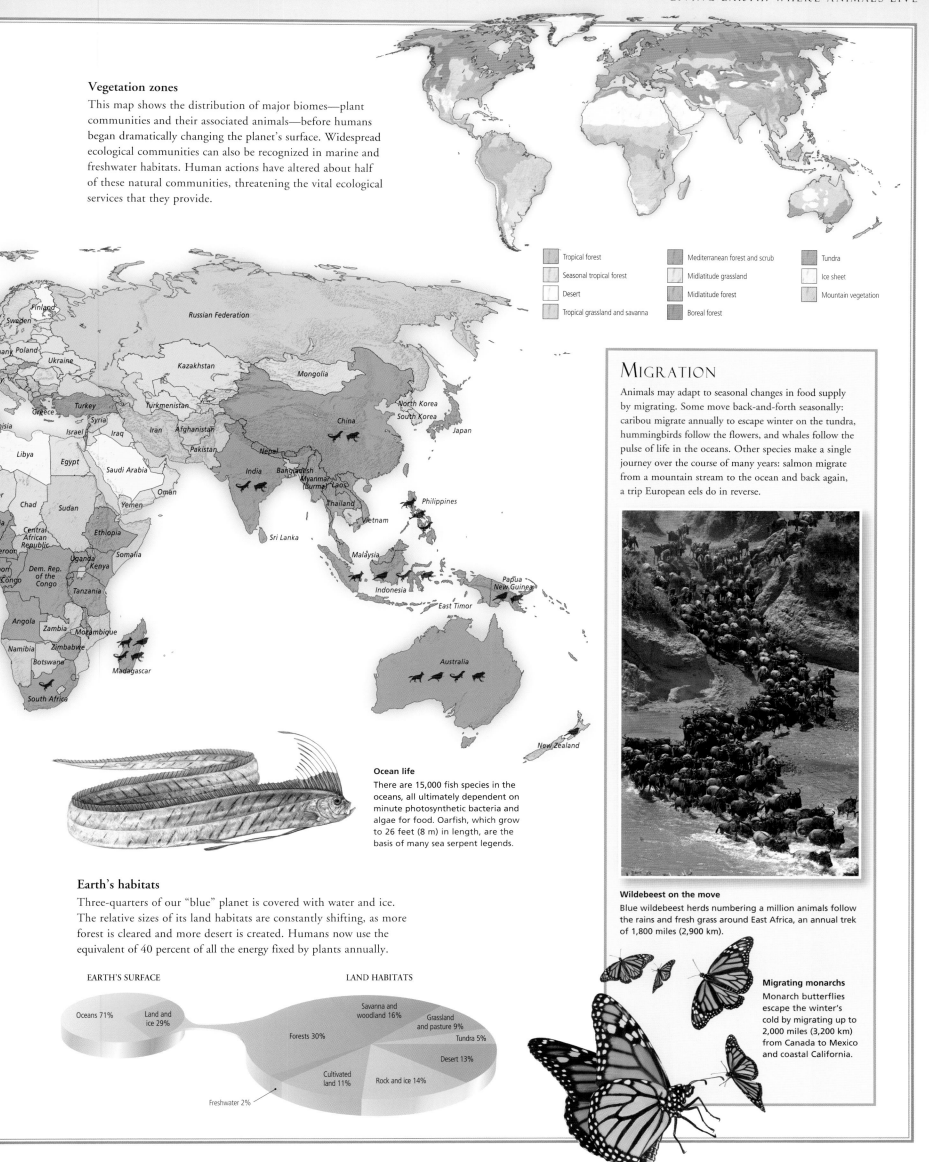

MIGRATION

Animals may adapt to seasonal changes in food supply by migrating. Some move back-and-forth seasonally: caribou migrate annually to escape winter on the tundra, hummingbirds follow the flowers, and whales follow the pulse of life in the oceans. Other species make a single journey over the course of many years: salmon migrate from a mountain stream to the ocean and back again, a trip European eels do in reverse.

Ocean life
There are 15,000 fish species in the oceans, all ultimately dependent on minute photosynthetic bacteria and algae for food. Oarfish, which grow to 26 feet (8 m) in length, are the basis of many sea serpent legends.

Wildebeest on the move
Blue wildebeest herds numbering a million animals follow the rains and fresh grass around East Africa, an annual trek of 1,800 miles (2,900 km).

Earth's habitats

Three-quarters of our "blue" planet is covered with water and ice. The relative sizes of its land habitats are constantly shifting, as more forest is cleared and more desert is created. Humans now use the equivalent of 40 percent of all the energy fixed by plants annually.

EARTH'S SURFACE

Oceans 71%

Land and ice 29%

LAND HABITATS

Savanna and woodland 16%

Grassland and pasture 9%

Forests 30%

Tundra 5%

Desert 13%

Cultivated land 11%

Rock and ice 14%

Freshwater 2%

Migrating monarchs
Monarch butterflies escape the winter's cold by migrating up to 2,000 miles (3,200 km) from Canada to Mexico and coastal California.

BALANCING ACT

Nature is very good at providing us with food, water, and oxygen, the essentials of life. Energy is captured from sunlight, and shared with community members. Minerals are converted into useful nutrients and body tissues, then carefully recycled. At first glance nature seems perfectly organized, with plants to feed the herbivorous animals, predators to hunt the herbivores, and fungi to clean up after them, but this image of nature is too simple. Competition and cooperation are actually more important than the "tooth and claw" of a few fierce animals. Many species are totally dependent on others; most trees, for example, must live symbiotically with microscopic fungi in order to grow and defend themselves. Although natural communities may appear balanced and harmonious, they are in fact constantly changing in membership, as individual species come and go and as the environment changes. Ecology is the study of all these interactions: the study of our home.

Competition between species
Lions may stalk and kill their prey but must compete with other species, such as hyenas and vultures, for the food. Competition for space and resources is a hallmark of community ecology.

Harvester ant

Competition within species
These male stag beetles are fighting over a female. Competition between individuals over resources underpins much animal behavior. In social species, such as ants and humans, related individuals may cooperate to enhance their competitiveness.

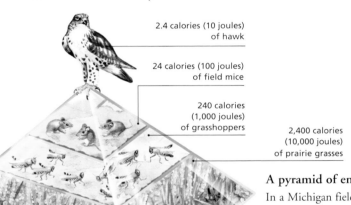

2.4 calories (10 joules) of hawk

24 calories (100 joules) of field mice

240 calories (1,000 joules) of grasshoppers

2,400 calories (10,000 joules) of prairie grasses

A pyramid of energy
In a Michigan field, sunlight is transformed into plant tissue that feeds grasshoppers and, in turn, field mice and hawks. As energy transfer between levels of the food chain is imperfect, fewer animals are supported at higher levels and the community has a pyramid-shaped structure.

FOOD WEB ROLES

Producers

Decomposers and scavengers

Herbivores

Carnivores

Top carnivores

Acacia tree

Impala

Organization of nature

Ecologists recognize five levels of complexity ranging from the individual animal to the entire biosphere. It is clear that no animal can survive without lots of others; it is less clear how many species can be lost and how many communities can be destroyed before the biosphere fails to provide the ecological services we take for granted.

Organism
This level involves the individual, such as the lar, or white-handed, gibbon of Asia's rain forests, as well as its interactions with other members of its own species, other species, and the environment.

Population
A population comprises the members of a species living in one place. Lar gibbons live in monogamous family groups. Adult pairs defend a territory and sing to advertise their presence.

Community
All the populations of many interdependent species living in one place and all their ecological interactions make up a community. The lar gibbon is part of the rain-forest canopy community.

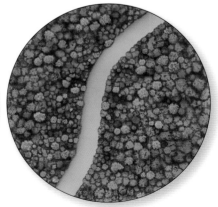

Biome
A biome is an association of similar communities distributed over large areas. The major biomes, such as tropical rain forest, are usually named after the dominant vegetation type.

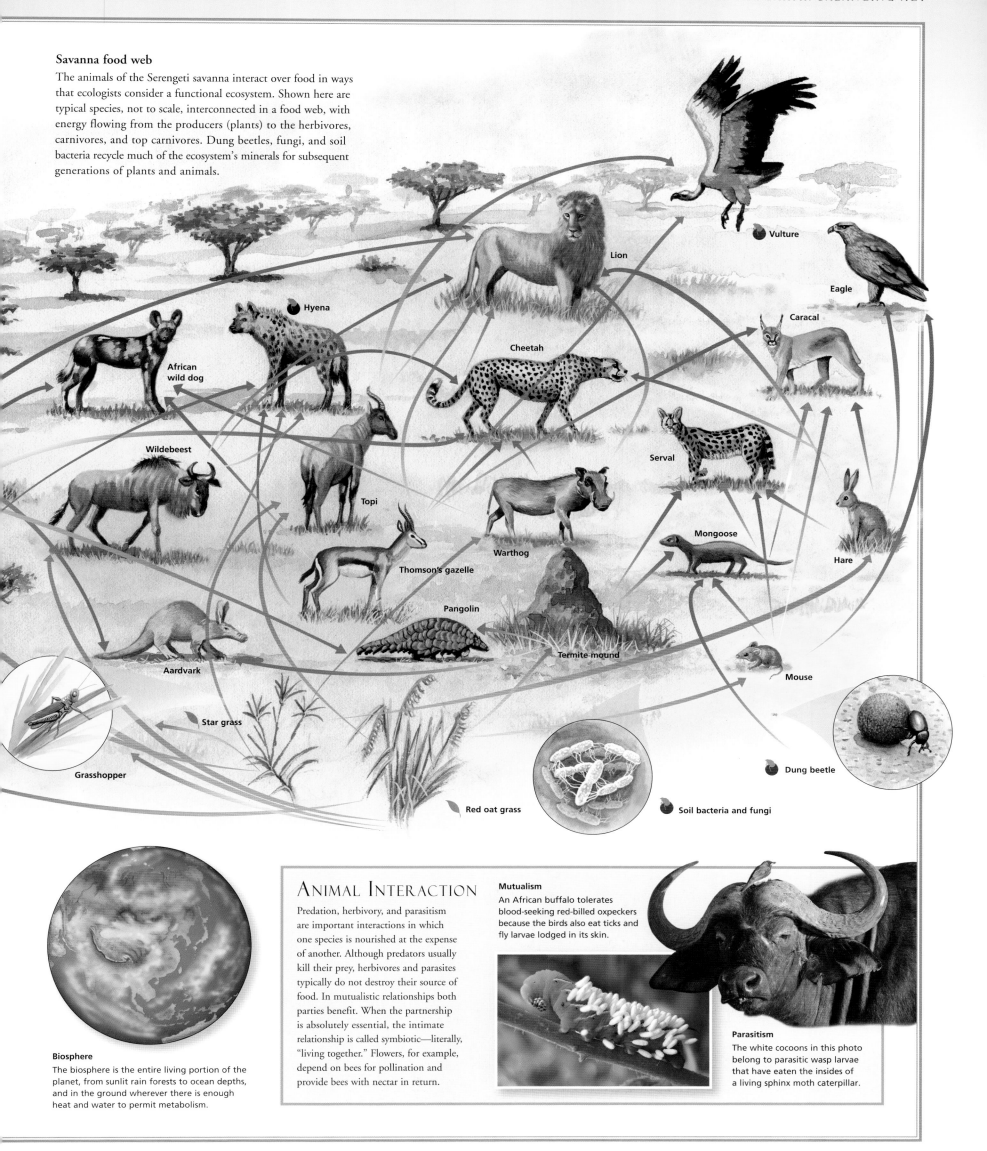

Savanna food web

The animals of the Serengeti savanna interact over food in ways that ecologists consider a functional ecosystem. Shown here are typical species, not to scale, interconnected in a food web, with energy flowing from the producers (plants) to the herbivores, carnivores, and top carnivores. Dung beetles, fungi, and soil bacteria recycle much of the ecosystem's minerals for subsequent generations of plants and animals.

Vulture

Eagle

Lion

Caracal

Hyena

Cheetah

African wild dog

Serval

Wildebeest

Topi

Warthog

Mongoose

Thomson's gazelle

Hare

Pangolin

Aardvark

Termite-mound

Mouse

Star grass

Dung beetle

Grasshopper

Red oat grass

Soil bacteria and fungi

Biosphere
The biosphere is the entire living portion of the planet, from sunlit rain forests to ocean depths, and in the ground wherever there is enough heat and water to permit metabolism.

ANIMAL INTERACTION

Predation, herbivory, and parasitism are important interactions in which one species is nourished at the expense of another. Although predators usually kill their prey, herbivores and parasites typically do not destroy their source of food. In mutualistic relationships both parties benefit. When the partnership is absolutely essential, the intimate relationship is called symbiotic—literally, "living together." Flowers, for example, depend on bees for pollination and provide bees with nectar in return.

Mutualism
An African buffalo tolerates blood-seeking red-billed oxpeckers because the birds also eat ticks and fly larvae lodged in its skin.

Parasitism
The white cocoons in this photo belong to parasitic wasp larvae that have eaten the insides of a living sphinx moth caterpillar.

Forest Habitats

At least one trillion trees cover 30 percent of the land's surface, and two-thirds of all animals are forest dwellers. From the lush vegetation of the tropics to the snow-covered conifers of the north, forests grow in a wide range of climates. Their three-dimensional structure provides different microhabitats that feed and shelter an extraordinary diversity of wildlife. Some species spend their entire lives in the canopy, climbing, swinging, gliding, or flying from branch to branch. Forests play a vital role in the health of our planet. Through exchanges of energy, water, and carbon dioxide, they influence climates on a regional and global scale. Much of the world's original forest has been cleared for cropland or pasture. Reforestation efforts are under way but natural regrowth supports not even half the original biodiversity, and plantation forests support even less. Forest management, especially in the tropics, will help to determine both how much wildlife is lost and how much warmer the planet will become.

The world's forests

Determined largely by climate and soil, the major forest types occur across Earth in roughly horizontal bands that merge into one another. Year-round warmth and high rainfall near the equator result in lush evergreen rain forests. Further north and south, trees cope with seasonal temperature and rainfall variation by dropping leaves or becoming dormant. The most northern forest is boreal, where hardy conifers endure bitter winters.

Boreal forest
The boreal forest, or taiga, is Earth's largest biome. It is dominated by evergreen conifer (needle-leaf) trees such as firs, spruce, and pines. The moose is a year-round resident.

Forest wildlife

A million species of forest animals show exquisite adaptations to the trees in which they feed, shelter, and reproduce. Just moving around without falling out of the trees can be challenging. Although all forest wildlife is directly or indirectly dependent on trees, few species actually eat the woody trunks and branches; those that appear to, such as termites, rely on bacteria and fungi to break down the wood's indigestible cellulose.

Northern flicker
This North American woodpecker spends more time on the forest floor catching ants than it does drumming on tree trunks for insect larvae.

Carpet python
Arboreal snakes such as the Australian carpet python wait for days to feed on birds and mammals. At night they can detect prey by body temperature.

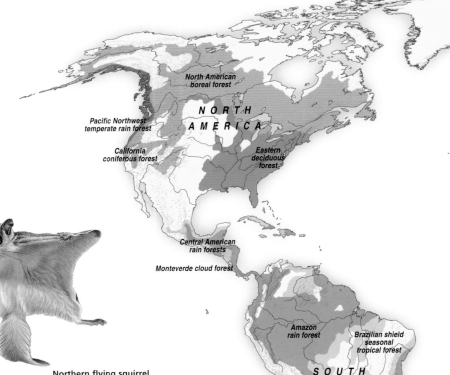

Northern flying squirrel
This nocturnal rodent can glide from tree to tree using a pair of furry membranes that extend between its front and rear legs.

Red-eyed tree frog
Climbing easily with sucker-padded toes, this amphibian spends most of its life in the trees of the always-humid tropical rain forest.

Disappearing forests

The largest cause of species extinction is the loss of 27,000 square miles (70,000 km²) of forest to logging and agriculture each year. Nearly half the forests that were present 2,000 years ago are gone. Frontier forests are undisturbed areas that are large enough to maintain their biodiversity. Efforts to set aside remaining forests are often frustrated; protected areas act like "honeypots" and attract poor settlers to their edges.

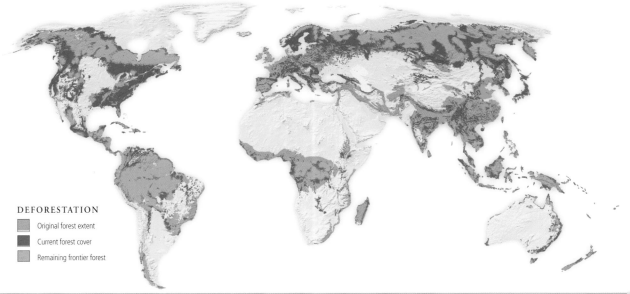

DEFORESTATION
- Original forest extent
- Current forest cover
- Remaining frontier forest

Temperate deciduous forest
A blaze of colors precedes leaf-fall as the forest prepares for winter dormancy. Spring begins with a wildflower show on the forest floor until new leaves provide shade again.

Temperate rain forest
High rainfall, coastal fog, and mild winters characterize these cool wet forests. In North America's Pacific Northwest, tall conifers are festooned with mosses, lichens, and ferns.

Seasonal tropical forest
In seasonal tropical areas, such as Indonesia's Komodo Island, the forest trees lose their leaves during the hot dry season. Komodo dragons stalk prey on the open forest floor.

Tropical rain forest
Ever-wet rain forests are home to more species of animals than any other biome. Scarlet macaws live high in the forest canopy, which is closed 100 feet (30 m) above the ground.

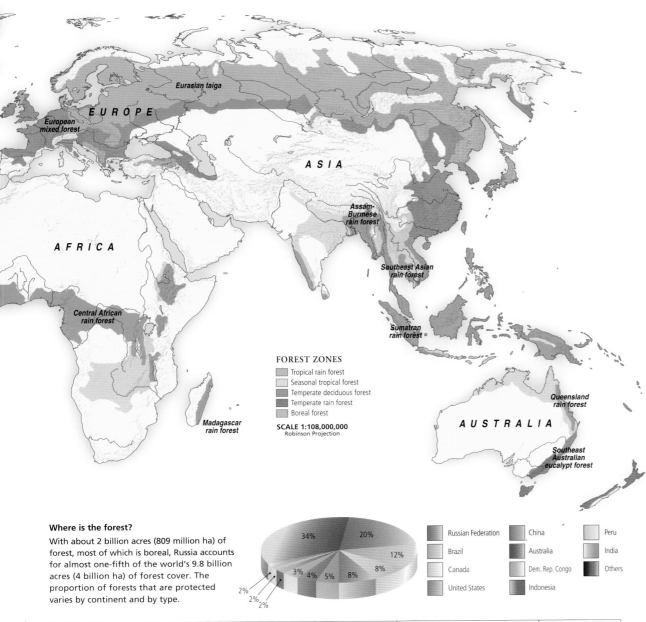

FOREST ZONES
- Tropical rain forest
- Seasonal tropical forest
- Temperate deciduous forest
- Temperate rain forest
- Boreal forest

SCALE 1:108,000,000
Robinson Projection

CARBON STORAGE

Of the 8.8 billion tons (8 billion t) of carbon dioxide released into the atmosphere by humans each year, about one-fifth comes from deforestation, and the rest comes from fossil fuel use. Through photosynthesis, forests absorb 37.5 percent of this carbon dioxide. The oceans absorb the same amount, but the remaining 25 percent stays in the atmosphere and is the major cause of global warming. By storing carbon, the world's forests provide a vital ecological service.

Vanishing rain forest
Forest loss reduces both carbon storage and biodiversity. In this satellite image, pale green and tan deforested tracts break up the darker green Amazon rain forest.

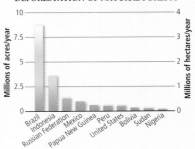

DEFORESTATION OF NATURAL FORESTS

The big emitters
Although the United States emits 25 percent of the world's carbon emissions, mostly from fossil fuel use, Brazil and Indonesia are the largest contributors based on deforestation.

Where is the forest?
With about 2 billion acres (809 million ha) of forest, most of which is boreal, Russia accounts for almost one-fifth of the world's 9.8 billion acres (4 billion ha) of forest cover. The proportion of forests that are protected varies by continent and by type.

Pie chart: 34%, 20%, 12%, 8%, 8%, 5%, 4%, 3%, 2%, 2%, 2%

- Russian Federation
- Brazil
- Canada
- United States
- China
- Australia
- Dem. Rep. Congo
- Indonesia
- Peru
- India
- Others

REGION	TROPICAL FOREST	PROTECTED	NON-TROPICAL FOREST	PROTECTED
Europe (incl. Russia)	Nil	n/a	3,828,000 sq. miles (9,914,000 km²)	3%
North America	1,700 sq. miles (4,400 km²)	7%	2,649,000 sq. miles (6,837,000 km²)	9%
Central & South America	2,669,000 sq. miles (6,914,000 km²)	12%	233,000 sq. miles (605,000 km²)	11%
Asia	814,000 sq. miles (2,108,000 km²)	16%	510,000 sq. miles (1,321,000 km²)	5%
Africa & Middle East	1,731,000 sq. miles (4,482,000 km²)	9%	70,000 sq. miles (180,000 km²)	3%
Australasia & Oceania	207,000 sq. miles (536,000 km²)	9%	105,000 sq. miles (271,000 km²)	19%

Grassland Habitats

Earth's great grasslands still cover about 10 percent of the land. Most of a grassland community's biomass lies below the ground in a rich, nutrient-storing root-mat, or sod. This enables grasses and herbs to survive and quickly recover from frequent drought and fire. Seasonality dominates the ecology. Animals usually feed and reproduce during the rainy season, and switch to survival mode (or migrate) during the hot dry season or cold season. Historically, grasslands were home to vast herds of grazing and browsing mammals, but today these populations can be found only in Africa. The grasses themselves depend on grazing, and without large numbers of herbivores, the vegetation changes to scrub or thorny woodland. Taking advantage of the fertile soil, humans have converted half the grassland biome for crops, grazing, and urban development. The remaining grasslands and their wildlife are also threatened by growing human populations and the increasing numbers of domestic sheep, goats, and cattle.

The world's grasslands

Known as savannas, or llanos in South America, the grasslands bordering the tropics often include scattered trees. They are warm year-round but have a pronounced dry season. The temperate grasslands are treeless plains with hot dry summers and cold winters. They are called prairies in North America, pampas in South America, veldt in South Africa, and steppe in Eurasia. The large herbivores associated with grasslands include North American bison, South American guanacos, African gazelles, Asian wild horses, and Australian kangaroos.

NORTH AMERICA

Urban 19%
Remaining grasslands 10%
Croplands 71%

SOUTH AMERICA

Urban 6%
Remaining grasslands 22%
Croplands 72%

THE LOST PRAIRIES

The great interior plains of the United States were once a sea of grass extending thousands of miles, home to about 60 million bison. Between 1830 and 2000, the prairies' extent shrank by two-thirds, and the bison were hunted down to about 100 animals. European settlers converted almost all the eastern tallgrass prairie to cornfields, while further west they farmed wheat, cattle, and sheep. Non-native plants invaded and now account for up to 90 percent of vegetation.

ORIGINAL PRAIRIE COVER

CURRENT PRAIRIE COVER

- Tallgrass prairie
- Midgrass prairie
- Shortgrass prairie

Fire on the steppe

Wildfire is an essential component of grassland ecology, helping to break down dead matter, recycle nutrients, and prevent shrubs from taking over. In many grassland regions, farmers also deliberately light fires to clear land for agriculture or to regenerate pasture for grazing animals. In this false-color satellite image of Central Asia's Kazakhstan steppe, vegetation appears green, burned areas are deep reddish brown, and the red dots represent burning fires.

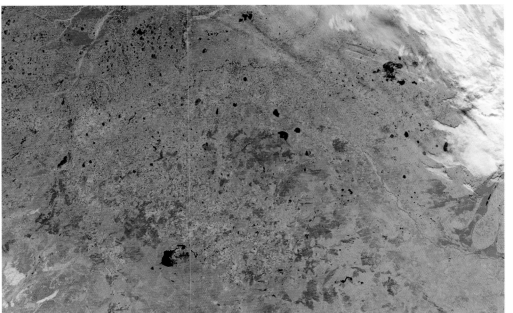

Region	Grassland & Savanna Area	Name
Europe (incl. Russia)	541,000 sq. miles (1,401,000 km²)	Steppe
North America	675,000 sq. miles (1,749,000 km²)	Prairie
Central & South America	1,911,000 sq. miles (4,950,000 km²)	Pampas
Asia	10,253,000 sq. miles (26,555,000 km²)	Steppe
Africa & Middle East	3,958,000 sq. miles (10,251,000 km²)	Savanna
Australasia & Oceania	1,186,000 sq. miles (3,072,000 km²)	Grassland

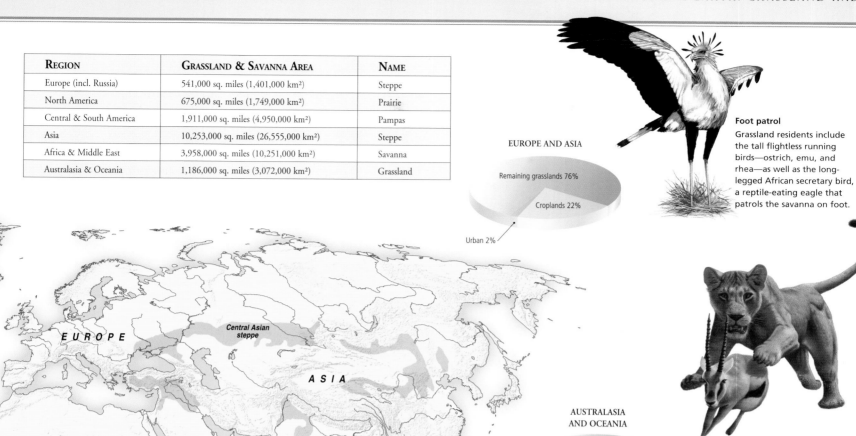

Foot patrol
Grassland residents include the tall flightless running birds—ostrich, emu, and rhea—as well as the long-legged African secretary bird, a reptile-eating eagle that patrols the savanna on foot.

EUROPE AND ASIA

Remaining grasslands 76%

Croplands 22%

Urban 2%

AUSTRALASIA AND OCEANIA

Remaining grasslands 59%

Croplands 39%

Urban 2%

Predator and prey
Motionless and hidden in the grass, a lioness can get within pouncing distance of the very wary and fleet-footed Thomson's gazelle.

GRASSLAND ZONES
☐ Tropical grassland (savanna)
☐ Temperate grassland
SCALE 1:108,000,000
Robinson Projection

AFRICA

Remaining grasslands 77%

Croplands 22%

Urban 1%

Outback grazer
Adapted to Australia's driest grasslands, the red kangaroo times its activities to the daily temperature regime, and its reproduction to the sporadic rainfall.

Grassland wildlife

Hot dry summers and cold winters with little food present grassland animals with challenges. With no trees to hide in, many predators and prey have adopted the burrowing habit and the ability to run fast. The huge standing crop of vegetation is regrown annually and supports large populations of vertebrate and invertebrate herbivores. Grasshoppers and their alter-egos, plague locusts, are notorious residents.

Burrower
Many grassland mammals and birds, such as America's burrowing owl (left), live underground, where they can hide from predators and escape the heat of summer and the cold of winter.

Termite eater
Termites are responsible for 90 percent of the decomposition of dead grass. The South American giant anteater visits termite mounds to feed on these abundant insects.

Grazing herds
Large grazing herds once characterized most grasslands but they survive only in parts of Africa, where zebras, wildebeest, and gazelles feed sequentially to reduce competition.

DRY HABITATS

Life as we know it depends on water, so animals face special challenges when they inhabit areas of little rain and extreme temperatures. In hot deserts, daytime temperatures regularly exceed 100°F (38°C) and the ground surface may reach 170°F (77°C). In cold deserts, water may be frozen and unavailable. Under such conditions, there is little vegetation and limited animal life. Few animals are about during the day. Most shelter beneath the sand or in whatever shade is available. Desert animals often have coats and scales that resist desiccation, and many use evaporative heat-loss mechanisms such as panting and sweating to keep the body and brain cool. A few animals become dormant and estivate for months or even years. At night the desert comes alive as its animals emerge and feed. Rain, when it comes, brings about a sudden transformation as desert plants bloom briefly and animals quickly reproduce. Then most animals go back into hiding and patiently await the next life-sustaining storm.

Western scrub jay
In summer in its chaparral or semidesert habitat, this bird gets all its water from its food, seeks shade at midday, and sheds heat from its unfeathered feet.

Hyperarid to humid
Much of the global land surface is already arid or semiarid. These areas have little topsoil and are susceptible to wind-erosion. Global warming and poor land-use practices are likely to increase the proportion of drylands, with significant negative consequences for both people and wild animals.

WORLD ARIDITY

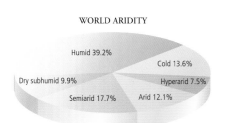

Humid 39.2%
Cold 13.6%
Dry subhumid 9.9%
Hyperarid 7.5%
Semiarid 17.7%
Arid 12.1%

DRY ZONES
- Desert
- Semidesert
- Coastal scrub
- ☀ Hot desert
- ☼ Cold desert

SCALE 1:108,000,000
Robinson Projection

The world's dry zones
Drylands circle the globe in two bands 20 to 30 degrees north and south of the equator. Deserts cover about 13 percent of Earth's land, but up to one-third of the land can be called arid or semiarid. Desert and semidesert biomes merge into grasslands, thornwoods, and coastal scrub (Mediterranean-type vegetation such as maquis, chaparral, fynbos, and mallee).

NORTH AMERICA

Great Basin
Mojave Desert
Californian chaparral
Sonoran Desert
Chihuahuan Desert

SOUTH AMERICA

Peruvian Desert
Atacama Desert
Chilean mattoral
Patagonian Desert

DESERTIFICATION

A decline in land productivity called desertification is occurring at the edges of many drylands. The major causes are climate change, overgrazing, poor soil management in croplands, and local human population growth. Currently, about 30 million acres (12 million ha) of agricultural land become useless each year. As the 1930s "dust bowl" in North America's Great Plains and the 1980s Sahelian drought show, desertification can destroy human societies and wildlife habitats.

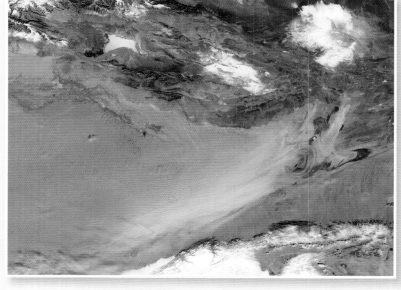

Dust storm
Poor management of drylands is increasing dust storms, such as this one over the sand dunes of China's Taklimakan Desert. By removing soil and organic matter, dust storms reduce agricultural productivity at desert margins.

DESERTIFICATION RISK
- Low
- Moderate
- High
- Very high
- Desert
- Not vulnerable

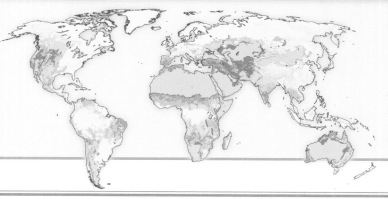

A drier world
Significant areas of grassland are at risk of desertification as a result of global warming and local land-use practices.

Southern grasshopper mouse
This nocturnal burrower obtains its water from its meals of other mice, scorpions, and beetles. The male stands and sings loudly to advertise his territory.

Greater roadrunner
Roadrunners sun themselves in the morning to warm up without burning food calories. Later they stand in the shade, spread their wings, and pant to stay cool.

DESERT	REGION	TYPE	AREA
Sahara	Northern Africa	Hot	3,500,000 sq. miles (9,100,000 km²)
Arabian	Arabian Peninsula	Hot	1,000,000 sq. miles (2,600,000 km²)
Gobi	China, Mongolia	Cold	500,000 sq. miles (1,300,000 km²)
Patagonian	Argentina	Cold	260,000 sq. miles (670,000 km²)
Great Victoria	Australia	Hot	250,000 sq. miles (650,000 km²)

Bactrian camel
Gobi desert camels have broad feet, long eyelashes, and closeable nostrils to deal with sand. Two fatty humps provide metabolic water.

EUROPE

ASIA

Mediterranean maquis

Karakum Desert

☼ Gobi Desert

☼ Taklimakan Desert

Iranian Desert

☀ Lut Desert

Thar Desert

☀ Sahara Desert

AFRICA

Arabian Desert

Namib Desert ☼

Kalahari Desert

South African fynbos

Great Sandy Desert ☀

AUSTRALIA

Simpson Desert ☀

Great Victoria Desert

Southern Australian mallee

Central bearded dragon
This lizard's display scares away predators. The color of its scales can slightly lighten or darken to optimize its temperature regulation.

Fog-basking beetle
This Namibian beetle emerges from the sand at night and climbs a dune to bask head-down in the passing fog, gathering water that then trickles to its mouth.

Burchell's sandgrouse
This desert bird has the habit of "belly wetting" when it drinks at a pool just after sunrise; it then carries the water to its chicks.

Indian wild asses
These wild asses can survive in the barren desert of northwest India as long as they live within a couple of miles of a waterhole.

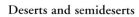

Deserts and semideserts

Semidesert regions (such as the Galápagos Islands, right, with giant tortoise) receive less than 10 inches (250 mm) of rain annually and feature well-spaced cacti and thorn scrub. True deserts (such as the Namib Desert, far right) receive less than 2 inches (50 mm) of rain annually and support few plants, and years or decades may pass between rains. The Namib's sidewinding adder hides during the day with only its eyes and nostrils above the sand.

Frozen Habitats

The last ice age ended only 18,000 years ago, and many cold-adapted species from that time survive around the polar ice caps and on polar and alpine tundra. The treeless polar tundra is underlain by frozen soil known as permafrost, and characterized by a short cool summer and a long frigid winter when the sun never rises. Animals require special adaptations to survive in frozen habitats year-round. Many species are migratory and walk, swim, or fly toward the equator to escape the bitter winter cold. Some that stay, such as polar bears, shelter in snow caves and live off their body fat; others, such as lemmings, burrow beneath the snow, where they nibble on what is left of the vegetation. Insulation, physiological adaptations, and social behavior enable penguins to overwinter on Antarctica's ice. Within days of the sun's return to polar regions, life is in full swing as newborns and hatchlings must be rushed though their development during the two- to four-month-long summer day.

Ice and tundra habitats

The three major ice caps cover all the Antarctic continent and Greenland with ice up to 16,000 feet (5,000 m) thick. The Arctic tundra remains extensive but is changing rapidly as the planet becomes warmer. In the southern hemisphere, tundra occurs on subantarctic islands. Alpine tundra is found in restricted mountainous areas of all continents and is associated with glaciers in a few places.

FROZEN ZONES
- Arctic tundra
- Alpine tundra
- Polar ice

SCALE 1:96,000,000
Robinson Projection

Warmer Poles

The polar regions are warming at three times the rate of the tropics. The 50-year decline in Antarctic winter sea ice (below) and the projected loss of Arctic permafrost and ice cover (right) are illustrative. Sea levels are projected to rise 3 to 6 feet (1–2 m) this century, but if all the world's 7.2 million cubic miles (30 million km³) of ice caps and glaciers melt, global sea levels could rise by as much as 256 feet (78 m).

Loss of Arctic permafrost
This map shows the projected impact of global warming on Arctic permafrost and ice cover. Animals such as caribou and walrus, which depend on tundra and sea ice, will face new stresses.

ARCTIC WARMING
- Current permafrost area
- Projected permafrost area 2100
- Current sea ice
- Projected sea ice 2070–90

Antarctic sea ice decline
Life around Antarctica depends on winter sea ice, which is shrinking every year. The algae that shelter beneath the ice provide for the growth of populations of shrimplike krill, which in turn sustain penguins, seals, and whales.

(Graph: x-axis 1850 to 2000; left y-axis MSA (uEq/L) 0.02 to 0.14; right y-axis Sea ice extent (degrees of latitude) 57 to 62)

- MSA* ice core record
- MSA long-term trend
- Sea ice extent satellite data

* MSA (methanesulphonic acid) is produced by phytoplankton and associated with sea ice extent.

Summer in Siberia

Still-frozen lakes dot the tundra east of the Lena River delta in Siberia, and cracked sea ice connects the New Siberia Islands to the mainland. The platform of sea ice enables polar bears to hunt seals, and as it melts with global warming, the bears and their cubs will starve. The lakes and permafrost are also melting and releasing methane, a potent greenhouse gas, and further contributing to climate change.

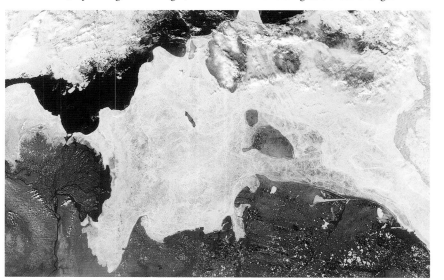

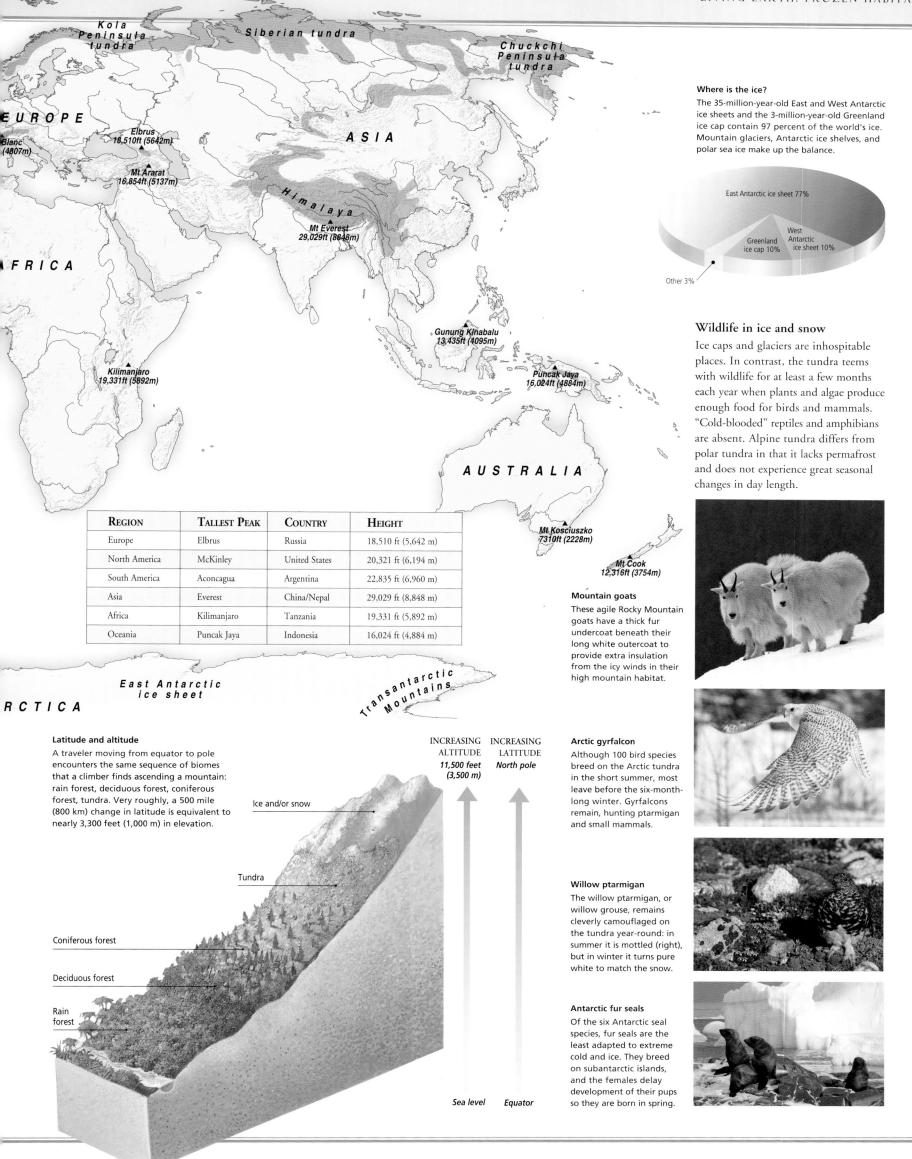

Kola
Peninsula
tundra

Siberian tundra

Chuckchi
Peninsula
tundra

EUROPE

Blanc
(4807m)

Elbrus
18,510ft (5642m)

Mt Ararat
16,854ft (5137m)

ASIA

AFRICA

Himalaya

Mt Everest
29,029ft (8848m)

Kilimanjaro
19,331ft (5892m)

Gunung Kinabalu
13,435ft (4095m)

Puncak Jaya
16,024ft (4884m)

AUSTRALIA

Mt Kosciuszko
7310ft (2228m)

Mt Cook
12,316ft (3754m)

East Antarctic
ice sheet

Transantarctic
Mountains

ARCTICA

Where is the ice?

The 35-million-year-old East and West Antarctic ice sheets and the 3-million-year-old Greenland ice cap contain 97 percent of the world's ice. Mountain glaciers, Antarctic ice shelves, and polar sea ice make up the balance.

East Antarctic ice sheet 77%

Greenland
ice cap 10%

West
Antarctic
ice sheet 10%

Other 3%

Wildlife in ice and snow

Ice caps and glaciers are inhospitable places. In contrast, the tundra teems with wildlife for at least a few months each year when plants and algae produce enough food for birds and mammals. "Cold-blooded" reptiles and amphibians are absent. Alpine tundra differs from polar tundra in that it lacks permafrost and does not experience great seasonal changes in day length.

Region	Tallest Peak	Country	Height
Europe	Elbrus	Russia	18,510 ft (5,642 m)
North America	McKinley	United States	20,321 ft (6,194 m)
South America	Aconcagua	Argentina	22,835 ft (6,960 m)
Asia	Everest	China/Nepal	29,029 ft (8,848 m)
Africa	Kilimanjaro	Tanzania	19,331 ft (5,892 m)
Oceania	Puncak Jaya	Indonesia	16,024 ft (4,884 m)

Mountain goats
These agile Rocky Mountain goats have a thick fur undercoat beneath their long white outercoat to provide extra insulation from the icy winds in their high mountain habitat.

Latitude and altitude

A traveler moving from equator to pole encounters the same sequence of biomes that a climber finds ascending a mountain: rain forest, deciduous forest, coniferous forest, tundra. Very roughly, a 500 mile (800 km) change in latitude is equivalent to nearly 3,300 feet (1,000 m) in elevation.

Ice and/or snow

Tundra

Coniferous forest

Deciduous forest

Rain
forest

INCREASING
ALTITUDE
11,500 feet
(3,500 m)

INCREASING
LATITUDE
North pole

Sea level

Equator

Arctic gyrfalcon
Although 100 bird species breed on the Arctic tundra in the short summer, most leave before the six-month-long winter. Gyrfalcons remain, hunting ptarmigan and small mammals.

Willow ptarmigan
The willow ptarmigan, or willow grouse, remains cleverly camouflaged on the tundra year-round: in summer it is mottled (right), but in winter it turns pure white to match the snow.

Antarctic fur seals
Of the six Antarctic seal species, fur seals are the least adapted to extreme cold and ice. They breed on subantarctic islands, and the females delay development of their pups so they are born in spring.

Aquatic Habitats

Aquatic habitats span a greater range of physical conditions than are found on land, so life in water is even more diverse. Coral reefs rival rain forests in terms of complexity, and salt marshes are among the most productive ecosystems on the planet. Compared to our intensive study of terrestrial life, however, aquatic habitats are relatively unexplored and they continue to surprise us. Tiny planktonic algae in sunlit ocean water, and not land plants, are responsible for producing most of the oxygen that land animals depend on. Life thrives in total darkness on the deep ocean floor where 660°F (350°C) water and hydrogen sulfide are released from underwater volcanic vents. One-fifth of the world's much-loved coral reefs are already gone, and half are doomed by present trends. Wetlands store 20 percent of the world's carbon and, if they continue to be destroyed, could release their carbon dioxide as a planet-warming "carbon bomb." Clearly, it is time to pay more attention to aquatic habitats.

Freshwater and marine habitats

Animals in aquatic habitats may be either permanent residents or visitors with adaptations to both land and water. Many more types of animals are found in salt water than in fresh, as oceans are the ancestral habitat of all lifeforms and are easier to live in metabolically. Nevertheless, freshwater ponds, lakes, rivers, and wetlands are the permanent home of diverse invertebrates, fish, waterfowl, and other vertebrates.

Ponds and lakes
Living between worlds, painted turtles must warm up in the sun before feeding in cool water. But when the water freezes in winter, turtles hibernate in the pond's muddy bottom.

HUMAN IMPACT ON THE OCEANS

- Very low impact
- Low impact
- Medium impact
- High impact
- Very high impact

The cost of human activities

Humans have destroyed much freshwater and coastal habitat, sacrificing clean water, flood control, and biodiversity in the process. Most oceanic communities have been damaged by overfishing, habitat destruction, pollution, and global warming. Chemicals discharged by polluted rivers are linked to large dead zones in coastal seas, where there is not enough oxygen to support life, and to the increased frequency of the noxious plankton blooms known as red tides.

Wetland protection

Adopted in 1971, the Ramsar Convention on Wetlands of International Importance supports conservation efforts at 1,759 freshwater, estuarine, and coastal marine sites in 158 countries. Wetlands that shelter migratory waterfowl are given particular attention.

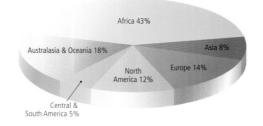

1,759 RAMSAR SITES PROTECT
398 MILLION ACRES (161 MILLION HA) OF WETLANDS

- Africa 43%
- Australasia & Oceania 18%
- Asia 8%
- North America 12%
- Europe 14%
- Central & South America 5%

Aquatic animals

Aquatic animals all need to obtain oxygen and food, and to avoid predators in order to reproduce. Bottom dwellers (benthos) take advantage of the "rain" of food from above, but they may live in total darkness. Open-water animals must swim (nekton) or float (plankton), or they will sink to their deaths. Life around the water's edge (littoral or intertidal zone) is richest, but the risks of predation are higher.

Blue-ringed octopus
This small tide-pool octopus is usually well-camouflaged, but quickly flashes its bright colors when disturbed, a warning that its venomous bite is deadly.

Common dolphin
Keen eyesight, excellent communication skills, and cooperative behavior allow pods of dolphins to hunt for schools of small fish in the open ocean.

Sockeye salmon
Sockeye hatchlings migrate from their mountain-stream birthplace to the ocean, where they feed for years before returning to the same stream to reproduce and die.

Wetlands
Wetlands and the rivers that feed them are highly productive habitats that support many invertebrates, fish, and birds. Roseate spoonbills hunt crustaceans and fish in shallow water.

Mangroves
Mangroves receive nutrients from both land and sea and support great numbers of algae, plants, invertebrates, and fish, as well as birds such as this yellow-crowned night heron.

Coral reefs
Corals grow in warm, clear, nutrient-poor seas, but a symbiosis between the coral animals and algae fuels their great productivity. A reef's structure provides niches for many animals.

Oceans
Oceanic fish tend to specialize as bottom-, surface-, or mid-water feeders. The head of the scalloped hammerhead shark has sensory organs that guide it to buried stingrays.

The world's waters

The great rivers, lakes, and wetlands are treasure troves of freshwater life that harbor thousands of fish species, amphibians, and aquatic turtles, snakes, birds, and mammals. Salt marshes and mangroves anchor the coastlines, serve as fish nurseries, and sustain millions of birds. Ocean habitats themselves are partitioned according to water temperature, light, depth, and nutrients (concentrated in upwelling zones). Coral reefs are the fragile crown jewels of the aquatic world.

AQUATIC HABITATS

- Major river
- Lake
- Wetland
- Salt marsh
- Mangrove
- Coral reef
- Deep-sea coral
- Continental shelf
- Upwelling zone
- Open ocean

SCALE 1:104,000,000
Robinson Projection

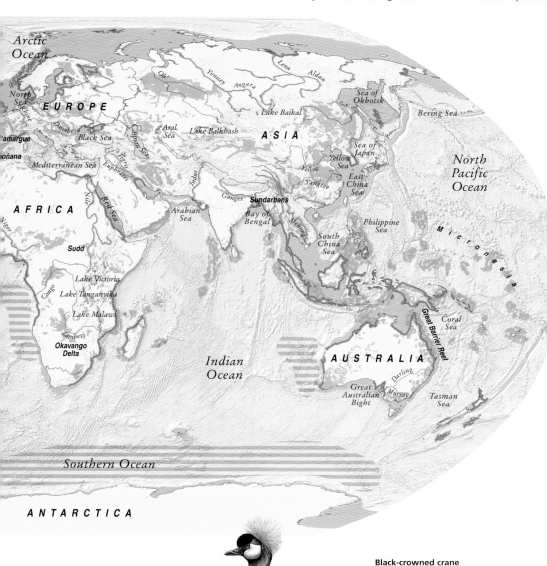

ALL WATER ON EARTH

Oceans 97.5%

Fresh water 2.5%

Ice caps and glaciers 79%

Groundwater 20%

Accessible surface fresh water 1%

Water in lakes 52%

Water in soil 38%

Water in rivers 1%

Water vapor in atmosphere 8%

Water in living organisims 1%

Where is the water?
The vast majority of water on our blue planet is salty. Less than 3 percent is fresh water, and most of this is locked up as either ice or groundwater. Less than 0.3 percent sustains life in lakes, rivers, and wetlands.

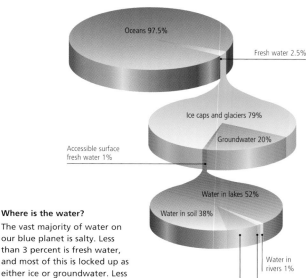

Mudpuppy
This bottom-feeding carnivore spends its life in ponds and lakes. Although it develops legs, it never loses its gills like other adult salamanders do.

Black-crowned crane
Permanent and seasonally flooded wetlands are vital to breeding river fish. Tall wading birds, such as cranes, take advantage of the bounty.

Sail-tailed water lizard
When threatened by a predator, this Central American lizard can make a quick escape. Fringed toes give its feet enough area to run across the surface of streams.

DEEP-SEA VENTS

Not all life is dependent on sunlight. About 8,000 feet (2,400 m) below the surface of the sea, hydrothermal vent communities feature 6-foot (2-m) giant tube worms (right) and depend on bacteria that use superheated sulfide-rich water for energy. Scientists have recently found similar microbial life living in very hot groundwater in rock cracks up to 6 miles (10 km) below the surface of land, ice, and sea around the world.

Human Habitats

Our complicated relationship with wild animals plays out in human-dominated rural and urban environments. On the one hand, our agricultural practices have disturbed ecosystems and replaced natural vegetation with monocultures, opening the door for invasive species and allowing some animals to become pests. On the other hand, a growing number of people want to reconnect with nature and are feeding birds and mammals in gardens and parks. Changing attitudes, coupled with the movement of people from rural areas to cities, reduces pressure on remaining wildlife habitats. Humans have already co-opted nearly half of Earth's surface, so the ultimate fate of wildlife is tied to our use of land. If urbanization continues throughout the 21st century and we manage rural areas in more sustainable ways, wildlife will have a future. Until that time, most people will only encounter nature around their urban homes. Although urban areas seem to be unnatural habitats for animals, they play an important role both in educating the public about wildlife and in maintaining the world's ecological balance.

Eastern gray squirrel
This tree squirrel has learned to live with humans and their dogs in urban parks in its native America and in Europe.

European starling
Insectivorous European starlings have become pests in North America and Australia, where their flocks damage orchards and displace native birds.

Migratory locusts
Warm, wet weather may cause grasshoppers to transform en masse into plague locusts. The resulting swarm of billions of insects severely damages crops.

Largest Populations (2010)		Fastest-growing Countries* (2005–2010)	
Country	Population	Country	Annual Growth
China	1,347,563,498	Liberia	4.5%
India	1,184,090,490	Burundi	3.9%
United States	309,162,581	Afghanistan	3.85%
Indonesia	242,968,342	Western Sahara	3.72%
Brazil	201,103,330	Timor-Leste	3.5%
Pakistan	179,659,223	Niger	3.49%
Bangladesh	159,765,367	Eritrea	3.24%
Nigeria	152,217,341	Uganda	3.24%
Russia	139,390,205	Democratic Republic of the Congo	3.22%
Japan	126,804,433	Occupied Palestinian Territory	3.18%

* Countries with more than 100,000 inhabitants

Other 37%
Arable and permanent cropland 12%
Permanent pasture 27%
Forest 24%

Global land use
Humans have converted 35 percent of land to agriculture, and 40 percent of its biological productivity for their own use. Much of this use is unsustainable, and agriculture will need to use less land more intensively in future.

Earth at night

Our planet glows in the darkness of space. This composite satellite image of Earth at night illustrates the extent of urbanization. The United States, Europe, and Japan are brightly lit by their cities, while the interiors of Africa, Asia, Australia, and South America remain, for now, dark and lightly populated. Of the world's 18 megacities (cities with more than 10 million people), 14 are located in developing countries. Half the global human population lives in cities and towns.

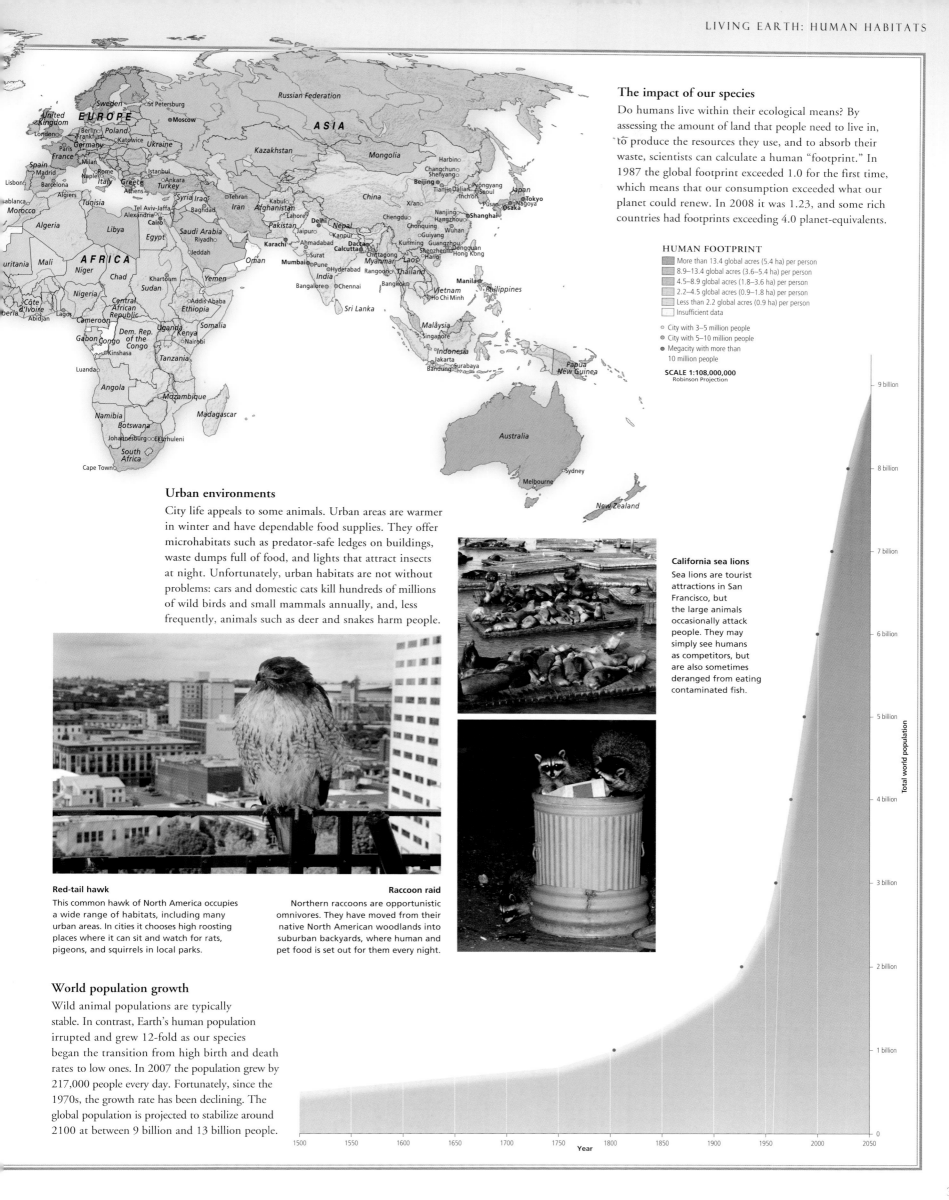

The impact of our species

Do humans live within their ecological means? By assessing the amount of land that people need to live in, to produce the resources they use, and to absorb their waste, scientists can calculate a human "footprint." In 1987 the global footprint exceeded 1.0 for the first time, which means that our consumption exceeded what our planet could renew. In 2008 it was 1.23, and some rich countries had footprints exceeding 4.0 planet-equivalents.

HUMAN FOOTPRINT
- More than 13.4 global acres (5.4 ha) per person
- 8.9–13.4 global acres (3.6–5.4 ha) per person
- 4.5–8.9 global acres (1.8–3.6 ha) per person
- 2.2–4.5 global acres (0.9–1.8 ha) per person
- Less than 2.2 global acres (0.9 ha) per person
- Insufficient data

○ City with 3–5 million people
◎ City with 5–10 million people
● Megacity with more than 10 million people

SCALE 1:108,000,000
Robinson Projection

Urban environments

City life appeals to some animals. Urban areas are warmer in winter and have dependable food supplies. They offer microhabitats such as predator-safe ledges on buildings, waste dumps full of food, and lights that attract insects at night. Unfortunately, urban habitats are not without problems: cars and domestic cats kill hundreds of millions of wild birds and small mammals annually, and, less frequently, animals such as deer and snakes harm people.

California sea lions
Sea lions are tourist attractions in San Francisco, but the large animals occasionally attack people. They may simply see humans as competitors, but are also sometimes deranged from eating contaminated fish.

Red-tail hawk
This common hawk of North America occupies a wide range of habitats, including many urban areas. In cities it chooses high roosting places where it can sit and watch for rats, pigeons, and squirrels in local parks.

Raccoon raid
Northern raccoons are opportunistic omnivores. They have moved from their native North American woodlands into suburban backyards, where human and pet food is set out for them every night.

World population growth

Wild animal populations are typically stable. In contrast, Earth's human population irrupted and grew 12-fold as our species began the transition from high birth and death rates to low ones. In 2007 the population grew by 217,000 people every day. Fortunately, since the 1970s, the growth rate has been declining. The global population is projected to stabilize around 2100 at between 9 billion and 13 billion people.

33

THREATS TO WILDLIFE

Human activities have taken a heavy toll on nature. Throughout the last 100,000 years a wave of extinctions followed the arrival of humans on each continent or island. Wildlife species are endangered by habitat alteration, the introduction of invasive species, pollution, overhunting, and human-caused global warming. All these threats are amplified by human population growth. Although the impacts per person are hardest on nature in developing countries, population growth anywhere and everywhere has a negative global impact. Several hundred species of vertebrates have gone extinct since 1650. The current annual extinction rate is estimated to be 10,000 times higher than the background rate over the last 60 million years. Thousands of species, mostly unnamed insects, are lost each year, and conservationists mount heroic efforts to save a few charismatic animals in zoos and protected areas. By 2100 half the larger species are likely to be threatened and many of them will lose the battle. Very few species are deliberately targeted for extinction. Most are simply the innocent victims of our presence and activities.

Extinction risk

The distribution of extinction risk varies by country. The interest in conservation is uneven, and monitoring efforts tend to focus on terrestrial vertebrates and often ignore plants and invertebrates. Some countries stand out in a tally of threatened species because their governments keep better records, but in reality the risks are highest in tropical countries, which have high biodiversity. Island nations and countries with rapidly growing human populations are especially dangerous places for animals to live.

Cook Islands

79 extinctions
French Polynesia

THREATENED ANIMAL SPECIES

0–49	**Extinctions since 1600***
50–99	10–29
100–199	30–50
200–299	More than 50
300–399	* including species extinct in wild
More than 400	**SCALE 1:98,000,000** Robinson Projection

236 extinctions
United States of America

Passenger pigeon
Once the most common bird in North America, this gregarious species went extinct in 1914 as a result of overhunting and habitat alteration.

Global warming

Largely as a result of human activities, our planet is getting warmer. The expected annual surface warming during the 21st century is 5.4°F (3°C) in the tropics and up to 14.4°F (8°C) in polar regions. Many species are already responding by moving poleward or up mountainsides, and becoming active earlier in the spring. Some animals restricted to isolated mountaintops are already going extinct, and ice-dependent species such as polar bears and penguins are vulnerable.

PROJECTED INCREASE IN SURFACE TEMPERATURE BY 2099

0–1.8°F (0–1°C)	3.6–5.4°F (2–3°C)	7.2–9°F (4–5°C)	10.8–12.6°F (6–7°C)
1.8–3.6°F (1–2°C)	5.4–7.2°F (3–4°C)	9–10.8°F (5–6°C)	12.6–14.4°F (7–8°C)

Critically endangered animals

The International Union for the Conservation of Nature (IUCN) maintains the Red List of Threatened Species. Population size and rates of harvesting and habitat destruction are prime indicators of risk, but some types of species—for example, island animals, large animals, top predators, fearless animals—are more extinction-prone than others. Even abundant colonial species can be driven extinct if their breeding behavior is disturbed. The animals illustrated here are all listed as critically endangered.

Orange-bellied parrot
Devastated by habitat alteration and competition with introduced birds, only 180 orange-bellied parrots remain in the wild. They breed in Tasmania and winter in southeastern Australia.

Orangutan
Orangutans are declining rapidly because of logging and palm oil cultivation. The Sumatran orangutan is critically endangered, with only 6,600 individuals left.

Baiji
Also known as the Yangtze river dolphin, this species was last seen in 2004 and is functionally extinct as a result of water pollution and fishing practices.

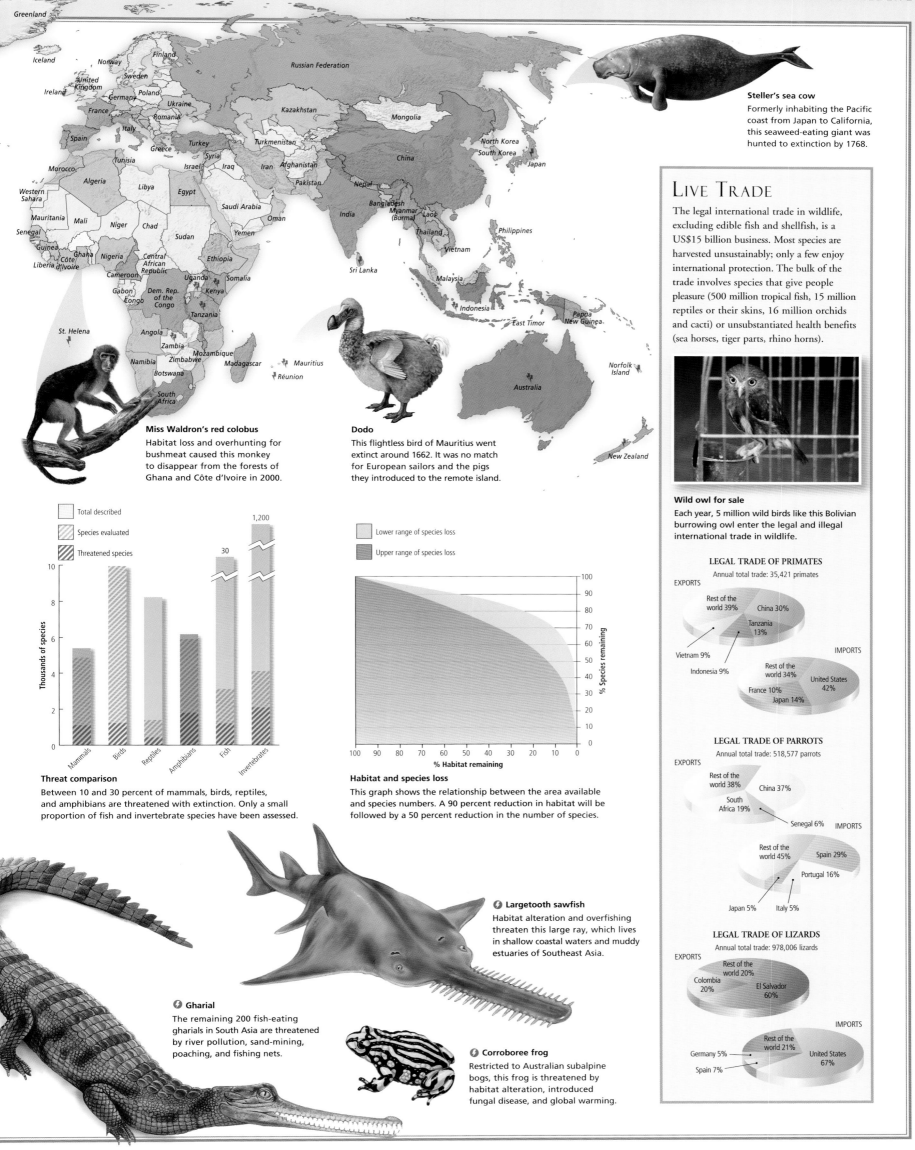

Steller's sea cow
Formerly inhabiting the Pacific coast from Japan to California, this seaweed-eating giant was hunted to extinction by 1768.

LIVE TRADE

The legal international trade in wildlife, excluding edible fish and shellfish, is a US$15 billion business. Most species are harvested unsustainably; only a few enjoy international protection. The bulk of the trade involves species that give people pleasure (500 million tropical fish, 15 million reptiles or their skins, 16 million orchids and cacti) or unsubstantiated health benefits (sea horses, tiger parts, rhino horns).

Wild owl for sale
Each year, 5 million wild birds like this Bolivian burrowing owl enter the legal and illegal international trade in wildlife.

LEGAL TRADE OF PRIMATES
Annual total trade: 35,421 primates

EXPORTS
Rest of the world 39%
China 30%
Tanzania 13%
Vietnam 9%
Indonesia 9%

IMPORTS
Rest of the world 34%
United States 42%
France 10%
Japan 14%

LEGAL TRADE OF PARROTS
Annual total trade: 518,577 parrots

EXPORTS
Rest of the world 38%
China 37%
South Africa 19%
Senegal 6%

IMPORTS
Rest of the world 45%
Spain 29%
Portugal 16%
Japan 5%
Italy 5%

LEGAL TRADE OF LIZARDS
Annual total trade: 978,006 lizards

EXPORTS
Rest of the world 20%
Colombia 20%
El Salvador 60%

IMPORTS
Rest of the world 21%
United States 67%
Germany 5%
Spain 7%

Miss Waldron's red colobus
Habitat loss and overhunting for bushmeat caused this monkey to disappear from the forests of Ghana and Côte d'Ivoire in 2000.

Dodo
This flightless bird of Mauritius went extinct around 1662. It was no match for European sailors and the pigs they introduced to the remote island.

Threat comparison

Total described
Species evaluated
Threatened species

Thousands of species

Mammals / Birds / Reptiles / Amphibians / Fish / Invertebrates

1,200
30
10
8
6
4
2
0

Between 10 and 30 percent of mammals, birds, reptiles, and amphibians are threatened with extinction. Only a small proportion of fish and invertebrate species have been assessed.

Habitat and species loss

Lower range of species loss
Upper range of species loss

% Species remaining
% Habitat remaining

This graph shows the relationship between the area available and species numbers. A 90 percent reduction in habitat will be followed by a 50 percent reduction in the number of species.

Largetooth sawfish
Habitat alteration and overfishing threaten this large ray, which lives in shallow coastal waters and muddy estuaries of Southeast Asia.

Gharial
The remaining 200 fish-eating gharials in South Asia are threatened by river pollution, sand-mining, poaching, and fishing nets.

Corroboree frog
Restricted to Australian subalpine bogs, this frog is threatened by habitat alteration, introduced fungal disease, and global warming.

CONSERVATION

The most effective response to the biodiversity crisis is to create the largest possible protected areas. About 10 percent of ice-free lands are now reserved for wildlife. National parks alone are not enough, however, as animals do not recognize reserve boundaries and they are affected by what humans do around each reserve. The attitudes of local people to wildlife are vitally important, so projects that benefit them are an essential part of conservation. Environmental NGOs (non-government organizations), with their armies of supporters, have successfully integrated human development into conservation efforts, especially when governments lack the will or funds to act. Protected areas provide us with all sorts of ecological services, including oxygen, clean air and water, medicines, and recreation. As the value of nature's services exceeds US$33 trillion per year—twice the value of all other human activities—wildlife conservation directly affects our well-being.

Wildlife tourism
The tourism industry is worth US$600 billion per year, and about 20 percent of this is wildlife-focused or ecotourism. Although tourists can harm wildlife habitat, well-planned activities benefit both local people and wildlife.

Biodiversity hotspots

More than half the planet's species occur in only 2.3 percent of its land area. Conservation International's 34 global hotspots, indicated on the map, contain an extremely large proportion of the world's biodiversity. Protecting these areas would help conserve many species found nowhere else, including 50 percent of endemic vascular plants and 42 percent of endemic vertebrates. When more widely distributed species are also considered, these small areas contain 77 percent of all terrestrial vertebrate species.

- Biodiversity hotspots
- % Percentage of original vegetation remaining

SCALE 1:90,000,000
Robinson Projection

NORTH AMERICA

California Floristic Province 25%

Madrean Pine-Oak Woodlands 20%

Caribbean Islands 10%

Mesoamerica 20%

Tumbes-Chocó-Magdalena 24%

SOUTH AMERICA

Tropical Andes 25%

Cerrado 22%

Atlantic Forest 8%

Chilean Winter Rainfall-Valdivian Forests 30%

Guinean Forests of West Africa 15%

Iberian lynx
Habitat conversion, declining wild rabbit populations, and fatal traffic accidents threaten the last hundred of these cats in Spain, even in Doñana National Park.

Resplendent quetzal
Restricted to montane cloud forests and declining in numbers, males still make "joy flights" in Costa Rican national parks.

Spectacled bear
The only neotropical bear survives in generally unprotected Andean forests. It is killed for its valuable gall bladder and because it raids crops.

Pygmy hippopotamus
Perhaps 2,000 of these hippos survive in Liberia and nearby countries, but their riverine forest habitat is fast disappearing.

PROTECTED AREAS
- Less than 1%
- 1–5%
- 5–10%
- 10–20%
- More than 20%
- Insufficient data

Parks and reserves

Countries vary in how much land they have reserved for wildlife, and national parks are no guarantee of protection—nearly half are affected by the activities of indigenous people who have long lived inside the park boundaries, poor settlers, poachers, loggers, and developers. Creating buffer zones around parks and habitat corridors between reserves will help to address the needs of wildlife.

Wasteful harvest
The great white shark is legally protected in many areas, but it is still among the 250,000 sharks killed daily for sport, for their fins (for Chinese soup), and as accidental bycatch of other fisheries.

Ivory trade
Poaching reduced African elephant populations from about 20 million to 500,000. The 1989 CITES (Convention on International Trade in Endangered Species) ban on ivory trade reversed the trend, but elephant conservation remains challenging.

HOTSPOT FACTS

First outlined by British ecologist Norman Myers in 1988, the biodiversity hotspot concept has been refined by Conservation International, which identifies the following 34 hotspots (also shown on map). All these hotspots are home to high numbers of endemic species and face serious threats.

Endemic threatened birds
Endemic threatened mammals
Endemic threatened amphibians

Atlantic Forest: Tropical rain forest
55 21 14

California Floristic Province: Chaparral to sequoia forest
4 5 8

Cape Floristic Region: Evergreen shrublands
0 1 7

Caribbean Islands: Montane forests to cactus shrublands
48 18 143

Caucasus: Arid vegetation
0 2 2

Cerrado: Woodland-savanna
10 4 2

Chilean Winter Rainfall-Valdivian Forests: Coastal to alpine forests
6 5 15

Coastal Forests of Eastern Africa: Moist and dry forests
2 6 4

East Melanesian Islands: Volcanic islands, diverse vegetation
33 20 5

Eastern Afromontane: Mountains and lakes
35 48 30

Guinean Forests of West Africa: Lowland forests
31 35 49

Himalaya: High mountains
8 4 4

Horn of Africa: Arid bushland and grassland
9 8 1

Indo-Burma: Tropical forests and rivers
18 25 35

Irano-Anatolian: Mountains and basins
0 3 2

Japan: Subtropical to northern temperate island habitats
10 21 19

Madagascar and Indian Ocean Islands: Isolated island habitats
57 51 61

Madrean Pine-Oak Woodlands: Rugged mountains and canyons
7 2 36

Maputaland-Pondoland-Albany: Warm temperate forests
0 2 6

Mediterranean Basin: Maquis shrublands
9 11 14

Mesoamerica: Dry and moist forests
31 29 232

Mountains of Central Asia: Glaciers to desert
0 3 1

Mountains of Southwest China: Temperate to alpine mountains
2 3 3

New Caledonia: Pacific islands
7 3 0

New Zealand: Mountainous islands
63 3 4

Philippines: Rain-forest fragments
56 47 48

Polynesia-Micronesia: Diverse island habitats
90 8 1

Southwest Australia: Forest to heath
3 6 3

Succulent Karoo: Arid succulent flora
0 1 1

Sundaland: Tropical rain forests
43 60 59

Tropical Andes: Montane cloud forests
110 14 363

Tumbes-Chocó-Magdalena: Coastal habitats
21 7 8

Wallacea: Tropical rain forests
49 44 7

Western Ghats and Sri Lanka: Tropical forests to grasslands
10 14 87

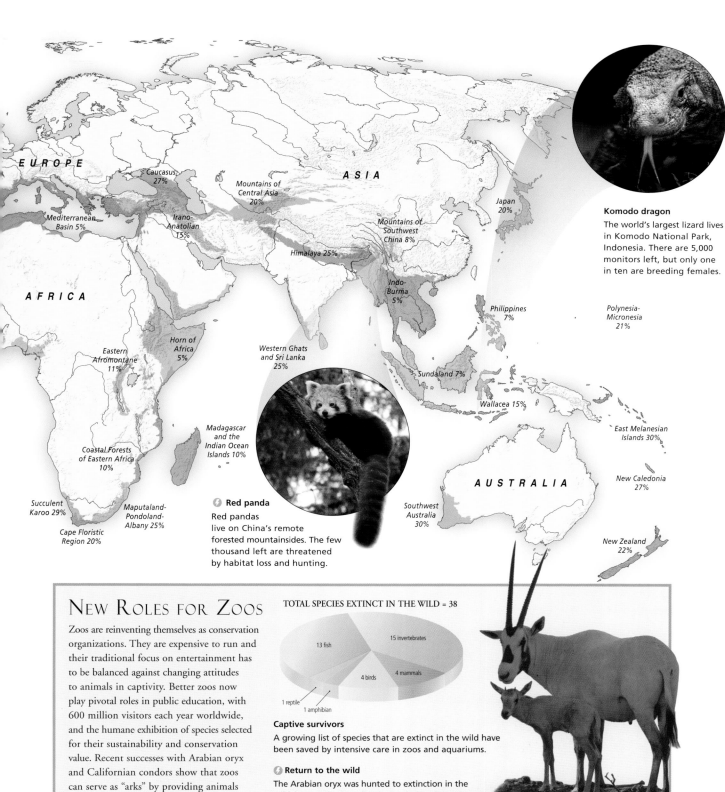

EUROPE

ASIA

Caucasus 27%

Mountains of Central Asia 20%

Mediterranean Basin 5%

Irano-Anatolian 15%

Himalaya 25%

Mountains of Southwest China 8%

Japan 20%

AFRICA

Indo-Burma 5%

Philippines 7%

Polynesia-Micronesia 21%

Eastern Afromontane 11%

Horn of Africa 5%

Western Ghats and Sri Lanka 25%

Sundaland 7%

Wallacea 15%

East Melanesian Islands 30%

Coastal Forests of Eastern Africa 10%

Madagascar and the Indian Ocean Islands 10%

AUSTRALIA

New Caledonia 27%

Succulent Karoo 29%

Maputaland-Pondoland-Albany 25%

Cape Floristic Region 20%

Southwest Australia 30%

New Zealand 22%

Komodo dragon
The world's largest lizard lives in Komodo National Park, Indonesia. There are 5,000 monitors left, but only one in ten are breeding females.

Red panda
Red pandas live on China's remote forested mountainsides. The few thousand left are threatened by habitat loss and hunting.

NEW ROLES FOR ZOOS

Zoos are reinventing themselves as conservation organizations. They are expensive to run and their traditional focus on entertainment has to be balanced against changing attitudes to animals in captivity. Better zoos now play pivotal roles in public education, with 600 million visitors each year worldwide, and the humane exhibition of species selected for their sustainability and conservation value. Recent successes with Arabian oryx and Californian condors show that zoos can serve as "arks" by providing animals for reintroduction into the wild.

TOTAL SPECIES EXTINT IN THE WILD = 38

15 invertebrates
13 fish
4 mammals
4 birds
1 reptile
1 amphibian

Captive survivors
A growing list of species that are extinct in the wild have been saved by intensive care in zoos and aquariums.

Return to the wild
The Arabian oryx was hunted to extinction in the wild, but captive breeding in North American zoos allowed its reintroduction to the Arabian Peninsula.

Deep in the deciduous forests of Germany, a red deer stag stands guard among females. Stags such as this one collect a harem, which they rigorously defend against other males throughout the mating season. Red deer are browsers, feeding on grasses, leaves, shoots, and buds. They range across Western Europe.

EUROPE

EUROPE

With an area of 3.9 million square miles (10.2 million km²), Europe makes up less than 7 percent of Earth's land. Topography can vary greatly in relatively small areas. Mountains dominate the south, descending into hills before flattening into broad plains in the north. Uplands and mountains curve along the western edge of Britain and Ireland and eastward into Norway. Mixed forest once covered much of Europe, but more than half has been lost because of the long-time presence of humans. This has led to widespread disruption of native wildlife—some species have become extinct, others are confined to habitat pockets. The large predatory mammals such as bear, wolf, and lynx have experienced the greatest impact from the spread of urban areas but herbivores, including red deer, moose, chamois, and ibex are well-represented. Europe has a diversity of bird species, from large raptors, to migratory waterfowl, to tiny passerines. Many different species of marine mammals and fish inhabit the Mediterranean Sea and coastal waters.

CLIMATE ZONES
- Semiarid
- Mediterranean
- Subtropical
- Temperate
- Continental
- Cold temperate
- Subpolar
- Highland

Climate

Polar winds are largely responsible for the cold winters experienced by northern Europe, which also records shorter, cooler summers than southern climates. More temperate conditions in western Europe are largely because of the Gulf Stream, which carries warm water to Europe's coastline and heats the prevailing westerly winds. More dramatic weather extremes—from bitingly cold winters to scorching summers—are common across the eastern interior. Southern Europe generally enjoys warm, dry summers and mild, wet winters.

Deciduous Woodlands
Five vegetation zones layer the broad swath of deciduous woodlands that sweep across Europe, providing many types of habitat for wildlife, such as badgers, to choose from.

The Mediterranean
A monkey, devil ray, viper, and bone-eating vulture are some of the more unusual animal species found in and around the Mediterranean Sea.

River Valleys
Dozens of major rivers drain the continent and support the entire spectrum of animal life, from tiny invertebrates to fish, birds, and mammals, such as this river otter.

Coniferous Forests of Northern Europe
Only wildlife species that are well adapted to the conditions can survive on the limited vegetation, and withstand the severe climate, of the far north coniferous forests.

VEGETATION ZONES
- Midlatitude forest
- Boreal forest
- Mountain vegetation
- Midlatitude grassland
- Tundra
- Mediterranean forest and scrub
- Ice sheet

Vegetation

Broadleaf deciduous forests of oak, ash, elm, beech, and birch once covered most of western and central Europe. Large areas of Scandinavia, northwestern Russia, and alpine mountain regions continue to support boreal forests of fir, spruce, and pine. On the tundra of the far north, mosses, small shrubs, and summer wildflowers grow on the permanently frozen soils. Dry areas of eastern Europe are swathed in grasslands.

Mountain Ranges
Born from continental collision, Europe boasts some of the steepest and most rugged mountain ranges on the planet where living relics from the Ice Age still dwell.

Life Along the Shore
The seashore varies dramatically along Europe's relatively long coastline, ranging from rocky tidepools to sandy dunes, and animals take advantage of the selection.

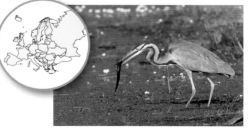

Marshes and Wetlands
Every country in Europe boasts a wetland or marsh, and no habitat is more productive in terms of supporting every link in the wildlife food chain.

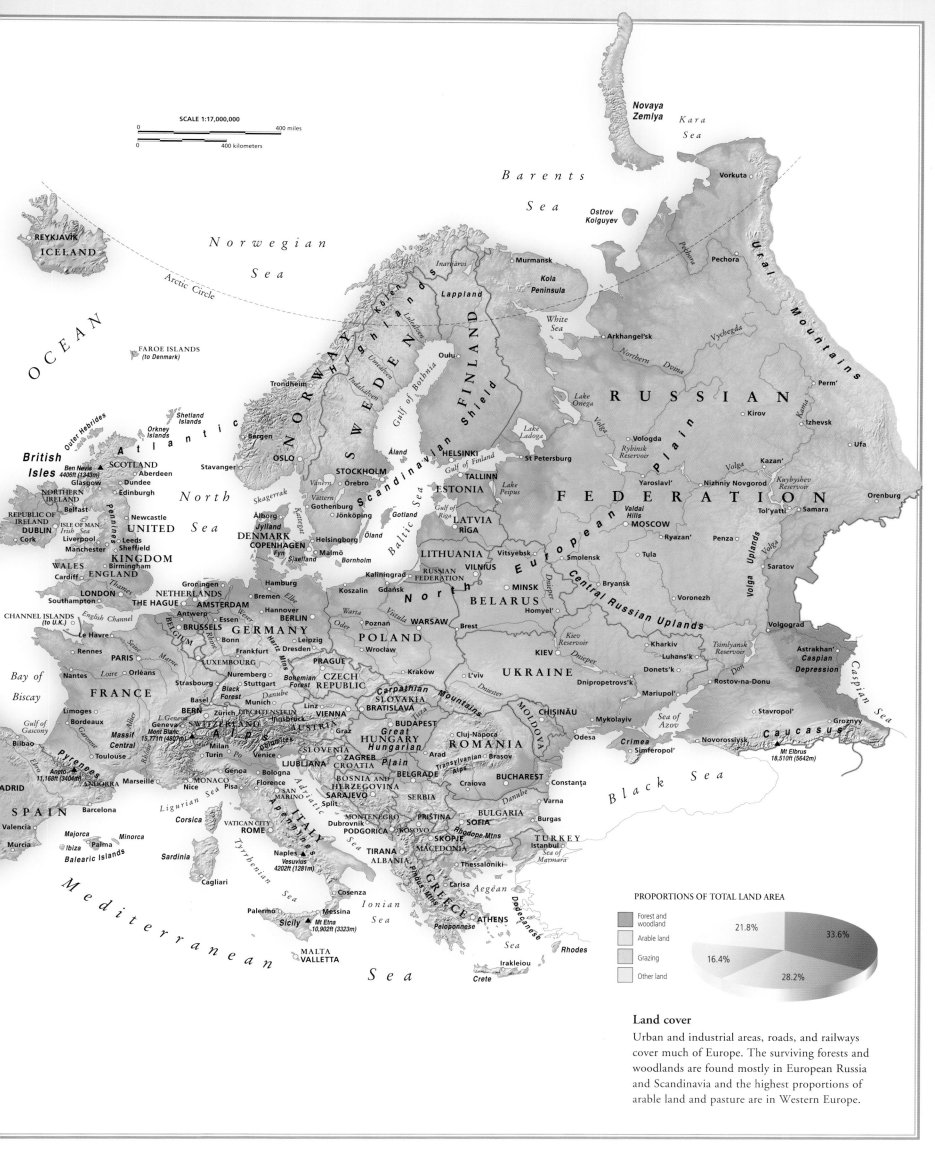

SCALE 1:17,000,000

0   400 miles

0   400 kilometers

Barents

Sea

Novaya
Zemlya

Kara
Sea

Ostrov
Kolguyev

Vorkuta

Norwegian

Sea

REYKJAVÍK
ICELAND

OCEAN

Arctic Circle

Murmansk

Kola
Peninsula

Lappland

White
Sea

Arkhangel'sk

Pechora

Pechora

Vychegda

Ural Mountains

Perm'

FAROE ISLANDS
(to Denmark)

Trondheim

Bergen

Oulu

Lake
Onega

Northern
Dvina

RUSSIAN

Kirov

Izhevsk

Ufa

Atlantic

Shetland
Islands

Orkney
Islands

Outer Hebrides

British
Isles

SCOTLAND
Ben Nevis
4406ft (1343m)

Aberdeen

Glasgow

Dundee

Edinburgh

Stavanger

OSLO

STOCKHOLM

Örebro

Vänern

HELSINKI

Åland

Gulf of Finland

Lake
Ladoga

St Petersburg

Vologda

Rybinsk
Reservoir

Yaroslavl'

Nizhniy Novgorod

Kazan'

Kuybyshev
Reservoir

Tol'yatti

Samara

Orenburg

FEDERATION

North

Sea

NORTHERN
IRELAND

Belfast

REPUBLIC OF
IRELAND

DUBLIN

Cork

ISLE OF MAN

Irish Sea

Liverpool

Manchester

Newcastle

Leeds

Sheffield

UNITED

KINGDOM

WALES

Cardiff

ENGLAND

Birmingham

Skagerrak

Gothenburg

Jönköping

TALLINN

ESTONIA

Gotland

LATVIA

RIGA

Lake
Peipus

Valdai
Hills

MOSCOW

Ryazan'

Penza

Saratov

Vitsyebsk

Smolensk

Tula

Kattegat

Ålborg

Jylland

DENMARK
COPENHAGEN

Helsingborg

Malmö

Fyn

Sjælland

Bornholm

Öland

Baltic Sea

Gulf of
Riga

LITHUANIA

VILNIUS

Kaliningrad

RUSSIAN
FEDERATION

Koszalin

Gdańsk

MINSK

BELARUS

Homyel'

Bryansk

Voronezh

Volgograd

Volga Uplands

Volga

LONDON

Southampton

CHANNEL ISLANDS
(to U.K.)

English Channel

Le Havre

Rennes

PARIS

Thames

Groningen

NETHERLANDS

AMSTERDAM

THE HAGUE

Antwerp

Essen

BELGIUM

BRUSSELS

LUXEMBOURG

Hamburg

Bremen

Hannover

GERMANY

BERLIN

Elbe

Weser

Oder

Warta

Poznań

Vistula

WARSAW

POLAND

Wrocław

Brest

KIEV

Kiev
Reservoir

Dnieper

UKRAINE

L'viv

Kharkiv

Luhans'k

Donets'k

Tsimlyansk
Reservoir

Rostov-na-Donu

Don

Astrakhan'
Caspian
Depression

Caspian Sea

North European Plain

Central Russian Uplands

Bay of
Biscay

Seine

Marne

Loire

Orléans

Nantes

FRANCE

Limoges

Gulf of
Gascony

Bordeaux

Garonne

Toulouse

Allier

Frankfurt

Bonn

Leipzig

Dresden

Harz Mts

Nuremberg

Stuttgart

Strasbourg

Basel

Black
Forest

Munich

Linz

PRAGUE

Bohemian
Forest

CZECH
REPUBLIC

SLOVAKIA

BRATISLAVA

Kraków

Danube

Carpathian

VIENNA

Graz

Mountains

Tisza

CHIŞINĂU

MOLDOVA

Dniester

Mykolayiv

Odesa

Sea of
Azov

Mariupol'

Dnipropetrovs'k

Stavropol'

Groznyy

Novorossiysk

Caucasus

Mt Elbrus
18,510ft (5642m)

ADRID

SPAIN

Bilbao

Ebro

Pyrenees

Aneto
11,168ft (3404m)

ANDORRA

Marseille

Rhône

BERN

L.Geneva

Geneva

Zürich LIECHTENSTEIN

Mont Blanc
15,771ft (4807m)

SWITZERLAND

Innsbruck

AUSTRIA

ALPS

Dolomites

SLOVENIA

LJUBLJANA

ZAGREB

CROATIA

Great
Hungarian
Plain

HUNGARY

BUDAPEST

Arad

Cluj-Napoca

ROMANIA

Transylvanian
Alps

Braşov

BUCHAREST

Craiova

Danube

Constanţa

Varna

Burgas

Black Sea

Crimea

Simferopol'

Milan

Turin

Po

Venice

Bologna

Genoa

Pisa

Florence

Ligurian
Sea

Nice

MONACO

VATICAN CITY

ROME

Corsica

Sardinia

Cagliari

Palermo

Sicily

Mt Etna
10,902ft (3323m)

Messina

Tyrrhenian
Sea

SAN
MARINO

Adriatic
Sea

Split

BOSNIA AND
HERZEGOVINA

SARAJEVO

Dubrovnik

MONTENEGRO

PODGORICA

BELGRADE

SERBIA

Apennines

Naples

Vesuvius
4202ft (1281m)

Cosenza

Ionian
Sea

ITALY

MALTA
VALLETTA

PRIŠTINA

KOSOVO

SKOPJE

MACEDONIA

TIRANA

ALBANIA

BULGARIA

SOFIA

Rhodope Mtns

Thessaloniki

TURKEY

Istanbul

Sea of
Marmara

Pindus Mtns

GREECE

ATHENS

Findus Mtns

Larisa

Aegean
Sea

Dodecanese

Rhodes

Sea

Irakleiou

Crete

Peloponnese

Valencia

Murcia

Majorca

Palma

Ibiza

Minorca

Balearic Islands

Mediterranean

Sea

CHANNEL ISLANDS
(to U.K.)

Cardiff

Pennines

NORWAY

SWEDEN

Lofoten Islands

Kjolen

Highlands

Lulealven

Umeälven

Indalsälven

Gulf of
Bothnia

FINLAND

Inarijärvi

Scandinavian Shield

Volga

Kursk

Ros toslav'

Orël

PROPORTIONS OF TOTAL LAND AREA

Forest and
woodland

Arable land

Grazing

Other land

21.8%

33.6%

16.4%

28.2%

Land cover

Urban and industrial areas, roads, and railways
cover much of Europe. The surviving forests and
woodlands are found mostly in European Russia
and Scandinavia and the highest proportions of
arable land and pasture are in Western Europe.

DECIDUOUS WOODLANDS

Europe's deciduous woodlands extend from as far north as Scotland, south to France, and east to the Urals. The term deciduous describes trees such as the oak, elm, birch, lime, and alder, which lose their leaves in autumn. Much of the broad swath of deciduous woodlands that once covered the continent was cleared long ago for agriculture and pastures, towns, and cities. What remains are pockets of woodland protected within preserves and parks. Woodlands have an average temperature of 50°F (10°C) and annual rainfall of 30–60 inches (762–1,524 mm). The relatively mild weather, with warm to cool summers and moderately cold winters, is because of the moderating effects of the Atlantic Ocean. The five vegetation strata of the woodlands—trees, small trees and saplings, shrubs, herbs, and the ground zone—provide habitats for a variety of wildlife. Woodland animals range from deer to small mammals and birds. When flowers are in bloom numerous delicate butterflies appear.

SCALE 1:32,000,000

0   500 miles

0   500 kilometers

Butterflies

Deciduous trees and flowering plants in open glades and meadows provide a plentiful food source for caterpillars and butterflies. Many of Europe's 576 butterfly species are found here.

White letter hairstreak
Satyrium album

Map butterfly
Araschnia levana

Lesser purple emperor
Apatura ilia

Silver-washed fritillary
Argynnis paphia

Camberwell beauty
Nymphalis antiopa

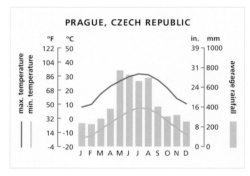

PRAGUE, CZECH REPUBLIC

Raccoon dog
Though the raccoon dog resembles a raccoon, it is a member of the dog family, Canidae. Small rodents are its preferred food but it is an omnivore, so can seek food widely. It hibernates in winter.

Red fox
The red fox has keen senses of sight, smell and hearing, earning it a reputation for intelligence. A skilled hunter, it is capable of feeding on a wide variety of prey.

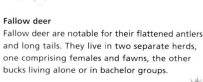

Fallow deer
Fallow deer are notable for their flattened antlers and long tails. They live in two separate herds, one comprising females and fawns, the other bucks living alone or in bachelor groups.

Red squirrel
Sciurus vulgaris

Little owl
Athene noctua

Black woodpecker
Dryocopus martius

Badger
Meles meles

European mole
Talpa europaea

Clouded yellow butterfly
Colias croceus

The deciduous forest

A single tree can support myriad species of wildlife. Red squirrel and black woodpecker nest in cavities in mature trees that also provide an abundant source of seeds and insects. The little owl perches on the high limbs while looking for prey. The soft soil beneath a tree makes digging easier for the badger and European mole.

CONSERVATION WATCH

The long tail of the red squirrel helps it balance when jumping from tree to tree and provides winter warmth. Although the red squirrel is common in many parts of Europe, the introduction of the North American gray squirrel has driven the red species from much of its range in Britain. Conservation efforts are underway.

SPRING

Life in the woodlands is dominated by the changing of the seasons. Plants and animals must be able to survive the winter, then take full advantage of the spring, when the days lengthen and the temperature rises, to propagate and perpetuate their species. First come the wildflowers that bloom before the canopy of leaves shades them from sunlight. The flowers provide food for insects, which, in turn, attract migrating birds that arrive from their wintering grounds to breed and raise their young.

Bluebells
Bell-shaped and slightly fragrant, the bluebell blooms in woodlands all along the Atlantic seaboard, from Scotland to Spain. Some of its ingredients are being tested for their medicinal properties.

THE EUROPEAN BADGER

The badger is an Old World member of the weasel family that also includes the otter and pine marten, and dates back 2.4 million years. There are nine species of badger globally, but only *Meles meles* occurs in the wild in Europe. It is found throughout the British Isles and on the continent, though not in northern Scandinavia or the Mediterranean islands. The badger prefers to live in woodlands and grassy fields. While it resides in complex burrow systems, often in locations that experience cold winters and deep snowfalls, it does not hibernate. Animals enter into a state of torpor that can last for several weeks, living off fat reserves accumulated during the rest of the year. Much of the badger's survival success is because of its highly opportunistic and omnivorous feeding habits, which often bring it into conflict with farmers. The badger requires large territories of up to 405 acres (164 ha) in which to forage.

BADGER'S DIET

A forager rather than hunter, the nocturnal badger spends half its time looking for food, relying on its keen sense of smell and hearing. Though it has carnivorous incisors, its molars are flattened for grinding, making it a true omnivore. Its diet ranges from acorns, fruits, seeds, and mushrooms to earthworms, insects, reptiles, birds, and small mammals. It even eats carrion.

COMPOSITION OF DIET

Insects 24%
Earthworms 35%
Cereals 18%
Fruits 9%
Birds 6%
Mammals 8%

Worms
Earthworms make up much of the badger's diet, especially in grassy fields on damp nights when a badger can suck up to 200 wigglers in one sitting.

Fruit
Badgers feast seasonally, eating tree fruit that falls to the ground, including apples and pears, as well as stripping berries from bushes.

Baby hedgehogs
A hedgehog's spiny fur and its ability to roll into a tight ball are no defense against a hungry badger, which relies on its powerful front claws to pry open its prickly prey.

Sett
The communal burrow, or sett, has numerous entrances, passages, and chambers. It is typically constructed on sloping ground in woodland or on the periphery of a field. Spoil piles of dirt mark its entrances. Setts are often used for decades and continually grow in size and complexity.

Fresh bedding
Badgers line their beds with insulating grass or leaves, which they drag backward into the den. The vegetation is changed regularly and occasionally spread out at the sett's entrance in the morning to air in the sunlight for an hour or two.

Taking to water
While the badger can swim, it prefers walking around ponds and lakes or crossing over streams and canals using fallen trees as bridges. When forced to swim it paddles with its front paws much like a dog.

A proficient digger

The badger's digging ability is legendary. Stories of the animal outpacing humans with shovels abound. Scientists estimate badgers had moved almost 27.5 tons (25 t) of soil at one 1,000-foot-long (305-m) tunnel network. Long claws break up earth; webbed front feet scoop it out. Badgers remove the soil by pushing it out with their back legs, and are capable of carrying large rocks.

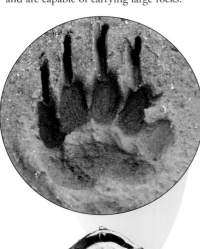

Family group
Highly communal badgers live in clans, generally containing up to 12 individuals. Cubs are weaned by six months and will forage with sows, often initiating play with other cubs and adults. Non-breeding sows sometimes serve as babysitters. Badgers use scent and vocalization to recognize clan members.

Predator
Full-grown badgers don't have any natural predators, though bears and wolves sometimes kill them to reduce competition for food. Cubs, however, are prey to the bears and wolves, as well as lynx and wolverines. The eagle owl (right) and golden eagle also eat young badgers.

Claws
The badger has five toes on each foot, with broad plantar pads and bare soles. The front claws can be as long as 2 inches (5 cm). A badger often places its back foot exactly where its front foot has stepped.

ASKHAM BRYAN
LEARNING RESOURCES

RIVER VALLEYS

The islands of Ireland and Britain and the European continent are etched with major rivers that form fertile valleys, including the Guadalquivir, Ebro, Loire, Danube, Vistula, Biebrza, Volga, and Lemmenjoki. River valleys are biologically important, creating a wide spectrum of ecosystems, from brackish lagoons at the mouth to freshwater springs at the source. The sheer variety of habitats supports a vast array of wildlife. The mix of water and lush vegetation are both a home and a source of food for insects, amphibians, reptiles, birds, and mammals. River valleys also serve as wildlife corridors, providing anadromous fish such as Atlantic salmon access to freshwater spawning grounds, and migrating waterfowl a road map as well as a resting spot in fall and spring. Both predator and prey are drawn by water. While rich in species, river valleys are also among the landscapes most impacted by human activity. Farming, industrialization, and the construction of dams have all taken their toll.

SCALE 1:30,000,000

Ebro River

Spain's longest river, the Ebro, springs from the Cantabrian Mountains in the north and flows 565 miles (910 km) southeast to the Mediterranean coast. Fed by more than 200 tributaries, the Ebro discharges more water than any other Spanish river.

Layers of life

A cross-section of a river valley reveals layers of life, each reliant on the other. Water supports nutrients and vegetation in the river and along its banks. This first link in the food chain leads to insects, invertebrates, fish, birds, and mammals. No two river valleys are the same, so speciation occurs. Climate, topography, and humans help determine which species are found where.

Wild boar
The wild boar is a highly aggressive omnivore. Adult males sport large tusks that are sharpened by grinding and used as weapons. Females guard their numerous young. The stiff bristles of the boar's fur are used to make hairbrushes.

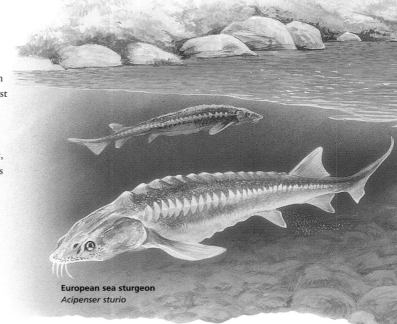

European sea sturgeon
Acipenser sturio

FLAMINGOS

The greater flamingo lives in colonies numbering in the hundreds. The birds flock to shallow river mouths along the Mediterranean Sea because the mix of fresh and salt water makes for a rich stew of nutrients. These nutrients, in turn, generate large amounts of algae, insect life, and crustaceans, which are the bird's favorite foods.

Flamingo
The greater flamingo is the tallest of six flamingo species and dates back 30 million years.

Vistula River

Poland's longest river drains an enormous area measuring 75,000 square miles (194,250 km²), or nearly half the country's landmass. Industrialization and farming have brought changes but the Vistula still retains a semi-natural character for much of its length. The river valley supports more than 1,000 plant species. Bordering forests and meadows provide homes for the Eurasian lynx and other mammals.

European beaver
Once hunted to near extinction for its fur and scent glands, which are thought to have medicinal properties, this largest of European rodents is semi-aquatic. It dams streams with sticks and mud and creates lodges where it can find protection from predators. The dams also help to create ponds for easier access to food.

European kingfisher
The common, or European, kingfisher hunts for fish from an overhanging perch or while hovering above water. Small fish are swallowed immediately, head-first, while bigger fish are carried to a tree limb and beaten against it. A pair may have to catch 100 fish a day to feed their hungry nestlings.

Muskrat
Ondatra zibethica

Common rabbit
Oryctolagus cuniculus

Black stork
Ciconia nigra

Souslik
Citillus citillus

WARSAW, POLAND

RIVER VALLEY	COUNTRY	WILDLIFE SPECIES
Ebro	Spain	Auduoin's gull, catfish
Loire	France	Little bittern, wild cat
Danube	Germany-Ukraine	White pelican, sturgeon
Vistula	Poland	Beaver, pine marten
Volga	Russia	Great white egret, Volga lamprey
Lemmenjoki	Finland	Reindeer, Siberian jay

European hedgehog
Erinaceus europaeus

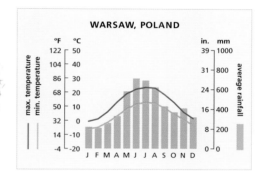

Danube River

The Danube drains the Black Forest in Germany and flows 1,770 miles (2,850 km) across 10 countries to the Black Sea. The river basin supports a diverse range of habitats and is home to many species of flora and fauna, including 100 types of fish. Five species of sturgeon swim its waters.

Black stork
A wading bird, the black stork feeds in the shallow waters of rivers, marshes, and ponds. This broad-winged bird flies with its long neck outstretched and migrates to Africa for the winter.

Eurasian otter
The Eurasian otter is well-adapted to aquatic life, with its slim body, webbed toes, and rudder-like tail. The otter can close its ears and nostrils while underwater and uses its sensitive whiskers to detect the movement of its prey.

THE DELTA OF COTA DONANA

The Guadalquivir is the second longest river in Spain and drains an area of 22,400 square miles (58,000 km²). It begins in the Cazorla Mountains and empties into the Gulf of Cádiz. Its delta is a complex system of marshes, dunes, and coastal lagoons. Much of the delta is protected as Doñana National Park, a UNESCO World Heritage site. One of the largest and best-known wetlands in Europe, Doñana is a land of contrasts, lying at the crossroads of two continents and influenced by both the Atlantic Ocean and the Mediterranean Sea. The array of habitats translates into a rich concentration of wildlife. Some 750 plant species live here, along with 20 species of fish, 10 amphibians, 19 reptiles, and 30 mammals, including the rare Iberian lynx, small-spotted genet, and wildcat. More than half of Europe's birds occur here, many of them in huge numbers, including flocks of up to 70,000 greylag geese and 200,000 teal.

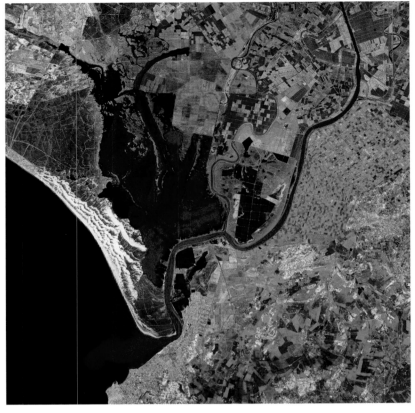

Waters teem with life
Birds flock to the delta's shallow, brackish waters because they are nutrient-rich and full of food, including shrimp, crabs, insects, and larvae. Wading birds, such as egrets and herons, have an advantage over smaller, short-legged shorebirds, such as plovers and sandpipers.

Greater flamingo
Greater flamingos are social birds, forming colonies numbering up to 300 individuals. They can travel 373 miles (600 km) in a single night when migrating, preferably in cloudless skies and with favorable tailwinds.

Polecat
The polecat is related to the weasel, mink, otter, and stout. Mostly nocturnal, it feeds on rodents, amphibians, and birds, and makes its den in stream banks or under tree roots.

Horseshoe bat
Mediterranean horseshoe bats live in colonies called clouds, roosting in caves and tunnels where the average temperature is 50°F (10°C). They use echolocation to find their prey.

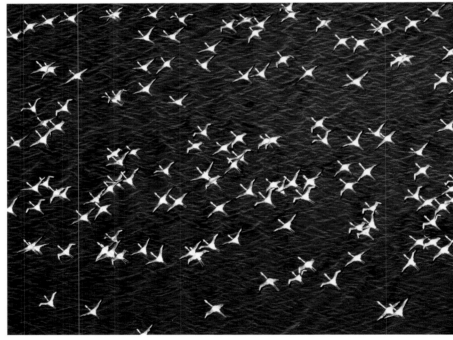

Spiny-footed lizard
The spiny-footed lizard owes its name to the comblike spines along its back legs, which allow it to run on sand. This species is found widely in the Mediterranean.

BIRD BEAKS

Birds have evolved to occupy certain niches, even in the same ecosystem, such as a delta. The most important function of a bird's bill is feeding, and it is shaped according to what the bird eats. For waterbirds, long, pointed bills suit probing and spearing; flat bills are adapted for straining and scooping.

Common spoonbill
The convex upper bill acts like an airfoil, creating swirling currents that suspend crustaceans and fish when swept from side to side in the water.

Common spoonbill
The common, or black-billed, spoonbill occurs in the intertidal flats and shallows of fresh and saltwater wetlands. It sweeps its bill from side to side in its quest to trap tiny fish.

Glossy ibis
The ibis uses its long, down-curved beak to probe in the mud for frogs, fish, insects, and snails. Nostrils at the base of the beak allow the bird to breathe.

Glossy ibis
The glossy ibis breeds in the warmer regions of Europe, where it nests colonially in trees. A strong flier and gregarious feeder, this widespread species migrates to Africa for the winter.

Purple heron
The 5-inch-long (13-cm) spiky beak of the purple heron is used to seize or harpoon prey. Food is swallowed whole.

Eurasian curlew
Females have longer decurved beaks than males, measuring up to 6 inches (15 cm). They feed by probing sand and mud for insects.

Lataste's viper
Lataste's viper is one of five venomous snakes found in Spain. Stout with a triangular head, it is recognizable by the wavy or zigzag stripe that runs along its back.

European weasel
It may be small, but the European weasel is known as a ferocious species. Medieval legend recognizes the weasel for killing the mythical basilisk.

Greater flamingo
The flamingo's keel-shaped bill is lined with rows of keratinous plates covered with tiny hairs. This enables the bird to filter invertebrates in a similar fashion to baleen whales.

MOUNTAIN RANGES

Like folds in skin, the European continent is creased with mountain ranges. They were created by the collision of jigsaw puzzle-shaped tectonic plates that form Earth's crust. Between five and 30 million years ago the northward-moving African plate slammed into the more stable European plate, pushing up sediments that once lay beneath a separating ocean made extinct by the collision. Collectively, the Alps, Scandes, Pyrenees, Carpathians, Rhodopes, Urals, Caucasia, and Dinaric landforms constitute what is known as the alpine biogeographic region. While the mountainous areas share common features, their varying gradients, climate, and soil types have influenced the distribution and diversity of species. The result is an amazing array of wildlife that includes 129 mammal species, 359 birds, 40 amphibians, and 65 reptiles. Plant life is also rich on the continent. The 5,000 species of vascular plants comprise half of all plant types native to Europe.

SCALE 1:25,000,000

0 — 400 miles
0 — 400 kilometers

Apollo butterfly
The beautiful Apollo butterfly, with distinctive "eye" marks on its wings, can be found in flowery alpine meadows as high as 6,400 feet (1,950 m). Life in a rugged mountain habitat has led to the development of many subspecies, some restricted to a single alpine valley. Medium-sized and tail-less, the Apollo has three pairs of walking legs.

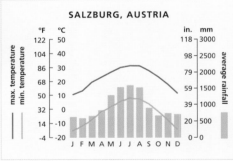

SALZBURG, AUSTRIA

Eagle wing
Eagle wings are a miracle in lightweight design. Bones are hollow and primary feathers spread like fingers to reduce drag. Most of the power for flying comes from the downward stroke.

Wildcat
Once found throughout Europe, the wildcat dates back to the Early Pleistocene. Hunting and habitat loss have reduced its range and numbers. It is generally solitary and is one-third larger, and has a thicker coat, than its direct descendant, the domestic cat.

European brown bear
Brown bears once occurred throughout Europe, but were driven almost to extinction. Protecting habitat and raising cubs in captivity has helped. Today, about 55,000 bears survive, most in Eastern Europe and Russia.

Golden eagle

Everything about an eagle is perfectly designed for hunting, from its keen eyesight, powerful wings, and aerodynamic feathers, to its sharp beak and talons. Eagles use several methods for capturing prey, but soaring and swooping are the most common. Snatching the animal by the head with one foot, the eagle drives the talons of its other foot into the prey's lungs as it carries it away.

RELICS OF THE GLACIERS

Plant and animal species that survived the Ice Age are known as glacial relics. A mountainous region of Poland, now protected as Karkonoski National Park, has a high proportion of glacial relics, including the arctic whorl snail, Sudetic wolf spider, and the bird known as the ring ouzel.

Rivers of ice
Glaciers are rivers of ice, always moving and churning up rocky debris. When they melt or retreat, they leave this debris behind in moraines.

Dotterel
A small wader, a member of the plover family, the migrating dotterel winters in the semiarid deserts of North Africa and the Middle East and breeds in the Alps and northern Europe, nesting in a bare ground scrape. The males are responsible for incubation.

Red kite
An extremely agile flier, the red kite has a small body relative to its wing size. If a predator approaches its nest the mother will signal her young to "play dead."

Tengmalm's owl
A small, ancient bird, Tengmalm's owl is found in boreal forests. It builds its nest in a tree cavity drilled by woodpeckers and successive generations occupy the same site. The male sings to attract a mate.

Dormouse
The dormouse's feet are adapted for grasping trees; the soles have cushioned pads and the toes have curved claws. Its hind feet can be turned backward, which allows it to dangle from a branch.

THE MOUNTAINEERS

Animals that live in the mountains have developed special physical characteristics that help them cope in a challenging environment marked by severe cold, rugged topography and reduced oxygen. With the exception of some insects, most of the animals living at altitude are warm-blooded. These animals adapt to the cold by hibernating in winter, such as the marmot; migrating to lower, warmer areas; or huddling together in burrows, such as the snow vole. Mountain animals tend to have shorter appendages in order to reduce heat loss, such as the alpine hare, which has smaller ears than its lowland counterpart. Animals such as the ibex have larger lungs and more blood cells because of the increased pressure and lack of oxygen at higher altitudes. Other physical adaptations include special hooves such as those of the chamois, to aid in climbing, or the footpads of the lynx, which are broad and well-furred compared to other felines as an adaptation for walking on snow.

Alpine hare
The hare's brown coat turns white before winter, providing camouflage from predators and greater warmth. Shorter daylight hours trigger hormones that inhibit the production of brown pigment in the new coat. The hollow white hairs improve insulation and allow more sunlight to be absorbed.

Marmot den
As sociable animals, marmots live in large burrows with several generations of their family. They excavate the burrow using their forepaws and hind feet and remove stones with their teeth. Entrances are sited between large rocks to avoid detection and flooding, and living areas are lined with dried grass. Burrows are enlarged to accommodate new generations; the newborn remain in the burrow for their first 40 days.

Tunnel to one
of several exits

Concealed
entrance

On guard

Nesting
chamber

CHAMOIS AND IBEX

Split hooves that can spread enable chamois and ibex to climb near-vertical cliffs and smooth, slick rock faces. The hooves have a hard, thin rim surrounding a soft and sponge-like interior, and these cushioned pads can grip slippery surfaces. Well-developed leg muscles and a low center of gravity aid in climbing and jumping. A chamois can leap as high as 6.5 feet (2 m) and as long as 20 feet (6 m).

Chamois
In summer, herds of chamois graze in alpine meadows above 6,000 feet (1,800 m). As winter approaches, they descend to shelter in forests near steep cliffs. Chamois were once hunted for their hides.

Ibex
Horn size distinguishes male and female ibex. The defensive horns start growing at sexual maturity and never stop, reaching lengths up to 3 feet (1 m) in the male.

Snow vole
Relatively large compared to other species, the snow vole is generally found above the timberline in high rocky mountainsides above 5,000 feet (1,500 m). Though voles burrow under rocks, they do not hibernate in winter.

Eurasian lynx
Mainly nocturnal and solitary, the Eurasian lynx is seldom seen or heard. A highly efficient hunter, it preys on rabbits, rodents, and deer in a hunting territory of some 20 square miles (50 km²). It can live up to 17 years in the wild.

Fresh grass is brought into the den

THE MEDITERRANEAN

An enclosed sea, the Mediterranean covers nearly 1 million square miles (2.6 million km²), with a coastline that extends 28,500 miles (46,000 km) and runs through 22 countries. The Mediterranean Sea represents only one percent of the planet's ocean surface, yet it contains approximately six percent of its marine species. Its rocky reefs, seagrass meadows, and upwelling areas support enormous biological diversity. Marine mammals include the fin whale, harbor porpoise, and striped dolphin, and shark species occurring in the Mediterranean include the great white and blue sharks. Coastal and inland areas are also important habitats for wildlife, with wading and shorebirds dependent upon shallow estuaries, and mammals ranging in size from tiny mice to 200-pound (90-kg) deer found in the oak, pine, and wild olive forests. Wildlife, however, is under extreme pressure from human activities, including coastal development, overfishing, agricultural and industrial runoff, and wildfire.

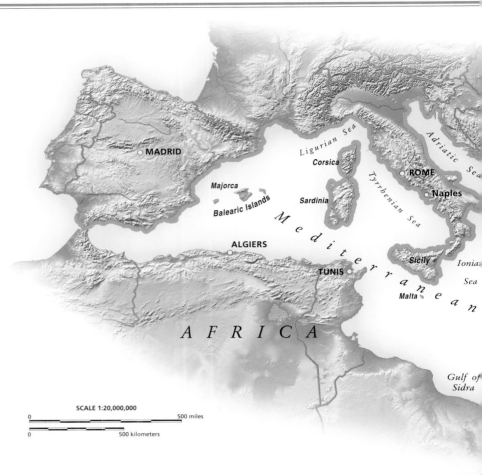

SCALE 1:20,000,000

WILDFIRES

Wildfires are commonplace throughout the Mediterranean. On average, 50,000 fires sweep through as many as 2.47 million acres (1 million ha) of forest and woodland every year. Up to 95 percent are caused by people. Hot, dry summers and a buildup of fuel compound the problem. Natural wildfires keep forests healthy and ensure plant diversity, but too much burning can impoverish habitat and contribute to climate change.

Forest fire
Wildfires have devastating effects on animals, from those with limited mobility, such as snails, snakes, and tortoises, to small and large mammals. Though birds can escape the flames, they lose their food supply of seeds, insects, and rodents.

Italian wall lizard
The Italian wall lizard, typical of the small reptiles at risk from wildfires, is found throughout the Mediterranean and as far away as Japan and the United States. It has been successful at adapting to new environments.

⚡ CONSERVATION WATCH

The Mediterranean monk seal is one of the most endangered marine mammals in the world, with fewer than 600 individuals in existence. They were once hunted for their pelts and blubber, which was turned into oil, and commercial fishermen considered them pests. The establishment of protected marine zones now holds the key to their continued survival.

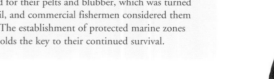

Sharks

The Mediterranean Sea has one of the greatest diversities of sharks on the planet, but a high proportion are endangered. Of the 71 species of sharks and rays found here, 30 are deemed threatened with extinction, including the great white, shortfin mako, and porbeagle sharks.

Mako shark
Isurus oxyrinchus

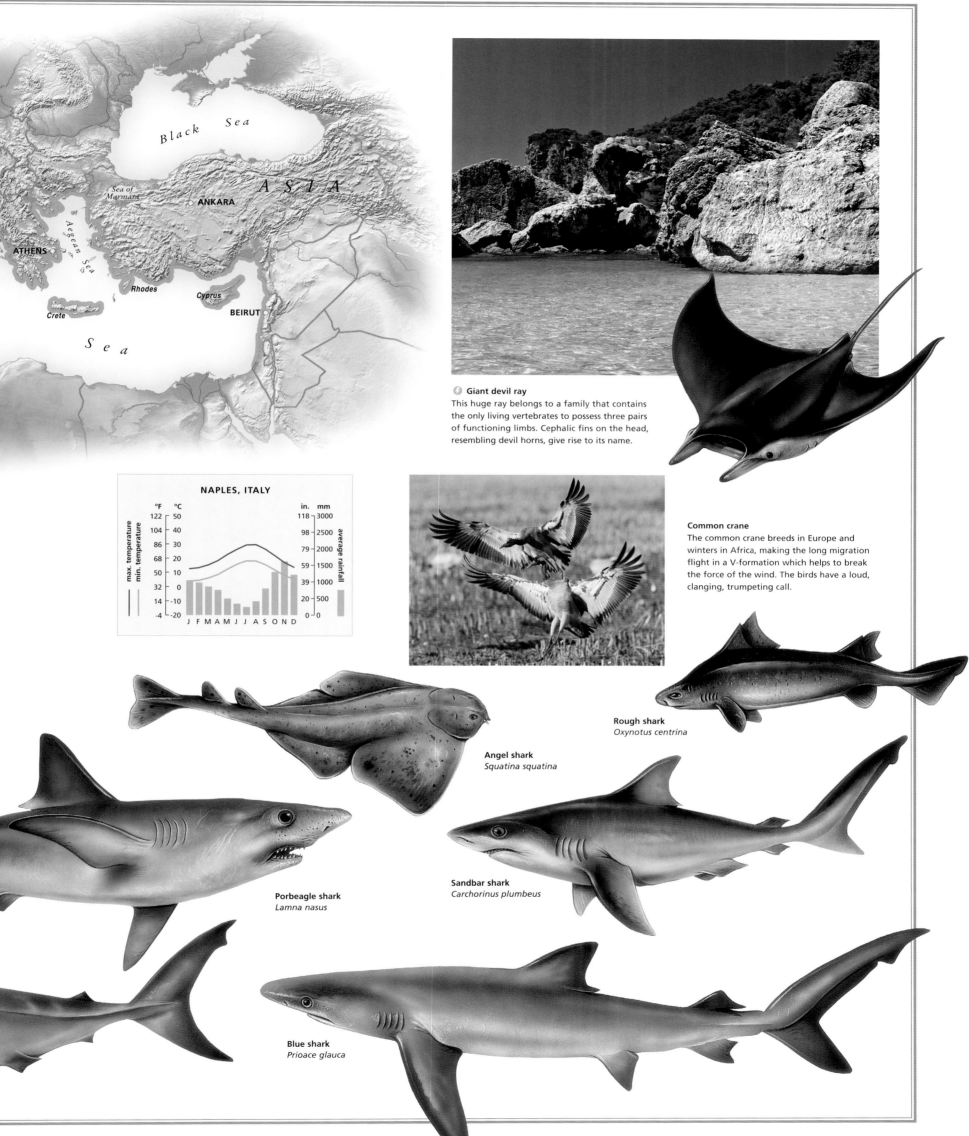

Giant devil ray
This huge ray belongs to a family that contains the only living vertebrates to possess three pairs of functioning limbs. Cephalic fins on the head, resembling devil horns, give rise to its name.

NAPLES, ITALY

Common crane
The common crane breeds in Europe and winters in Africa, making the long migration flight in a V-formation which helps to break the force of the wind. The birds have a loud, clanging, trumpeting call.

Rough shark
Oxynotus centrina

Angel shark
Squatina squatina

Porbeagle shark
Lamna nasus

Sandbar shark
Carchorinus plumbeus

Blue shark
Prioace glauca

THE MEDITERRANEAN

MEDITERRANEAN ISLANDS

Five thousand islands, ranging from tiny islets to enormous Sicily, pepper the Mediterranean, making it one of the largest island groups in the world. Variations in size as well as altitude, geology, and isolation produce a wide range of habitats that support a diverse array of species. The limited or non-existent exchange of genetic material between island and mainland species has resulted in an exceptionally high rate of endemism. Isolation has also helped some ancient island plant species survive the last glacial period, when their mainland relatives perished. More than 125 plant species, 10 bird species, and the Cyprus mouflon, a wild sheep, are found on Cyprus and nowhere else. The islands also serve as resting and refueling stops for birds migrating between Europe and Africa. More than 100 different species, including the red-footed falcon and golden oriole, visit Corsica.

Eleonora's falcon
The medium-sized Eleonora's falcon lives in colonies of 100 pairs or more on rocky cliffs in Greece. It winters in Madagascar and is named for the 14th-century Sardinian princess who introduced laws to protect it. In the Middle Ages, falcons were trained and used for hunting.

Bearded vulture
Also known as the Lammergeier, this vulture inhabits high mountains. It feeds almost exclusively on bones, swallowing small ones whole and allowing gastric fluids to digest them. It smashes larger bones on rocks.

Sardinian wild deer
About 1,500 endemic Sardinian red deer live in mountainous areas of Sardinia. Once close to extinction, the deer is now protected and numbers are growing. Males compete for harems, first by bellowing and trying to chase competitors away, then by battling with their antlers.

Barbary Macaque

The vulnerable Barbary macaque, commonly, but mistakenly called an ape, is the only wild primate found in Europe. It is restricted to Gibraltar, and though there is fossil evidence of the species in other parts of Europe, the 100 surviving macaques actually descended from North African populations that were introduced by the British from the 18th century. The British Army has assumed responsibility for the macaque's care.

Common dolphin
Common dolphins are distinguished from other dolphins by their unique crisscross color pattern: dark on the back, light grey on the flank, with a pale yellow thoracic patch and white abdomen. They live in large schools and jump and splash together.

Island	Area in sq miles (km²)	Population
Sicily	9,926 (25,708)	5,017,509
Sardinia	9,301 (24,090)	1,655,677
Cyprus	3,572 (9,252)	788,457
Corsica	3,351 (8,680)	281,000
Crete	3,219 (8,336)	623,666

Blue tit
On Corsica, blue tits line their nests with aromatic plants, such as mint, lavender, and citronella, to help protect their chicks from blowflies, mosquitoes, and other blood-sucking parasites. The herbal potpourri, which parents constantly replenish, is also thought to repel fungi and bacteria.

CONSERVATION WATCH

Hunting and competition from livestock left the population of Cyprus's largest wild land mammal, the mouflon, down to just a few dozen by the beginning of the 20th century. The population has increased, in part, because of the establishment of special watering holes that protect the mouflon from diseases carried by domestic cattle, sheep, and goats.

EUROPE
FLYWAYS OF EUROPE

The migration of billions of birds across thousands of miles every year is one of the world's most magnificent natural phenomena. Migrants traveling in huge numbers follow overlapping flyways that loop between breeding grounds in the north and wintering grounds in the south. Species ranging in size from enormous white stork to tiny blackcap fly between Europe and Africa. They cross over two land bridges—one across the Middle East and down the east coast of Africa, and the other over Gibraltar and down the west coast of Africa. The aerial highways that link breeding and wintering areas also include a network of stop-over sites, where migrants can rest and refuel before continuing their journey. Flyways tend to follow coastlines and north–south river valleys. They may be only a few hundred yards wide at certain points, such as mountain passes and straits like the Bosporus; in other places they measure hundreds of miles across.

WINGSPANS

A bird's wingspan is measured from the tip of one fully extended wing across the body to the tip of the other wing. Feathers provide insulation and help streamline the body and wings, making the bird aerodynamic. Birds adjust their wingspan to control flight.

White stork *60 inches (150 cm)*
Riding on thermals of hot air, the white stork has a wingspan twice the length of its body.

Northern lapwing *28 inches (70 cm)*
Migration is often wind-assisted for the northern lapwing, whose wings make a lapping sound.

Eurasian teal *20 inches (55 cm)*
This dabbling duck flies in large flocks. Fast wing beats make the flocks appear to twist in flight.

Swallow *13 inches (33 cm)*
Swallows are fast and acrobatic fliers that prey on insects, which they catch mid-flight.

Wood warbler *9 inches (22 cm)*
The entire population of wood warblers flies to tropical Africa to escape harsh European winters.

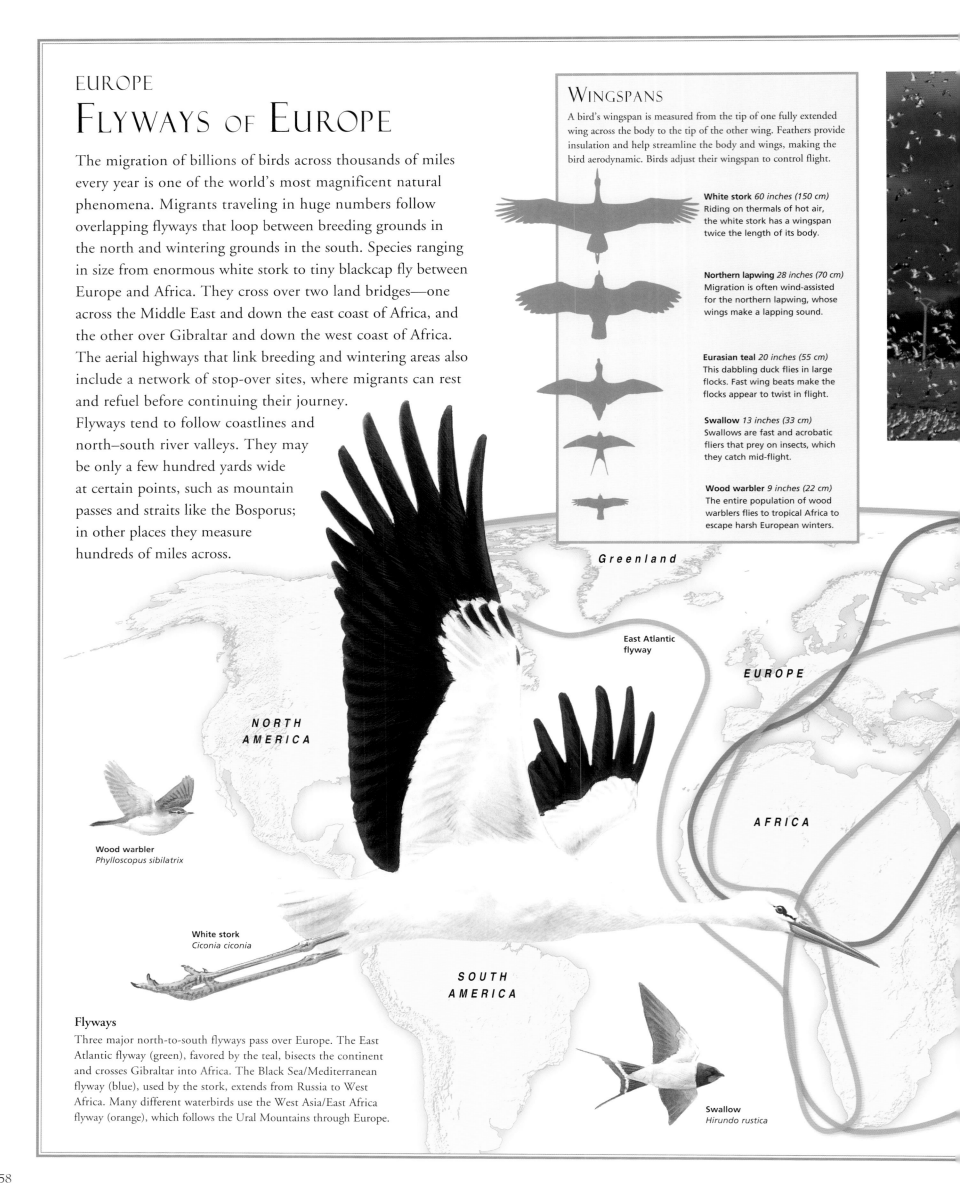

Greenland

East Atlantic flyway

EUROPE

AFRICA

NORTH AMERICA

Wood warbler
Phylloscopus sibilatrix

White stork
Ciconia ciconia

SOUTH AMERICA

Swallow
Hirundo rustica

Flyways
Three major north-to-south flyways pass over Europe. The East Atlantic flyway (green), favored by the teal, bisects the continent and crosses Gibraltar into Africa. The Black Sea/Mediterranean flyway (blue), used by the stork, extends from Russia to West Africa. Many different waterbirds use the West Asia/East Africa flyway (orange), which follows the Ural Mountains through Europe.

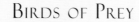

BIRDS OF PREY

Bird-eating raptors and owls prey on migrating species. The peregrine falcon nests near wetlands that attract large flocks of shorebirds and waterfowl to ensure an abundance of food for its young. Golden eagles time their own migration with that of prey species, such as warblers and songbirds. Another bird-eater is the European eagle owl. It nests on cliffs that overlook forests and open fields so that it can capture passing birds.

Blackcap
Sylvia atricapilla

Flock of plovers
Birds flock for defense, to locate food, and to navigate during migration. The coordinated movements of flocks such as these plovers result from the second-to-second decisions of individual birds reacting to their neighbors.

Osprey
The osprey snatches fish from shallow depths. Before hitting the water, it thrusts its talons forward, pushes out its breast, and holds its wings back, ready to clutch its catch headfirst.

Eurasian teal
Anas crecca

Peregrine falcon
The peregrine falcon can reach speeds of up to 200 miles per hour (320 km/h) as it dive-bombs its prey, usually medium-sized birds, such as pigeons, ducks, and shorebirds. As strong as it is speedy, a peregrine can carry off prey half its own body weight.

ASIA

**Black sea/
Mediterranean flyway**

Lanner falcon
Lanner falcon, also called Feldegg's falcon, resides in southeast Europe and breeds in Africa. It hunts by horizontal pursuit rather than diving from above, and is one of the few raptors that attack its prey head on, often resorting to ambush. Bats are favorite targets.

**West Asia/
East Africa flyway**

Northern lapwing
Vanellus vanellus

*Indian
Ocean*

SPECIES	WINTERING AREA	MIGRATION DISTANCE
Swallow	South Africa	5,600 miles (9,000 km)
Wood warbler	Central Africa	4,660 miles (7,500 km)
Eurasian teal	East Africa	3,400 miles (5,500 km)
White stork	East Africa	3,400 miles (5,500 km)
Blackcap	East Africa	3,400 miles (5,500 km)
Northern lapwing	North Africa	1,900 miles (3,000 km)

CONIFEROUS FORESTS OF NORTHERN EUROPE

The coniferous forest, or taiga, stretches across the upper part of Europe in a green band bordered by tundra to the north and deciduous trees to the south. It gets its name from the dominant vegetation: cone-bearing trees, including pine and spruce, that possess needles instead of leaves. The advantage of needles is that they contain little sap and do not freeze during the long, cold winters, when average temperatures drop below freezing for half the year. Needles are also dark and can better absorb what little sunlight there is present. Since they are not deciduous, the trees do not need to expend energy regenerating during the short growing season. The lack of plant diversity compared to other European biomes translates into fewer animal species, too. Resident mammals that have adapted to the harsh conditions include hearty specialists, such as moose, bears, lynx, and pine marten.

SCALE 1:30,000,000

Great gray owl
The scientific name for one of the world's largest owls, the great gray, is *Strix nebulosa*, derived from the Latin word meaning misty or foggy. It pants when hot and cools off by exposing its skin.

FOREST	COUNTRY	WILDLIFE SPECIES
Bohemian	Czech Republic, Austria, Germany	Wolf, hazel grouse
Bavarian	Germany	Bison, lynx
Trillemarka	Norway	Siberian jay, golden eagle
Pokka-Pulju	Finland	White-backed woodpecker, flying squirrel

European wolf
Wolves still survive in many European countries despite centuries of hunting and habitat loss. This highly social animal forms packs comprising the extended family of a dominant male.

Red deer
Only male red deer have antlers. Made of bone, the antlers grow about one inch (2.5 cm) a day from spring until they are shed in winter. Red deer graze in the early morning and late evening. They do not migrate.

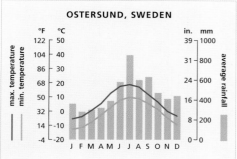

OSTERSUND, SWEDEN

Pine marten
Semi-retractable claws allow the pine marten to climb trees. A bushy tail helps it balance when scurrying from limb to limb, and fur on the soles of its paws aids insulation and creates built-in snowshoes for winter.

Black grouse
Black grouse, also known as blackgame, engage in an elaborate courtship ritual. Cocks fan their lyre-shaped tails and make a bubbling, spitting call while competing for hens.

Whooper swan
Whooper swans mate for life, jointly building a nest beside a shallow lake or slow-moving river. The male stands guard while the female incubates the eggs. The cygnets live with their parents for their first year, all migrating to warmer lands for winter.

Alpine newt
Though an amphibian, the alpine newt lacks webbed toes and spends much of its time on land, usually in undergrowth. It moves to the cool water of forest pools during the spawning season.

MOOSE

The largest of the deer family, moose are one of Europe's oldest species. Stone Age hunters depicted them in cave paintings. They are ideally suited to survival in northern forests from Norway to Russia—long legs ease travel through bogs and deep snow, especially when chased by wolves and bears. Moose defend themselves by flailing and kicking, their large size acting as a deterrent to would-be predators.

Adult male
Bulls grow antlers in summer. During the rut, August–October, they splash urine-soaked mud on hairy skin flaps under their jaws to attract females. They battle other males to win a mate.

Female and calf
Cows reach sexual maturity at 1.5 years. The gestation period varies, lasting anywhere between 215 and 243 days. Twins are common and mothers fiercely defend their calves.

LIFE ALONG THE SHORE

At 202,500 miles (325,900 km), Europe's shoreline is relatively long in relation to its land area compared to other continents. With a wide continental shelf, the seashore varies dramatically, ranging from rocky coastlines to sandy beaches to muddy tidal flats. Saltmarshes, coastal dunes, estuaries, and bays are some of the habitats that support an enormous variety of plants and animals. Tidal pools form along the rocky coastline and provide oases for limpets, mussels, crabs, and fish. Bivalve mollusks burrow under the surface on sandy beaches. Deposits of mud and silt in the sheltered waters of estuaries and bays are high in nutrients and provide homes for worms and other invertebrates. These, in turn, satisfy waders and shorebirds, such as the heron, stilt, oystercatcher, and stork. The coastline is also delicate. Development and changing land use threatens wildlife habitat, and erosion is a problem. Europe's coastlines are retreating, on average, by 1.6 to 6 feet (0.5–1.8 m) each year.

SCALE 1:30,000,000

0   400 miles

0   400 kilometers

Little gull
The aptly named little gull is the smallest gull in the world. Often mistaken for a tern because of its size, coloring, and behavior, it snatches insects from the air and plucks food off the water. Highly migratory, the little gull nests in floating vegetation among reeds.

Sea urchin
The purple sea urchin's spines offer it protection from predatory fish as it feeds on kelp and other marine plants. Strong rasping teeth also allow the sea urchin to break off coral polyps and it can cause considerable damage. Sea urchins, like starfish, belong to the echinoderm group of invertebrates.

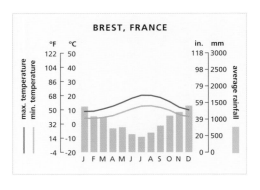

BREST, FRANCE

Starfish
Starfish are spiny-skinned animals called echinoderms with five or more "arms" that radiate from a disk. The common starfish is the most familiar. It is typically 4 to 12 inches (10–30 cm) in diameter and orange, pale brown, or violet in color. Others include the spiny sun star, sand starfish, and cushion star.

Sea slug
Sea slugs are essentially snails that have lost their shells or are in the process of losing them. There are hundreds of species, ranging from spectacular multicolored fanlike nudibranchs to primitive bubble shells. A muscular foot that produces sticky mucus aids their crawling movement.

Life in a tidal pool

Inside a tidal pool the environment is always changing with the movement of the sun, wind, and tide. Survival means avoiding being washed away or drying out. The hardiest animals, namely barnacles and whelks, live in the splash zone. Starfish and sea urchins cling to the middle zone and tiny fish stick to deeper pools. Hermit crabs and sea anemones dwell on the bottom.

Starfish underside
Tubelike feet aid starfish locomotion and feeding. The central mouth leads to two stomachs, one of which can be everted so the starfish can digest food outside its body.

Anemone
A sea anemone's body is a column with a single opening, used to ingest food and expel wastes. When touched, surrounding tentacles inject a poison and hold the prey for digestion.

Herring gull
A common gull found throughout the North Atlantic, the herring gull can drink either freshwater or sea water. It excretes the salt through special glands located above its eyes. A scavenger, the gull's call is a loud, clear bugle.

European harbor seal
Common harbor seals can be found from Ireland to the east coast of Sweden and north from Holland to the Arctic. They have two sets of flippers. The pectorals have five webbed digits with claws used for grooming and defense. The hind flippers are kicked for forward propulsion.

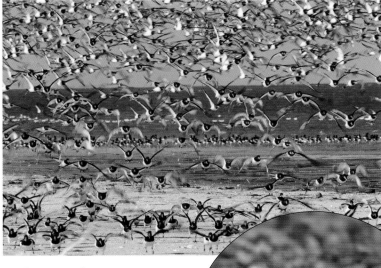

Eurasian oystercatcher
The tip of the oystercatcher's bill changes shape. Most of the year it is broad so that the coastal bird can pry open mollusks and hammer through shells. By the time the oystercatchers move inland to breed the tip has worn down to a point perfectly shaped for digging up worms.

SHORELINE CREATURES AND THEIR HABITAT	
CREATURES	**HABITAT**
Common moon jellyfish	Bay
Gray sea slug	Rocky shore
Chiton	Rocky shore
Little egret	Estuary
Harbor porpoise	Bay

Marshes and Wetlands

Wetlands are either continuously submerged or intermittently inundated by seasonal flooding or daily tides. Enormously diverse in size and shape according to their origins and geographical location, they include marshes, fens, bogs, peatlands, ponds, and coastal estuaries. Wetlands occur in every country in Europe. One-eighth of the United Kingdom's entire landmass is covered in wetlands. Among the most biologically diverse habitats on Earth, nearly 900 European wetlands have been declared of international importance. Dynamic, complex, and renowned for their high levels of endemic species, they are a sanctuary for a wide variety of plants, invertebrates, fish, amphibians, reptiles, and mammals, as well as a high concentration of birds, including millions of migratory and sedentary waterfowl. Wetlands play an important role in maintaining an ecological balance, serving as the planet's natural kidneys by filtering runoff as well as controlling erosion and floods. They also act as buffers from storms.

Life in a marshland

The entire food chain is represented in a marsh, from plant to prey to predator. The sediment-rich water promotes algal and plant growth, which nourishes invertebrates, insects, and fish. These serve as food for purple heron and semi-aquatic rodents, such as the water shrew and muskrat, which, in turn, provide sustenance for birds of prey, such as the marsh harrier.

SCALE 1:20,000,000

0 — 400 miles

0 — 400 kilometers

CORK, IRELAND

Purple heron
Ardea purpurea

Muskrat
Ondatra zibethicus

Water shrew
Noemys fodiens

European perch
Perca fluviatilis

COUNTRY	TERRITORY AREA IN ACRES (HA)	WETLAND AREA IN ACRES (HA)
France	134,828,000 (54,563,000)	3,953,700 (1,600,000)
Sweden	101,542,500 (41,092,800)	26,440,300 (10,700,000)
United Kingdom	59,698,200 (24,159,000)	7,355,300 (2,976,585)
Estonia	10,674,500 (4,320,000)	3,325,800 (1,345,900)
Slovenia	5,005,400 (2,025,600)	296,500 (120,000)

Marsh harrier
Circus aeruginosus

Azure damselfly
Coenagrion puella

Wigeon

The wigeon is a dabbling duck, so named because it grazes by upending on the water surface rather than diving. When spooked, wigeons can spring straight up to take flight. During the breeding season males sport colorful plumage, with pink breasts and a yellow crown stripe.

DRAGONFLY

Dragonflies spend most of their lives as larvae underwater. They metamorphose by crawling onto plants. Exposed to air, their skin splits and the adult dragonflies emerge. Dragonflies have two pairs of wings and can fly at a speed of 100 body-lengths per second.

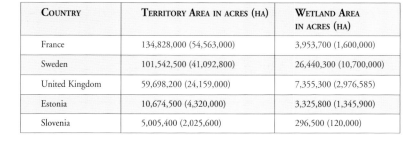

Dalmatian pelican

The largest of seven pelican species, the Dalmatian can be distinguished from the more common white pelican by its size, curly nape feathers, and light ash plumage. It catches fish in its huge bill pouch. Habitat loss has made it vulnerable to extinction.

Horned lark

Known as the shore lark in the United Kingdom, this small bird winters on seashore flats, then heads inland to breed. Its nest, on the open ground, is lined with grass and one side often has a flat doorstep of pebbles.

Water shrew

The water shrew lives in shallow burrow systems, often with underwater entrances. A fast swimmer, it uses hairs on the underside of its tail as a rudder. Venomous saliva helps immobilize prey, ranging from aquatic larvae and insects to small fish, frogs, slugs, and snails.

The bald eagle is found throughout North America and as far south as Mexico. This swooping bald eagle spreads its wings to slow its descent as it prepares to land on the Kenai Peninsula, Alaska. These eagles feed mainly on fish that they pluck from the water, but are also known to steal food from other birds.

NORTH AMERICA

NORTH AMERICA

Mysterious evergreen woods, parched deserts, temperate rain forests, vast grassy plains, snow-capped mountain peaks, oak forests bursting with life, swamps, and sandy beaches; all are found in North America. From northern Mexico through the United States and Canada, the continent is extraordinarily varied climatically and topographically, and this is reflected in its diverse flora and fauna. North America shares some of its wildlife wealth with other continents; awesome brown bears and moose haunt Eurasia, and pumas prey on white-tailed deer in South America. Many of its most beautiful songbirds migrate to and from North America every year. But many animals are unique, from pronghorns and bison to spotted salamanders and Gila monsters. However, humans have taken a huge toll on this land. Some species, such as passenger pigeons, have disappeared entirely and some habitats, including sagebrush and grasslands, are mere shadows of their former glory.

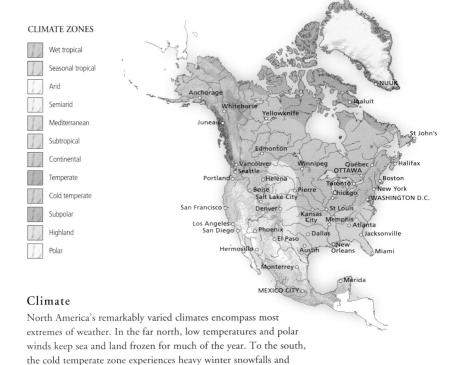

CLIMATE ZONES

- Wet tropical
- Seasonal tropical
- Arid
- Semiarid
- Mediterranean
- Subtropical
- Continental
- Temperate
- Cold temperate
- Subpolar
- Highland
- Polar

Climate

North America's remarkably varied climates encompass most extremes of weather. In the far north, low temperatures and polar winds keep sea and land frozen for much of the year. To the south, the cold temperate zone experiences heavy winter snowfalls and short summers. Winter snow is also abundant in the northeastern USA, where summers are hot and humid. The greatest aridity occurs in the southwestern USA and northwestern Mexico.

The Boreal Forest
Vast, cold, and remote, the boreal coniferous forest shrouds northern North America from sea to sea below the Arctic and supports a small but splendid wildlife assemblage.

The Great Plains
The vast expanse of grasses that flowed through the center of North America has nearly vanished, but traces of its glory remain in remnant bison herds and prairie dog towns.

VEGETATION ZONES

- Tropical forest
- Seasonal tropical forest
- Desert
- Tropical grassland
- Mediterranean forest and scrub
- Midlatitude grassland
- Midlatitude forest
- Boreal forest
- Tundra
- Mountain vegetation
- Ice sheet

Pacific Northwest Coniferous Forest
Boasting the tallest trees on Earth, the Pacific Northwest coniferous forest teems with wildlife, from fish in its coursing rivers to insects living in the treetops.

The Great Basin
The forbidding extremes of the Great Basin, a cold desert dominated by sagebrush and species that depend on it, are succumbing to human and plant invaders.

Natural Vegetation

A permanent cover of ice swathes most of Greenland. South of the arctic tundra—a barren region of bogs, mosses, and scattered conifers—a huge belt of boreal forest blankets most of Canada and reaches southward along the western ranges. Grasslands flank the Rocky Mountains, stretching across the interior to the broadleaved forests of the east, merging with Mediterranean scrub near the west coast. Deserts extend from the southwestern USA across much of northern Mexico.

The Rocky Mountains
The Rocky Mountains' tall peaks and low basins are the home of some of the continent's most spectacular wildlife including bison, bears, bobcats, and wolves.

Deserts of the Southwest
In the hot, dry expanses of the deserts of the southwest, diverse plants and animals have evolved ingenious strategies for conserving water and keeping cool.

Eastern Deciduous Forest
Rolling mountains and majestic trees that burst into brilliant fall colors define the eastern deciduous forest, where songbirds, salamanders, and flowering shrubs abound.

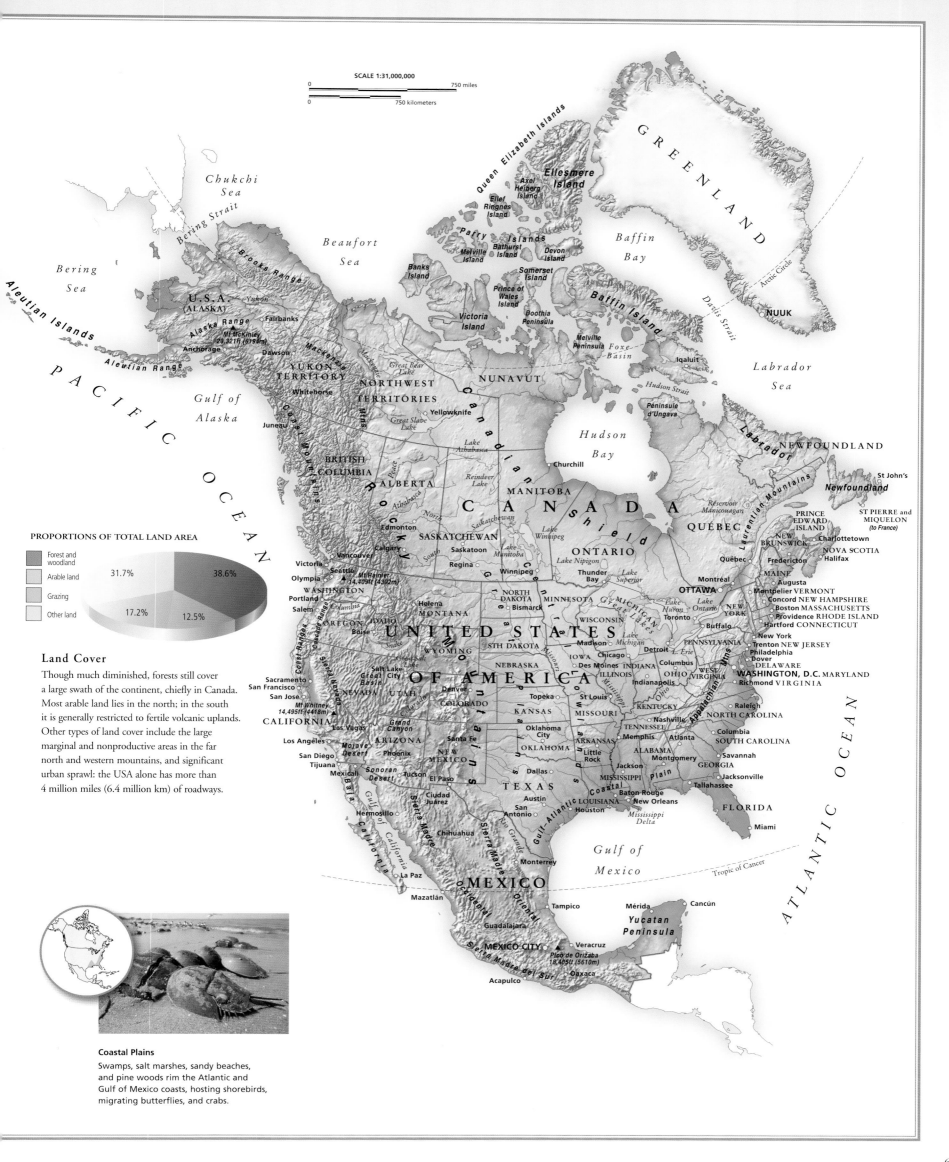

SCALE 1:31,000,000

0   750 miles

0   750 kilometers

G R E E N L A N D

Chukchi Sea

Bering Strait

Beaufort Sea

Baffin Bay

Bering Sea

Aleutian Islands

P A C I F I C   O C E A N

Queen Elizabeth Islands

Axel Heiberg Island
Ellef Ringnes Island
Ellesmere Island
Melville Island
Bathurst Island
Devon Island
Parry Islands
Banks Island
Somerset Island
Prince of Wales Island
Boothia Peninsula
Victoria Island
Melville Peninsula
Foxe Basin
Iqaluit

Arctic Circle

NUUK

Davis Strait

Labrador Sea

U.S.A. (ALASKA)
Yukon
Fairbanks
Brooks Range
Mt McKinley 20,321ft (6194m)
Alaska Range
Anchorage
Dawson
Juneau
Gulf of Alaska
Aleutian Range
Coast Mountains
YUKON TERRITORY
Whitehorse
Mackenzie
Great Bear Lake
NORTHWEST TERRITORIES
Yellowknife
Great Slave Lake
NUNAVUT
Hudson Strait
Péninsule d'Ungava
Labrador

Hudson Bay
Churchill

NEWFOUNDLAND
St John's
Newfoundland

BRITISH COLUMBIA
ALBERTA
Peace
Athabasca
Lake Athabasca
Reindeer Lake
North
South
Saskatchewan
Vancouver
Victoria
Seattle
Olympia
Edmonton
Calgary
Regina
SASKATCHEWAN
Saskatoon
MANITOBA
Lake Winnipeg
Lake Manitoba
Winnipeg
ONTARIO
Lake Nipigon
Thunder Bay
Lake Superior
C A N A D A
Canadian Shield
Réservoir Manicouagan
QUÉBEC
Laurentian Mountains
PRINCE EDWARD ISLAND
ST PIERRE and MIQUELON (to France)
Charlottetown
NOVA SCOTIA
NEW BRUNSWICK
Fredericton
Halifax
Québec
Montréal
OTTAWA
MAINE
Augusta

Portland
Salem
WASHINGTON
Coast Ranges
Cascade Range
Columbia
OREGON
Mt Rainier 14,405ft (4392m)
Helena
MONTANA
IDAHO
Boise
Snake
NORTH DAKOTA
Bismarck
MINNESOTA
Great Lakes
Lake Michigan
Lake Huron
WISCONSIN
Madison
Milwaukee
Lake Ontario
Toronto
Buffalo
Lake Erie
VERMONT
Montpelier
NEW HAMPSHIRE
Concord
MASSACHUSETTS
Boston
RHODE ISLAND
Providence
CONNECTICUT
Hartford

Sacramento
San Francisco
San Jose
Mt Whitney 14,495ft (4418m)
CALIFORNIA
NEVADA
UTAH
Salt Lake City
Great Basin
Great Salt Lake
WYOMING
U N I T E D   S T A T E S
STH DAKOTA
NEBRASKA
IOWA
Des Moines
Chicago
ILLINOIS
Colorado
Denver
COLORADO
O F   A M E R I C A
Rocky Mountains
Topeka
KANSAS
MISSOURI
St Louis
INDIANA
Indianapolis
OHIO
Columbus
Detroit
PENNSYLVANIA
Appalachian Mtns
NEW YORK
New York
NEW JERSEY
Trenton
Philadelphia
DELAWARE
Dover
WASHINGTON, D.C. MARYLAND
Richmond VIRGINIA
WEST VIRGINIA

Las Vegas
Los Angeles
San Diego
Tijuana
Mexicali
Mojave Desert
ARIZONA
Phoenix
Tucson
Sonoran Desert
NEW MEXICO
Santa Fe
Grand Canyon
Colorado
OKLAHOMA
Oklahoma City
ARKANSAS
Little Rock
KENTUCKY
Nashville
TENNESSEE
Memphis
Mississippi
NORTH CAROLINA
Raleigh
Columbia
SOUTH CAROLINA
Atlanta
GEORGIA
Savannah

El Paso
Ciudad Juárez
Chihuahua
TEXAS
Dallas
Austin
San Antonio
Houston
LOUISIANA
Jackson
MISSISSIPPI
ALABAMA
Montgomery
Baton Rouge
New Orleans
Gulf-Atlantic Coastal Plain
Mississippi Delta
FLORIDA
Jacksonville
Tallahassee
Miami

Gulf of California
Sierra Madre Occidental
Hermosillo
Baja California
La Paz
Mazatlán
Guadalajara
MEXICO
Sierra Madre Oriental
Monterrey
Tampico
Rio Grande
Gulf of Mexico
Tropic of Cancer
Mérida
Cancún
Yucatan Peninsula
Veracruz
MEXICO CITY
Pico de Orizaba 18,405ft (5610m)
Sierra Madre del Sur
Acapulco
Oaxaca

A T L A N T I C   O C E A N

PROPORTIONS OF TOTAL LAND AREA

■ Forest and woodland
□ Arable land
□ Grazing
□ Other land

38.6%
31.7%
17.2%
12.5%

Land Cover

Though much diminished, forests still cover
a large swath of the continent, chiefly in Canada.
Most arable land lies in the north; in the south
it is generally restricted to fertile volcanic uplands.
Other types of land cover include the large
marginal and nonproductive areas in the far
north and western mountains, and significant
urban sprawl: the USA alone has more than
4 million miles (6.4 million km) of roadways.

Coastal Plains

Swamps, salt marshes, sandy beaches,
and pine woods rim the Atlantic and
Gulf of Mexico coasts, hosting shorebirds,
migrating butterflies, and crabs.

THE BOREAL FOREST

Covering about one-quarter of North America, the boreal forest stretches from the interior of Alaska to the fringes of Newfoundland. Named for the Greek god of the North Wind, Boreas, this forest is also called taiga, a Russian word meaning "land of little sticks." Long, cold, snowy winters and infertile soils prevent the spruce, fir, and other coniferous trees that dominate this landscape from growing taller than about 50 feet (15 m). Along with these evergreens, birch, aspen, and a few other hardy deciduous trees thrive, all adapted to the natural fires that regularly ravage the forest. The harsh climate limits wildlife diversity, but about 85 mammal species make their homes here, and the boreal forest in summer abounds in breeding migratory birds, when some 3 billion birds of about 300 species feast on its abundant insects. Few people live in the boreal forest, but it is threatened by resource extraction, pollution, and global warming, which could create warmer and drier conditions, insect outbreaks, and more frequent fires.

SCALE 1:35,000,000
0   500 miles
0   500 kilometers

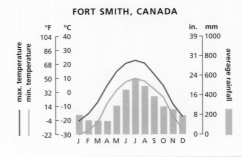

FORT SMITH, CANADA

Common loon
The haunting, wailing calls of breeding common loons emanate from boreal forest lakes and rivers across Canada and Alaska, the northernmost lower 48 US states, and into Yellowstone National Park. These fish-eating water birds rarely go ashore except to mate or to lay and incubate eggs.

Wetlands

Countless lakes, ponds, bogs, and other wetlands dot the boreal forest. More than 13 million migratory ducks breed, feed, and rest in these wetland habitats, as do millions of other waterbirds, including loons, grebes, cranes, and kingfishers. Wetlands and the boreal forest's many rivers are also home to about 130 species of fish and aquatic mammals, such as beavers, whose dams actually create wetlands.

Eared grebe
Eared grebes breed in large, raucous colonies in shallow wetlands in the western boreal forest and other parts of western North America. In summer, they hunt for aquatic insects and spiders on the water's surface and also dive underwater for them.

Whooping crane
Nearly the entire world population of endangered whooping cranes, about 70 breeding pairs, summers in the boreal forest wetlands of Canada's Wood Buffalo National Park and its surrounds. Living 20 to 30 years, whooping cranes raise only one chick a year.

Moose
The boreal forest is the primary habitat of the moose, the largest of all deer. In a sense, moose manage the boreal forest. They graze extensively on the forest's aspens and other deciduous trees, preferring them to conifers. As a result, moose grazing makes room for spruces and other conifers to grow.

CONSERVATION WATCH

The boreal forest is a stronghold of the
solitary wolverine, which ranges widely.
It was never abundant but is declining
in most of its North American range,
and may be extinct elsewhere. Trapping
for their fur and poisoning, largely by
ranchers, has taken a toll on wolverines,
which are easily disturbed and prefer to
live and breed in remote wildernesses.

Least weasel
Least weasels prefer to live and hunt in grassy
meadows intermixed with forest. Their long,
slender bodies enable them to follow mice
and voles into their burrows and, in winter,
through tunnels in the snow. This weasel
needs to eat one or two prey a day, equal
to about half its body weight.

Hungry hunters

Seven of North America's 11 species of mustelids live
in various boreal forest habitats. These luxuriously-furred
carnivores range from tiny least weasels, which weigh
just one or two ounces (28–56 g), to husky wolverines
that weigh up to 500 times more. Predators with
voracious appetites, mustelids eat almost any animal
they can catch as well as feeding on carrion.

Mink
Neovison vison

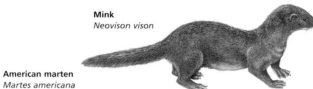

American marten
Martes americana

Least weasel
Mustela vison

Fisher
Martes pennanti

Wolverine
Gulo gulo

Porcupine
A North American porcupine is studded
with about 30,000 barb-tipped quills for
protection. If a predator attacks, the
porcupine drives its quills into the assailant,
injuring and sometimes killing the victim.

Northern river otter
Excellent swimmers and divers, semi-aquatic northern river otters ply the
rivers and lakes of the boreal forest. They hunt, usually alone and at night,
for fish, frogs, turtles, birds, eggs, and sometimes muskrats. A layer of oil
underlying their thick fur insulates their bodies in cold water.

NORTH AMERICA
CARIBOU ON THE MOVE

Caribou, known as reindeer outside of North America, are superbly adapted to life in the cold boreal forest as well as the high Arctic tundra. Two subspecies occupy parts of the North American boreal forest. The woodland caribou lives here year-round in small groups, while barrenland caribou live further north. Barrenland caribou migrate in huge herds as far as 3,100 miles (5,000 km) a year between summer tundra calving grounds and winter boreal forest habitats. Woodland caribou may migrate too, but over much shorter distances of 9 to 50 miles (15–80 km) within the forest. Their numbers have steadily declined over the past century, disappearing entirely from most of the more southerly sections of their former range. Logging, mining, oil exploration, roads, and other human impacts on the boreal forest are the major reasons for this decline. Barrenland caribou are more secure, but climate change threatens the security of both this subspecies and its woodland counterpart.

CONSERVATION WATCH

Summer brings swarms of mosquitoes and black, bot, and warble flies that disturb caribou foraging and force them into patches of snow, where there are fewer insects. Higher summer temperatures because of global warming will boost insect numbers, which may compromise caribou health and reproduction.

Swimmers
Always on the move, whether migrating or just grazing, caribou are not deterred by lakes or rivers. They are strong swimmers, reaching speeds of up to six miles per hour (10 km/h) and air trapped between their double layer of fur aids buoyancy. A dip also brings some relief from pesky biting insects.

Beaufort Sea

Prudhoe Bay
Kaktovik
Mackenzie Bay
Arctic Circle
Fort Yukon
Fort McPherson
Peel
Yukon
ALASKA
Anchorage
U.S.A.
CANADA
YUKON TERRITORY
Whitehorse

Grazing
A caribou's summer fare consists of a variety of grasses, flowering plants, leaves of willows and birches, and even mushrooms. Caribou shed their antlers every alternate year and, unique among deer, females bear them, too.

ADAPTED TO LIFE IN THE SNOW

Traveling through the deep snow that blankets the boreal forest for most of the year is hard work that requires a lot of energy. Some mammals, including Canada lynx, snowshoe hares, and caribou, have evolved "snowshoes." Specific adaptations make their feet extra large and this keeps them from sinking far into the snow. The willow ptarmigan, a forest bird, has evolved a different strategy: its feet are densely feathered.

Canada lynx
Medium-sized cats with tufted ears and keen eyesight, Canada lynx specialize in hunting snowshoe hares, which make up about 80 percent of their diet. Predator and prey are so closely linked that fluctuations in hare populations are mirrored in lynx numbers.

Lynx paw
The Canada lynx's paws are huge for the cat's size. They are furred above and below, serving to improve insulation, much like a pair of mittens.

Snowshoe hare paw
Very large hind feet covered in dense fur and stiff hairs, and long toes that spread widely, allow a snowshoe hare to race over deep snow.

The hunted
Even snowshoes and fur that turns from brown to white to blend into the winter snow do not keep snowshoe hares from the jaws of Canada lynx. The hares dine on willow and aspen, which defend themselves with nasty chemicals when the hares over-browse.

On the move

The caribou that make up the Porcupine Herd spend most of the year on the move. They travel north on fairly fixed routes from their boreal forest wintering habitat, to calve in the northern foothills of the Brooks Range and on the Alaskan Coastal Plains. In the fall they return along more diffuse routes.

Porcupine Herd Migration route

Mackenzie

NORTHWEST TERRITORIES

Shoveling for food
Green food is scarce in the boreal forest winter and the lichen that makes up much of the caribou's winter diet is buried beneath snow. Caribou use their sharp-edged hooves to shovel off the snow. This requires a lot of energy, so caribou try to steal the patches others have cleared.

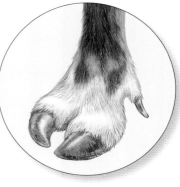

Caribou paw
Two large, half-moon-shaped front toes and two smaller back toes spread to make a caribou's hooves wide and long. This enables it to tiptoe through snow without getting bogged.

Pacific Northwest Coniferous Forest

Stretching 1,300 miles (2,090 km) along the coast from Alaska to northern California, and just 40 to 75 miles (65–120 km) wide, the Pacific Northwest coniferous forest of North America is one of the richest forests on Earth. Mild temperatures and abundant rainfall of 30 to 115 inches (760–2,900 mm) per year combine to produce dense stands of towering, long-lived evergreen trees, such as Douglas fir, western hemlock, western red cedar, sitka spruce, and coast redwood. These coastal old-growth forests, through which many rivers course, are home to a diverse array of wildlife. Some species, such as the northern spotted owl and the Pacific giant salamander, are found nowhere else, and scientists are regularly discovering new species of insects and spiders in the forest canopy. Brown bears grow fat on the abundant salmon and trout that ply the rivers, while orcas lurk offshore seeking prey. Logging, dams built for hydroelectric power, and other human activities pose the major threats to this habitat.

SEATTLE, WASHINGTON, USA

SCALE 1:34,000,000

0 — 500 miles
0 — 500 kilometers

Bald eagle
The majestic bald eagle uses its strong legs and powerful toes, tipped with sharp talons, to snatch salmon and trout, its favorite prey. This large raptor depends on old-growth coniferous or deciduous forest near large bodies of water. It roosts, perches, and builds its immense nest, which can weigh a ton (1,000 kg), in forest trees.

Pacific banana slug
The second-largest land-living slug does, indeed, reach the size of a banana. The Pacific banana slug inhabits the Pacific Coast's coniferous rain forests, where it eats fungus, dead leaves, and animal droppings on the moist forest floor.

Marbled murrelet

Shy and secretive, marbled murrelets nest in coastal forest trees, usually selecting the largest trees available. They hunt small fish offshore, sometimes traveling 12 miles (19 km) or more from their nest to forage. In pursuit of a meal, murrelets often work synchronously in pairs at shallow depths, "flying" through the water by using their muscular wings like flippers and their webbed feet to steer.

Brown bear
Pacific coastal brown bears enjoy a food bonanza in summer, feasting on the abundant salmon swimming upriver to spawn. With food so plentiful, the usually solitary bears gather in numbers at prime fishing spots, often where waterfalls and other obstructions slow the fish down.

Fish diet
The high-protein, high-fat salmon diet on the Pacific coast produces the largest brown bears in the world. Adult males reach a massive 1,300 pounds (600 kg) or more, and may stand 9 feet (2.8 m) tall. When hunting is good, these bears can eat 10 large salmon a day.

Salmon in stages

A female sockeye salmon lays eggs in the same river in which it hatched years before. Eggs hatch as alevin with the yolk sac still attached. Days later, an alevin becomes a free-swimming fry and, later, a parr that lives in freshwater for several years. A silver-colored smolt is ready to enter the sea, where it will grow into a large adult. Adults returning to rivers to spawn have red bodies and green heads.

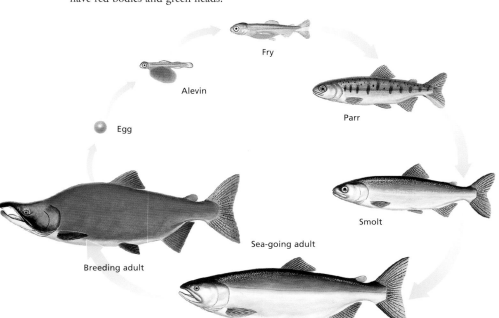

Fry

Alevin

Egg

Parr

Smolt

Sea-going adult

Breeding adult

Sockeye salmon
At four or so years old, male and female sockeye salmon leave the ocean and enter rivers to breed, returning to the same systems in which they hatched. By then, both sexes have turned bright red on their back and sides, a signature of their adult breeding status.

THE ROCKY MOUNTAINS

The Rocky Mountains divide North America in half. Stretching from Alberta, in Canada, to New Mexico in the United States, and varying from 60 to 350 miles (95–563 km) wide, the Rockies include 100 different ranges. The highest peaks reach 14,400 feet (4,390 m) but among them are large, low basins and troughs. Habitat diversity is enormous, ranging from snow-capped peaks to alpine meadows to boreal and deciduous forest and arid steppes, but coniferous forest dominates in the generally cool, dry climate. Wildlife diversity is limited in the Rockies. Relatively few insects, amphibians, and reptiles live here, and many of the fish species in the region's plentiful lakes and rivers have been introduced. However, at the heart of the Rockies, in Yellowstone National Park, exists the most impressive array of large mammals in North America. Bison, moose, elk, bighorn sheep, mountain goats, mule and white-tailed deer, pronghorn, grizzly and black bears, gray wolves, coyotes, pumas, wolverines, Canada lynx, bobcats, and more come together in this region.

SCALE 1:35,000,000

0 — 500 miles

0 — 500 kilometers

Common raven
The common raven is one of the Rockies' most conspicuous birds. Sociable and seemingly fearless, it is often seen scavenging gray wolf kills and will even swoop or chase these carnivores to steal a bite for its hungry nestlings.

Western rattlesnake
Although armed with deadly venom, western rattlesnakes are not aggressive and are seldom seen. In hot weather they hunt at night and spend cold winters hibernating in caves and other animals' burrows. Females give birth to up to 20 young in the fall.

Rattle structure
Each segment of the rattle is composed of tough skin that is not shed. The loosely interlocking rattles bounce against each other when the snake vibrates its tail.

JASPER, ALBERTA, CANADA

Numerous trout species

The lakes and streams of Yellowstone National Park, many of which were once fishless, are now home to about a dozen native fish species, including cutthroat trout and Arctic grayling. Four species of trout—rainbow, brown, brook, and lake—were also introduced for sport fishing from the late 19th century to the mid-20th century. The non-natives are now outcompeting the natives, some of which have sharply declined.

Cutthroat trout

Native cutthroat swim the same streams as non-native rainbows, which have robbed them of food and habitat. Consequently, the cutthroat is now highly vulnerable.

Mountain goat

Spending most of their time on severely steep, rocky slopes in alpine areas of the northern Rockies, where they are safe from predators, mountain goats nibble small plants that grow among the rocks. Powerful front legs help them to climb and descend the steep slopes, and rough pads on the undersides of their split hooves provide traction. The hooves are capable of pinching around a rock edge or spreading out for braking.

Mule deer
Mule deer prefer drier habitats than the white-tailed deer that also inhabit the Rocky Mountains. During most of the year, mule deer live in small groups of two or three, feeding on a wide range of plant species. When food is scarce in winter, larger groups gather at food sources.

American beaver
Energetic American beavers build lodges of tree branches and trunks they fell using their chisel-shaped front teeth. Their lips close behind their front teeth so they can carry branches underwater without fluid entering their lungs. Beavers have dense fur and webbed hind feet.

COYOTE

Adaptable and opportunistic, coyotes thrive almost everywhere in North America, from the high Rockies to large cities such as Washington DC. They took advantage of the extermination of gray wolves to expand well beyond their original, mostly western, range. However, where wolves reign, as they do once again in Yellowstone National Park, coyote numbers have decreased.

Facial expressions
Among other signals, such as vocalizations and postures, social coyotes use a variety of facial expressions to communicate. They may live alone, in breeding pairs, or packs of several individuals.

Playful

Combative

Defensive

Friendly

THE GRAY WOLF

Gray wolves once prowled throughout North America, coast to coast from the Arctic to central Mexico. They are still relatively abundant in Alaska and Canada but extermination programs and habitat loss over several hundred years combined to nearly eliminate these predators from the lower 48 US states. By the 1930s only a small number remained in a few northern strongholds. However, in 1995 and 1996, amid great controversy, 66 wolves were reintroduced to Yellowstone National Park and central Idaho, where they had not bred since 1926. By 2007, these wolf populations had increased to about 1,500 animals. Conservation programs and natural re-colonization from Canada have led to growing wolf numbers in Minnesota, Wisconsin, and Michigan. Efforts to reintroduce the Mexican gray wolf subspecies in the southwest, however, have thus far met with little success. The ecology of Yellowstone, where the wolves' impact has been best studied, has changed dramatically as wolves have flourished on meals of abundant elk.

Former range

Current range

CONSERVATION WATCH

Success can have a price. In 2008, the US government removed the thriving Rocky Mountains wolf population from its Endangered Species List. The population in Minnesota, Wisconsin, and Michigan, numbering about 4,000, was "de-listed" in 2007. Conservationists fear that state wildlife agencies may be less careful stewards of a species once persecuted as vermin.

Wolf cubs
A breeding wolf pair produces a litter of five to six cubs in spring or summer after mating about two months earlier. Born helpless, the cubs remain in a den for two months before joining the pack's hunting forays a few weeks later. Cubs do not hunt themselves until aged eight months.

Leaders of the pack
Wolves prey mostly on elk, mule deer, and white-tailed deer. They generally hunt in packs of five to 10 or more members, led by a dominant breeding pair, most often accompanied by members of their own recent litters. But a pair or even a single wolf can bring down elk and deer alone, so the benefit of pack hunting may lie in the pair sharing the surplus of their kills with their young.

Howling
The haunting sound of wolves howling can be heard up to 10 miles (15 km) away, and sometimes wolves howl to reunite stray members of the pack. Wolf packs also howl together at dusk, before heading out to hunt, which may reinforce the bonds between family members.

CASCADING EFFECTS OF WOLF REINTRODUCTION

Elk form about 90 percent of the prey of Yellowstone's wolves. As a result, their numbers are about half what they were before wolves returned. With fewer elk browsing, streamside vegetation including willows, aspens, and cottonwoods, is flourishing where once it was disappearing. Wolves have also reduced coyote numbers, which has led to greater survival rates among pronghorn calves, the coyotes' favorite prey. Other species have similarly been advantaged or disadvantaged by the return of the wolves.

Top scavenger
The presence of wolves helps grizzly bears, which are able to usurp wolf kills. Stolen carcasses are especially important to grizzlies when they emerge, starving, from winter hibernation. Scavenging ravens and eagles are increasing, too.

Birds abound
The recovery of willows and other streamside vegetation that was once overbrowsed by elk has improved the prospects for songbirds that nest in this habitat. Species such as the yellow warbler are increasing in number.

Hunting party
Although bison are harder to kill, wolves increasingly hunt them as elk numbers diminish. Large packs such as this one may be the key to wolves' success in bringing down these huge beasts.

More moose
Willow regrowth has provided new habitat for American beavers, which prefer to eat small willow trees. New beaver dams, in turn, have created more habitat for water-loving moose.

Return of the aspen
Aspen stands were once abundant along streams, but stopped growing about the same time as wolves disappeared from Yellowstone. With the wolves' return, aspen are again thriving.

Rodents on the rise
Semi-aquatic muskrats have found new homes in ponds created by beaver dams, as have river otters. More rodents taking up residence means more prey for foxes and birds of prey.

THE GREAT PLAINS

The Great Plains cover an immense swath of the continent's center, stretching about 1,000 miles (1,600 km) east from the foothills of the Rocky Mountains. Once a vast, largely treeless dry sea of perennial grasses, most of the Great Plains now form some of the world's best agricultural land, covered in fields of wheat and corn, and cattle. Though the plains may seem monotonous, closer inspection reveals a landscape of great diversity. The climate is dry, with rainfall of 24 inches (610 mm) at most recorded each year, but rainfall increases from west to east, dividing the region into western short-grass prairie, eastern tall-grass prairie, and mixed grass in between. Topography ranges from pancake flat to rolling hills. Amid the grassy expanses, trees and shrubs flourish along streams. Bison, whose enormous herds once thundered across the plains and supported the region's wolves and grizzly bears, typify this near-vanished ecosystem.

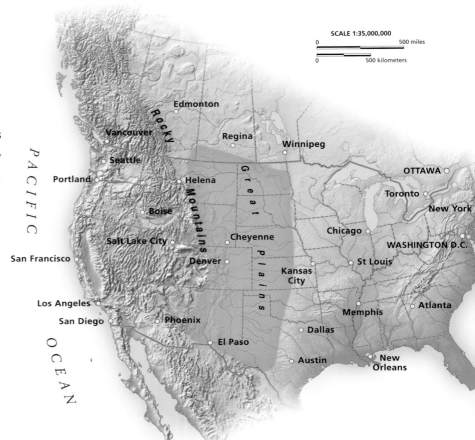

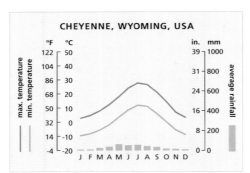

CHEYENNE, WYOMING, USA

American bison
The largest male bison reach the size of a small car, and can run at speeds of up to 40 miles per hour (64 km/h). The beasts are front-loaded: their head and shoulders are massive while their rear ends are relatively slender. In combat over females, two males may charge each other, butting heads with such force that one may be flipped head over heels.

Bobcat
Shy and secretive, bobcats thrive in agricultural areas with some natural vegetation or rocky outcrops that provide shelter. Cottontail rabbits, pocket gophers, wood rats, and ground hogs are among their favorite prey, but these cats will also take deer fawns or birds.

Greater short-horned lizard
These lizards defend themselves from coyotes and other predators by squirting blood from their eyes. The blood contains formic acid, obtained from the bodies of their primary food—ants.

Bison's head and neck
A bison's massive head is supported by a short yet wide neck and a large muscular hump between its shoulder blades, connected by a heavy ligament. A bison swings its strong head back and forth to sweep feeding areas clear of snow as deep as two to three feet (60–90 cm).

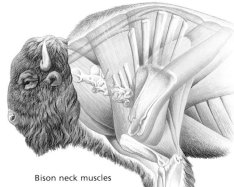

Bison neck muscles

CONSERVATION WATCH
The long, paddle-shaped snouts that give the American paddlefish its name are densely spotted with electrical sensors. These enable a paddlefish to locate its zooplankton prey in murky water by sensing its electric field. This exquisite sensory system, however, has not protected the paddlefish from overfishing, dams that block access to spawning grounds, and water pollution. The species is considered vulnerable to extinction.

Temperature extremes
Winters on the windswept Great Plains are brutally cold; summers are scorching hot. A bison's winter coat, with 10 times as many hairs as a cow's, helps keep it from freezing to death when temperatures plummet. The deep black fur, which absorbs the heat of the sun, is shed in summer but bison still have to pant to lose heat. If they failed to do so, they would not survive.

Bird life
The Great Plains host about 300 species of breeding migratory birds in summer, such as lark buntings, as well as permanent residents, such as greater sage grouse. Here the birds find, or once did, abundant grasshoppers and other insects, seeds, and herbs to feed their nestlings. However, with so much of the prairie gone, most of these species are in decline.

Western meadowlark
Sturnela neglecta

Grasshopper sparrow
Ammodramus savannarum

Lark bunting
Calamospiza melanocorys

Greater sage grouse
Centrocercus urophasianus

Snakeweed grasshopper
Hesperotettix viridis

THE GREAT PLAINS
PRAIRIE DOGS

More than 5 billion black-tailed prairie dogs once colonized the Great Plains, living in aggregations large enough to be called towns. The largest recorded single town numbered some 400 million of these burrowing rodents, spread over 25,000 square miles (65,000 km²). Four other less-widespread prairie dog species also inhabit the United States and Mexico. Vegetation shorn by the herbivorous animals and the pockmarks of their mounded burrow entrances make even the small towns that remain today conspicuous in the landscape. The animals themselves, which are active during the day, are conspicuous too. Scientists call prairie dogs keystone species because so many other species are affected by their presence. Many predators, such as coyotes and golden eagles, eat them. Burrowing owls, rabbits, snakes, insects, and others occupy their burrows, and prairie dog burrowing churns up the soil so it can better support plants. In turn, the plants attract grazers, such as pronghorn and bison, many rodents, and rabbits.

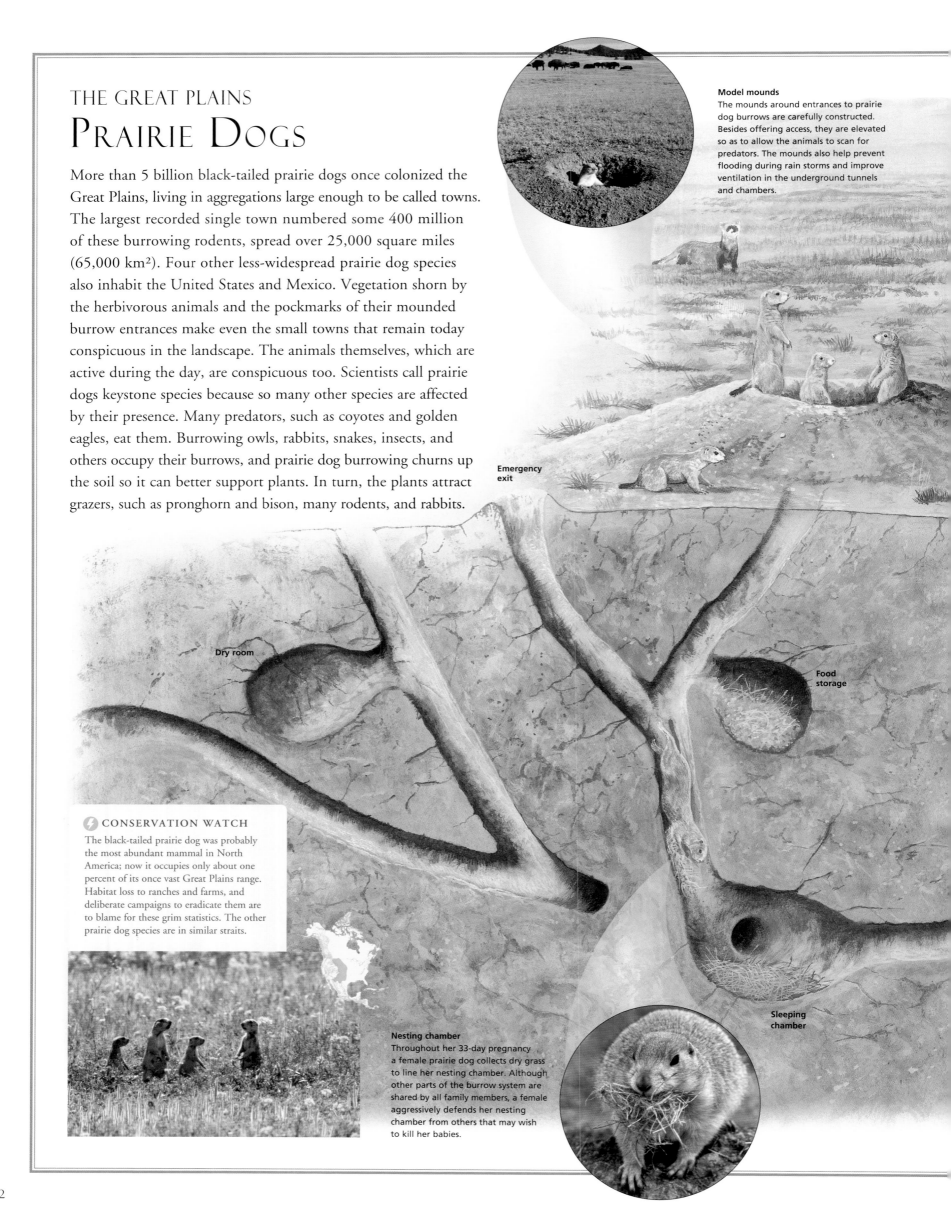

Model mounds
The mounds around entrances to prairie dog burrows are carefully constructed. Besides offering access, they are elevated so as to allow the animals to scan for predators. The mounds also help prevent flooding during rain storms and improve ventilation in the underground tunnels and chambers.

Emergency exit

Dry room

Food storage

⚡ CONSERVATION WATCH

The black-tailed prairie dog was probably the most abundant mammal in North America; now it occupies only about one percent of its once vast Great Plains range. Habitat loss to ranches and farms, and deliberate campaigns to eradicate them are to blame for these grim statistics. The other prairie dog species are in similar straits.

Nesting chamber
Throughout her 33-day pregnancy a female prairie dog collects dry grass to line her nesting chamber. Although other parts of the burrow system are shared by all family members, a female aggressively defends her nesting chamber from others that may wish to kill her babies.

Sleeping chamber

Home underground

A prairie dog town is divided into coteries—social groups of an adult male, two or three adult females, and one or two youngsters. Coteries defend territories that include their underground burrow system, which the rodents use to escape predators and bad weather, raise young, and spend the night. Multiple entrances give way to tunnels as long as 110 feet (33 m) and as deep as 16 feet (5 m).

Listening room

Toilet

Dry room

Nursery chamber

Alarmed
With so many prairie dogs active at the same time, a few are always on the lookout for predators. On sighting a threat, a prairie dog instantly sounds the alarm, calling to alert others before diving into the burrow for its own protection.

PRAIRIE DOG PREDATORS

Only about half of the prairie dogs that emerge from their natal burrows live more than a year, although males can reach five years of age and females eight years. Disease, such as flea-borne bubonic plague, and many predators, from carnivores to birds of prey to snakes, take their toll on prairie dogs of all ages. Juveniles and subadults are particularly vulnerable to predation.

Aerial attack
Prowling slowly over the plains, the medium-sized northern harrier is just one of 10 or so day-hunting birds that feasts on prairie dogs.

Tunnel invaders
Black-footed ferrets live in prairie dog burrows and eat their hosts. They have lithe bodies that easily slink through tunnels to find a meal. The decline of prairie dogs, coupled with disease, almost rendered the ferrets extinct. The species was saved only by a zoo breeding program.

Night visitors
American badgers use their strong claws to dig their own complex burrow systems, but also visit prairie dog towns in search of food. Hunting at night, a badger may dig into a prairie dog burrow to catch one of its sleeping occupants unawares.

The newborn
Born in a special nesting chamber in the burrow system, a prairie dog litter ranges in size from one to eight. Newborns are blind, naked, and helpless, but just 40 days later youngsters emerge into the plains' sunshine and begin eating independently.

THE GREAT BASIN

North America's only cold desert south of the Arctic, the Great Basin, covers most of Nevada and parts of California, Idaho, Utah, Wyoming, and Oregon. At altitudes of 3,900–5,250 feet (1,200–1,600 m) in the rain shadow of western mountains, this is a land of extremes. The precipitation range is 4–12 inches (100–305 mm), mostly in the form of snow, but years of severe drought may be followed by wet years. Winter temperatures rarely climb above freezing and summer nights can be frosty, but summer days may be as hot as 90°F (32°C) with frequent violent thunderstorms. Dominated by sagebrush, the Great Basin appears desolate but 800 plant species eke out a living here and animal life is surprisingly abundant. A curious feature of the Great Basin is that its rivers and streams do not drain to the sea. Water is lost only to evaporation, so most of the fish species known here are found nowhere else. Human population growth, wildfires, and invasive species are threats to this habitat.

SCALE 1:35,000,000

0   500 miles

0   500 kilometers

Animal	Top Speed in mph (km/h)
Pronghorn	62 (100)
Black-tail jackrabbit	40 (65)
Coyote	40 (65)
Gray wolf	40 (65)
Mule deer	38 (61)
Puma	35 (56)
Brown bear	30 (48)
Bighorn sheep	30 (48)

Black-tailed jackrabbit
The black-tailed jackrabbit thrives in the Great Basin desert thanks, in part, to its amazing thermoregulation abilities. By increasing or decreasing blood flow to its enormous ears, the jackrabbit can either store or lose heat, thereby enabling it to regulate its body temperature. The jackrabbit is also most active after dusk.

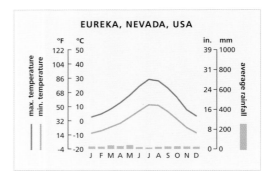

EUREKA, NEVADA, USA

Wild horses
They seem a timeless emblem of the Great Basin but wild horses did not exist here until about 1680. Domestic horses that arrived with the Spanish were soon adopted by Native Americans. Today, the Great Basin hosts the largest number of wild horses, 50,000–75,000, which are descended from released and escaped animals. At one time, herds in the west may have been several million strong.

THE PRONGHORN

Speedy hoofed mammals, able to race across the range at up to 62 miles per hour (100 km/h), pronghorns are a uniquely North American enigma. Scientists are unsure as to their closest relatives, but cows, deer, or giraffes are all possibilities. Adapted to arid and semiarid habitats, pronghorns range widely and migrate seasonally in search of nutritious food and to escape deep snow or drought.

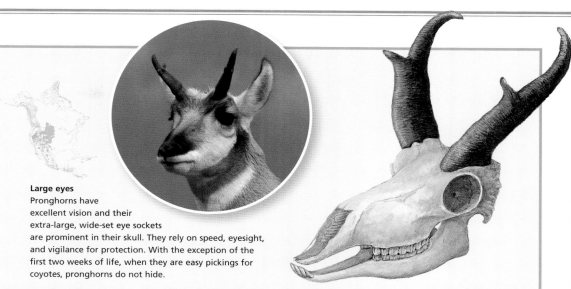

Exceptional speed

It remains a puzzle why pronghorns run so fast, clocking up speeds way beyond those required to escape any living predator they might encounter. One intriguing theory is that they evolved alongside speedier hunters, such as the American cheetah, which are now extinct.

Large eyes

Pronghorns have excellent vision and their extra-large, wide-set eye sockets are prominent in their skull. They rely on speed, eyesight, and vigilance for protection. With the exception of the first two weeks of life, when they are easy pickings for coyotes, pronghorns do not hide.

CONSERVATION WATCH

Hunting, habitat loss, and competition with wild horses and domestic livestock, especially sheep that transmit diseases, all conspired to reduce bighorn sheep numbers by 90 percent by the early 1900s. Some populations were completely eliminated. Protection and translocation programs have helped them recover, but several bighorn populations remain endangered.

Puma

Though not as fast as a pronghorn, a puma can catch one in broken, bushy terrain. It is harder for pronghorns to reach top speeds in these environments and they offer cover for a puma to stealthily approach its quarry.

SAGEBRUSH COUNTRY

The country dominated by big sagebrush once blanketed more than 23,000 square miles (60,000 km²) of western North America. This arid, high-elevation habitat is a mosaic of sagebrush species, grasses, shrubs, small green plants, and wildflowers, interspersed with woodlands, streams, and wetlands. Some animals evolved in sagebrush habitats and many, such as the sage grouse and sage vole, can live nowhere else. They get sustenance from sagebrush's soft, evergreen leaves, seek shelter under its branches, or both. But the sagebrush country and its 350 associated plants and animals are imperiled. People have eliminated about half the sagebrush habitat and what remains is influenced to varying degrees by human activities. Much sagebrush was simply destroyed, to be replaced by farms and forage more palatable to the cattle that arrived in the late 1800s. Invasive exotic cheatgrass and other weeds have edged out still more, and a host of other impacts have degraded or denuded the unique sagebrush country.

Cheatgrass
A native of Asia, cheatgrass has successfully invaded sagebrush country. This annual plant produces vast numbers of seeds that can survive five years of drought. Seeds also germinate and grow roots faster than perennial natives, quickly taking up vital water. Cheatgrass provides little or no nutrition except for a brief period in the spring so it is useless as food for mule deer and other grazers.

SAGEBRUSH IN THE GREAT BASIN

Current sagebrush habitat

Agriculture/ industry/ urban

Other habitats

Big sagebrush
Big sagebrush is found only in the dryland of western North America. Growing up to 10 feet (3 m) tall, but usually shorter, it can live as long as 100 years, however wildfires usually cut short its life. The silvery-gray shrub has brilliant yellow flowers in late summer, and year-round bears soft green leaves with fine hairs that may help keep the plant cool and conserve water.

Sagebrush community
Many animals rely on sagebrush habitats for survival in all or part of their range. Among the mammals and birds, pronghorns, pygmy rabbits, and white-tailed prairie dogs feed on sagebrush, as do Gunnison sage grouse and sage sparrows. In turn, ferruginous hawks hunt the rabbits, jackrabbits, and prairie dogs.

SAGEBRUSH COUNTRY ANIMALS

Mammals 20%

Reptiles 13%

Birds 21%

Invertebrates 46%

Spiders 36%

Aphids 26%

Beetles 11%

Ants 11%

Gall midges 16%

Sagebrush checkerspot
Female butterflies lay their eggs under the leaves of host plants in the sagebrush community. Caterpillars feed in groups on leaves and flowers.

Brewer's sparrow
Brewer's sparrows are abundant in summer in remaining Great Basin sagebrush habitats, but their numbers are declining.

Brown-headed cowbird
Recent additions to the sagebrush community, brown-headed cowbirds arrived only after farms and ranches appeared and created suitable feeding habitat for them.

Desert spiny lizard
The shy desert spiny lizard often shelters in desert woodrat nests and hunts by day for insects.

Desert woodrat
Desert woodrats are common in sagebrush habitats, where they eat leaves and other vegetation.

CONSERVATION WATCH

With greater sage grouse almost entirely dependent on sagebrush, it is not surprising that as sagebrush habitat has declined, so too have the grouse. The population of these large, showy birds has fallen by about one-third in the past 40 or so years and they have completely disappeared from five states and one province they once called home.

Greater sage grouse
Greater sage grouse eat sagebrush all year and in winter it comprises their entire diet. Females nest under a sagebrush canopy, insects attracted to sagebrush are fed to chicks, and the canopy conceals them from predators.

Mule deer
Named for their large ears, mule deer rely on sagebrush in many parts of their western range to get them through the harsh winter, when other plants are scarce. However, their diet is diverse, including hundreds of plants and shrubs, berries, and acorns.

DESERTS OF THE SOUTHWEST

The Mojave, Sonoran, and Chihuahuan deserts comprise the hot deserts of southwestern United States and northern Mexico. At fairly high elevations, the Mojave is a transition from the Great Basin and is the smallest of the deserts. From 1.5 to almost 11 inches (38–279 mm) of precipitation falls here and summer temperatures average 86–104°F (30–40°C). Its low elevation makes the Sonoran the hottest of these deserts. Summer temperatures soar to more than 105°F (40°C) and rainfall ranges from none to two inches (50 mm) a year in the driest western part of this desert. The Chihuahuan is the largest desert and fairly temperate because of its high elevation, annual rainfall of 6–16 inches (152–406 mm), and average annual temperatures of 65°F (18°C). Despite harsh conditions, many desert-adapted plants and animals populate these arid expanses. Some, such as the saguaro cactus and desert tortoises, live nowhere else.

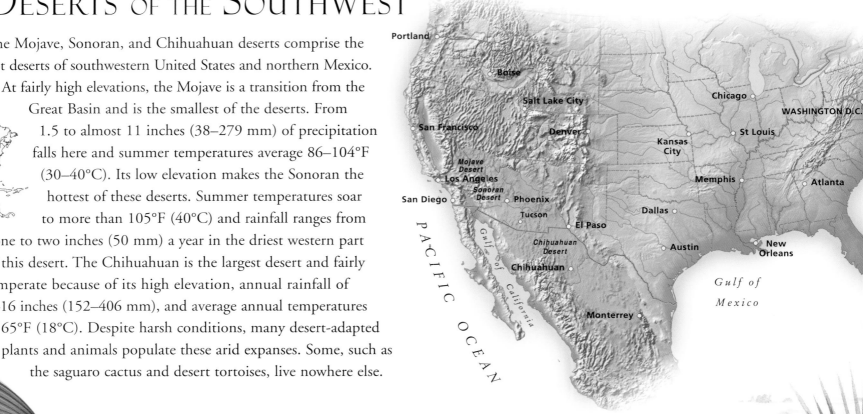

TUCSON, ARIZONA, USA

SCALE 1:30,000,000

Hummingbirds
More hummingbird species live in the southwest deserts than anywhere else in the United States and Canada. Southwestern Arizona boasts 15 species of these birds, which occur only in the New World. Costa's hummingbird breeds and winters here, sipping nectar from flowers.

Curved-billed thrasher
Common in the Sonoran and Chihuahuan deserts, the curved-billed thrasher builds a deep, grass-lined cup nest in cholla cacti. Breeding pairs share nest construction, incubation, and chick feeding responsibilities.

Burrowing owls
Burrowing owls may be year-long residents or winter migrants from more northerly extremes. These small owls nest and store food in other animals' burrows, such as those of desert tortoises. The owls hunt for insects, scorpions, rodents, frogs and toads, reptiles, and birds.

Ringtails
Although cat-like in appearance, ringtails are closely related to raccoons. Agile climbers, they scamper up and down canyon sides and trees. Their ankles rotate 180 degrees so they can easily descend a tree headfirst.

Desert dominants

Major vegetation types distinguish the three southwest deserts. Cacti are rare in the Mojave, where creosote bush and bur sage dominate. Joshua trees are prominent here and most plants are perennial shrubs, many found nowhere else in the world. In the Sonoran, creosote bush and bur sage occur at low elevations, but higher elevations host blue palo verde, ironweed, agave, and many cacti species. Prickly pear, yucca, and acacias characterize the Chihuahuan.

American agave
Found in the Sonoran and Chihuahuan deserts, the American agave blooms just once, then dies. Hummingbirds and insects drink the flower's nectar; birds and small mammals eat its seeds.

Chuckwalla
A large, robust lizard, the chuckwalla spends its mornings basking and its afternoons foraging. If it is cool, hot, or threatened, the lizard retreats to a rock crevice. If a predator approaches, it puffs up its body so that it cannot be dislodged.

CONSERVATION WATCH

Gila monsters and closely related beaded lizards are the only venomous lizards but their toxic bite has not stopped them declining in the face of threats posed by urban sprawl, pets, and cars. Fearful of the beasts, people often move them away from their neighborhoods and few, if any, of these lizards survive.

Desert tortoise

The only land turtle in its southwestern desert range, the football-sized desert tortoise spends most of its time in a burrow. It may go two years without a meal, even though its diet of green plants and wildflowers is its only source of water. Males often fight when they meet, using a horn on their shell to try to flip over their opponent. Fires, disease, urban sprawl, vehicle traffic, and skyrocketing numbers of ravens that eat hatchlings all threaten desert tortoises. Females do not breed until 15–20 years old.

DESERTS OF THE SOUTHWEST
SAGUARO CACTUS COMMUNITY

Found only in the Sonoran Desert, the saguaro cactus is a central component of this ecosystem and used by a variety of desert dwellers, including people. Birds such as gilded flickers dig nest holes in its flesh and Harris's hawks build stick nests in its arms. Abandoned nest holes are inhabited by other birds, such as finches and sparrows, and hawk nests are often reused by ravens and great horned owls. Bats, birds, and insects, especially bees, sip nectar from the cacti's large flowers and provide vital pollination services in return. Coyotes, jackrabbits, cactus wrens, and others eat its nutritious, water-rich fruit and seeds, then play their part in dispersing the seeds. Native Americans also eat the fruit, and once used the saguaro's strong ribs to construct houses. The cactus owes its success to amazing adaptations for storing and utilizing the region's scant water supplies.

Sonoran Desert
The satellite image of the Sonoran Desert shows the Salton Sea (bottom left) and the Gulf of California (right).

Saguaro cactus
With its tall, thick, trunk-bearing arms upturned toward the sky, the saguaro cactus dominates the Sonoran Desert landscape. These stately cacti grow as high as 50 feet (15 m) but attain that height slowly, after more than 125 years of growth. They do not begin to sprout arms until they are 65 to 75 years old and do not flower until about 35 years of age.

Southern long-nosed bat
Southern long-nosed bats specialize in eating the nectar and pollen of desert plants, such as agave and saguaro cactus. Flitting between flowers, the bats pollinate the plants. Some species, such as the organ pipe cactus, could not reproduce without them.

Nest hole
A Gila woodpecker pair digs a nest hole in a saguaro but will not make use of it for several months, until the inner pulp has dried into a solid casing around the hole.

Vantage point
Peering out of its secure nest cavity, a Gila woodpecker can survey the landscape for potential predators, such as bobcats, coyotes, foxes, hawks, and snakes.

Insect hunting
Gila woodpeckers leave the shelter of their holes to hunt for insects on the saguaro. Males probe the trunk and main branches; females focus on the edges.

Gila woodpecker
Permanent desert residents, Gila woodpeckers depend on saguaro cacti for nesting sites and for the insects that live on their trunks and branches. These birds help the cacti by cutting away flesh infected by disease-causing insect larvae.

Cactus wrens
These small birds, which get all the water they need from juicy insects and fruit, build their nests in cacti. The spines keep predators at bay, protecting eggs, nestlings, and adults. Cactus wrens are often seen singing from a perch atop a tall agave.

Greater earless lizard
These lizards are fast-moving, heat-loving reptiles that are active by day. They tunnel under the sand to seek shelter from heat and to nest. Scientists speculate that they lack external ear openings to keep sand out of their ears.

Kangaroo rat
Merriam's kangaroo rats hop across the sandy desert at night, gathering seeds of plants, such as mesquite and creosote bush. They store the seeds in their fat cheek pouches and, once full, cache the seeds in small sandy holes within their home range.

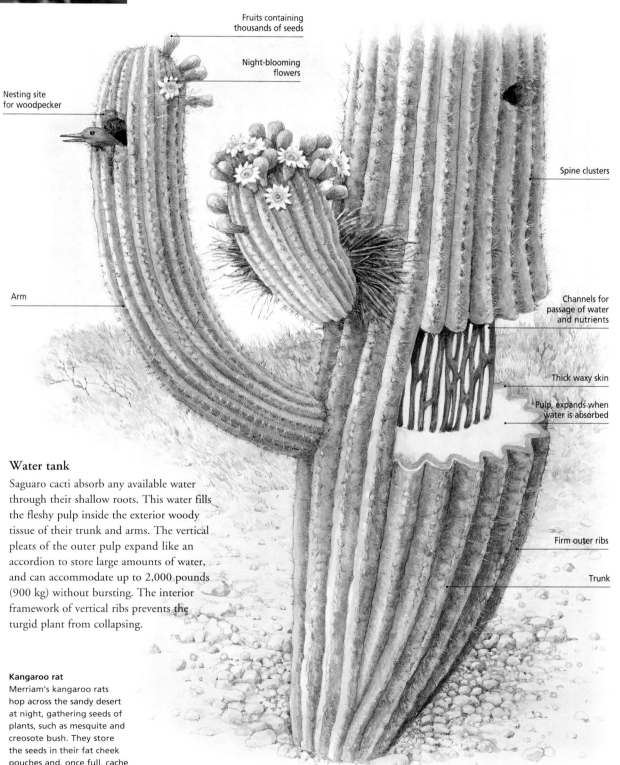

Fruits containing thousands of seeds

Night-blooming flowers

Nesting site for woodpecker

Arm

Spine clusters

Channels for passage of water and nutrients

Thick waxy skin

Pulp, expands when water is absorbed

Firm outer ribs

Trunk

Water tank
Saguaro cacti absorb any available water through their shallow roots. This water fills the fleshy pulp inside the exterior woody tissue of their trunk and arms. The vertical pleats of the outer pulp expand like an accordion to store large amounts of water, and can accommodate up to 2,000 pounds (900 kg) without bursting. The interior framework of vertical ribs prevents the turgid plant from collapsing.

EASTERN DECIDUOUS FOREST AND THE APPALACHIANS

The great eastern deciduous forest was once unbroken from central Florida to northern New England and southeastern Canada, and west to the Mississippi River. Dominated by tall trees that drop their leaves in the fall, such as oaks, maples, beech, chestnuts, and hickory, this forest boasts a rich understory of smaller trees, bushes, shrubs, ferns, fungi, and green plants. Winters are cold, but fall and spring are mild, and summers are long and warm. Water is abundant, with high levels of precipitation year-round. The Appalachian Mountains, which extend from Labrador, in Canada, to Alabama, in the United States, bisect and define this region. The diversity of wildlife in eastern deciduous forests is outstanding, with especially rich bird and amphibian faunas. Much of the forest was logged and farmed between the 1600s and the late 1800s. As the economy changed and many farmers moved west, farms were abandoned. Large fragments of forest have returned, but major urban and suburban centers dominate this region.

INDIANAPOLIS, INDIANA, USA

Striped skunk
Striped skunks emit a foul-smelling spray from their anal glands when threatened but that does not deter great horned owls from preying on them. Many skunks in eastern North America are also killed by vehicles and disease, such as rabies.

American black bear
The only bear in eastern North America is the American black bear, which overlaps with brown bears elsewhere. The black bear occupies diverse habitats, from deciduous forests and rain forests to swamps, tundra, and even suburbia.

Wild turkey
Habitat loss and hunting eliminated the wild turkey from the forests of the eastern United States by the early 1900s, but it has rebounded, thanks to protection and reintroductions. Traveling in noisy flocks, these birds forage on the ground for nuts.

Eastern chipmunk
Chattering eastern chipmunks are conspicuous members of the eastern forest community during summer. To endure cold winters, they hibernate in burrows, waking every few days to consume some of the nuts and seeds they cached in the fall.

Forest flier

Widely distributed in northern North America, the northern flying squirrel is found in isolated populations in the southern Appalachians, where it overlaps with the smaller southern flying squirrel. Mushrooms and other fungi are their favorite foods and the squirrels help disperse fungal spores throughout their forested habitats. Active only at night, they forage on the ground and in the treetops, where they are hunted by predators, such as owls and hawks.

Parachuting
Flying squirrels do not fly, but glide 65–295 feet (20–90 m) from tree to tree. The gliding membrane that stretches between their limbs, called a patagium, acts like a parachute. It keeps the squirrel aloft after it launches itself from on high.

Bobcat
While bobcats are fairly common in eastern forests they are seldom seen. Spending the day sheltering in rocky outcrops, brush piles, and dense bushes, they prowl the forest at night in search of a meal. Cottontail rabbits are favorites, but bobcats also prey on mice and white-tailed deer.

THE RACCOON

Northern raccoons are North America's ultimate generalist carnivores. With catholic tastes, they find food almost anywhere, from fields and forests to urban backyards, and shelter under porches as well as in tree holes and dens. Bobcats and foxes are among their predators in eastern forests, while the raccoons, themselves, prey on small mammals, birds, crustaceans, fish, mollusks, and insects, as well as eating fruit, seeds, and carrion.

Handy paws
The skeleton of a raccoon's forepaw bears a striking resemblance to that of a human hand, giving it great manual dexterity. It moves its forepaws through streams and ponds, plucking out crayfish and other aquatic creatures with its "fingers."

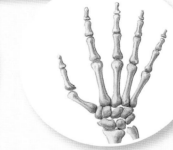

Raccoon paw   Human hand

Deciduous forest landscape

Autumn leaves in the eastern deciduous forest clothe the landscape in brilliant yellows, rich golds, and reds as vibrant as the feathers of a northern cardinal. However, this spectacle presages the tough winter, when food becomes scarce for many animals.

Northern cardinal
Cardinalis cardinalis

EASTERN DECIDUOUS FOREST AND THE APPALACHIANS
OAK FORESTS

The eastern United States is dominated by hardwood forests, of which oak forests are the main type. About 30 oak species live here in various associations with maples, beech, hickory, northern conifers, pines, and southern evergreens. Oaks flourish in areas disturbed by both natural and man-made fires, which were frequent in this part of North America until wildfire suppression programs were introduced. Fires removed other tall trees, whose shade prevented oak seedlings from thriving. Today, without fires, oaks have a hard time replacing themselves. Gypsy moth larvae, introduced insect pests that defoliate oaks and other eastern hardwoods, add to the stress on these forest ecosystems. Oaks produce huge crops of hard, nutritious seeds called acorns, although the size of the crop varies from year to year. Acorns, or mast, are a critical food source for about 50 species of mammals and birds. In addition, oak trees offer leafy forage for plant-eaters and provide shelter for many species.

- Oak–Pine
- Oak–Chestnut
- Oak–Hickory

American robin
American robins nest in small trees under the canopy of oak forests as well as in urban backyards. They forage for earthworms between trees and also eat berries. One of the first birds to breed in the spring, the robin produces up to three clutches of three or four chicks per year.

Acorn harvest
White-tailed deer, black bears, squirrels, mice, turkeys, grackles, blue jays, and woodpeckers are among the many species that depend on acorns for fall and winter survival. Animals that store acorns in larders to tide them over the winter are important in dispersing the acorns throughout the forest.

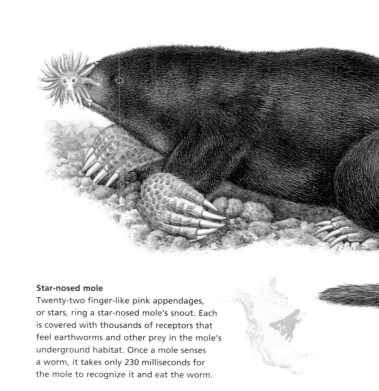

Star-nosed mole
Twenty-two finger-like pink appendages, or stars, ring a star-nosed mole's snout. Each is covered with thousands of receptors that feel earthworms and other prey in the mole's underground habitat. Once a mole senses a worm, it takes only 230 milliseconds for the mole to recognize it and eat the worm.

Blue jay

Raucous, boldly colored blue jays are year-round residents of the eastern deciduous forest. To survive winter, they collect and cache thousands of acorns, beechnuts, and pecans in the fall, storing the nuts in the ground. These birds also eat insects, green vegetation, and birds' eggs.

Virginia opossum

The only marsupial in North America north of Mexico, the Virginia opossum is best known for its habit of "playing possum" (acting dead) in response to danger. Although it lives just a year or two, the opossum has high rates of reproduction. A litter averages seven to nine young.

ECOLOGICAL INTERACTION

Oak trees produce bumper crops of acorns every two to six years, and few in between. Acorn eaters, such as white-tailed deer, white-footed mice, and chipmunks, flourish in the good acorn years, as do their ticks. This raises the risk of humans catching Lyme disease from a tick's bite. On the positive side, chipmunks prey on gypsy moths, an invasive species that defoliates oak trees.

White-tailed deer
Odocoileus virginianus

White-footed mouse
Peromyscus leucopus

Chipmunk
Tamius minimus

Acorn
Quercus velutina

Black-legged tick
Ixodes scapularis

Gypsy moth
Lymantria dispar

White-tailed deer

The only hoofed mammal in the eastern deciduous forest today, the white-tailed deer has recovered from habitat loss and overhunting. With forest returning, hunting now carefully managed, and the absence of their one-time wolf predator, the deer are considered "over abundant."

EASTERN DECIDUOUS FOREST AND THE APPALACHIANS
FOREST SALAMANDERS

At least 55 species of salamander, more than are found anywhere else on Earth, live in the forests of the southern Appalachian Mountains. About 20 are exclusive to the mountains. What is more, the group of lungless salamanders, which breathe through their skin, evolved here and, numbering 34 species, dominate the salamander fauna. The once-towering peaks of the ancient Appalachian range have eroded into gentle ridges and valleys. This process isolated salamanders, which rarely venture far from where they hatch, in different watersheds and on mountaintops, where they evolved into new species. For the same reason, this well-watered region is also rich in freshwater fish, turtles, mussels, crayfish, and insects. Because they live in and along streams and in other moist places under rocks, logs, and on the forest floor, salamanders are threatened by water pollution and habitat degradation. Even small changes due to global warming loom large for salamander species with restricted ranges.

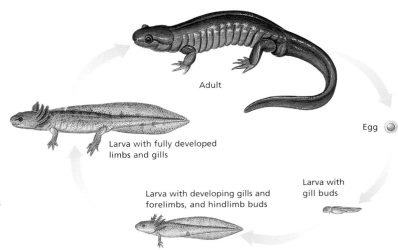

Adult

Larva with fully developed limbs and gills

Egg

Larva with gill buds

Larva with developing gills and forelimbs, and hindlimb buds

Metamorphosis

Many salamanders lay their eggs in water. The eggs hatch into larvae, which have gills and swim in search of prey, such as aquatic insects and their larvae. When salamander larvae reach a certain size they begin the process of metamorphosis, to change their body to better suit life on land. They grow tails and sprout legs and, except in the lungless species, develop lungs. In some salamander species, this transformation takes place within the egg.

Insect haven

Insects abound in the eastern deciduous forest, from the lofty heights of the canopy to the forest floor. Although mostly small, their combined weight probably exceeds that of the remaining animal life combined. Moths, butterflies, and their caterpillars are important food for many forest birds. Fierce yellowjacket wasps also prey on caterpillars, flies, and bees. Salamanders eat beetles and a host of other insects and their larvae.

Mudpuppy
Necturus maculosus

Striped hawk moth
Hyles livornica

Lunar moth
Actius luna

Common yellowjacket
Paravespula vulgaris

Long-tailed salamander
Eurycea longicauda

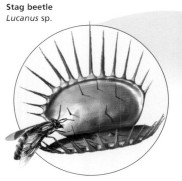

Stag beetle
Lucanus sp.

Venus flytrap
The Venus flytrap, a carnivorous plant, lures insects to its two-part leaves ringed with spiny teeth, with bright color and sweet secretions.

Red salamander
The red salamander eats small insects, worms, and other invertebrates, as well as smaller salamanders. It takes just 11 milliseconds to snatch prey using its long tongue, which is supported by a skeleton and tipped with a sticky pad.

Spotted salamander
Found only in deciduous forest, the spotted salamander spends much of its time hiding under logs or within the burrows of other animals. However, on a few warm, wet spring evenings these salamanders emerge in large numbers and migrate to small ponds to breed.

Salamanders

The salamanders of eastern North America range from the diminutive pigmy salamander, which is not as long as a small finger, to the arm's-length eastern hellbender. Whatever their size and secretive habits, salamanders are key players in their ecosystems. They are predators, prey, and nutrient recyclers. Many eat tiny insects, linking these creatures in the food chain to larger vertebrates, such as the birds and mammals that eat salamanders.

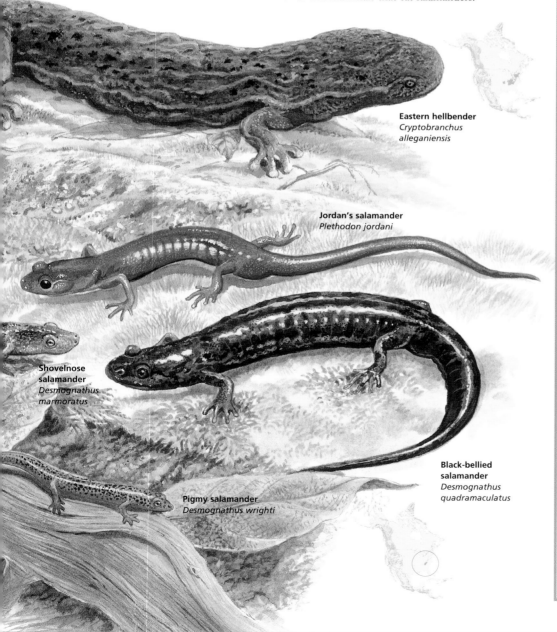

Eastern hellbender
Cryptobranchus alleganiensis

Jordan's salamander
Plethodon jordani

Shovelnose salamander
Desmognathus marmoratus

Black-bellied salamander
Desmognathus quadramaculatus

Pigmy salamander
Desmognathus wrighti

FRUITFUL FUNGI

More than 2,000 species of mushroom, or fungi, are found in the damp forests of the Smoky Mountains National Park. Some live on organic material, such as leaf litter and animal dung, hastening its breakdown. Others enjoy a symbiotic relationship with trees. Called mycorrhizzae, these fungi extract carbohydrates from the tree and, in return, provide it with nutrients that it could not extract from the soil.

Witches' butter
Witches' butter is a kind of jelly fungi, a species whose fruiting bodies are gelatinous and often irregularly shaped. Found on oaks, beech, alder, and other deciduous tree wood, witches' butter is actually a parasite on other fungi that live on decaying wood.

Collared earthstars
Collared earthstars grow in the leaf litter of the deciduous forest, usually in groups. Visible in the foreground are newly sprouted fruiting bodies (mushrooms), with pointed tips, and an older earthstar, with the rounded top and collar that gives the species its name.

Shelf fungi
Shelf, or bracket, fungi, like the sulfur shelf, grows on dead oak wood as well as on living trunks, where it is a pathogen known as brown rot. The sulfur shelf is also known as the chicken of the woods. When cooked, its taste and texture are reminiscent of chicken.

THE COASTAL PLAINS

The Atlantic and Gulf of Mexico coastal plains encompass pine woodlands, moist deciduous forest, cypress swamps, salt and brackish marshes, and sandy beaches. Running along the coast from New York, around Florida, and west to east Texas, the plains are characterized by frequent fires, sandy soils, and wetlands. Chesapeake Bay, the largest estuary in the United States, is a prominent feature of the Atlantic coastal plains. Its 64,000-square-mile (165,760-km²) watershed includes parts of six states and the District of Columbia. However, little of the diverse natural plains habitats remains intact. They are now densely populated and, apart from major urbanization, have been logged and converted to agriculture, and beachside areas have been developed for recreation. Still, the coastal plains are rich in wildlife, especially migratory birds that frequent them during stopovers on their lengthy journeys between winter homes in South America and breeding sites as far north as the Arctic.

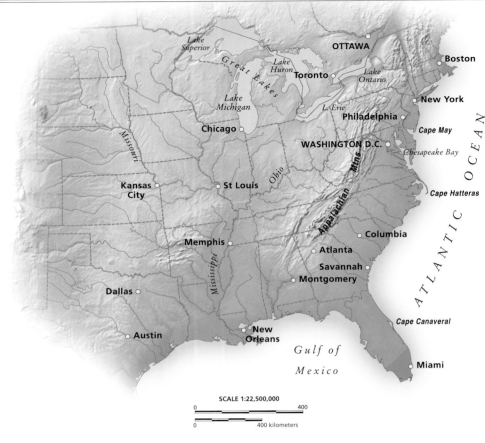

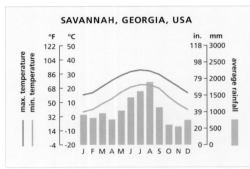

SAVANNAH, GEORGIA, USA

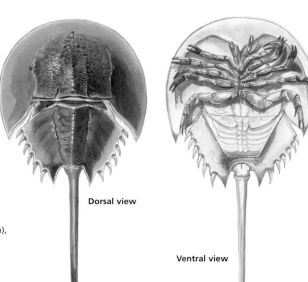

CONSERVATION WATCH

An isolated subspecies of the puma, the Florida panther lives in the swamps of south Florida. Pumas once ranged throughout eastern North America but hunting and habitat loss eliminated them from all but this retreat. Less than 100 of the critically endangered cats remain and they risk collisions with speeding vehicles.

Least bittern

The tiny least bittern has the uncanny ability to disappear among the reeds in which it forages. An alarmed least bittern will stand very tall, with its bill pointed skyward, to imitate a reed. It even sways in the wind, much like the reeds do.

Ancient species

Horseshoe crabs are an ancient species, some 540 million years old. They existed even before flowering plants and dinosaurs, and have changed little since. The North American species spawns on Atlantic beaches in spring. The massive clutches of eggs feed as many as a million shorebirds during their northward migration. Nesting sea turtles and fish also partake of the feast.

Dorsal view

Ventral view

Horseshoe crab

Female horseshoe crabs, with an average width of 9.5 inches (24 cm), are about 60 percent larger than their male counterparts. The first of six paired appendages on its underside is used to place food into the crab's central mouth.

Great blue heron
The largest heron in North America, the great blue heron, stands more than 4 feet (1.2 m) tall. Males and females perform elaborate courtship rituals to secure their bond before nesting begins. They raise their crests, puff their feathers, and joust with their bills.

Black skimmer
The black skimmer's large red and black bill is unusual in that the lower mandible is distinctly longer than the upper. Flying low over the surface of the water, these seabirds skim the water with their lower mandible to catch small fish. They often hunt at night.

Yellow-crested night heron
Rather large, hulking birds, yellow-crested night herons often nest in colonies, where they build stick nests overhanging water. These birds were nearly eliminated from the coastal plains of the United States in the late 1800s and early 1900s. Hunters killed and sold them as meat and their beautiful plumes decorated women's hats.

Nine-banded armadillo
Its body covered in shell-like plates, the nine-banded armadillo has expanded its range in the southeastern United States. First seen north of the Rio Grande, Texas, in about 1850, it has since ventured as far north as Kansas and Nebraska, and east to Florida.

Canebrakes for cover
Thickets of North American bamboos, called canes, once stood 20 feet (6 m) tall and stretched for miles along the coastal plains. Cut down to make way for farming, these thickets now survive only in scattered stands. They make a great wildlife habitat, providing cover, food, or both, for birds and mammals, and food for the caterpillars of moths and butterflies.

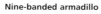

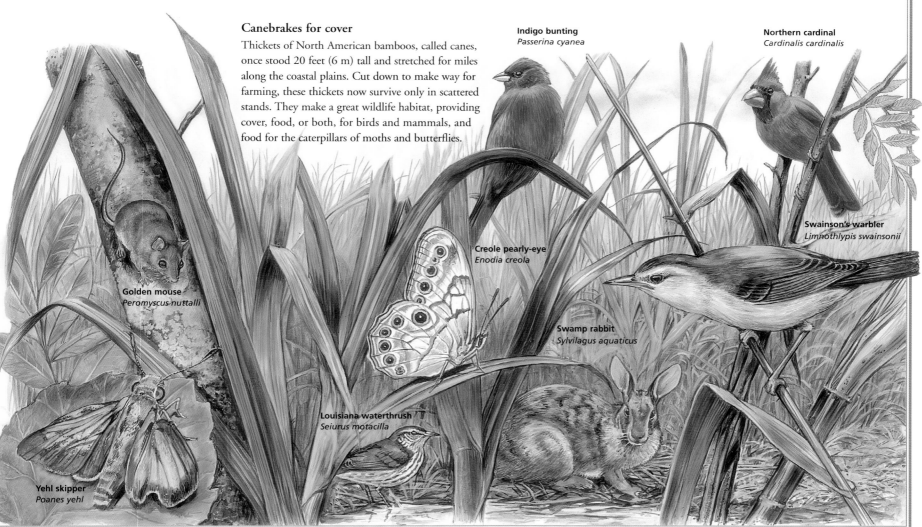

Indigo bunting
Passerina cyanea

Northern cardinal
Cardinalis cardinalis

Swainson's warbler
Limnothlypis swainsonii

Creole pearly-eye
Enodia creola

Golden mouse
Peromyscus nuttalli

Swamp rabbit
Sylvilagus aquaticus

Louisiana waterthrush
Seiurus motacilla

Yehl skipper
Poanes yehl

THE COASTAL PLAINS
BIRD MIGRATION

Birds have migrated across the Americas for millions of years. Some 200 species breed in summer in North America as far north as the Arctic Circle, when insect and plant food is abundant. They wing their way south as far as Tierra del Fuego, at the southern tip of South America, to avoid the meager fare available to them in winter, then retrace their flight the next spring. It is a spectacular phenomenon involving billions of birds in spring and fall, with huge numbers of these winged wanderers converging on a few choice stopover spots, such as Cape May, New Jersey. A million migratory shorebirds break their journey here in spring to feast on horseshoe crab eggs. But the fall is even more amazing. Funneled by geography, tens of thousands of migrating seabirds, raptors, and songbirds pour into this small peninsula on a single autumn day. However, many of the warblers and other migrants that pass through are in trouble, beset by habitat loss and fragmentation.

Red-winged blackbirds
Found throughout North and Central America south of the Arctic, red-winged blackbirds are the continent's most abundant birds. Some populations do not migrate but others, namely those that breed in Canada and northern United States, migrate to the south. Huge feeding flocks of several million birds may form during winter.

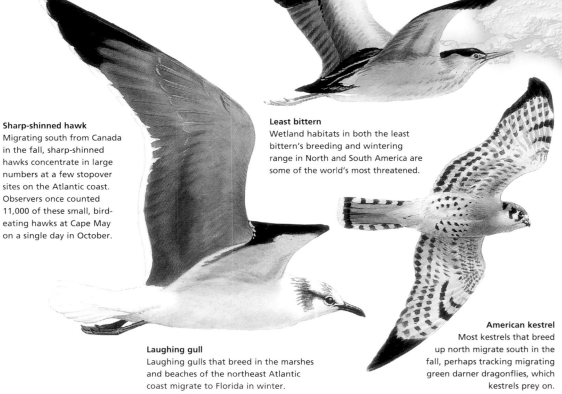

Sharp-shinned hawk
Migrating south from Canada in the fall, sharp-shinned hawks concentrate in large numbers at a few stopover sites on the Atlantic coast. Observers once counted 11,000 of these small, bird-eating hawks at Cape May on a single day in October.

Least bittern
Wetland habitats in both the least bittern's breeding and wintering range in North and South America are some of the world's most threatened.

American kestrel
Most kestrels that breed up north migrate south in the fall, perhaps tracking migrating green darner dragonflies, which kestrels prey on.

Laughing gull
Laughing gulls that breed in the marshes and beaches of the northeast Atlantic coast migrate to Florida in winter.

Piping plover
Diminutive piping plovers nest on Atlantic beaches and migrate in winter to similar habitats further south, from North Carolina to Mexico and the Caribbean. These ground-nesting birds are endangered due to habitat loss and human disturbance.

Black-throated blue warbler
Climate change threatens birds such as the black-throated blue warbler because it may influence food availability at breeding, stopover, and wintering sites.

Rose-breasted grosbeak
Rose-breasted grosbeaks that breed in the eastern parts of their range follow the Atlantic flyway through Central America and northwest South America to winter in southern Mexico. Those breeding in the north and west follow the Mississippi flyway.

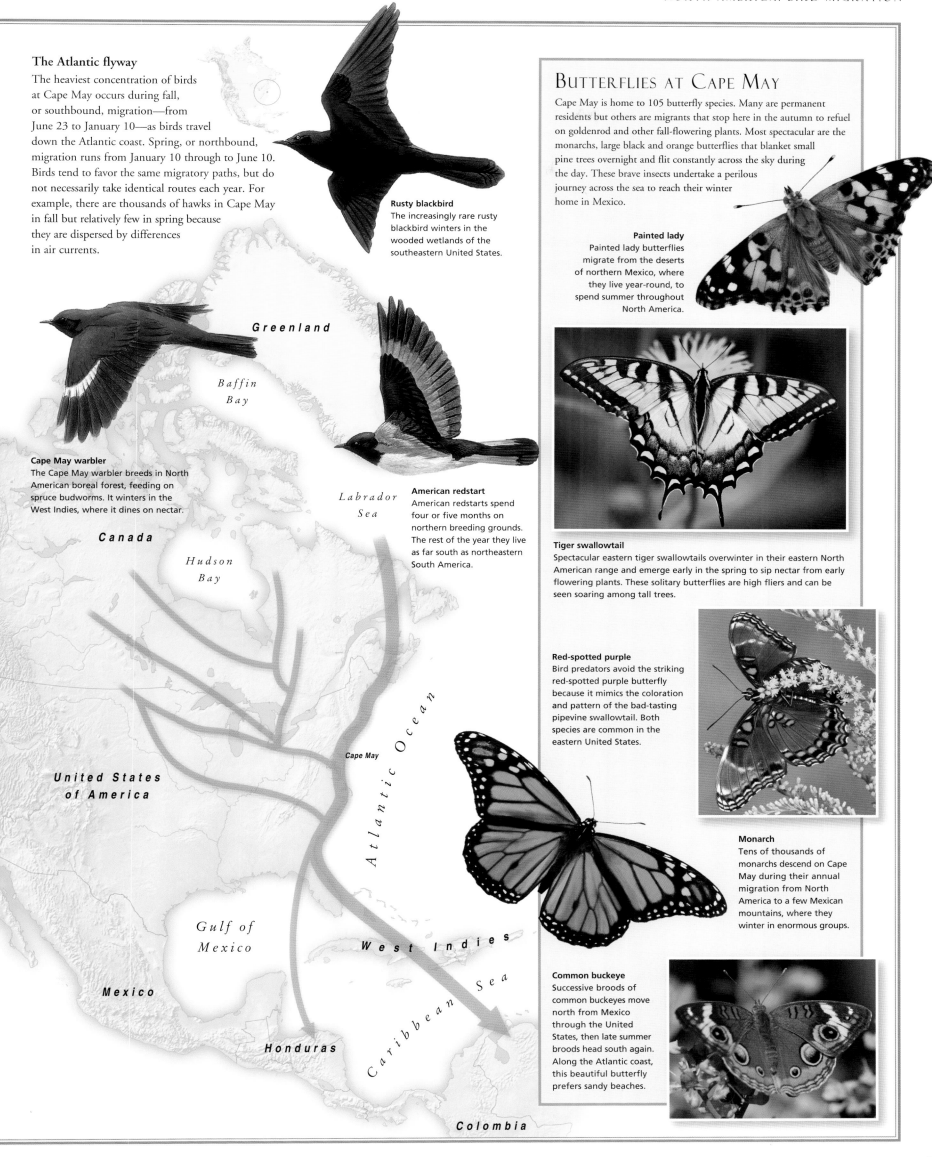

The Atlantic flyway
The heaviest concentration of birds at Cape May occurs during fall, or southbound, migration—from June 23 to January 10—as birds travel down the Atlantic coast. Spring, or northbound, migration runs from January 10 through to June 10. Birds tend to favor the same migratory paths, but do not necessarily take identical routes each year. For example, there are thousands of hawks in Cape May in fall but relatively few in spring because they are dispersed by differences in air currents.

Rusty blackbird
The increasingly rare rusty blackbird winters in the wooded wetlands of the southeastern United States.

Cape May warbler
The Cape May warbler breeds in North American boreal forest, feeding on spruce budworms. It winters in the West Indies, where it dines on nectar.

American redstart
American redstarts spend four or five months on northern breeding grounds. The rest of the year they live as far south as northeastern South America.

Greenland

Baffin Bay

Labrador Sea

Canada

Hudson Bay

Atlantic Ocean

United States of America

Cape May

Gulf of Mexico

West Indies

Caribbean Sea

Mexico

Honduras

Colombia

BUTTERFLIES AT CAPE MAY
Cape May is home to 105 butterfly species. Many are permanent residents but others are migrants that stop here in the autumn to refuel on goldenrod and other fall-flowering plants. Most spectacular are the monarchs, large black and orange butterflies that blanket small pine trees overnight and flit constantly across the sky during the day. These brave insects undertake a perilous journey across the sea to reach their winter home in Mexico.

Painted lady
Painted lady butterflies migrate from the deserts of northern Mexico, where they live year-round, to spend summer throughout North America.

Tiger swallowtail
Spectacular eastern tiger swallowtails overwinter in their eastern North American range and emerge early in the spring to sip nectar from early flowering plants. These solitary butterflies are high fliers and can be seen soaring among tall trees.

Red-spotted purple
Bird predators avoid the striking red-spotted purple butterfly because it mimics the coloration and pattern of the bad-tasting pipevine swallowtail. Both species are common in the eastern United States.

Monarch
Tens of thousands of monarchs descend on Cape May during their annual migration from North America to a few Mexican mountains, where they winter in enormous groups.

Common buckeye
Successive broods of common buckeyes move north from Mexico through the United States, then late summer broods head south again. Along the Atlantic coast, this beautiful butterfly prefers sandy beaches.

This remarkably colored red-eyed tree frog clasps a heliconia in a Costa Rican rain forest. Most tree frogs have adhesive pads on their fingers and toes that help them stick to leaves and branches. Some even have an opposable first finger, like a thumb, that allows them to grasp twigs and stems.

CENTRAL &
SOUTH AMERICA

CENTRAL & SOUTH AMERICA

Highly distinctive species from every class in the animal kingdom are found in Central and South America. Biodiversity is particularly remarkable in Central America, which supports around 7 percent of Earth's species on less than one-half a percent of its land. The spectacular landscapes in which these animals live, dramatically exemplified by the continent's physical geography, are every bit as varied. The region is dominated by large river systems and wetlands, but also renowned for its imposing mountain chains and volcanoes, deserts, lakes, vast grasslands, and tropical forests. Coastal and marine life is abundant amid the tropical coral reefs, mangroves, and seagrass beds. At its southernmost tip South America also supports sea ice.

Central America
Located at the junction of two continental masses and the world's largest oceans, this region is rich in biodiversity.

The Gran Chaco
Climatic extremes and wooded grasslands that become swamps in the rainy season are typical of this region.

Amazon Rain Forest
The largest rain forest in the world, which crosses nine international borders, features wildlife and ecosystems barely seen elsewhere.

Patagonia
Dramatic mountainous landscape at America's southern extreme adjoins the rugged coast, where Antarctic animals are regular visitors.

The Andes Wilderness
Low valleys grazed by camelids and snowy peaks patrolled by the spectacular condor typify the wild beauty of these mountains.

Life in the Caribbean
Shallow warm waters harbor magnificent coral reefs and their resident turtles, fish, and crustaceans in the stunning Caribbean.

The Galápagos Islands
The fascinating species found here are supremely adapted to the harsh life on one of Earth's major tropical archipelagos.

CLIMATE ZONES
- Wet tropical
- Seasonal tropical
- Arid
- Semiarid
- Mediterranean
- Subtropical
- Temperate
- Subpolar
- Highland

Climate

The northwest coast, parts of the northeast and east coasts, and much of the Amazon Basin experience hot, wet weather year-round. Moist onshore winds are the main drivers of the subtropical conditions that extend down the east coast. Cold ocean currents off the west coast dry the air, producing an arid coastal strip. Conditions vary across the Andes; generally it is hot and wet in the north, hot and dry in the center, and cold and wet in the far south. Patagonia, east of the Andes, has low rainfall.

VEGETATION ZONES
- Tropical forest
- Seasonal tropical forest
- Desert
- Tropical grassland
- Mediterranean forest and scrub
- Midlatitude grassland
- Midlatitude forest
- Mountain vegetation

Vegetation

Amazon rain forests extend over much of the great river basin, giving way to cloud forest in the Andes and tropical deciduous woodlands in the north and east. The savanna grasslands that characterize the Gran Chaco and the Brazilian Highlands merge to the southeast with more temperate grasses on the Pampas. Thick stands of temperate rain forest occur on the southern Andes but the Central Andes and Patagonia are sparsely vegetated. The Atacama Desert is virtually devoid of plant life.

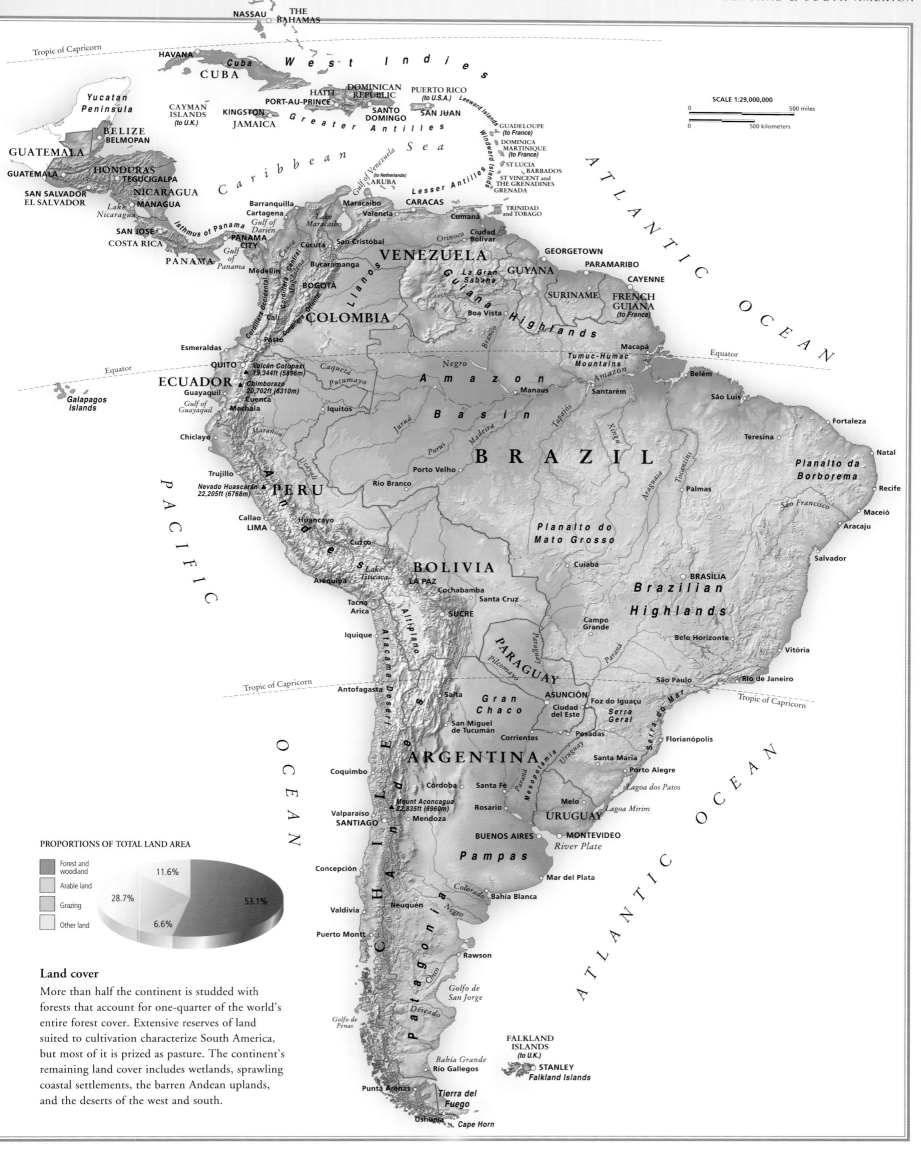

PROPORTIONS OF TOTAL LAND AREA

Forest and woodland
Arable land
Grazing
Other land

11.6%
28.7%
6.6%
53.1%

Land cover

More than half the continent is studded with forests that account for one-quarter of the world's entire forest cover. Extensive reserves of land suited to cultivation characterize South America, but most of it is prized as pasture. The continent's remaining land cover includes wetlands, sprawling coastal settlements, the barren Andean uplands, and the deserts of the west and south.

CENTRAL AMERICA

The near-equatorial isthmus of Central America connects the South and North of the American continent and serves as a terrestrial bridge between the Pacific and Atlantic oceans. This narrow strip of land, measuring 202,000 square miles (523,000 km²), formed 3 million years ago and is today the territory of seven countries: Guatemala, Honduras, El Salvador, Belize, Nicaragua, Costa Rica, and Panama. It holds a greater concentration of plant and animal life than anywhere else in the world. Central America is characterized by contrasting landscapes, ranging from dry, sea-level forests to those shrouded in mist, and from lofty peaks and coastal marshes to fertile valleys that continue to be shaped by volcanic activity. The abundant natural bounty here includes rivers and lakes, islands, thermal springs, lagoons, estuaries, beaches, and reefs. Distinct climates meet and merge in Central America as a result of topography rather than seasonal change. Average annual temperatures fall within the narrow range of 65–86°F (18–30°C).

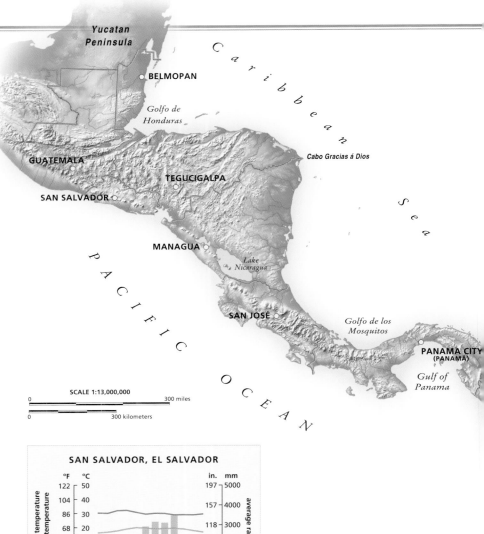

SCALE 1:13,000,000

SAN SALVADOR, EL SALVADOR

Capybara
The largest of all the 1,729 rodent species, the semi-aquatic capybara is extremely agile in the water, using its partly webbed toes like tiny paddles. Troops, containing up to 20 animals, live along riverbanks where young capybaras are sometimes preyed on by caimans. However, this adult has little to fear—it is too large a meal for the surrounding caimans, which are more likely to hunt for fish or frogs.

Scarlet macaws
Scarlet macaws are large, colorful parrots that are often seen perched on cliffs. Here they consume clay, which helps them digest poisonous chemicals found in the unripe fruit they feed on. Macaws fly in pairs or small groups and can reach speeds of 35 miles per hour (56 km/h).

Boa constrictor
The boa constrictor is a large, solitary snake with powerful muscles that allow it to squeeze its prey until it suffocates. The snake can open its jaws wide and swallows its prey whole, head-first. Strong acids in its stomach help the constrictor digest its meal.

White-faced capuchin
The white-faced capuchin is easy to spot in the wild. Small and inquisitive, it usually travels in groups from tree to tree with the aid of its prehensile tail. These monkeys forage for fruit and insects at all forest levels and communicate using chatters and shrieks.

Mantled howler monkey
The mantled howler monkey is often heard before it is seen. Even in dense rain forest its roars and piglike grunts travel for more than half a mile (0.8 km). A particularly large hyoid bone in the monkey's throat allows it to make such a resonant noise.

Tayra
The tayra is a mustelid related to the otter, but it lives in trees. It hunts small vertebrates, such as rabbits and lizards, and also feeds on carrion and fruits. Similar to a weasel, this skilled climber is able to jump from tree to tree when threatened.

TENT-MAKING BATS

Honduran white bats are among the few bat species that construct their own roosts. They bite the veins of large heliconia leaves until they collapse downward, forming a partially enclosed, tent-like space beneath which the bats hang upside down. These "tents" provide protection from jungle rains, sunlight, and predators such as snakes. One male and five or six females usually roost together.

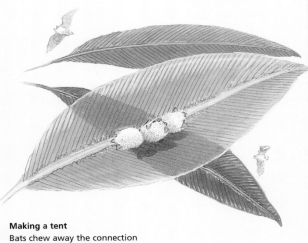

Making a tent
Bats chew away the connection between the midrib and edge of the leaf until it droops.

Protected roost
The little Honduran white bats roost in the tent they have created.

CENTRAL AMERICA
RAIN FORESTS

Central American rain forests are found in the tropical zone between the Tropic of Cancer and Tropic of Capricorn, where the weather is hot and humid year-round. Days and nights are of almost equal length and there is little seasonal variation, with an average temperature throughout the year of 80.6°F (27°C) and ample sunlight. Abundant rainfall, no less than four inches (100 mm) per month, is a result of cooling moisture produced by wind and ocean currents. Viewed from above, the tree canopy is an evergreen cover of towering trees that reach heights of 60 to 150 feet (20–50 m). These giants are laced with vines and lianas, and their trunks coated with epiphytes, bromeliads, and orchids. The forest's lower layers are densely planted with smaller trees and shrubs, and the deeply shaded forest floor is covered with decaying plant material. Birds of every size and color are found here, as are bats, monkeys, reptiles, ants, and many other insects that share a symbiotic relationship with plants as seed dispersers.

DEFORESTATION
- 1800
- 1960
- Present

Blue morpho butterfly
The blue morpho butterfly owes its coloring to tiny ridges on its wings that reflect light, giving it dazzling visibility. By contrast, the wing undersides are brown. Generally the butterfly rests with its wings closed to make it less visible to enemies.

FROGS AND TOADS

The frogs and toads of Central American rain forests include climbers that inhabit the canopy and ground-dwelling species that shelter in caves, burrows, or rock crevices. Most, however, live in ponds and streams. Their bulging eyes enable them to see in any direction, and their sticky tongues are adept at capturing insect prey. Rain forests echo with loud frog and toad calls during the mating season.

Harlequin frog
(Atelopus varius)

Poison dart frog
While some frogs rely on camouflage to remain unobtrusive, the brilliant red skin and blue legs of the poison dart frog serve as a warning to predators. The toxic excretions of this 2.3-inch (6-cm) frog were used by native people on the tips of their arrows.

Most tadpoles must stay in water, but the rain forest air is so moist that the poison dart frog can carry its young on its back.

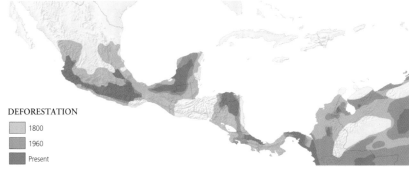

Golden toad
The golden toad, an endemic species of Costa Rica, is thought to be extinct in the wild. During the rainy season, hundreds of black females and yellow males used to gather in small ponds to mate. Females produced 200 to 400 eggs and, after hatching, the larvae remained in water for about five weeks as they progressed toward adulthood.

Red-eyed tree frog
(Agalychnis callidryas)

Three-toed sloth
Although sometimes taken for a primate, the brown-throated three-toed sloth is more closely related to the armadillo. Its movements and metabolism are slow; the sloth takes almost a month to digest a single meal and moves at an average speed of 1.2 miles per hour (2 km/h). Sloths are strictly arboreal and descend to the ground only to defecate.

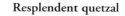

Resplendent quetzal

The quetzal is often found in wild avocado trees, the fruits of which it swallows whole. This bird constructs its nest in the cavity of a dead tree, choosing a soft trunk that is in an advanced state of decomposition. The two feathers that form its tail, which can be 23 inches (59 cm) long, protrude from the nest to protect them from damage.

Spectacled owl
White "glasses" in the region of its yellow eyes give the spectacled owl its name. Juveniles, such as the bird on the left, have the markings in reverse; it takes years to reach the full adult plumage of the bird on the right.

Kinkajou
The kinkajou is also known as the sugar bear because of its habit of eating honey, nectar, and sweet fruits. It licks nectar from flowers with its flexible tongue. Pollen that sticks to its fur is carried from flower to flower, making it an important pollinator.

Keel-billed toucan
Although it appears weighty, the keel-billed toucan's bill is light and hollow, and supported by thin rods of bone. The toucan employs its bill skillfully; using its feather-like tongue to catch insects and flick fruits down its throat.

Margay
An accomplished climber, the margay spends most of its life in the forest canopy. This agile cat has specially adapted claws and rotating ankle joints that enable it to climb down trees headfirst and run upside down beneath branches.

CENTRAL AMERICA
THE JAGUAR

The jaguar is a top terrestrial predator in Central and South America, and plays an important role in stabilizing ecosystems and regulating the populations of its prey species. Its survival depends on more than one habitat and its presence is also critical for other animals. The jaguar's range has severely contracted to Mexico and Central America, mainly in Costa Rica, northern Guatemala, and Belize. Some populations are also found in Mato Grosso, Brazil, and in the Pantanal, an ecoregion bordering Brazil, Bolivia, and Paraguay. Factors that influence the jaguar's future prospects include its persecution by humans, because it is seen as a threat to people and livestock; hunting for fur and sport; a shortage of prey; loss of habitat, including the conversion of land for cattle ranching; and inadequate protection measures. Its survival depends on an intimate understanding of its habitat, gathering population data for both the jaguar and its prey, monitoring disease, education to mitigate conflicts with cattle ranchers, and developing protection measures.

Climbing
Jaguars depend on forest for their survival; it is their original and preferred habitat for hunting. They climb trees to lie in wait for wild prey below. But because of forest loss as a result of new settlements and clearing for pasture, some jaguars now also kill domestic animals and livestock in areas close to human populations.

Present
Former

CONSERVATION WATCH
Historically, the jaguar's range stretched from the southwestern United States to southern Argentina, but today it is extinct in the United States and numbers have drastically declined in Mexico and Argentina. Recovery programs have included on-the-ground monitoring, predator controls, minimizing livestock conflicts, and creating jaguar reserves.

Swimming
The jaguar is an excellent swimmer and thrives near rivers, lakes, and streams. When hunting fish it stalks, under cover, on its target's blind spot, before leaping into the water to catch its prey. The jaguar is also capable of carrying a large kill while swimming.

Fish prey
Like other big cats, jaguars routinely catch fish for the proteins and essential fatty acids they contain. Apart from fish, cats rarely prey on small animals because of their relatively low nutritional value. However, rabbits are an exception, and are highly sought after by leopards.

Coat
The jaguar can be distinguished by the presence of small dots within the larger rosette markings on its magnificent coat. Each marking has a unique pattern that is like a fingerprint.

Leopard-like ancestors

Jaguars are thought to have evolved from leopard-like ancestors in Eurasia, and to have arrived on the American continent 1.8 million to 10,000 years ago via the Bering land bridge. The modern jaguar is smaller and has shorter legs than its cousin the leopard, although both these members of the genus *Panthera* have muscular bodies, roar, climb trees, and enjoy swimming. Female jaguars reach sexual maturity at the age of three and males at four years.

Offspring
Female jaguars bear a litter of one to four cubs after a gestation period of 91 to 111 days, with births peaking during the rainy season when prey is most abundant. The cubs are born blind but gain their sight at two weeks. Females mother the cubs for two years, after which time they are ready to find their own territory.

Teeth
Four canine teeth, up to 2 inches (5 cm) long, are used for killing, while the sharp, scissor-like carnassial teeth enable the jaguar to crush bones, or to hold meat and cut it at the same time.

Eyes
The pupils of the night-hunting jaguar can contract to mere slits and its night vision is up to seven times better than that of a human. It also has excellent binocular vision for judging distances.

PREY

Jaguars are known to eat more than 85 species of prey, taking advantage of the diversity of animals that are found in rain forests. They prefer to hunt at night, but may capture prey during the day if it is available. Jaguar prey ranges from domestic livestock to tapirs, deer, sloths, peccaries, capybaras, agoutis, crocodiles, snakes, monkeys, and fish. They can consume up to 55 pounds (25 kg) of meat in one sitting, followed by periods of famine.

Capybara
Because capybaras live in groups, a jaguar has a good chance of taking at least one while it feeds underwater, or catching one on land, where capybaras are less agile.

Sloth
Like many other predators, jaguars prey on sloths. A green coating of algae on the sloth's fur aids its camouflage in the rain forest canopy.

Baird's Tapir
Baird's tapir becomes active at dusk, foraging along riverbanks. It is easily detected by a stalking jaguar employing its highly effective night vision.

Amazon Rain Forest

The Amazon rain forest is the oldest and largest tropical forest in the world. It extends across the Amazon River basin, a region of 2.6 million square miles (6.7 million km²) drained by the Amazon River. Sixty-two percent of the basin is in Brazil but it also covers parts of Peru, Bolivia, French Guyana, Suriname, Guyana, Venezuela, Colombia, and Ecuador. This huge expanse of rain forest contains an amazing collection of wildlife, including amphibians, birds, insects, mammals, and reptiles. Tarantulas, caterpillars, scorpions, anacondas, caimans, jaguars, sloths, tamarins, toucans, and vampire bats all occur in this region. Although some soils in the Amazon rain forest have declined in fertility, the area is a web of diverse landscapes and ecosystems. Dense, jungle-like forests filled with towering trees merge with open forests shaded by palms and tangled with lianas. High humidity, abundant rainfall, and an average temperature of 75°F (24°C) are common characteristics across the basin.

SCALE 1:37,500,000

0 — 500 miles

0 — 500 kilometers

Big River Creatures

Amazon River waters have a high diversity of fish, estimated at more than 3,000 species. During each rainy season extensive forested areas adjacent to the river are flooded and many fish, reptiles, and mammals move into the newly flooded areas to feed, mainly on fallen fruits from the trees. They also reproduce here, returning to the main channels when the floodwaters recede.

Pink river dolphin
The pink river dolphin is the largest and most common of the world's five freshwater dolphins. It uses echolocation to find prey in the muddy rivers of flooded jungles. Age, water clarity, temperature, and location determine its body colors, which can vary from pink to gray or white.

Black caiman
The black caiman is the largest member of the Alligatorinae family. This predator lives along slow-moving rivers and lakes, and in the seasonally flooded savannas of the Amazon basin. Its prey includes capybaras, fish, turtles, and deer.

Amazon River
The Amazon River is the world's second longest river. Its 3,976-mile (6,400-km) course, which includes 15,000 tributaries, meanders from the Andes to the Atlantic Ocean. The Amazon is the source of almost 20 percent of all river water that flows into the oceans.

Giant river otter
Only a few thousand giant river otters are thought to survive in the wild because of hunting by humans. With a body length of 80 inches (2 m), this is the world's longest river otter. It propels itself through water using its powerful paddle-shaped tail.

Pirarucu
The carnivorous, air-breathing pirarucu, the world's largest freshwater fish, is thought to be 200 million years old. It can grow to up to 120 inches (3 m) in length and weigh up to 400 pounds (180 kg).

Rain forest

The Amazon rain forest can be divided vertically into four layers, each representing a unique ecosystem. At the emergent level, eagles and parrots inhabit the tallest trees. The broad crowns of these giants form the canopy, which is home to snakes, toucans, tree frogs, monkeys, parakeets, orchids, and bromeliads. In the understory, shrubs and ferns grow larger leaves to capture sunlight, but only a thin layer of decaying organic matter is found on the forest floor.

EMERGENTS

Orange-winged amazon
(*Amazona amazonicas*)

Pygmy marmoset
Inhabitants of rain forests canopies, pygmy marmosets are the smallest monkeys. Habitat destruction does not seem to have affected these primates, but some populations have declined because of the pet trade. Public education is aimed at reducing human disturbances and helping to monitor the trade.

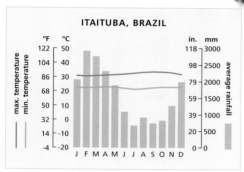

ITAITUBA, BRAZIL

CANOPY

Black spider monkey
(*Ateles belzebuth*)

Maned three-toed sloth
(*Bradypus torquatus*)

Orange-winged amazon
(*Amazona amazonicas*)

UNDERSTORY

Channel bill toucan
(*Ramphastos Vitellinus*)

Hoatzin
The hoatzin, which belongs to a primitive bird family, lives in flocks of 50 or more. These birds perch on low or middle branches that overhang water, and eat green leaves and buds. They have a large food-storage pouch and esophagus for converting plant carbohydrates into sugars they can digest.

CONSERVATION WATCH

Since 1970, more than 232,000 square miles (600,000 km²) of Amazon rain forest has been destroyed, occupied, or altered by human activity. It continues to be threatened by hunting, unsustainable logging, illegal gold mining, agriculture and cattle ranching, dam construction, fire, and gas and oil mining operations. At the current rate of loss, 55 percent of the rain forest could be gone by 2030.

FOREST FLOOR

Green anaconda
(*Eunectes murinus*)

AMAZON RAIN FOREST
LIFE IN THE TREETOPS

Most of the species diversity within tropical rain forests is concentrated in the canopy, just below the top, emergent, layer. This dense ceiling of closely spaced trees, which rarely interlock, stretches for vast distances. Canopy dwellers are well-adapted to deal with the forest openings by climbing, jumping, or flying. It is estimated that biodiversity within the canopy includes 40 percent of all plant and animal species globally. Some of the world's loudest birds and primates, which rely on sound signals to communicate because the dense leaf cover precludes visual territorial displays, are found here. Other important species are bats and small mammals that coexist with a high number of insects and their allies. These, in turn, have evolved camouflage coloration to protect themselves from birds of prey, lizards, and frogs. All creatures of the canopy are adapted to take advantage of treetop resources, such as nesting sites, transit routes, hiding places, and a diet of insects, fruits, seeds, flowers, and leaves.

Toucan barbet
The colorful toucan barbet hops from branch to branch, feeding on a diet of insects and fruit, from the ground right up to the forest canopy. Its distinctive call is a repetition of short, foghorn-like notes. Breeding pairs nest in hollows in dead trees.

Storing carbon, releasing oxygen
Forest canopies absorb carbon dioxide from the atmosphere and convert it into oxygen. The canopy thereby plays an important part in global climate regulation because it enables the exchange of heat, water vapor, and atmospheric gases.

Common fruit bat
Fruit bats digest food quickly, without microbial fermentation in the stomach, so they must constantly forage for meals. As a consequence, these bats are a key species in the pollination of tropical fruits, and many plants rely on fruit bats for the dispersal of seeds.

Julia butterfly
A yellow-orange tropical butterfly with long forewings, the Julia butterfly is a fast-flying, long-lived species. It is active during the day, feeding on the nectar of flowers, such as lantana and shepherd's needle.

Hairy protection
Julia butterfly females lay their eggs on new passionflowers, the leaves of which nourish their larvae. Caterpillars rely on their short antennae to locate food, and defend themselves with fine, irritating bristles that lodge in the skin of their predators.

Emperor tamarin
The emperor tamarin lives in groups and communicates using strident squeaks. The male is an attentive father, assisting at the birth of its offspring and taking responsibility for their grooming and transportation. This tiny monkey is territorial and fiercely defends its area.

Red howler monkey
The red howler monkey travels through the forest by clambering along tree branches and lianas, but also descends to the ground, where it walks and runs. It is most active in the morning and evening. Its calls carry more than 1.5 miles (3 km) through the forest.

Versicolored barbet
The versicolored barbet, which is distinguished by the bristles that border its heavy bill, is a member of the Ramphastidae family and is closely related to toucans. Like all fruit-eating species, this arboreal bird plays an important role in seed dispersal, regurgitating seed pits throughout the forest.

⚡ CONSERVATION WATCH
The pied tamarin, which has one of the smallest ranges of any primate, is dying out in the forests of the Amazon. Its habitat has been reduced, and is now fragmented and isolated because of urban expansion and agriculture. This small monkey, which weighs just 0.9 pounds (400 g), lives in groups of two to 10, and has a lifespan of just nine years.

Brown-eared woolly opossum
The woolly opossum's large, protruding eyes face forward, giving it a monkey-like appearance. Its hands and feet are adapted for climbing and gripping, and its flexible prehensile tail provides extra support. It is usually solitary, but opossums gather where fruit is plentiful.

Orange-winged parrot
The sociable orange-winged parrot moves through the crowns of tall trees searching for ripe fruits and nuts. True to its name, this parrot has a brilliant orange patch on its wings, visible as it flies over the forest at dawn.

Harpy eagle
The largest and most powerful raptor of the tropical rain forest is the harpy eagle, which preys upon tree-dwelling mammals. Like other birds of prey, it brings green twigs to its nest to protect its young from insects and parasites, and to ensure a cooler home environment.

THE ANDES WILDERNESS

The Andes is the world's longest mountain range. It stretches for 5,000 miles (8,000 km) and mountain peaks reach higher than 12,000 feet (3,600 m) along half its length. The mountain system forms the western border of South America and extends through Colombia, Venezuela, Ecuador, Peru, Bolivia, Chile, and Argentina. Glaciers, snow-capped volcanoes, desert plateaus, cloud forests, deep gorges incised by rivers, and peaceful valleys characterize the landscape. Conifers and ferns abound and wildlife is richly varied: 50 percent of the plant and animal species found here are unique to the area. The movement of sedimentary rocks and tectonic forces that helped form the Andes some 199 million years ago continue to cause earthquakes and volcanic eruptions even today. The weather varies significantly, depending on the location, elevation, and proximity to the sea. It ranges from wet and warm conditions averaging 64°F (18°C) to freezing temperatures above the snow line.

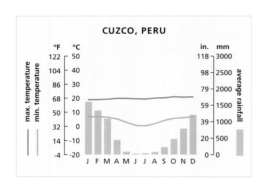

SCALE 1:37,500,000

0   500 miles

0   500 kilometers

CUZCO, PERU

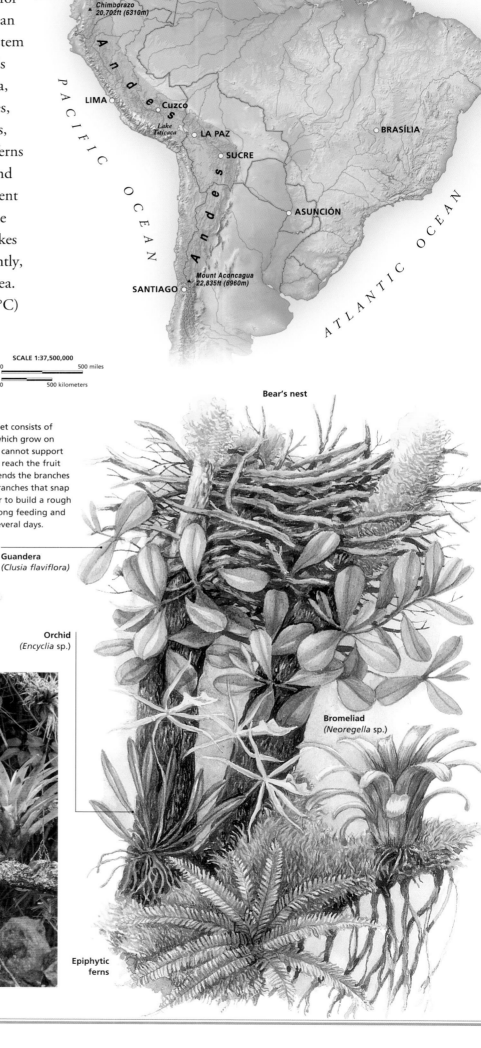

Bear's nest

Treetop platform

The spectacled bear's diet consists of fruits and bromeliads, which grow on high tree branches that cannot support the animal's weight. To reach the fruit and flowers, the bear bends the branches toward itself. Smaller branches that snap off are used by the bear to build a rough nest that serves as a strong feeding and sleeping platform for several days.

Guandera
(Clusia flaviflora)

Orchid
(Encyclia sp.)

Bromeliad
(Neoregella sp.)

Epiphytic ferns

Spectacled bear

The spectacled or Andean bear lives mainly in cloud forests. It is the only representative of the family Ursidae in South America and the only surviving member of the genus *Tremarctos,* thanks largely to its ability to climb even the tallest trees. It has good eyesight and is named for the markings around its eyes.

Rugged beauty
Spectacular granite pillars and black sedimentary peaks dominate the rugged Andean landscape in locations such as Torres del Paine National Park, in Chile. Aconcagua, the highest point in the Americas and the tallest peak in the world outside Asia, is another iconic Andean view.

Taruca
Throughout the day, taruca of both sexes and all ages gather in tight-knit herds, led by an adult female. During the summer months the herds move up to higher slopes, but in winter these animals, also known as huemul, shelter in the lower valleys of the Andes.

Andean cock-of-the-rock
The female cock-of-the-rock builds a shallow nest of mud and vegetation on rock walls, hence the bird's name. The polygamous males compete in a mating ritual that includes dances, gymnastics, plumage displays, and vocal challenges.

CONSERVATION WATCH

The Brazilian tapir, a large animal with a distinctive fleshy snout, prefers water to land. Its peaceful nature and meaty physique make it a favorite hunting target. However, the tapir is now vulnerable because of such illegal hunting, combined with the destruction of its tropical forest habitat. After a gestation of 400 days, females produce just one offspring.

Andean red fox
A long-lived solitary hunter, the Andean red fox is one the greatest predators of this region. It hunts mostly small mammals but also takes poultry and livestock, bringing it into conflict with farmers. The fox is under pressure from hunters, who prize its fur.

Giant anteater
As its name suggests, the giant anteater feeds voraciously on ants and termites, consuming up to 30,000 in a day. It claws open termite mounds and uses its tubular snout and long sticky tongue to gather up insects. Though generally docile, it can defend itself against pumas and jaguars.

THE ANDES WILDERNESS
THE CONDOR

Considered to be the largest flying bird, the Andean condor is in danger of extinction across a significant portion of its range. Its decline has been most marked since 1973, in part caused by aggressive hunting, loss of habitat and therefore food, air pollution, water contamination, and collisions with structures such as power lines. The condor's vulnerability to threats is undoubtedly increased by its slow rate of reproduction and years spent reaching breeding maturity. Population decline has been most dramatic in Ecuador, Venezuela, and Peru. Biologists estimate that a few thousand birds remain in the wild, concentrated mostly along the southern section of the Andes mountains. This bird of prey and its close cousin, the California condor, are part of the New World vultures, a family more closely related to storks than to the vultures of Africa. Standing nearly 3 feet (90 cm) tall, the condor feeds on the carrion of animals such as deer, elk, cows, and llamas.

PREY ON NEWBORNS

Condors prefer open areas to search for carrion, newborns, and dying animals, which are their main food sources. If a meal has been particularly large, they may have to spend hours on the ground or perched on a low branch before they are able to take off again. Condors can travel 200 miles (320 km) a day soaring at great heights while foraging for food. They are able to survive without a meal for at least two weeks.

Puma
The puma is one of the main carnivorous predators in the Andes, but even this successful hunter must protect its cubs from condors that circle overhead.

Northern pudu
The world's smallest deer, the 12-inch (30-cm) tall pudu is one of the condor's favorite meals. It also feeds on the remains of sheep, llama, vicuña, cattle, seals, and the eggs of seabirds.

Carrion diet

Condors are not hunters. They locate carrion by sight or by following smaller birds. This helps other scavengers because the condor is capable of tearing through the tough hides of some carcasses. The only member of the genus *Vultur*, the condor can live for up to 50 years and mates for life. It communicates by grunting and hissing.

Dining
The average weight of a condor is 30 pounds (15 kg) and it can eat up to 4.5 pounds (2 kg) in one sitting. Older condors eat before the younger birds.

The largest bird of prey

Condors are well-adapted carcass feeders. Since they are not outfitted to stalk, their feet have rounded claws instead of the sharp talons of raptors. Bare skin on a condor's head and neck keeps it safe from bacteria when it sticks its heads into carcasses, and its beak is tailored for tearing fleshy tissue.

Naked head
A naked head and neck enables the condor to feed off carcasses without soiling its feathers. Blood vessels concentrated over the head help to radiate heat and keep the bird cool.

Feet
The condor has strong legs but relatively weak, blunt nails that are more like toenails than talons. The feet are thus better adapted to walking than grasping.

Inflatable neck
Condors do not possess vocal cords, so they inflate air sacs in their neck when agitated or excited. This gives them the appearance of being larger than they really are.

In flight
Condors flap their wings to lift off the ground, but rarely do so when flying. Instead, they rely on thermal air currents to stay aloft. A condor's wingspan can exceed 10 feet (3 m), which enables it to fly in a way that expends as little energy as possible.

CONSERVATION WATCH

Efforts are being made to breed condors in captivity for return to the wild as part of the American Zoo and Aquarium Association's Species Survival Plan program. Thirty-nine condors reared in North America and Colombia have been reintroduced to Peru, Colombia, and Venezuela. Colombian biologists satellite-tracking the birds found that they survived and are now breeding—a major milestone.

Galapagos Islands

Nineteen islands and more than 40 islets comprise the Galápagos archipelago, located in the Pacific Ocean some 620 miles (1,000 km) off the coast of Ecuador. It has changed little in millions of years. Ongoing seismic and volcanic activity reflects the processes that formed the islands, which, together with their isolation, led to the development of some of the most unusual species on Earth. All the Galápagos reptiles, half the birds, 32 percent of the plants and 25 percent of the fish, as well as many invertebrates, are found nowhere else. Ocean currents, the merging of cold and warmer waters, warm air temperatures, high rainfall, and a lack of predators have all contributed to the evolution of this unique suite of species. Endemic mockingbirds, seabirds, finches, and marine life inspired Charles Darwin's theory of evolution following his visit in 1835. The islands are now a World Heritage site and protected within the Galápagos National Park.

SCALE 1:3,000,000

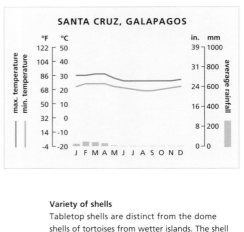

SANTA CRUZ, GALAPAGOS

Galápagos hawk
A permanent resident found only in the Galápagos, the Galápagos hawk often uses tortoises as observation posts from which to sight prey, such as giant centipedes, locusts, small lava lizards, snakes, and rodents. It also takes small marine and land iguanas, hatchling tortoises, and sea turtles.

Giant tortoises
Eleven of the 13 subspecies of giant tortoise that evolved from a single species survive today. Five live on Isabela Island, separated by wide lava fields; five are found on Santa Cruz, San Salvador, San Cristobal, Pinzon, and Española islands, respectively; and the Pinta tortoise can be seen at the Charles Darwin Research Station, Santa Cruz. Each species has a different shell, or carapace, and has evolved adaptations to suit the environment in which it lives.

Variety of shells
Tabletop shells are distinct from the dome shells of tortoises from wetter islands. The shell of the smaller saddle-backed tortoise allows it to extend its head high to feed. Tabletop shells afford more protection than saddle-backs, but domed shells provide the most protection.

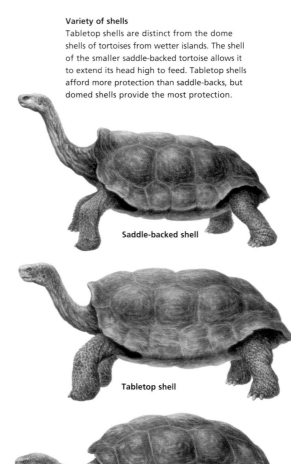

Saddle-backed shell

Tabletop shell

Domed shell

Saddle-backed shell ventral view

Domed shell ventral view

Galápagos land iguana
Galápagos land iguanas are vegetarians, subsisting mostly on the fruit and pads of *Opuntia* cactus. They use their front feet to scrape away larger cactus thorns, then gulp down cactus fruit in a few swallows. These iguanas live in dry areas and in the mornings they bask in the hot equatorial sun.

Blue-footed booby
Male blue-footed boobies pick up their distinctive blue feet and perform an exaggerated step-walk during their courtship dance. The world's 40,000 breeding pairs, half of which inhabit the Galápagos Islands, breed opportunistically.

FINCHES

Thirteen species of finch, belonging to four genera, live on the Galápagos Islands. All evolved from a single pair of birds similar to the blue-black grassquit finch commonly found along the Pacific Coast of South America. Finches have bills of varying size and shape, suited to their particular diet and lifestyle. According to Darwin's theory of evolution, beaks changed as the birds developed different tastes for fruits, seeds, or insects.

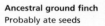

Ancestral ground finch
Probably ate seeds

Marine iguana
The only seagoing lizard, the marine iguana develops its colors with age. Young iguanas are black, while adults can be shades of green, red, gray, or black, depending on their island home. Males favor sunny, rocky shores during the day, where sea breezes keep them cool.

Sharp-billed finch
Pecks seabirds to drink blood

Tree finch
Feeds on insects

Warbler finch
Extracts insects from twigs

Animal Types	No. of Species
Giant tortoises	13
Lava lizards	7
Iguanas	3
Land reptiles	23
Insects	1,600

Woodpecker finch
Raps rotten wood for insects

Sea lion
Graceful and inquisitive, sea lions always seem to be playing with something, whether it is with each other, marine iguanas, penguins, or red crabs. They often splash brown pelicans, which share a similar diet that includes mussels, clams, anchovies, and sardines.

Tree finch
Feeds on plant material

Large ground finch
Cracks and eats large seeds

Large cactus ground finch
Feeds on cactus flowers and seeds

THE GRAN CHACO

One of the major wooded grasslands of South America, the Gran Chaco comprises savannas and thorn forests so impenetrable that until relatively recently they had barely been explored. The region covers a total of 250 square miles (650 km²), extending northward from the foothill plains of Argentina into western Paraguay, eastern Bolivia, and a small area of southwestern Brazil. The Chaco is divided into the Boreal, Central, and Austral regions by its two main rivers, the Pilcomayo and Bermejo. As this region is a low, flat, alluvial plain, the climate is hot and dry in summer, but river flooding during the rainy season converts large areas into swamps. The resident wildlife continues to amaze scientists, with animals such as the Chacoan peccary, rediscovered in 1975, and at least 18 species of armadillo. However, the Chaco is threatened by unrestricted forest clearing, overgrazing, cattle ranching, oil and gas exploration, and road construction.

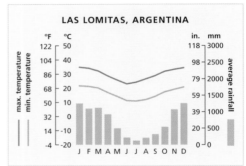

Nine-banded armadillo
Solitary and nocturnal, but more diurnal during winter, the nine-banded armadillo can have between seven and nine bands. It can jump up to 4 feet (1.2 m) straight into the air to escape predators. The armadillo's armored skin is composed of hard, bony plates. Since it cannot store large reserves of body fat to keep warm, it forages actively and often grunts as it searches for food.

To defend itself from predators the three-banded armadillo rolls into a tight ball using its thick bony plating like armor.

Three-banded armadillo
Contrary to popular belief, the nine-banded armadillo is incapable of rolling completely into a ball; it has too many bony dermal plates. Only the three-banded armadillo is capable of this.

Guira cuckoo
The Guira cuckoo is a large ground-feeding bird that gives off a sharp, penetrating smell. It inhabits scrubby and open areas, and bands of six to 18 individuals perch, feed, and roost together.

Maned wolf
The maned wolf looks like a cross between a wolf and a fox. It has evolved long legs for roaming long distances in tall grass. This wolf takes one partner for life, but only interacts with its mate during the breeding season. Just 1,500 maned wolves remain in the wild, and numbers continue to decline because of threats such as habitat loss, agriculture, and hunting.

Paradox frog
The tadpoles of the paradox frog may be four times the length of the adult. The frog lives amid vegetation at the bottom of lakes, ponds, and lagoons, where it feeds on larvae and insects at night. Its skin secretions are being used to treat diabetes.

Blue-fronted parrot
In parrot society, the blue-fronted parrot is regarded as one of the best talkers and singers. It uses a repertoire of whistles, shrieks, and yapping notes. Active, intelligent, and graceful, this bird is commonly kept as a pet.

Burrowing owl
The burrowing owl may be spotted standing near its burrow, which can consist of a labyrinth of tunnels. In this undergound refuge the owl breeds, nests, and sleeps during the day. The tunnel also serves as protection and can be used to trap prey.

Chacoan peccary
The Chacoan peccary emits a strong odor from a scent gland on its back when frightened or to mark its territory. It is the largest of the four peccary species that live in South America, and is distinguished by its long bristles and shaggy appearance. The Chacoan peccary was thought to be extinct until 1975, when it was rediscovered.

PATAGONIA

At the southern end of the American continent, stretching from the Atlantic to the Pacific Ocean through the Andes, is geographically diverse and dramatic Patagonia. It is a region of immense beauty, and includes habitats as varied as treeless plains, forests, snow-capped mountains, large deserts, fertile valleys, wide seashores, impressive lakes, and gigantic glaciers. Its climate is equally variable, from long cold winters averaging 36°F (2°C) to scorching summers, when temperatures reach 105°F (40°C). The Andes in Patagonia receive 80 inches (2,000 mm) of rain annually, but the land becomes drier near the Atlantic zone, with only 8 inches (200 mm) recorded. Some parts of Patagonia preserve untouched vegetation, others are sparsely populated, while the human influences of ranching and mining prevail elsewhere. Vastly different environments across the region result in an abundance of rare vertebrates, from wild grazing mammals to the puma, Andean cat, river otter, and gray fox. Patagonia is also noted for its coastal and marine animals, freshwater fish, and birds.

SCALE 1:35,000,000

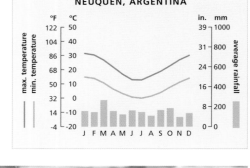

NEUQUEN, ARGENTINA

Antarctic accent

Patagonia is renowned for its rugged coastlines, which are rich in animals that depend on the sea, such as great colonies of Magellanic penguins, seals, and sea lions. The climate is mostly temperate, but it becomes colder to the south. The meeting of cool air from the Antarctic with moist Pacific air masses, combined with low sea-surface temperatures, accounts for the region's high rainfall.

Southern elephant seal
The southern elephant seal is so named for its enormous size and the bull's habit of inflating its trunk to impress rivals. The female comes ashore to give birth and does not leave the beach until her pup is weaned, losing weight as her offspring thrives.

Magellanic penguins
Magellanic penguins enact a courtship ritual with the same partner every six months, when they return to breed at the rookery where they were born. Parents share the task of incubating the eggs for 42 days, then raise the chicks together for the next 29 days.

Species	Onshore Sighting
Killer whale or orca	February to April and October to November
Southern elephant seal	August to March
Black-browed albatross	September
Magellanic penguin	September to April
Southern right whale	June to December
Dark dolphin	December to March
South American sea lion	April to November
Commerson's dolphin	April to December

Geoffroy's cat
A small, solitary wild cat, Geoffroy's cat has razor-sharp claws that help it climb trees. These claws are also used to stab and secure prey, such as small lizards, rodents, insects, frogs, and fish. Humans are the cat's only predators.

Patagonian mara
The mara is a large rodent, the fourth largest in the world, yet belongs to the guinea-pig family. Its hind legs are slightly larger than its front legs, giving it the ability to make agile jumps. The mara is also able to run fast and is capable of reaching speeds of 28 miles per hour (45 km/h).

Southern viscacha
Populations of the southern viscacha, a medium-sized rodent, have greatly declined because of illegal hunting for its woolly coat and for its meat. It is extremely agile, often running with no difficulty on rocky territories, where it lives in burrows.

Patagonian gray fox
The survival of the Patagonian gray fox has depended on its ability to eat everything from meat and fruit to eggs and carrion. When eating cooperatively, foxes without litters bring food to families with pups. This fox evolved from the wolf family 6 to 7 million years ago.

PATAGONIA
BIRDS OF THE PAMPAS

The Pampas is one of the richest grazing lowland areas in the world, but also one of the most endangered habitats on Earth. Found primarily in Argentina and Uruguay, it covers an area of 300,000 square miles (800,000 km²) from the Andes mountains to the Atlantic Ocean. With a humid and moist climate, the northern region has an average temperature of 64°F (18°C) and well distributed rainfall throughout the year produces fertile soils suitable for agriculture. To the south, the semiarid Pampas is known for its marshes and wetlands. Grasshoppers are one of the most abundant herbivores throughout the Pampas, but it is also home to rodents, deer, viscachas, and marsupials such as opossums. Migration has enabled birds to adapt to life in these windy grasslands. Marine and coastal birds make a stopover in the region to feed and rest, and more than 300 bird species have been recorded here, including 18 species of stork, ibis, heron, gull, and spoonbill. Land birds are not as common, but among the most notable are the tinamou and rhea.

⚡ CONSERVATION WATCH

There are only a few hundred white-winged nightjars left in Brazil and about 50 in Paraguay. Populations have declined as a result of the destruction of tropical savanna and open grasslands, the spread of invasive grasses, fire, the expansion of eucalyptus plantations, and the impacts of agriculture.

Greater rhea
The greater rhea is the largest South American bird. Although flightless, it can run at speeds of 37 miles per hour (60 km/h). Males mate with multiple females, who each lay eggs in the nest he has prepared. It is then his task to incubate the 30 to 60 eggs and to take care of the striped chicks that hatch.

Great pampas finch
The great pampas finch feeds on seeds and grain. It lives near marshes and in association with tall grasses and shrubs, and is usually seen in a bush calling, or on top of a tree or branch singing. It belongs to one of the most diverse terrestrial vertebrate orders, the Passeriformes, which encompass more than half of all bird species.

Baby toucan
Toco toucans nest high in tree cavities or holes made by woodpeckers. Three to four young fledge some 50 days after hatching and receive care for about eight weeks.

OCEANS OF GRASS

This treeless region comprises a continuous terrain made up of different grasses. Its distinctive vegetation is the tall, coarse-leaved pampas grass, with feathery spikes extending some 8 feet (2.5 m). Only trefoils, flowers, and other herbs grow between its tussocks. Grasses are categorized into hard pastures, which include the large, tussock-forming species, and soft pasture species with more tender undergrowth of greater nutritional value to grazers. Vertebrates are the main seed-eaters because the tall grass grants them refuge from carnivorous predators.

Uruguayan pampas grass
(*Cortaderia selloana*)

Tussock paspalum
(*Paspalum quadrifarium*)

Wild cane
(*Gynerium sagittatum*)

Puna grass
(*Achnatherum caudatum*)

Buff-necked ibis
The buff-necked ibis, also known as the white-throated ibis, uses its curved bill to feed on insects, reptiles, frogs, and small mammals and is easy to spot on the pampas.

Chalk-browed mockingbird
The chalk-browed mockingbird is skilled at imitating the melodies of other birds. During the breeding season the male performs a nuptial dance that involves flying from branch to branch and landing slowly with its tail splayed.

Toco toucan
The toco toucan is the largest of nearly 40 species in the toucan family. It feeds on fruit, but when nesting it also consumes a variety of insects as a source of protein. The toucan resides in the jungle canopy and actively flies in noisy flocks of six birds.

CENTRAL & SOUTH AMERICA
LLAMAS AND RELATIVES

The South American or New World camelids originated in North America 45 to 40 million years ago. They belong to the Camelidae family composed of llamas, alpacas, guanacos, and vicuñas, although the term llama is commonly used to refer to all four races. Their habitat includes near-waterless environments located in cool, dry mountain valleys and the Altiplano—the high Andean plateau distinguished by its steep, rocky mountain ledges that extends through Bolivia, Peru, Argentina, and Chile. Camelids are adapted to life at high altitude: thick wool coats protect them from the cold temperatures, and their extra-large lungs and hearts supply their bodies with sufficient oxygen to cope with the thin air. Throughout history, these mammals have played important roles in the culture and economies of indigenous communities. While the guanaco and vicuña live in the wild, the llama and alpaca were domesticated between 4000 and 3500/¥ and used for transportation, milk, meat, and fiber.

Grass grazing
These llamas are grazing along a line of snow-capped volcanoes in the Paranicota Volcano Shadows, located in the Chilean Altiplano on the border with Bolivia. This remote, harsh, and cold region is also home to condors, pumas, and flamingos.

Curious camelids

Camelids are herbivores that use their protruding lower incisor teeth and cleft upper lip to snip grass and tear off leaves. They have long legs, necks, and eyelashes, and slender heads. Camelids lack functional hooves and, instead, have feet made up of just two toes covered by a nail. These social herd animals require little water and can rest on their stomachs by bending their hind limbs when seated. They move their front and back legs on the same side in unison when walking.

Guanaco
Considered as ancestors of llamas and alpacas, guanacos can survive for long periods without drinking. While grass constitutes the bulk of their diet, they also graze on trees and range from sea level to elevations of 13,000 feet (4,000 m).

Vicuña
Mountain-grazing vicuñas range from elevations of 10,000 to 16,000 feet (3,000–5,000 m). They use one territory for day foraging and a higher, and therefore safer, territory for sleeping. Their fleece once clothed Inca royalty.

Habitat under threat
The ice fields of southern Patagonia are the natural home of guanacos, as well as foxes, rheas, maras, armadillos, wild cats, and bats. Since the early 1980s, this ecosystem has been severely threatened by overgrazing from introduced sheep and livestock.

PREDATOR

Pumas are the main predators of llamas. A puma stalks a llama before ambushing it. Leaping from the ground, the puma typically pounces on the llama's back and breaks its neck. Until the puma has finished its meal, it covers the carcass with leaves and twigs to hide it from hungry competitors.

ANIMAL	FINENESS OF WOOL (IN MICRONS)
Vicuña	6–10
Alpaca	10–27.7
Merino	12–20
Angora rabbit	13
Cashmere	15–19
Yak	15–19
Camel	16–25
Guanaco	16–18
Llama	20–40
Chinchilla	21
Mohair	25–45

Small intestine

Third stomach chamber

First stomach chamber

Second stomach chamber behind first

Digestion
Llamas have a three-chambered stomach and chew their cud, a mouthful of swallowed food that is regurgitated from the first stomach. Once swallowed, the cud moves to the next two chambers to be fully digested, thereby extracting as much energy as possible from the food. Llamas spit their mouth contents or a foul-smelling fluid from their first stomach chamber to defend themselves.

Wool
A llama's coat consists of a double layer of fibers. About 20 percent is the protective outer coat of long and coarse guard hairs, while the inner layer comprises short, wavy fibers that are fine and soft.

Alpaca
The most numerous camelid, the alpaca, is reared in the Andean mountains for its fiber, which is finer than cashmere. Most concentrated in the southern highlands of Puno, the alpaca can be distinguished by its fringe.

Llama
The llama was one of the first animals to be domesticated, some 4000 years ago. As pack animals, they can carry loads of 50 to 75 pounds (25–35 kg) and cover up to 20 miles (30 km) in a day.

129

THE CARIBBEAN SEA

The warm, tropical waters of the Caribbean Sea cover
an area of about 1,050,000 square miles (2,700,000 km²).
This sea is renowned for its coral reefs and clear waters.
The Atlantic meets the Caribbean in the Anegada
Passage that lies between the Lesser Antilles and
Virgin Islands, and the Windward Passage between
Cuba and Haiti. A nursery ground for an array
of marine animals, the Caribbean Sea is home to
saltwater crocodiles, dozens of species of stony corals,
sea snails, spiny lobsters, and more than 500 species of fish.
Red mangroves are one of the key habitats of the region,
providing food and shelter, above and below the water,
for creatures such as manatees, kingfishers, crabs, egrets,
common black hawks, and boa constrictors. Mangroves,
fringing the shores, also protect against land erosion and
storm damage, and filter pollutants.

SAN JUAN, PUERTO RICO

SCALE 1:20,000,000

Whale shark
Fishermen once feared the whale shark, the
biggest fish in the world. However, it was
eventually discovered that the species is not
a man-eater but feeds on plankton by sucking
in huge quantities of plankton-rich water,
then expelling the water through its gills.

Cuban tody
The Cuban tody is endemic to Cuba and
the oldest survivor of five tody species
confined to the Greater Antilles. The bird
often appears inactive as it feeds on flies
from a perch. However, its bright red throat
bristles when issuing its "tot-tot-tot" call.

O C E A N

Leeward Islands
SAN JUAN

Lesser Antilles

Windward Islands

ARACAS

Mesoamerican Reef

The world's second largest reef system, the Mesoamerican Reef covers the northern end of the Yucatan Peninsula in Mexico, the coasts of Belize and Guatemala, and stretches to the Bay Islands in northern Honduras. This tropical region hosts productive ecosystems, such as barrier and fringing reefs, atolls, patch reefs, and seagrass beds. It is at risk from rising water temperatures and increasing tourism.

West Indian manatee
Ancient mariners mistook manatees for sirens or mermaids, perhaps because of their long tails. This gentle mammal can swim vertically or upside down, and dense bones enable it to stay suspended at, or below, the water's surface.

Reef octopus
The Caribbean reef octopus is able to squeeze its body through tiny cracks in the reef. It can maneuver its head, beak, and each of its eight arms through a space the size of a keyhole.

Parrotfish
The parrotfish grazes on algae that grows on rocks or coral, pulverizing the algae with its grinding teeth to aid digestion. It later excretes the undigested coral, which then forms much of the sand in the fish's range.

Barracuda
Barracudas live around the margins of coral reefs. They are formidable predators. The barracuda's projecting lower jaw is spiked with knifelike teeth and its silvery coloration reduces its visibility to prey, enabling it to herd fish schools into shallow water.

SOLENODON

The solenodon is one of the world's few poisonous mammals. It lives in burrows and is nocturnal. Although it resembles a rat, it can be distinguished by its elongated, flexible snout. Endemic to Cuba, the solenodon inflicts its venomous bite when fighting, provoked, or agitated by one of its own kind.

Grooved tooth
Venomous saliva is secreted by the submaxillary gland that flows through the grooved second lower incisor, which delivers the poisonous bite.

This Bengal tiger, charging through the water at the mouth of the Ganges River, India, is a skilled swimmer. It can swim rivers more than 3 miles (5 km) wide and is a formidable predator. Its large canines, long, sharp, retractable claws, and massive forelimbs and shoulders allow it to single-handedly overpower prey much bigger than itself.

ASIA

ASIA

Asia is the world's largest continent, covering 8.6 percent of Earth's surface area. It is bounded on the east by the Pacific Ocean, on the south by the Indian Ocean, and on the north by the Arctic Ocean. Asia stretches from north of the Arctic Circle to south of the equator—from east to west, Asia stretches nearly halfway around the world. This vast area has many different kinds of climate, with some of the coldest and some of the hottest, some of the wettest and some of the driest places on Earth. The subregions of Asia include West Asia, Central Asia, South Asia, Southeast Asia, Eastern Asia, and Russia. The high, cold deserts of Central Asia are known for their vast areas of barren landscape. Several biogeographic areas are considered biodiversity hot spots, harboring unique plants and animals. Among the many rivers that traverse the Asian continent, 32 rivers exceed 1,000 miles (1,600 km) in length. The Yangtze River in China is the longest at 3,915 miles (6,300 km).

CLIMATE ZONES

- Wet tropical
- Seasonal tropica
- Arid
- Semiarid
- Mediterranean
- Subtropical
- Continental
- Cold temperate
- Subpolar
- Highland

Climate

The Malay Archipelago and Malay Peninsula climate is dominated by heat and humidity. Southern Asia and the Indochina Peninsula experience more seasonal rains, often associated with monsoonal winds. The arid interior owes its temperature extremes largely to the Himalaya, which block moisture-bearing winds. A band of almost constant high pressure creates hot, arid conditions in the southwest. Cold polar air prevails in the north.

The Steppes of Central Asia
The steppes are Asia's unique grassland ecosystem that harbors grazing herbivores and burrowing rodents. The flat-bottomed lakes here attract numerous waterbirds.

The Himalayas
This is the world's longest and highest mountain range. About one-third of the mountain animals in the world occur here, and are well adapted for the environment.

VEGETATION ZONES

- Tropical forest
- Seasonal tropical forest
- Desert
- Tropical grassland
- Mediterranean forest and scrub
- Midlatitude grassland
- Midlatitude forest
- Boreal forest
- Tundra
- Mountain vegetation

The Siberian Wilderness
The Siberian wilderness is the world's largest remaining wilderness, dominated by taiga forests. The wildlife here includes carnivores such as the brown bear and the Siberian tiger.

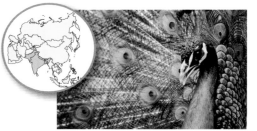

The Indian Subcontinent
The junction between the east and the west, this region has a great diversity of natural forest and wetland ecosystems that harbor a rich wildlife.

Vegetation

The Arctic Ocean is flanked by a strip of tundra. To its south, stretching from the Urals to northern Japan, is a broad belt of coniferous forest that yields to deciduous and mixed forests that extend down the east coast, steppe grasslands, and scrub. Either sparse, arid-adapted plants or none at all typify large areas of the interior and southwest. In Southeast Asia, high rainfall supports some of the most extensive tropical forests in the world.

Hot and Cold Deserts
These are semiarid areas with extremely harsh climates. Many of the wildlife species here burrow underground for insulation against the extreme heat and aridity.

The Mountains of Southwest China
This region is known to be the most botanically rich temperate region in the world. Many species of rare and threatened wildlife, including the giant panda, live here.

East Asia
Located at the intersection of three of Earth's tectonic plates, this region contains numerous volcanoes, hot springs, and mountains, and is prone to earthquakes.

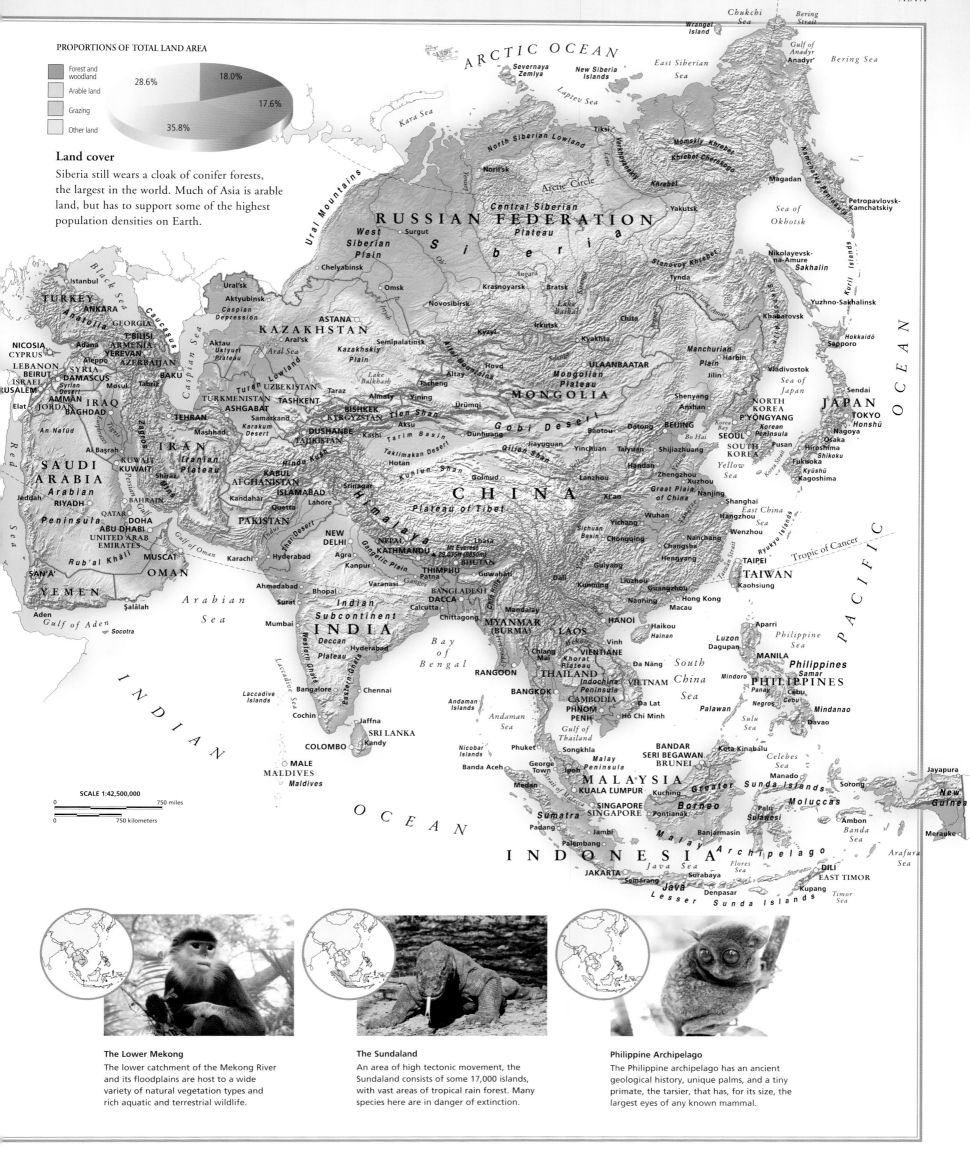

PROPORTIONS OF TOTAL LAND AREA

- Forest and woodland
- Arable land
- Grazing
- Other land

18.0%
28.6%
17.6%
35.8%

Land cover

Siberia still wears a cloak of conifer forests, the largest in the world. Much of Asia is arable land, but has to support some of the highest population densities on Earth.

SCALE 1:42,500,000

0 — 750 miles

0 — 750 kilometers

The Lower Mekong

The lower catchment of the Mekong River and its floodplains are host to a wide variety of natural vegetation types and rich aquatic and terrestrial wildlife.

The Sundaland

An area of high tectonic movement, the Sundaland consists of some 17,000 islands, with vast areas of tropical rain forest. Many species here are in danger of extinction.

Philippine Archipelago

The Philippine archipelago has an ancient geological history, unique palms, and a tiny primate, the tarsier, that has, for its size, the largest eyes of any known mammal.

The Steppes of Central Asia

The steppes are a unique grassland ecosystem that occurs in the lower slopes, foothills, and basins of Central Asia's mountain ranges. These areas may be semidesert, or covered with grasses and shrubs, depending on the season and the latitude. The climate is continental and temperate, with hot, windy summers, periodic droughts, and cold winters. The topography in some parts of this region can be either completely flat, low plain or a gently hilly plain–plateau. Several large rivers, such as the Ural and the Irtysh, and their tributaries, cross the region and there is an abundance of wetlands that include many flat-bottomed lakes. Compact turf or cushion-like vegetation is common here and several endemic species of tulips grow in the meadow zones. The wildlife is dominated by grazing species, such as antelope, sheep, and wild horses, and small burrowing rodents such as hamsters, voles, and lemmings. Several species of water birds also inhabit the wetlands or are seasonal visitors.

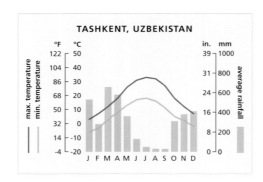

Great bustard
A large, ground-dwelling bird, the great bustard has an omnivorous diet, feeding on seeds, insects, worms, and frogs. The males develop a gular pouch and long white whiskers during the breeding season and carry out a flamboyant display to attract females.

Ground Dwellers

The small ground-dwelling animals of the steppe include a variety of rodents such as ground squirrels, hamsters, voles, jerboas, and marmots, and lagomorphs such as pikas and hares. They contribute to the natural disturbance regime in the steppes because their burrowing habits cause the recycling of nutrients, which sustains the ecosystem.

Steppe lemming
Lemmings eat shoots, leaves, and seeds and are most active at night. Solitary by nature they live in burrows on the steppes but do not hibernate. Litters range from four to 10 pups. Populations undergo phases of rapid growth and subsequent crashes.

Black-bellied hamster
This, the largest species of hamster, lives solitarily in burrows. Stores of cereal grains, seeds, and peas are kept in its winter burrow, which can reach more than six feet (2 m) below the surface.

Saiga antelope

The saiga is recognizable by its over-sized, flexible nose, which is thought to warm the air as it breathes in winter and to filter out the dust in summer. Saigas occur in large herds that move across the semidesert steppes grazing on several species of plants, including some that are poisonous to other animals. Males compete for females, fighting with their horns and head-butting.

High-altitude steppes
The high steppes of Central Asia can be a challenging environment for both animals and plants. Cold winters cause the surface water to freeze and the flat, open terrain exposes all living things to strong winds. Vegetation is low-growing and hardy.

Wild horses of the steppe
Przewalski's horse is the last surviving subspecies of wild horse. Compared with the domestic horse this animal is stockily built, with a large head, shorter legs, and a muscular body. In the wild it lives in a social group comprising a dominant stallion, a dominant lead mare, other mares, and their offspring.

CONSERVATION WATCH

Przewalski's horse once roamed freely on the steppe along the Mongolia–China border. The wild population declined in the 20th century because of hunting, harsh climate, and habitat loss. It was dying out in Mongolia in the 1960s and was designated "extinct in the wild." These horses have since been bred in captivity and have recently been reintroduced in Mongolia.

THE SIBERIAN WILDERNESS

The Siberian wilderness is the world's largest remaining wilderness and provides a safe home for many species of plants and animals. The climate is continental, with hot summers, above 104°F (40°C), and extremely cold winters, below -76°F (-60°C). The average annual temperature is below freezing, but the snow cover is relatively thin. Annual precipitation ranges from 16 to 24 inches (400–600 mm) in the west, decreasing to eight inches (200 mm) in the east. The area is dominated by taiga forests, characterized by coniferous trees such as spruce and pines. In taiga forests the trees are widely spaced, and carpets of mosses and lichens cover the ground. The wildlife here includes large herbivores such as moose and caribou (reindeer), and carnivores such as the red fox, lynx and wolves. Brown bears are also found here. Among the high upland ridges mountain goats and alpine sheep graze on rocky slopes, and small burrowing mammals such as lemmings and voles search for insects and fresh shoots.

ARCTIC OCEAN

SCALE 1:50,000,000

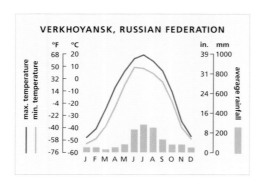

VERKHOYANSK, RUSSIAN FEDERATION

Siberian jay
The small-bodied Siberian jay is a widely distributed species in the wild coniferous forests of the north. It is commonly found in unspoilt forests with small natural clearings, marshy hollows, and ancient spruce trees. The birds have various alarm calls to warn others if predators are near.

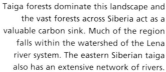

Remote forests
Taiga forests dominate this landscape and the vast forests across Siberia act as a valuable carbon sink. Much of the region falls within the watershed of the Lena river system. The eastern Siberian taiga also has an extensive network of rivers.

Hazel grouse
The hazel grouse can fly but does so only infrequently. It nests on the ground, laying a clutch of three to six eggs in a nest concealed by grasses. It feeds mostly on plants, but also eats insects in the breeding season. During the non-breeding season, males and females associate as loosely bound pairs.

Ural owl
The Ural owl, a medium- to large-sized bird, has a wide distribution in the taiga forests where it feeds at night on rodents and other medium-sized birds. It is an aggressive owl and will chase birds of prey from its territory. It nests in hollow tree trunks.

Siberian brown bear
This is a subspecies of the brown bear (*Ursus arctos*), and has a larger skull and luxuriant fur. It is generally a solitary animal and, when it meets other animals in its range, is usually aggressive. It has an omnivorous diet, feeding on plants, fish, insects, and small mammals.

Sable
A member of the Mustelidae family, this small carnivore was once hunted for its coat of thick fur, which was highly prized by fur traders. A careful, secretive predator with acute senses of smell and hearing, it feeds on birds, small mammals, and fish.

Reindeer
Reindeer are large herbivores that live in herds and travel long distances annually. They feed on the leaves of willows and birches, as well as grazing on sedges and grasses. During winter, when snow covers much of their range, their main food source is lichens.

⚡ CONSERVATION WATCH
The Siberian tiger is a rare subspecies that is confined to the Amur region in the Russian Far East where it preys primarily on wild boar and red deer. It is considered to be the largest wild cat in the world but is endangered, with only about 480 to 520 individuals occurring in the wild.

HOT AND COLD DESERTS

The hot and cold deserts of Central Asia are semiarid regions with extremely harsh climates. Wide temperature variations are experienced on a daily basis, with fiercely hot temperatures during the day and below freezing temperatures at night. The landscape in these areas consists of sand dunes, barren mountains, and pebble grounds that cover vast plains. The weather typically includes dry air, strong winds, extremely hot summer temperatures, and swirling dust storms. These deserts generally receive less than 10 inches (254 mm) of rainfall per year. The plant cover is sparse and is limited to species that are able to tolerate drought. Animals that live in desert regions have developed adaptations that allow them to cope with the lack of water, the extreme temperatures, and the shortage of food. Desert dwellers such as rodents and reptiles burrow underground, where they are insulated from the heat and aridity. They emerge at night to feed.

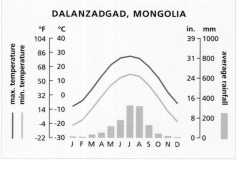

DALANZADGAD, MONGOLIA

Bactrian camel
The critically endangered Bactrian camel occurs in north-western China and Mongolia. It is identifiable by the two humps on its back, where it stores fat that can be converted into water and energy. These camels develop a thick, shaggy coat in winter.

Cold desert
A cold desert is one that has snow in winter, such as the Gobi Desert in China, with temperatures as low as -40°F (-40°C). The small animals that live here burrow underground to keep warm. These deserts are also home to animals such as gazelles, jerboas, Bactrian camels, and sand grouse.

Sand grouse
This ground-dwelling bird lives in semiarid grass-covered plains and sandy desert habitats, often with a cover of scrub, where it feeds on legume seeds. It nests in a ground scrape, where two or three greenish eggs with cryptic markings are laid. It is found in large flocks during the non-breeding season.

Gray monitor
The gray monitor is a burrowing lizard, widely distributed in deserts. It is active during the early hours of the day and feeds on vertebrates such as rodents, lizards, snakes, birds, frogs, and toads. It also eats eggs. These monitors become relatively inactive during the winter period.

SCALE 1:35,000,000

0   500 miles

0   500 kilometers

Lebetine viper
A large, venomous snake, the Lebetine viper has a wide distribution in dry and semiarid areas. It has a broad triangular head and a blunt, rounded snout. Primarily nocturnal or crepuscular, it hunts rodents and birds.

Hot desert
Hot deserts, such as the Thar Desert in India and Pakistan, are warm throughout the fall and spring seasons and extremely hot during the summer, when temperatures can rise to 129°F (54°C). These areas receive little rainfall during winter. The animals in hot deserts burrow to keep cool during the day.

LONG-EARED JERBOA

Jerboas are small jumping rodents in the Dipodidae family. The several species all have long hind legs, a long tail, and nocturnal feeding habits. The long-eared jerboa is recognizable by its exceptionally large ears. Classified as endangered, it is at home in the Gobi Desert in China.

Jerboa
The long-eared jerboa has the general appearance of a mouse but with long hind legs and feet. It has a tuft at the end of its tail.

Skeleton
The illustration of a jerboa skeleton reveals how long its hind legs are in relation to the rest of the body. It is these legs that give the jerboa its agile, jumping gait.

Jerboa burrow
The jerboa burrows in sand, where it digs with the aid of its fore feet, and throws the sand out with its long hind feet.

THE HIMALAYAS

The Himalayas, a massive mountain range in Asia, separates the Indian subcontinent from the Tibetan Plateau. The Himalayan system is the longest—1,490 miles (2,400 km) west to east—as well as the highest mountain range in the world. The climate here ranges from tropical at the base of the mountains to permanent ice and snow at the highest elevations. The distribution of plants and animals of the Himalayas varies with climate, rainfall, altitude, and soils. The vegetation varies from the unexplored tropical rain forests of the Eastern Himalayas, to the dense subtropical and alpine forests of the Central and Western Himalayas, to the sparse desert vegetation of the cold desert areas of the Transhimalaya. The wildlife is characterized by species adapted to life in cold and mountainous regions and about one-third of the mountain animal species in the world are found here. Many species of goat antelope, including the mountain goat, Himalayan tahr, chiru, and takin make this region their home.

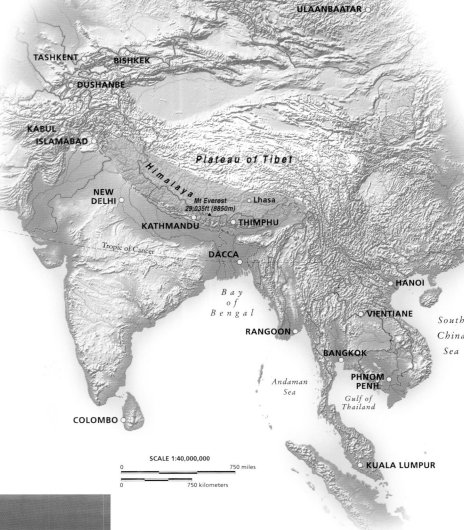

Chiru antelope
Chiru antelopes usually congregate in herds of more than 100 individuals and they live in the high mountain grassland and semidesert areas of the Tibetan plateau. The species has been over-exploited for its skin and is now endangered.

Indian wild ass
This is the largest among wild asses and is native to the high, cold habitat of the Tibetan Plateau. These animals live in cohesive herds of up to 400 individuals, led by an old female. Mature males are solitary, although they form, and defend, harems during the breeding season.

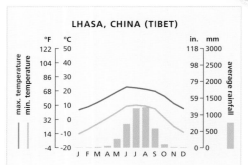

LHASA, CHINA (TIBET)

Markhor
The markhor is an Asian mountain goat found in the western Himalayas, at elevations as high as 11,800 feet (3,600 m), in scrub forests of oaks, pines, and junipers. Males are solitary; females and their young live in small herds.

Himalayan tahr
This is a wild goat species that inhabits the rugged wooded hills and mountain slopes in the Himalayas. The tahr spends the summers grazing in high pastures, then descends to lower elevations to form mixed-sex herds in the winter.

BIRDS OF THE MOUNTAINS

The diversity of habitats in the Himalayan region is reflected in the richness of its bird fauna, which includes many endemic species. Among the larger birds found here are kites, eagles, vultures, and pheasants. Many birds move to higher altitudes during the summer and return to the shelter of valleys during winter.

Monal pheasant
This large-sized pheasant is the national bird of Nepal. The males have a long, metallic green crest and brightly colored plumage. They occur in pairs during the breeding season and form large groups that roost communally during the winter.

Western tragopan
A medium-sized brightly plumaged pheasant found along the Himalayas, the western tragopan is considered the rarest of all living pheasants. It is mostly arboreal but also feeds on the ground.

Yak
Wild yaks live in treeless mountains and plateaus feeding on grasses, lichens, and other plants. Vegetation in their habitat is scarce, so they must travel great distances to find sufficient food. They live at altitudes between 10,500 and 17,500 feet (3,200–5,400 m) but are insulated by a thick coat of shaggy hair.

BIG CATS

The Asian big cats are the large mammalian top predators in Asia. They include the Asiatic lion, tiger, leopard, and the snow leopard. The Asiatic lion is restricted to the Gir Forest in the state of Gujarat in India's west. The tiger, with six subspecies, is more widely distributed across Asia. The Bengal tiger is found in the Indian subcontinent and Burma, the Siberian tiger occurs in eastern Siberia, the Indochinese tiger in the Mekong region, the Sumatran tiger in Sumatra (Indonesia), and the South China tiger—critically endangered—occurs in South China. There are seven subspecies of leopard distributed throughout Asia. The snow leopard is native to the rugged mountain ranges of Central Asia. The tiger, the largest and most powerful wild cat in the world, is a highly adaptable predator. As it is a territorial animal that needs large contiguous areas of habitat that support its prey, it often faces conflicts with humans. All the big cats in Asia are threatened with extinction today, because of loss of habitats, poaching, and increasing human–wildlife conflict.

🔵 **Sri Lankan leopard**
The Sri Lankan leopard is a subspecies of leopard endemic to Sri Lanka. A solitary hunter, it is the island's top mammalian predator and occurs widely in a variety of habitats, including dry monsoon forests, montane forests, thorn scrub, and lowland tropical rain forests.

🔵 **Bengal tigers fighting**
The Bengal tiger is a solitary and extremely territorial animal. Adult tigers guard their territories fiercely. Males in particular will not tolerate any incursions by other males into their territory, often leading to fights that can end in the death of one of them, or cause severe wounds to both.

Big Cat	Group Size	Litter Size	Life Expectancy in the Wild
Bengal tiger	Solitary	2–4	15–20 years
Sri Lankan leopard	Solitary	2–3	10–15 years
Asiatic lion	2–5	1–4	12–16 years
Snow leopard	Solitary	1–4	15–18 years

☐ Former range
■ Current range

🔵 **Asiatic lion**
The Asiatic lion is a subspecies of lion restricted to the Gir Forest National Park of western India. They are highly social animals that live in prides led, usually, by two adult females. The males are less social, and associate with the pride mostly for mating and during the hunting of large prey.

PREY

In the wild, tigers feed mostly on large and medium-sized prey, such as deer, sambar, and buffalo. However, if large prey is scarce they will often capture smaller prey, such as small mammals, ground-dwelling birds, and reptiles in order to feed themselves and their offspring. Depending on the habitat, tigers may also eat peafowl, monkeys, fish, porcupines, frogs, crabs, and large monitor lizards.

Careful capture
After a careful stalk, tigers make a short rush toward prey, such as this Indian muntjac, usually approaching from the side or back to avoid hooves and antlers.

Protecting the kill
If a kill is made in the open, a tiger usually drags the carcass, in this case that of an axis deer, into dense cover before beginning to feed.

Bengal tiger cubs
A tiger litter is made up of three or four cubs, which are raised by the mother. They remain in their birth den until they are about eight weeks old, then emerge to watch their mother hunt. They do not become independent of her for about 18 months.

CONSERVATION WATCH

The total wild population of the snow leopard is estimated to be 4–7,500 individuals. It lives in the rugged mountainous regions—up to 17,000 feet (5,180 m)—of Central Asia. Snow leopards are illegally hunted because of the high demand for their thick pelt. They also run into conflict with humans when they attack livestock, which happens when other prey is scarce.

THE INDIAN SUBCONTINENT

The Indian subcontinent is a large section of Asia consisting of countries lying mainly on the Indian tectonic plate. These include countries on the continental crust (India, Pakistan, Bangladesh, Nepal, and Bhutan), an island country on the continental shelf (Sri Lanka), and an island archipelago (the Maldives). The subcontinent has a tropical monsoon climate, with a wet and a dry season. Mainland India harbors a diversity of natural ecosystems, including forests, and an array of wetlands influenced by large rivers such as the Brahmaputra, Ganges, and Indus. A long mountain range, the Western Ghats, runs north to south along the western edge of the subcontinent. Many species of animals, including several endemic amphibians and reptiles live here. The ranges also serve as a wildlife corridor, allowing the seasonal migration of the endangered Asian elephant. The continental island of Sri Lanka is separated from southern India by the narrow Palk Strait. Although the plants and animals in Sri Lanka show affinities with those of peninsular India, many species on the island have evolved in isolation.

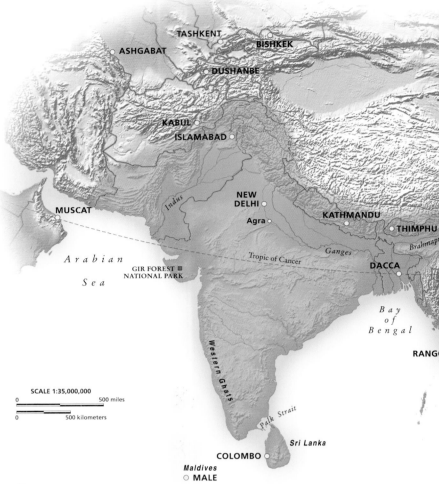

SCALE 1:35,000,000

Nilgai
The nilgai, closely related to wild cattle, is a large herbivore that generally lives in small herds of up to 20 individuals. Mature males have a gray–blue coat and are sometimes known as "blue bulls." The nilgai is able to live in dry conditions, sometimes surviving without water for several days, by deriving water only from the vegetation it feeds on.

Gaur
A species of wild cattle, the gaur is recognizable by its humped back and large body supported by slim white legs. It is the heaviest and most powerful of all wild cattle and lives in herds of up to 40 individuals, led by an old female. Adult males may be solitary.

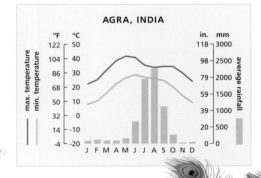

AGRA, INDIA

⚡ CONSERVATION WATCH

The Asian elephant is the largest terrestrial mammal in Asia. There are two subspecies in the region, occurring in peninsular India and Sri Lanka respectively. A small percentage of the adult males bear tusks. These elephants have a semi-prehensile "finger" at the tip of their trunk, which enables them to gather plant matter for feeding. They live in herds, led by an old female; mature males live a solitary life.

Animal Common Name	Population in India (% of world)
Tiger	60%
Asian elephant	50%
Asiatic lion	100%
One-horned rhinoceros	80%

Indian rhinoceros

Indian rhinoceros are generally solitary although their home ranges may overlap and they sometimes gather in small, short-term groups. These large herbivores have one horn, a good sense of smell, but poor eyesight. They can run at speeds of up to 25 miles per hour (40 km/h).

Peacock dance

The male peafowl, the "peacock" bears a group of colorful display feathers on its tail coverts. During the breeding season the peacock expands these feathers and performs a dance in front of peahens to entice them for mating. These feathers are shed annually during the non-breeding season.

Common langur

The common langur is a sub-arboreal species of monkey that spends much of its time on the ground. It lives in medium to large groups of 10 to 64 individuals led by a dominant male. The group is likely to have a home range of 495 to 2,965 acres (200–1,200 ha).

KING COBRA

The largest poisonous snake in the world, the king cobra feeds almost exclusively on other snakes. It hunts its prey during the day, and is able to swallow snakes that are much bigger than its own head. King cobras are capable of killing a human with a single bite.

Cobra–mongoose battles

The mongoose is a natural predator of cobras, including king cobras. When a cobra encounters a mongoose, it flattens its upper body by spreading its ribs, forming the distinctive hood on its neck. It emits a high-pitched hiss and strikes at the predator. The mongoose expands its fur and jumps around the cobra to avoid being bitten, waiting for the ideal moment to jump on the snake's neck to give it a lethal bite.

THE MOUNTAINS OF SOUTHWEST CHINA

This region stretches across 100,400 square miles (260,000 km²) of temperate to alpine mountains, characterized by extremely complex topography, ranging from less than 6,500 feet (2,000 m) above sea level in some valley floors to 24,800 feet (7,558 m) at the summit of Gongga Shan. Mountain ridges are oriented in a generally north–south direction. The area has a wide range of climatic conditions and temperatures. Tributaries of several temperate and tropical rivers originate from these mountains. There is also a wide variety of vegetation types, including broad-leaved and coniferous forests, bamboo groves, scrub communities, savanna, meadow, prairie, freshwater wetlands, and alpine scrub. The region is the most botanically rich temperate region in the world. The wild animals that make their home here include more than 200 mammals and 600 bird species, including many that are rare and globally threatened. The world's best-known flagship species for conservation, the giant panda, is restricted to the shrinking forests of this region.

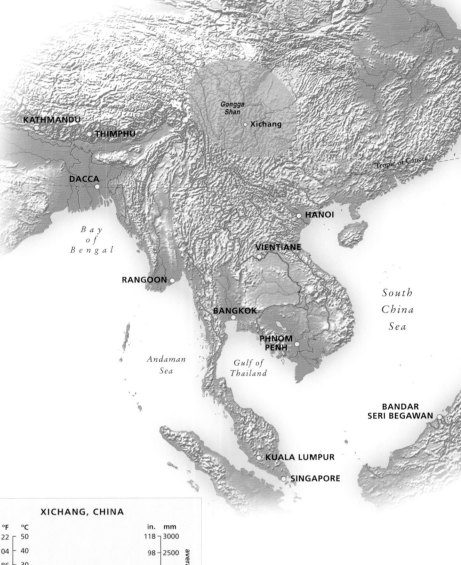

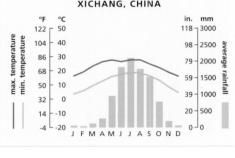
XICHANG, CHINA

Golden monkey
Golden monkeys are an arboreal species that inhabit temperate montane forests. These monkeys feed mainly on lichens and other plant matter, supplemented with insects. Found in groups of 20 to 30, they have a large home range of up to 15 square miles (40 km²).

Red goral
The red goral, the smallest of the currently recognized goral species, lives at high elevations of 6,500 to 13,000 feet (2,000–4,000 m). It feeds primarily on lichens, supplemented with tender stems, leaves, and twigs from shrubs. It is agile, moving easily and with speed over rough terrain.

Takin
The takin, a goat–antlope, is found in bamboo forests at altitudes of 6,500 to 14,500 feet (2–4,500 m). It feeds during the day on grasses, buds, and leaves. Takin gather in small herds in winter and herds of up to a hundred individuals in summer.

GIANT PANDA

Giant pandas live in dense bamboo and coniferous forests at altitudes of 5–10,000 feet (1,500–3,000 m). Their diet consists mainly of bamboo leaves, stalks, and roots, which they crush with their powerful jaws and teeth. A single adult panda must eat 20 to 40 pounds (9–18 kg) of food a day to survive, and spends up to 15 hours a day feeding. Although principally terrestrial, pandas can climb trees.

Baby panda

Female pandas give birth to one or two cubs weighing four to eight ounces (100–200 g) each, in a sheltered den. A female in general raises only one cub, if more than one is born.

Bamboo

Bamboo groves are one of the main vegetation types in the mountains of southwest China but they are subject to periodic die-off after mass flowering. The giant panda depends on bamboo species such as the umbrella bamboo.

Former range

Current range

⚡ Giant panda

The panda's thick, woolly coat keeps it warm in cool forests. Each adult has a defined territory and females are not tolerant of other females in their range. Giant pandas communicate through vocalization and scent marking of trees.

⚡ CONSERVATION WATCH

Red pandas, which are arboreal and generally solitary, occur in both deciduous and coniferous forests. They rest during the day in the branches of trees and in tree hollows. Their primary food is bamboo, but they also feed on berries, blossoms and leaves of other plants. They are threatened by deforestation and other human activities, and are classified as endangered.

THE SUNDALAND

The Sundaland covers the western half of the Indo-Malayan archipelago, and consists of some 17,000 equatorial islands. They are dominated by two of the largest islands in the world: Borneo 279,925 square miles (725,000 km²) and Sumatra 164,980 square miles (427,300 km²). Earthquakes and volcanic eruptions are a common natural hazard here; there are more than 20 active volcanoes on the island of Java. The landscape is dominated by lowland rain forests, which have several strata of vegetation. Sandy and rocky coastlines support scrubland, muddy shores are lined with mangrove forests, and large peat-swamp forests occur further inland. Montane forests, where plants such as mosses, lichens, and orchids are plentiful, occur at higher elevations. Higher still, scrubby subalpine forests are dominated by rhododendrons. Sundaland fauna is diverse, with nearly 3,000 species of vertebrates, one-third of them endemic. The Sundaland also has the highest number of species threatened with extinction in the Asian region.

SCALE 1:40,000,000

0 ——————————————— 750 miles

0 ——————————————— 750 kilometers

INDONESIAN MARINE LIFE

The waters around the Indonesian archipelago are relatively shallow and warm and the rich nutrients support a diversity of marine life. These waters also serve as an important migratory area for more than 30 species of marine mammals. More than one-third of all known whale and dolphin species can be found in the Indonesian seas, including the rare and endangered blue whale—the largest mammal in the world.

MALACCA, MALAYSIA

Marine turtles
Six of the world's seven marine turtle species are found in Indonesia. There are important nesting and foraging grounds on the many islands, and migration routes converge at the crossroads of the Pacific and Indian oceans.

Nudibranch
These are a group of marine slugs—mollusks without an external shell. A variety of colorful nudibranchs are found in the coral reefs around Indonesia. They store toxic chemicals in their body for their defense.

Tail
The dragon's muscular tail is as long as its body. It is used for balance and when capturing prey, and in fights with other males, especially when standing on its hind legs.

Red Helen butterfly
This large swallowtail butterfly is common in evergreen forests. It has a white patch on the upper hindwing, which is characteristic of the species. The larvae feed on plants of the Rutaceae family, which includes citrus plants.

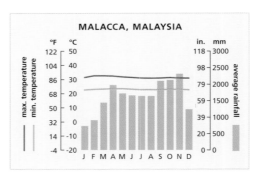

☉ Sumatran rhinoceros
The Sumatran rhinoceros is the smallest of the living rhino species. A solitary browser, it eats up to 110 pounds (50 kg) of leaves, saplings, twigs, and shoots a day. Individual bulls have territories as large as 20 square miles (50 km²).

Former range

Current range

Crested langur
The crested langur lives in groups of up to 50 individuals, which include a single adult male, several adult females, and immature individuals. It feeds mainly on leaves, supplemented with fruits, nuts, young shoots, and flowers. The young are born orange-colored and become gray as they grow.

Sun bear
This, the smallest member of the bear family, is a solitary, nocturnal omnivore. It feeds on termites, birds' eggs, vertebrates, fruits, insects, berries, and shoots. The sun bear spends much of its time in trees. It has a long, slender tongue that may be up to 10 inches (25 cm) long, which it uses to extract honey from beehives.

Komodo dragon

The world's largest lizard, the venomous Komodo dragon is restricted to Komodo and a few neighboring islands. Although these lizards usually feed on carrion, they have been known to kill large animals such as goats, deer, and cattle by ambushing them on paths through thick undergrowth. Previous belief that damaging bites were due to bacterial infection are now better understood as resulting from tissue-destroying venom.

Claws
Strong claws help the Komodo dragon dig burrows for resting. They are also used as weapons and to disembowel prey.

Skin
The scales in the dragon's skin, some of which are reinforced with bone, have sensory plaques connected to nerves that facilitate its sense of touch.

Tongue
The Komodo's sense of smell functions through its tongue, which samples the air then "smells" by touching the roof of its mouth.

TROPICAL RAIN FORESTS OF SOUTHEAST ASIA

Lowland tropical rain forests are forests that receive high rainfall, more than 80 inches (2,000 mm) annually, with a mean annual temperature of 75°F (24°C), and an average relative humidity of 85 percent. These forests occur in a belt around the equator, between the Tropic of Cancer and the Tropic of Capricorn, at elevations of less than 3,300 feet (1,000 m). Among the continents that harbor tropical rain forests, Asia is the second largest region, with Indonesia, Malaysia, and the Philippines all in the tropical zone. Tropical rain forests are characterized by a closed canopy formed by tall broadleaf evergreen trees, several layers of vegetation—the emergent overstory, canopy, sub-canopy, understory—a relatively open and shaded forest floor with a thick layer of litter, and many thousands of species of plants and animals. The diverse wildlife in tropical rain forests in southeast Asia is well adapted to live in the trees, and includes birds, arboreal amphibians, reptiles, and mammals.

Dipterocarp trees
The tropical lowland rain forests in Borneo are dominated by towering trees of the Dipterocarpaceae family, which often exceed 145 feet (45 m) in height. A majority of these dipterocarp species undergo a mass flowering event, occurring roughly every four years and coinciding with the onset of dry weather. At these times the forest canopy bursts into color.

THE ORANGUTAN

Among the great apes of the world, orangutans are the most arboreal, spending most of their time in trees. They are generally solitary, with large territories. A major portion of their diet consists of fruits, supplemented with young leaves, shoots, seeds, bark, flowers, insects, and small vertebrates. They are remarkably intelligent great apes and are known to use tools for feeding. In the evening they construct a "nest" in a tree, using leaves and branches, and rest there for the night.

Orangutan
Orangutans usually move by swinging from one branch to another. Their powerful arms, twice as long as their legs, enable them to easily bear their body weight, which is 100 to 200 pounds (45–90 kg).

Baby orangutan
Females give birth to a single offspring, and care for it for some six to seven years. Newborn infants weigh around three pounds (1.5 kg). They begin to take soft food from their mother's lips at about four months.

Hornbill nest

Hornbills nest in cavities in living trees. The male locates a possible site and invites the female to inspect it. Once she is satisfied with the choice of nest, the birds mate and the female then seals herself inside the nest chamber using rotten wood, clay, regurgitated food, and other materials supplied by the male. The sealing process usually takes three to seven days. The female lays her eggs, incubates them, then rears the chick inside the nesting cavity.

Epiphytic orchid
Phalenopsis sp.

Fern
Drymoglossum piloselloides

Delivering food
The male delivers food to its mate, and later to the chicks. In most large forest species, the female remains in the nest until the chick is fledged, a total period of incarceration of up to five months.

Flying frog
A large tree frog with brilliant colors, Wallace's flying frog is well adapted to life in the treetops. Its fingers and toes are webbed and a membrane of skin stretches between the limbs.

Flying lizard
This is an arboreal lizard that can spread out folds of skin attached to its movable ribs to form "wings" that it uses to glide from tree to tree over distances of more than 26 feet (8 m).

Regular body shape   Flattened for flying

Flying snake
These arboreal snakes are able to glide between trees, by flattening their bodies to up to twice their usual width from the back of the head to the vent.

White-handed gibbon
The white-handed gibbon is a small, tailless ape with dense, shaggy fur that varies from black to pale gray. It has long, slender arms and the upper side of its hands and feet are white. Its opposable thumb is used for climbing or grooming.

Rain forest life

An estimated 70 to 90 percent of life in the rain forest exists in the trees above the shaded forest floor. A variety of epiphytes, such as colorful orchids and mosses, occur in the trees. Arboreal animals such as flying squirrels, tree frogs, and flying lizards feed, nest, and rest among the foliage.

Gliding lemur
Galeopterus variegates

Orchid
Vanda sp.

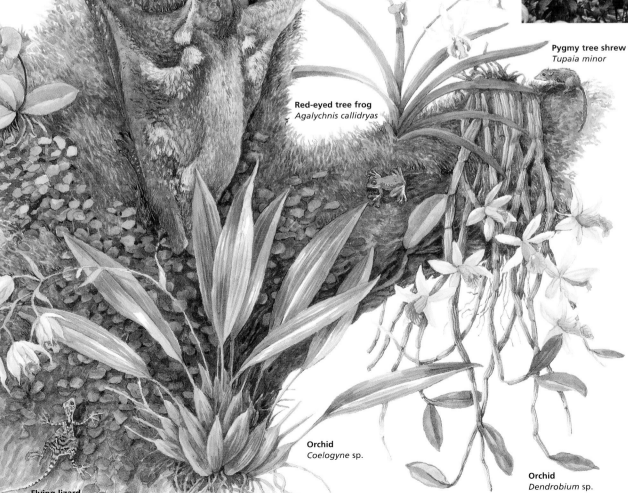

Red-eyed tree frog
Agalychnis callidryas

Pygmy tree shrew
Tupaia minor

Proboscis monkey
The male of this primate species has a distinct, enlarged, protruding nose, which can be up to seven inches (17 cm) long. It also has an enlarged belly. It is found in small groups of 10 to 32, living on a diet of seeds, leaves, shoots, and fruit.

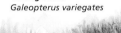

Slow loris
The slow loris, a nocturnal, arboreal primate, is known for its slow, deliberate movements and powerful grasp. It can be difficult to remove the slow loris from a branch. These animals live alone or in small family groups. As opportunistic carnivores, they typically eat insects, birds' eggs, and small vertebrates.

Orchid
Coelogyne sp.

Orchid
Dendrobium sp.

Flying lizard
Draco volans

East Asia

This region includes the Japanese archipelago, which consists of more than 3,000 islands, Korea, and southeast Russia. The archipelago sits at the intersection of three tectonic plates—resulting in numerous volcanoes, hot springs, mountains, and earthquakes. The area stretches from humid subtropics in the south to a temperate zone in the north. Vegetation on the islands of the Japanese archipelago ranges from boreal mixed forests of fir, spruce, and pine, to subtropical broadleaf evergreen forests and mangrove swamps. Higher elevations support alpine vegetation; subalpine vegetation and beech shrublands occur throughout the region. About half the mammal, reptile, and amphibian species in Japan are endemic. The long, north–south stretch of the Korean Peninsula and its complex topography have resulted in wide climatic variations. Wildlife here includes the roe deer, Amur goral, sable, brown bear, tiger, lynx, northern pika, water shrew, and Manchurian ring-necked pheasants. Species such as the black bear, mandarin vole, river deer, fairy pitta, and ring-necked pheasant are found in the lowlands.

SCALE 1:30,000,000

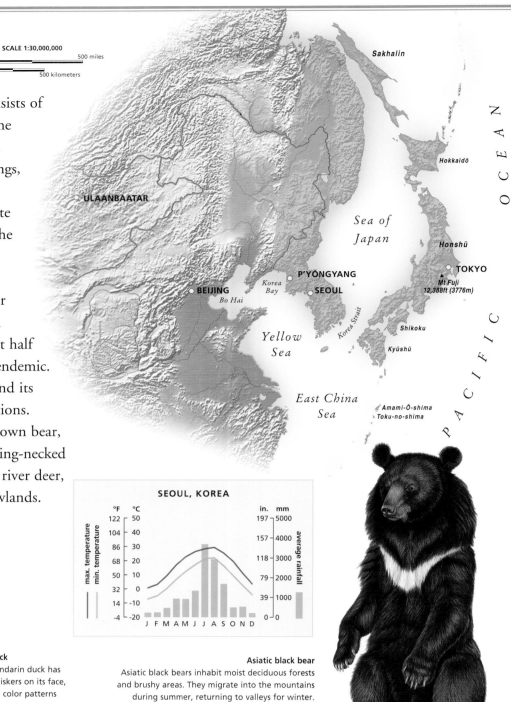

SEOUL, KOREA

Mandarin duck
The male mandarin duck has a red bill, whiskers on its face, and stunning color patterns on its body feathers. This duck breeds in wooded areas near shallow lakes, marshes, or ponds. It nests in cavities in trees close to water and feeds mainly on plants and seeds.

Asiatic black bear
Asiatic black bears inhabit moist deciduous forests and brushy areas. They migrate into the mountains during summer, returning to valleys for winter. They are excellent tree climbers and strong swimmers. They are sometimes known as "moon bears" because of the white patch on the chest.

Azure-winged magpie
A member of the crow family, the azure-winged magpie inhabits various types of coniferous and broadleaf forest, including parks and gardens. It feeds in family groups of up to 30 individuals and its diet includes seeds, nuts, invertebrates, and fruits. It nests in loose, open colonies with a single nest in each tree.

Oriental fire-bellied toad
This is a mostly aquatic frog, which spends much of its time in shallow pools. It has a brightly colored body, with bright green and black coloration on its back, and brilliant orange and black on its underside—warning predators of its toxicity. When disturbed, it secretes a milky toxin from its abdominal skin.

Amami rabbit
An endemic rabbit that is restricted to two islands in Japan, Amami-O-shima and Toku-no-shima, the amami rabbit is found mainly in dense old-growth forests. It has primitive morphological traits that resemble those found in fossils from the Miocene Epoch. It digs burrows for resting and breeding.

⚡ CONSERVATION WATCH

Red-crowned cranes are among the rarest cranes in the world and, weighing from 15 to 20 pounds (7–10 kg), are the heaviest. They breed in Siberia and parts of Mongolia and migrate to east Asia in the fall. Adults reinforce their pair bond in a synchronized courtship dance. They inhabit wetlands and have a broad diet that includes insects, frogs, and grasses.

Staying warm
These macaques have a thick coat of fur, which helps them withstand cold winter temperatures. Mothers protect their young from the cold by huddling closely together.

Japanese macaques

The Japanese macaque is an omnivorous, semi-terrestrial primate that lives in groups of 10 to 160. Its home range depends on the availability of food and is around one-and-a-half square miles (3.5 km²). It is an excellent swimmer, able to swim distances of 500 yards (0.5 km). In Shiga Heights, in central Japan, macaques remain near hot springs in winter, which helps to maintain their body temperature.

Mount Fuji
Among the many mountains in Japan, Mount Fuji is the highest, its summit reaching 12,400 feet (3,776 m). It is an active volcano, which last erupted about 300 years ago. Its symmetrical cone is covered with snow for several months of the year.

Japanese giant salamander
This, the second largest salamander in the world, grows up to five feet (1.5 m) in length. It is an aquatic species restricted to mountain streams that have clear, cool water. It has poor eyesight but feeds at night on insects, crabs, frogs, and fish.

THE LOWER MEKONG

The Lower Mekong region includes Laos, Cambodia, Vietnam, and southern parts of Thailand and Myanmar. It contains the lower catchment of the Mekong river and its floodplains. A wide variety of vegetation types is found in this region, including mixed wet evergreen, dry evergreen, deciduous, and montane forests. There are also patches of shrublands and woodlands on karst limestone outcrops and, in some coastal areas, scattered heath forests. Other distinctive, localized, vegetation formations include floodplain swamps, mangroves, and seasonally inundated grasslands. The area supports amazing bird diversity, some 1,300 species, and the largest waterbird populations in Southeast Asia. Four species of ungulates new to science have been discovered in this region over the past two decades. They include the Annamite muntjac, the large-antlered muntjac, the leaf deer, and the saola. The region also supports the highest diversity of freshwater turtles in the world.

SCALE 1:30,000,000

0 — 500 miles

0 — 500 kilometers

Big-headed turtle
This freshwater turtle is distinguished by its large head and long tail. It is found in rivers and streams and is also known to climb trees, using its beak. It cannot withdraw its head into its shell, but the top of the head is covered with a large bony scute for protection. It feeds on fish and snails.

White-throated kingfisher
Halcyon smyrnensis

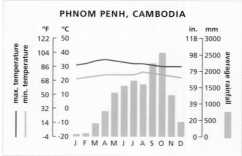
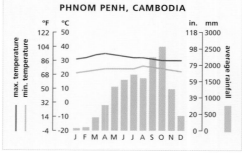

PHNOM PENH, CAMBODIA

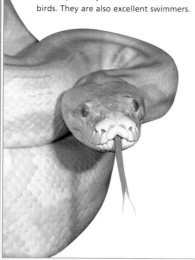

Burmese python
Burmese pythons are among the largest snakes on Earth. They may reach 23 feet (7 m) or more in length and can weigh up to 200 pounds (90 kg). They are nocturnal carnivores, killing by constriction, and survive primarily on small mammals and birds. They are also excellent swimmers.

The Mekong River
The Mekong is the longest river in Southeast Asia, with an estimated length of 2,703 miles (4,350 km), draining an area of 306,950 square miles (795,000 km²). The river links numerous habitats that attract a variety of animals. Islands in the river enhance habitat diversity, with sandy shores, shallow ponds, sediment flats, and reed beds.

Capped gibbon
Capped gibbons live together as monogamous pairs, spending most of their time in the trees. They eat mainly fruits, leaves, and small animals. The males are black; females are black on the belly and head but pale gray elsewhere.

Red-shanked douc monkey

This colorful arboreal monkey lives in primary and secondary evergreen forests and moist deciduous forests. It forms groups of 4 to 15 individuals, which socialize by grooming each other, led by dominant males. The monkeys communicate through facial expressions and vocalization. They feed on flowers, leaves, fruits, seeds, and buds.

Clouded leopard

This medium-sized wild cat has a tawny coat, bearing cloud-shaped patterns, and a stocky build. It is known to have the longest canine teeth, two inches (5 cm), of any living feline. It is tree-dwelling, solitary, and secretive.

⚡ CONSERVATION WATCH

The freshwater Siamese crocodile occurs in swamps, oxbow lakes, and slow-moving sections of streams and rivers. It feeds predominantly on fish, but also amphibians, reptiles, and possibly small mammals. Females construct a mound nest during the annual wet season and lay 20 to 50 eggs. The species is critically endangered in the wild because of habitat destruction, over-exploitation for farming, accidental entanglement and drowning in fishing nets, and hunting.

Eld's deer

The rare, medium-sized Eld's deer is found in dry dipterocarp forests. It lives in small groups of four to seven animals, but also gathers in herds of up to 50 individuals. Adult stags are solitary, joining herds during the rut. Eld's deer are active at dusk and rest at forest edges during the day.

Life in the river

Riverine wetlands along the Lower Mekong consist of a mosaic of habitat types, influenced by the movement of water over the riverbed. Sandbars, mudflats, perennial river channels, rock outcrops, waterfalls, deep pools, and rapids are all found here. The wildlife is richly varied. Crocodiles bask on the muddy banks, turtles and frogs hunt for insects, long-legged waders fish by the shore, and giant carp cruise the waters.

Black-necked crane
Grus nigricollis

Giant ibis
Pseudibis gigantean

Siamese crocodile
Crocodylus siamensis

Irrawaddy dolphin
Orcaella brevirostris

Siamese giant carp
Catlocarpio siamensis

Smooth-coated otter
Lutrogale perspicillata

Mekong wagtail
Motacilla samveasnae

Fishing cat
Prionailurus viverrinus

Giant Asian pond turtle
Heosemys grandis

Spiny-breasted giant frog
Paa fasciculispina

THE PHILIPPINE ARCHIPELAGO

The Philippine archipelago includes more than 7,100 islands covering 114,741 square miles (297,179 km²) in the Pacific Ocean. The isolated fragments of the archipelago have an ancient geological history—some date back 30 to 50 million years—and include 17 active volcanoes. The Philippines has a tropical climate with three pronounced seasons: wet (June–October); cool and dry (November–February); and hot and dry (March–May). The archipelago is within a typhoon belt and is affected by a number of cyclonic storms every year.

Once covered with thick tropical lowland rainforests, the islands have been cleared extensively and only isolated patches of forest remain today. There is still a rich diversity of vascular plants, about one-third of which is endemic, dominated by orchids, palms, begonias, and dipterocarps. Among the many terrestrial vertebrate species in the Philippines more than 50 percent are endemic. Birds are the largest vertebrate group, with more than 600 species found in the region.

SCALE 1:12,000,000

0   200 miles

0   200 kilometers

Tarsier

Just the size of a human fist, this small arboreal mammal is a forest-dweller. Its eyes cannot turn in their sockets but a special adaptation in its neck has enabled the tarsier to rotate its head through 180 degrees. Its eyes are considered to be, for its size, the largest of any known mammal. The tarsier is a solitary animal, with a specific home range, travelling up to a mile (1.5 km) across the forest. It is primarily an insectivore, but also feeds on lizards and birds.

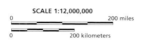

Tarsier hands and feet
The tarsier's second and third toes have sharp claws specially adapted for grooming. Its long digits are tipped with rounded pads that allow it to cling easily to trees.

Sleeping tarsier
The tarsier sleeps during the day, usually in dark hollows close to the ground, near the trunks of trees and shrubs deep in thick bushes and forests. These animals sleep in groups, or as solitary individuals, becoming active at night.

Cloud rat
A nocturnal, arboreal rodent, the cloud rat has large hind feet and long claws that facilitate its excellent tree-climbing ability. A herbivore, it feeds on leaves and flowers and is endemic to the island of Luzon in the Philippines, where it is found in the northern highlands.

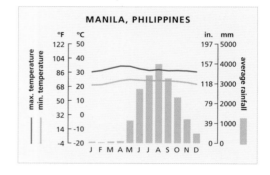

MANILA, PHILIPPINES

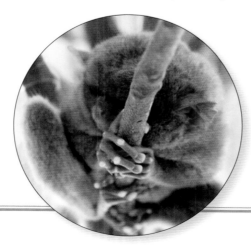

⚡ Philippine eagle

One of the largest and most powerful birds of prey, the Philippine eagle builds a large nest in emergent dipterocarp trees, about 98 feet (30 m) from the ground. The female lays only one egg and the parents care for the hatchling for about 20 months. Each breeding pair requires a home range of 9 to 19 square miles (25–50 km²).

⚡ CONSERVATION WATCH

The tamaraw, also known as the Mindoro dwarf buffalo, is a small hoofed mammal endemic to the island of Mindoro in the Philippines. It is the largest terrestrial mammal in the country, with an average height of three feet (1 m). It is a diurnal grazer that feeds on grass and bamboo shoots. Adults live a solitary, reclusive life.

⚡ Philippine crocodile

A relatively small freshwater crocodile endemic to the Philippines, the Philippine crocodile has a broad snout and heavy dorsal armor. It feeds on aquatic invertebrates, fish, and small vertebrates. The female constructs a small nest mound, where 7 to 20 eggs are laid.

Luzon mangrove snake

This is one of the biggest cat snake species, between six and eight feet (1.8–2.5 m) long, with vividly marked bold yellow bands on a black body. It is a nocturnal feeder and its prey includes small mammals, lizards, frogs, other snakes, and fish.

⚡ Visayan spotted deer

Endemic to the Philippines, this small, short-legged deer is found in steep dipterocarp forests that are relatively inaccessible to humans. It feeds at night, grazing on cogon grass and young low-growing leaves and buds within the forest.

GOLDEN-CAPPED FRUIT BAT

One of the largest fruit bats in the world, this species bears a patch of golden-tipped hairs on the top of its head. It roosts in colonies during the day and flies long distances, up to 25 miles (40 km) during the night in search of fruits, mainly the fruits of fig trees. It uses its excellent eyesight to locate food, rather than the echolocation used by other bat species.

⚡ Heavyweight bat

The golden-capped fruit bat is probably the heaviest bat in the world, weighing up to two-and-a-half pounds (1.2 kg).

Wide wingspan

This bat's wingspan is more than five feet (1.5 m). It may travel more than 25 miles (40 km) each night in search of food.

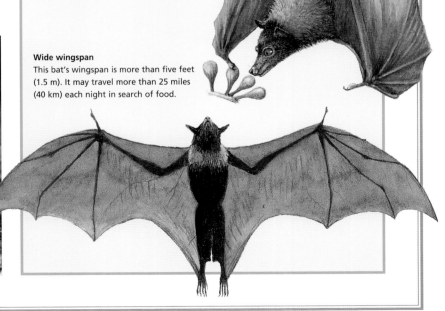

159

African elephants are the largest land animals on Earth. This herd
of African elephants moves through the Etosha National Park,
Namibia. Three-quarters of an elephant's life is devoted to feeding
or moving toward food or water. Female elephants, or cows, live in
family groups with their young, but adult bulls roam on their own.

AFRICA

AFRICA

Africa, the world's second largest continent at 11.7 million square miles (30.2 million km²) hangs below Europe like an enormous island. Historically connected to the rest of the Old World by a thin strip of land along the east of Egypt, Africa has unique fauna and flora. Much of the animals and plants consist of species that are widespread within, and sometimes between, the major habitat types—deserts in the north and south, wet forests in the center, savannas and grasslands between these forests and deserts, and the woodlands and scrub forests of the higher altitude plateaus in the east and southeast of Africa. But geological and climatological processes have, over the last few million years, produced areas of isolation—the Great Rift Valley, the fynbos of South Africa, the mountains of the Eastern Arc of Tanzania and Kenya, and the great island of Madagascar, where speciation has occurred in isolation, and evolution has produced rare and unusual animal and plant forms.

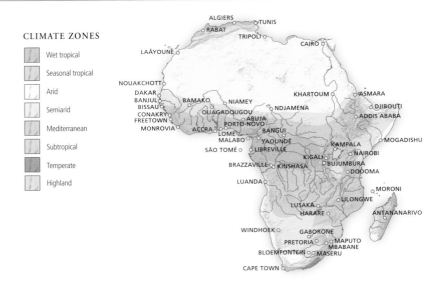

CLIMATE ZONES

- Wet tropical
- Seasonal tropical
- Arid
- Semiarid
- Mediterranean
- Subtropical
- Temperate
- Highland

Climate

The equator splices broadly similar climatic zones in Africa. Nearest the equator rainfall is regular and abundant; the duration of the wet season decreases the greater the distance from the equator. High pressure produces arid zones at 30 degrees north, creating the Sahara Desert, and 30 degrees south, where drier conditions are limited to the southwest.

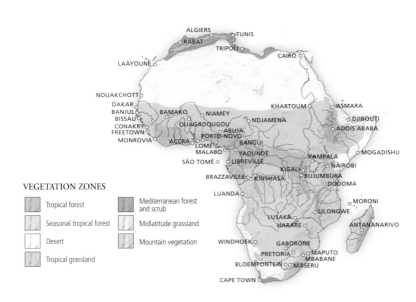

VEGETATION ZONES

- Tropical forest
- Seasonal tropical forest
- Desert
- Tropical grassland
- Mediterranean forest and scrub
- Midlatitude grassland
- Mountain vegetation

Vegetation

Abundant rain supports extensive tropical rain forests on Africa's west coast and in the Congo Basin. These are bounded by tropical woodlands and savannas, which cover almost half the continent and encircle an expanse of seasonal tropical forest in the south. To the north, the savanna yields to thorn woodlands and sparse grasses. Vegetation is scanty or nonexistent in the Sahara and much of the Namib Desert.

The Sahara and Sahel
The world's largest desert, the Sahara spans nearly the entire top of the continent. Animals are widely dispersed, but they are all adapted to living in the hottest place on Earth.

East African Savanna
Large groups of giraffes still find a home in the savannas of central and eastern Africa. The savannas are also home to the great migrations of antelopes, zebra, and buffalo.

The Congo Basin
Much of the Congo forest, the world's second largest tropical forest, remains intact and is home to many of humankind's closest ancestors—gorillas, chimpanzees, and bonobos.

Life in the Albertine Rift
An area of spectacular peaks, deep valleys, and diverse lakes, the Albertine Rift Valley is home to the famed mountain gorilla, and to thousands of unique plant and animal species.

The Ethiopian Highlands
The Ethiopian Highlands are high islands cut off from the rest of Africa by their altitude. The Simien and Bale mountains are home to many unique animals species.

The Miombo Woodlands
Little known, but one of the largest ecoregions in Africa, the Miombo woodlands, which provide a habitat for Africa's largest elephant herds, span much of south-central Africa.

The Okavango Delta
The Kavango River floods seasonally into a massive basin in northern Botswana, creating an inland swamp and lake. Hippopotamus and waterbirds abound.

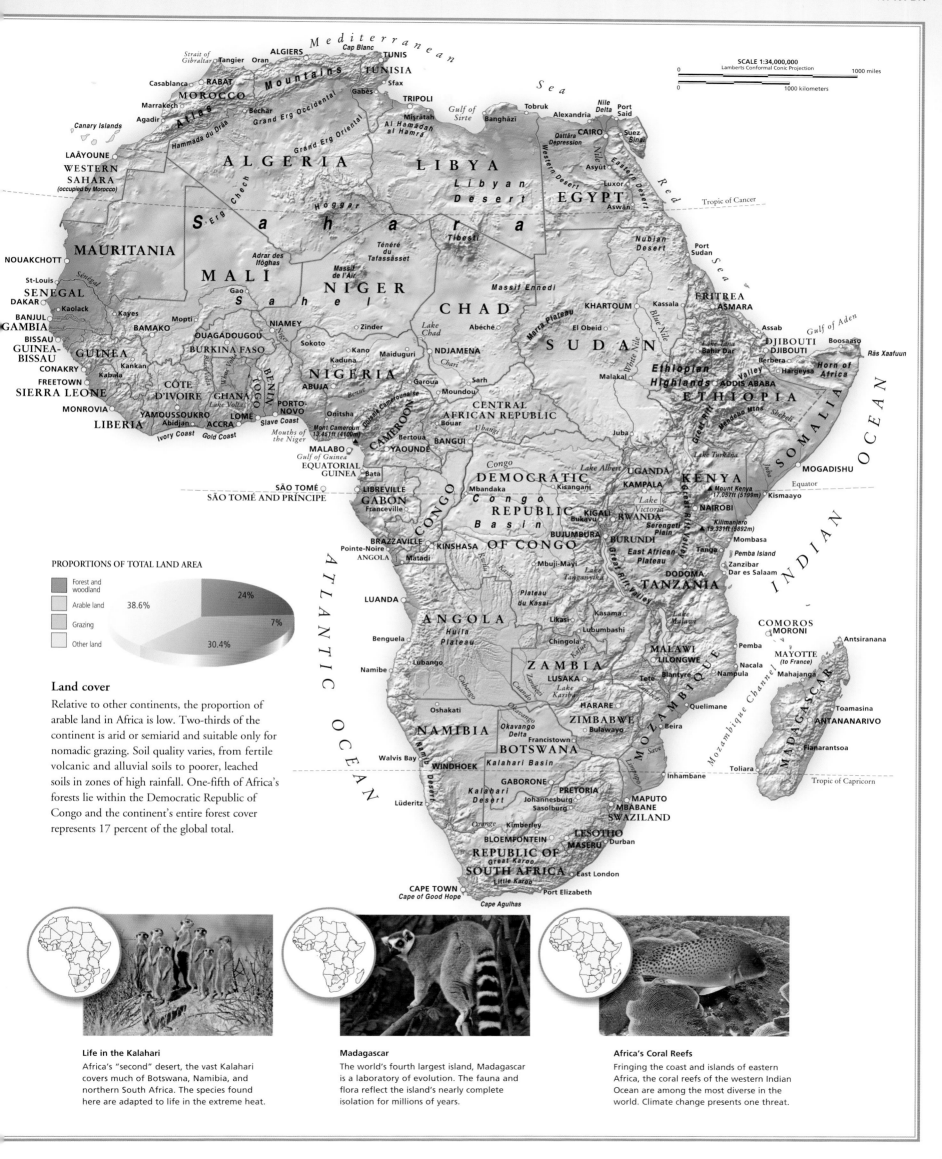

PROPORTIONS OF TOTAL LAND AREA

- Forest and woodland
- Arable land   38.6%
- Grazing
- Other land

24%

7%

30.4%

Land cover

Relative to other continents, the proportion of arable land in Africa is low. Two-thirds of the continent is arid or semiarid and suitable only for nomadic grazing. Soil quality varies, from fertile volcanic and alluvial soils to poorer, leached soils in zones of high rainfall. One-fifth of Africa's forests lie within the Democratic Republic of Congo and the continent's entire forest cover represents 17 percent of the global total.

Life in the Kalahari

Africa's "second" desert, the vast Kalahari covers much of Botswana, Namibia, and northern South Africa. The species found here are adapted to life in the extreme heat.

Madagascar

The world's fourth largest island, Madagascar is a laboratory of evolution. The fauna and flora reflect the island's nearly complete isolation for millions of years.

Africa's Coral Reefs

Fringing the coast and islands of eastern Africa, the coral reefs of the western Indian Ocean are among the most diverse in the world. Climate change presents one threat.

THE SAHARA AND SAHEL

Stretching from the Red Sea to the Atlantic Ocean, the Sahara covers 3.3 million square miles (8.6 million km²) in northern Africa and merges with the semiarid savanna of the Sahel at its southern extremity. Sculpted by strong winds, the Sahara landscape is characterized by mountains, valleys, and dunes. Although the most arid of ecosystems, it is dotted with isolated and variable water sources that sustain life. Temperature extremes pose a major challenge to desert wildlife. The world's highest temperature—136.4°F (58°C)—was recorded in the Libyan Sahara in 1922, yet subzero temperatures are also common. Most of the Sahara's 1,200 plant species are adapted to the heat and low rainfall, being short-lived or possessing thick, rubbery leaves. Diversity of animal species is low, with only 70 mammal species, 90 bird species, and 100 reptile species found across this vast area. Because of these low densities, desert animals are susceptible to hunting, which has decimated ostrich, addax, gazelle, and cheetah populations.

Desert oases

A wadi, or valley in Arabic, is a depression or streambed found in the desert, often at the base of a mountain or within a sheltered area. Wadis remain dry for most of the year but are transformed by heavy rains. Flooding produces lush vegetation that supports a variety of wildlife as well as nearby villagers. Although most desert animals are adapted to dry conditions, wadis are a critical source of succulent vegetation and fresh water.

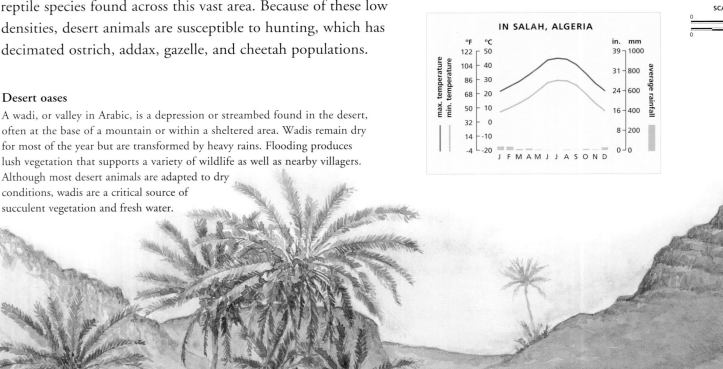

Ostrich
Struthio camelus

Slender-horned gazelles
Gazella leptoceros

Desert jerboa
Jaculus jaculus

Red-fronted gazelles
Gazella rufifrons

IN SALAH, ALGERIA

SCALE 1:45,000,000

⚡ CONSERVATION WATCH

With an estimated population of 9 to 12,000, the endangered Saharan subspecies of the cheetah is found only in Algeria, Morocco, and Niger. Numbers continue to fall as its prey base—small antelope—is destroyed by poaching and increased competition resulting from habitat loss. This brings cheetahs into conflict with sheep and camel herders.

Scimitar-horned oryx
Formerly found throughout North Africa, the scimitar-horned oryx once congregated in groups of more than 1,000 at water sources. It is now extinct in the wild because of habitat loss and hunting. Captive breeding and reintroductions provide hope that oryx will again roam the desert landscape.

Green Sahara
The Sahara, shadowed by the Atlas Mountains to the northwest, has been a desert for several million years. But during the last ice age, 20,000 to 5,000 years ago, large rivers, whose beds are visible even in today's satellite imagery, flowed across a greener landscape. Rock carvings and cave paintings from this era depict a broad savanna, home to zebras, gazelles, hippopotamus, and giraffes.

Rock hyrax
The rock hyrax is a small ungulate that has a unique call, which sounds like a woman screaming. Despite its size, it is closely related to the elephant and lives in rocky outcrops in colonies averaging 50 individuals. The hyrax's heavily furred feet are equipped with glands that produce sweat, which aids traction in its rocky habitat.

DESERT ADAPTATIONS

The desert is an extreme environment. Daytime Saharan temperatures often exceed 100°F (38°C) but drop 50°F (10°C) at night. With little available shade or water, wildlife must be able to cope with these temperature extremes, excessive dryness, and harsh sunlight. Many animals have evolved behavioral and physiological adaptations, such as sleeping in burrows by day, raising their body temperatures before sweating, and developing kidneys that conserve water.

Fennec fox
The smallest of foxes, the fennec, has large ears that help it to dissipate heat and detect prey. Its sandy coat reflects sunlight, blends into the landscape, and insulates the fox during cold nights, when it is active.

⚡ Addax
The addax obtains all of its water needs from plants and is adept at tracking and finding patches of desert vegetation after rain. Its broad hooves are adapted to travel over soft sand without sinking. The once healthy addax population has been reduced to less than 300 individuals.

Dorcas gazelle
The dorcas gazelle can live its entire life without tasting water, gaining moisture from the plants—primarily acacias—in its diet. The gazelle became completely nocturnal in response to heavy hunting.

THE CONGO BASIN

The Congo Basin forest spans six countries across about two-thirds of the African continent, from the Gulf of Guinea in the west, to the East African Rift in the east. The Congo is second only to the Amazon in size, covering more than 700,000 square miles (1.8 million km²), which includes 25 percent of the world's remaining tropical forest. Unlike much of the Amazon, the Congo is largely undeveloped, but increased road-building, agricultural expansion, mining, and forestry activity destroy up to 2 million acres (810,000 ha) a year and threaten the future of these forests. The Congo is not a single ecosystem but a patchwork of ecosystems that includes rivers, swamps, and flooded forests. The size of the forest basin is rivalled only by its diversity. More than 10,000 species of plants, 1,000 bird species, and 400 species of mammals, including forest elephants, four species of great ape, and a wide variety of forest antelopes and monkeys make their home here.

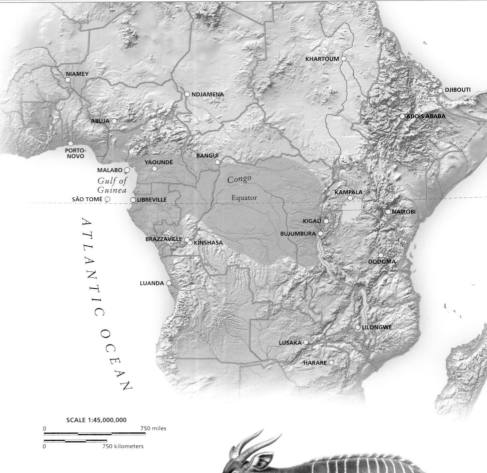

SCALE 1:45,000,000

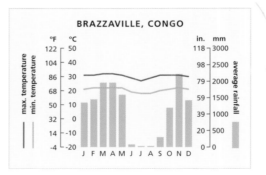

BRAZZAVILLE, CONGO

Red river hog
Traveling in large groups, or sounders, of up to several dozen animals, red river hogs use their strong snouts to dig for tubers and roots in the forest floor. Adept swimmers, they are often found in swamps. While adults are characterized by a red coat and contrasting black and white stripe down their back, piglets are darker.

Congo bongo
Easily recognized by its striped coat and the spiral horns sported by both sexes, the bongo is one of Africa's largest antelopes. Like other African herbivores, it prefers to graze on nutrient-rich grasses found in small forest clearings. Females are social; males solitary.

CONSERVATION WATCH

The okapi resembles a zebra but is in fact the only living relative of the giraffe. Not described by science until 1901, the okapi is found only in the north and east of the Democratic Republic of Congo, formerly Zaire. In the late 1980s, the government established the Okapi Wildlife Reserve to protect the species from hunting and habitat destruction. The initiative has been largely successful, despite near-constant civil war.

Lady Ross's turaco
A social bird that lives in flocks of up to 30 individuals, the Lady Ross's turaco emits a noisy call. Turacos mate while traveling in groups, and the male and female share responsibility for incubating the eggs. The bird's characteristic red crest can rise up to 2 inches (5 cm) when it is excited.

Giant swallowtail
The largest of hundreds of African butterfly species, the giant swallowtail has long, narrow wings. Females tend to remain in the canopy, where they lay their eggs, while males are more frequently encountered near streams on the forest floor, where they engage in territorial disputes.

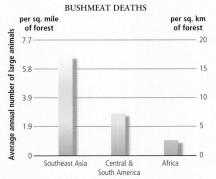

African gray parrot
With striking red tail feathers, the African gray parrot is endemic to the forests of central and western Africa and renowned for its mimicking ability. Studies suggest that up to 21 percent of these parrots are taken annually for the pet trade. As well, the trees they nest in are frequently harvested for their timber.

THE FACTS	
Area	More than 1.3 million sq miles (+3.4 million km²)
Number of countries	6
Length of Congo River	2,900 miles (4,700 km)
Habitat	Rain forest, woodland, swamp, savanna, freshwater
Estimate of mammal species	More than 400
Estimate of fish species	More than 700
Estimate of bird species	More than 1,000

Complete ecosystem
The Congo Basin's dense vegetation, rivers, and swamps, constitute a self-contained ecosystem. This structure, when combined with the hot and humid conditions, regulates water flow and creates a stable climate that has enabled the forest's biological diversity to evolve and endure.

Congo River
The Congo is the second-largest river in the world. It contains more than 4,000 islands and water may take six months to traverse the African continent. With more than 500 endemic fish species, the Congo's productive fisheries support millions of people.

BUSH MEAT

The number of Congo animals killed and sold as bush meat is growing, with estimates of more than 2 billion pounds (1 billion kg) being traded each year. This trade is facilitated by a growing network of logging roads that penetrate the forest, and many wildlife managers are calling for stricter legislation and improved management to curb unsustainable hunting.

BUSHMEAT DEATHS

Average annual number of large animals

per sq. mile of forest: 7.7, 5.8, 3.9, 1.9, 0

per sq. km of forest: 20, 15, 10, 5, 0

Southeast Asia | Central & South America | Africa

Blue duiker
One of the smallest species of antelope living in central Africa, blue duikers are commonly found in bush-meat markets. Hunting threatens not only the duiker but also its predators, which rely heavily on the duiker as a food source.

THE CONGO BASIN
PRIMATES OF THE CONGO

The forests of the Congo Basin are some of the most diverse and extensive tropical forests remaining in the world. Home to 33 of the 79 African primate species, these forests are also critical to primate evolution and conservation. However, it is not the number of species but their evolutionary and ecological significance that makes the primates of the Congo Basin so important. All of Africa's great apes, humankind's closest relatives, are found in the Congo—bonobos, gorillas, and chimpanzees. The smaller monkeys—colobus monkeys, drills, and guenons—are keystone species, eating fruits and spreading or dispersing their seeds, which helps regenerate the forest. The habitat is under increasing pressure from the timber and mining industries, but the single greatest threat to primates is the direct hunting by humans for food, with thousands of animals entering the bush-meat trade annually.

The Congo Basin
A mosaic of forests, swamps, woodlands, and flooded forests, this vast region stretches across central Africa. The Congo Basin's tropical forests are critical to storing carbon and preventing global warming. Rates of deforestation have been lower here than in other tropical forest areas of Asia and the Amazon, but threats and access to the area are increasing.

Skeleton
The ape skeleton reveals adaptations for both terrestrial walking and arboreal climbing, including a flat chest, short legs, long arms, no tail, and the ability to walk with weight bearing down on the knuckles.

Black and white colobus
Widely distributed across the Congo, the black and white colobus, like other colobines, has a specialized digestive tract that allows it to feed on a diet composed primarily of leaves.

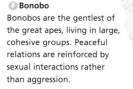

Bonobo
Bonobos are the gentlest of the great apes, living in large, cohesive groups. Peaceful relations are reinforced by sexual interactions rather than aggression.

Drill
With a restricted range in west Africa, the drill is one of the most endangered primates. Drills live in social units of up to 20 individuals, but groups may merge to form troops of up to 200 individuals. Males may be twice the size of females, some weighing 55 pounds (25 kg).

Chimpanzee
Chimpanzees are humans' closest relative and share 98 percent of our DNA. Highly intelligent, they are often observed using tools.

Mandrill
One of the largest and most striking of the terrestrial monkeys, mandrills are distinguished by the vibrant coloration of the snout and hindquarters of males. While males are higher ranking, the enduring bonds in these highly social animals, which form groups of up to 1,350 individuals, are among females.

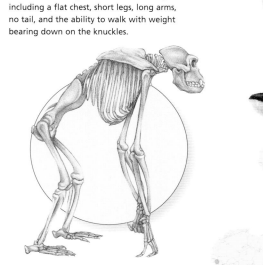

Playful

Frightened

Hungry

Submissive

Aggressive

Attentive

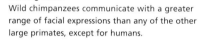

Making faces
Wild chimpanzees communicate with a greater range of facial expressions than any of the other large primates, except for humans.

Ebola virus
First identified in humans in 1976 in Africa, the ebola virus kills 50 to 90 percent of its human victims and it is equally dangerous for gorillas and chimpanzees. Recent outbreaks in the Congo Basin have decimated great ape populations and caused outbreaks in humans who have killed apes or scavenged the bush meat from carcasses. Scientists are testing vaccines that would protect people and apes alike.

⚡ CONSERVATION WATCH

In the late 1970s, hopes for the conservation of mountain gorillas were few. Populations were in decline and habitat shrinking. Since then, focused conservation action and a vibrant gorilla tourism program in Rwanda have led to stable or increasing populations and declining threats from poaching and habitat loss, despite years of military conflict and instability in many parts of the species' range.

⬤ Mountain gorilla
Mountain gorillas live in small groups of about nine individuals, led by a large silverback male. Although the largest of the primates, mountain gorillas are rarely aggressive and spend most of the day eating leaves and stems.

⬤ Western gorilla
The western gorilla has the widest distribution of any gorilla subspecies and is often found in swampy habitats or forest clearings feeding on fruits and herbs. A recent discovery has more than doubled population estimates that now stand at more than 200,000 gorillas.

THE ETHIOPIAN HIGHLANDS

The Ethiopian Highlands, sometimes referred to as "the roof of Africa," encompass a vast expanse of high-altitude habitat. They are mainly contained within modern-day Ethiopia—just 5 percent of their 200,000 square-mile area (518,000 km²) is in Eritrea and Somalia—and are divided by the Great Rift Valley into northwest and southeast sections. The base of the highlands is a plateau that formed 70 million years ago and begins at 5,000 feet (1,500 m), but rises to up to 15,000 feet (4,570 m), completely isolating the region's flora and fauna. National parks have been designated in the two best known areas—the Simien Mountains in the northwest and the Bale Mountains in the southeast. The region's unique flora and fauna bears its own name—Afromontane. Eleven percent of the highlands's 5,200 vascular plant species are endemic, including several species of wild coffee. The highlands are also home to 193 mammal species, 33 percent of them endemic; 59 species of amphibians, 39 percent of which are found nowhere else; 80 species of reptiles; and 680 bird species.

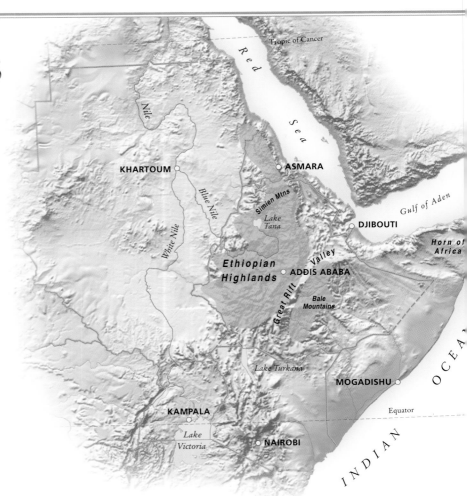

SCALE 1:25,000,000

Abyssinian blue-winged goose
This goose is primarily terrestrial, feeding on grasses and other plants. During the courtship ritual, the male struts around the female whistling and displaying its blue wings, its head arched over its back and its bill pointed skyward. The species is protected by local religious beliefs.

⚡ CONSERVATION WATCH

The Ethiopian wolf, an ancient lineage, is more closely related to the gray wolf than any African canid. The wolf is found in six isolated populations, with the largest single population of several hundred individuals surviving in the Bale Mountains. Habitat conversion is the primary cause of its decline, but domestic dogs also bring a multitude of threats to small wolf populations: disease, competition for prey, and hybridization.

ADDIS ABABA, ETHIOPIA

Rouget's rail
Typically found at high elevations, this bird is commonly associated with water, where it searches for aquatic insects, crustaceans, and snails. It is primarily threatened by the loss of its habitat to domestic livestock grazing and the collection, for building construction, of thatch, which degrades the rail's habitat.

Giant mole rat
The giant mole rat spends most of its day underground, only surfacing to gather plants. It may reach densities of up to 10 rats per acre (22 per ha) and forms a vital part of the diet of the Ethiopian wolf. Higher wolf densities correspond with large rat populations.

Gelada baboon

Found only in the high plateaus of Ethiopia, the gelada travels in small harems dominated by a large male. Dozens of these harems often gather to escape predators, with herds of up to 600 individuals sometimes sleeping on cliffs. Gelada are adapted to feeding on grasses in these open areas and tend to forage in an upright sitting position, shuffling along the ground. The chest skin is a dramatic red color, replacing the sexual signaling usually visible on the hindquarters of other baboons.

Walia ibex
The walia ibex, a mountain goat, is another rare endemic species of the Ethiopian Highlands. Closely related to the Nubian ibex, it has large horns, most prominent in the males. Once avidly hunted, it survives in the Simien Mountains, within a 400-strong remnant population.

Mountain nyala
The mountain nyala, only the males of which have spiraled horns, was the last African antelope to become known to science, in 1910. Its endangered status can, in part, be attributed to hunting for meat and medicinal use.

The Facts	
Area	200,000 sq. miles (520,000 km²)
Altitude	5,000–15,000 ft (1,500–4,600 m)
Habitat	Montane grassland, shrubland
Endemic mammals species	63
Endemic bird species	27
Endemic amphibian species	23

ASKHAM BRYAN

AFRICA
ENDEMIC BIRDS

More than 2,300 bird species, or 23 percent of the current list of 9,917 living birds worldwide, are found across the 58 countries that comprise Africa, Madagascar, and the African island nations. Sixty percent of these, or more than 1,400 bird species, are found nowhere else in the world. Like other continents, Africa has many species that are threatened with extinction—about 10 percent, or 234 of its birds, slightly less than the international average. But threats are increasing because of a growing population of 800 million people; advancing climate change; increased desertification in the Sahara; and competition for land, water, and wetlands. More than 5 billion birds migrate annually between Africa and Eurasia. Of 36 species that migrate between Africa and Britain, 20 have declined sharply since 1967 and two—the red-backed shrike and wryneck—have become extinct in Britain. Further evidence of problems can be found among the 522 migratory waterbirds on the African–Eurasian flyways, 41 percent of which are in decline.

Martial eagle
The largest of the African birds of prey, the martial eagle feeds on a variety of mammals and birds, ranging from hyraxes to antelope. Its slow reproduction rate—one egg every two years—makes the eagle vulnerable to population declines in areas where it comes into conflict with humans.

SECRETARY BIRD

The sole member of the family Sagittariidae, the secretary bird is endemic to sub-Saharan Africa. It can fly but spends more time hunting on the ground than other birds of prey—often covering 20 miles (30 km) on foot each day. It stomps on clumps of grass to flush out grasshoppers and lizards before chasing them down and, shielded by its large wings, will repeatedly strike a snake until it is stunned.

Impressive nest
Secretary birds forage separately but may roost together at night. Nests are enormous structures of interwoven sticks that often span 98 inches (2.5 m) across and 20 inches (0.5 m) deep. They may use the same nest for years.

Lesser kestrel
The migratory lesser kestrel spends the winter in the grasslands of sub-Saharan Africa. As a small falcon, it relies on its keen eyesight and gliding abilities to seek out prey, such as small rodents. Rather than build its own nest, the kestrel resumes the nests of other birds.

Distinctive crest
The secretary bird is easily recognized by the black, quill-like feathers that form a crest on the back of its head. It has the body of an eagle but stands on storklike legs.

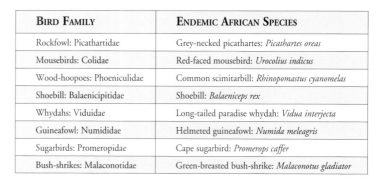

BIRD FAMILY	ENDEMIC AFRICAN SPECIES
Rockfowl: Picathartidae	Grey-necked picathartes: *Picathartes oreas*
Mousebirds: Colidae	Red-faced mousebird: *Urocolius indicus*
Wood-hoopoes: Phoeniculidae	Common scimitarbill: *Rhinopomastus cyanomelas*
Shoebill: Balaenicipitidae	Shoebill: *Balaeniceps rex*
Whydahs: Viduidae	Long-tailed paradise whydah: *Vidua interjecta*
Guineafowl: Numididae	Helmeted guineafowl: *Numida meleagris*
Sugarbirds: Promeropidae	Cape sugarbird: *Promerops caffer*
Bush-shrikes: Malaconotidae	Green-breasted bush-shrike: *Malaconotus gladiator*

Cape sparrows
Cape sparrows live in many habitats in southern Africa. They typically forage for insects on the ground and can be found in small groups or large flocks. They are monogamous and nest in loose colonies of up to 100 pairs with up to 15 nests in one tree.

Ostrich
Flightless birds such as the ostrich exist in many avian families around the world. As well as being the globe's largest bird, the ostrich is the only bird species with two-toed feet. Its long, strong legs make it one of the fastest animals on land, capable of reaching speeds of up to 45 miles per hour (72 km/h). Once widespread, its range is now restricted to western, eastern, and southwestern Africa.

Female ostrich
Unlike the black and white male, the female ostrich is a brownish-gray, which aids camouflage. Females will lay 12–14 eggs in a clutch, and up to four clutches a year. Males, because of their color, incubate at night. After 40 days, the young hatch, and clutches of several females often join together in large creches.

Yellow-billed hornbill
Like all hornbills, the yellow-billed species is characterized by a large, curved, colorful beak. Only males have a casque, or bony, air-filled cavity atop the bill, which serves to attract mates and broadcast their loud call. Southern yellow-billed hornbills forage on the ground for insects and build nests in the cavities of woodland trees.

Ground-hornbill
The southern ground-hornbill is a large, terrestrial, turkey-like bird with a booming call. It has bright red skin on its throat, accentuated by a blue patch on the female. Ground-hornbills often breed cooperatively and all family members may assist a female to rear her single chick.

EAST AFRICAN SAVANNA

Though considered the cradle of humankind, the savannas of East Africa are best known for their animals—elephants, giraffes, rhinoceros, wildebeest, impala, gazelles, lions, hyenas, and jackals, to name a few. Savanna across Central Africa is sandwiched between the Sahara Desert and Sahel to the north, and the Congo forest to the south, arcing down through South Sudan into Ethiopia, Kenya, and Somalia, before ending in northern Tanzania. Savanna vegetation ranges from dry forest and scrub to the spectacular grasslands of Tanzania's Serengeti and the Masai Mara of Kenya. With seasonal rainfall varying from 12 to 47 inches (300–1,200 mm) annually, animals often migrate, following the rains and subsequent grass growth. This open vegetation has been maintained for tens of thousands of years by virtue of the interaction between the rains, grazing by the abundant wildlife, and fires, both natural and lit by humans, that suppress the growth of dense, woody vegetation.

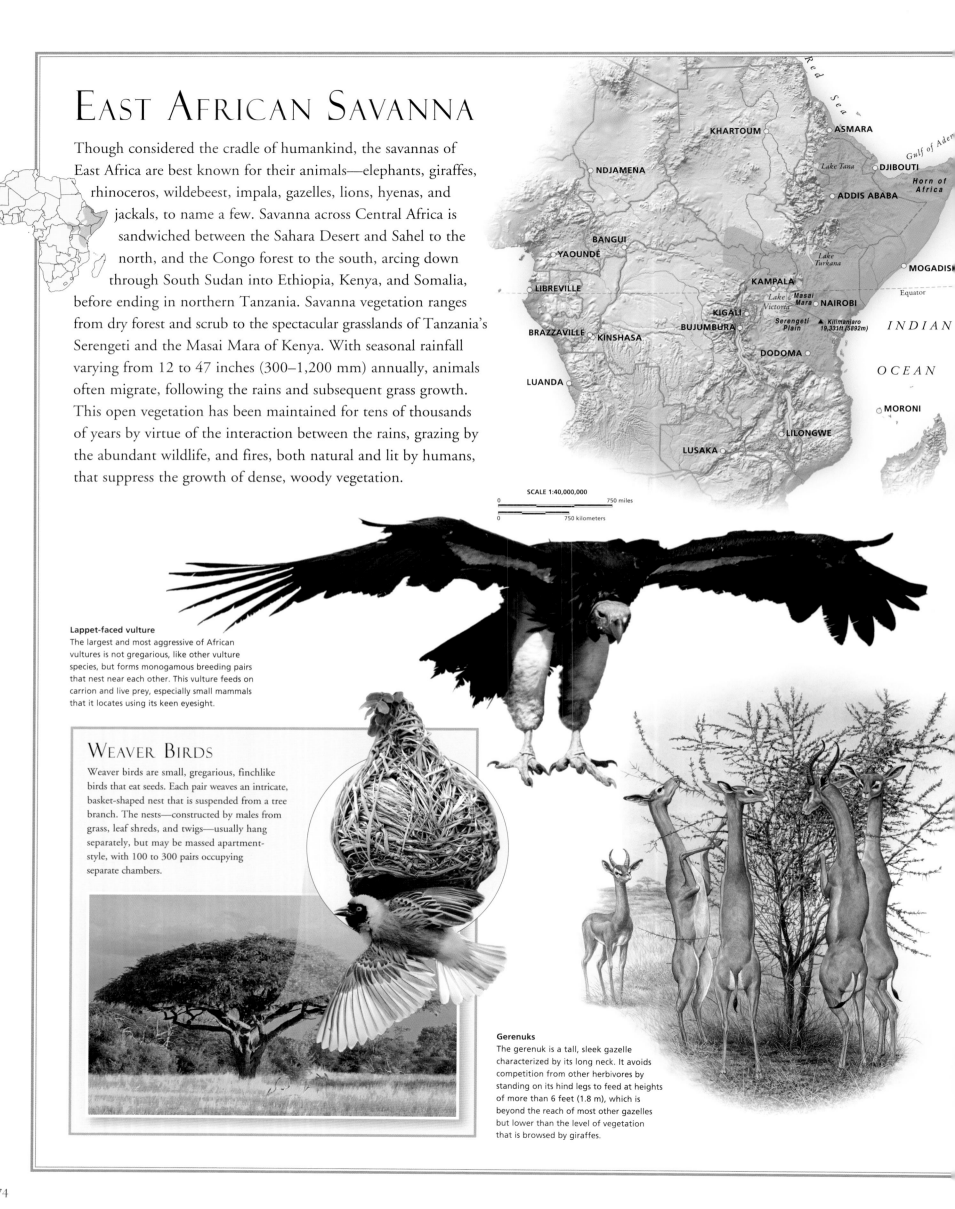

SCALE 1:40,000,000

0 — 750 miles
0 — 750 kilometers

Lappet-faced vulture
The largest and most aggressive of African vultures is not gregarious, like other vulture species, but forms monogamous breeding pairs that nest near each other. This vulture feeds on carrion and live prey, especially small mammals that it locates using its keen eyesight.

WEAVER BIRDS

Weaver birds are small, gregarious, finchlike birds that eat seeds. Each pair weaves an intricate, basket-shaped nest that is suspended from a tree branch. The nests—constructed by males from grass, leaf shreds, and twigs—usually hang separately, but may be massed apartment-style, with 100 to 300 pairs occupying separate chambers.

Gerenuks
The gerenuk is a tall, sleek gazelle characterized by its long neck. It avoids competition from other herbivores by standing on its hind legs to feed at heights of more than 6 feet (1.8 m), which is beyond the reach of most other gazelles but lower than the level of vegetation that is browsed by giraffes.

Savanna engineers

Elephants are often called ecosystem engineers because of their direct impacts, but termites may play a greater role in savanna structure and function. Termites, which are incredibly abundant, increase soil porosity, allowing water to infiltrate the soil. They also bring nutrients to the surface in tall mounds that may rise 6 to 9 feet (2–3 m) high. These nutrients influence larger scale patterns of vegetation, and hence animal distribution.

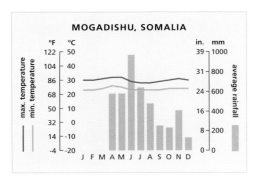

Safari ants
Safari or army ants may live in colonies of 20 million individuals. When food is scarce, columns containing up to 50 million ants from several colonies may form to find resources.

MOGADISHU, SOMALIA

African elephants
Males are primarily solitary so elephant societies are dominated by female groups, led by an old matriarch. Elephants rely on their good memory to recall widely dispersed water holes. They also communicate across distances using rumbling infrasound, which can carry for three miles (4.8 km).

Giraffe
At 18 feet (5.5 m) tall, the giraffe is the tallest land mammal. Recent genetic evidence suggests that there may be as many as six species of giraffe, with variations in color and pattern. Males swing their long necks in combat and when competing for partners.

Striped hyena
A skilled scavenger, the striped hyena has strong teeth and jaw muscles that allow it to crush and digest bones. It is primarily solitary but may rest in pairs. At kill sites, striped hyenas are outcompeted by lions and other carnivores.

EAST AFRICAN SAVANNA
GRASSLAND GRAZERS

From South Africa to just south of the Sahara, grassland ecosystems are dominated by hoofed animals, or ungulates, that come in a wide variety of shapes and sizes. Some of these animals browse or eat woody vegetation, but the greatest densities are among those species that live off seasonally abundant and nutritious grasses—the grazers. The largest grazer is the white rhinoceros, weighing in at 5,000 pounds (2,200 kg), while smaller grazing gazelles, such as the oribi, may weigh as little as 20 pounds (9 kg). In the Serengeti and other large grasslands, zebra eat the taller, rougher grasses, allowing wildebeest to follow in their wake and clip off the shorter, more nourishing grasses. This grazing pattern spurs new growth, and small gazelles such as the Grant's or Thomson's are among the first to dine on the lush, short swards of new grass. This succession of grazers enhances grassland productivity and may explain the abundance of wildlife in the savannas of Africa.

African buffalo
The African buffalo is one of Africa's most abundant of large herbivores. It usually lives in herds of up to a few hundred but buffalo sometimes congregate in their thousands. Although their sight and hearing is poor, a well developed sense of smell allows them to detect predators on the open plains.

Grazing succession
Grazing animals move gradually from raised slopes to lower, damper pockets in their search for good herbage. Larger animals such as zebra are followed by wildebeest, then the smaller gazelles.

 Zebra
 Wildebeest
Thomson's Gazelle

White-eared kob
Africa's best-kept secret was recently revealed when conservationists announced that more than 1.2 million white-eared kob, tiang antelope, and Mongalla gazelle continued to migrate in South Sudan, despite 30 years of civil war. The kob migration had not only survived, but thrived, with numbers rivaling those of the Serengeti.

CONSERVATION WATCH

The two subspecies of white rhino have different histories. Nearly extinct in the early 1900s, the southern white rhino has staged a remarkable recovery, with more than 10,000 now living in South Africa. However, the northern white is now virtually extinct, with only eight to 10 surviving in the wild. The declines are because of demand for rhino horn.

MIGRATION MILES

Each year 2 million animals follow a migration path around the vast plains of the Serengeti. More than one million wildebeest, half a million zebras, and tens of thousands of African buffalo and Thomson's gazelles make the annual move, covering more than 1,000 miles (1,600 km). Not all paths traverse national parks; migrating animals still spend up to 10 percent of their journey in unprotected areas.

River crossings
Lurking crocodiles and raging rapids pose the greatest hazards during river crossings. As many as 200,000 wildebeest die during each migration from being caught in stampedes, falling victim to predators, or drowning.

Grassland communities

Grasslands, dominated by large grazing ungulates above ground and termites below ground, host a diversity of other wildlife. Rodents can occur at densities equaling the grazers. Dozens of carnivore species—from small serval cats to hyenas, leopards, cheetahs, and lions—take advantage of the variety of prey, which ranges from elephants to mice. Birds are abundant, from small larks and nightjars to the world's largest bird, the ostrich.

Thomson's gazelle
The Thomson's gazelle is known for its graceful leaps, which often reach more than 8 feet (2.5 m) in height. When stalked by predators, it will bounce or "stot" to signal that it is escaping. During migration, males establish territories that they rigorously defend in the hope of herding passing females.

Zebra
The plains zebra (above), found across eastern and southern Africa, is one of three zebra species. Grevy's zebra, found only in northern Kenya and southern Ethiopia, has fine stripes and a white belly. The mountain zebra of South Africa and Namibia has wide stripes over its hindquarters. Studies suggest that a zebra's stripes may play a role in thermoregulation—the maintenance of a stable body temperature.

MIGRATION MAP

→ Migration routes

Mara R.
Kenya
4
3
5
Serengeti National Park
2
1
Tanzania

Lining up
A winding column of blue wildebeest crosses the Serengeti–Masai Mara Nature Reserve, tracing a route used annually as they migrate across the grasslands.

Birth on the run
Approximately 400,000 wildebeest are born in the rainy season preceding migration, but births also occur along the way, placing calves at great risk. However, youngsters can stand and run within an hour of birth.

Life in the Albertine Rift

Thirty-five million years ago, the African continent almost divided in two. This event created a 6,000-mile (9,600-km) long split, or fissure, known as the East African or Great Rift Valley. An area of spectacular peaks, deep valleys, and diverse lakes, the northern section of the rift, named the Albertine Rift for England's Prince Albert, stretches from the northern tip of Lake Albert to the southern tip of Lake Tanganyika and straddles five countries—the Democratic Republic of Congo, Uganda, Rwanda, Burundi, and Tanzania. Its geographic variety has produced spectacular biological diversity. The region is home to a vast array of vertebrate species: 39 percent of Africa's mammal species, 50 percent of its birds, 19 percent of its amphibians, 14 percent of its reptiles, and a high number of freshwater fish. Representatives of these five groups, alone, total more than 7,500 species. Many are found nowhere else on Earth and a high proportion are critically endangered due to habitat loss or change.

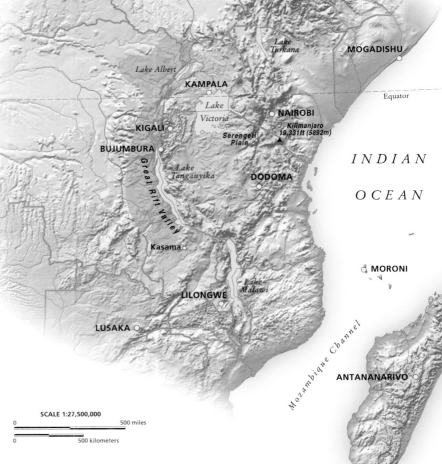

SCALE 1:27,500,000

Owl-faced monkey
Little is known about this endangered monkey. Limited to the forests of the Democratic Republic of Congo and Rwanda, it uses its elongated fingers to cling to bamboo. Infants are born with a yellowish-brown coat that darkens in colour as they mature.

High-altitude variety

The Albertine Rift is home to some of the world's most spectacular plants and animals. At altitudes above 10,000 feet (3,050 m), the giant lobelia provides nectar for many species of sunbirds. Mountain gorillas are visitors to areas dominated by heath at elevations of 9,000 to 12,000 feet (2,800–3,600 m).

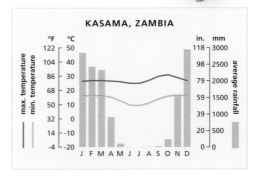

KASAMA, ZAMBIA

⚡ **CONSERVATION WATCH**
The golden monkey is so closely related to the blue monkey that they were mistakenly classed as a single species. With a soot-black coat, highlighted by a gold-orange mantle across its back and head, this endangered species is found only in the Virunga Volcanoes—home of the more famous mountain gorilla—and Nyungwe National Park, in Rwanda.

Mountain gorilla
Gorilla beringei beringei

Erica
Erica cruenta

Blue monkey
The paucity of hair on the faces of these silvery-gray furred monkeys gives them a blue appearance. They often feed and travel in groups with other primates, such as red-tailed monkeys, red colobus, and mangabeys. Such multiple species groups enhance efforts to discover new food sources and afford greater protection from predators.

Yellow-eyed black flycatchers
Melaenornis ardesiacus

Flamingos

Alkaline soda lakes have developed across this region as a result of the deposition of fine volcanic ash. The lakes are home to both the lesser and greater flamingos. Flamingos are filter feeders—they use their bills, which are lined with fine hairs, to strain water and capture small shrimplike animals. The prey contains a red pigment that gives flamingos their pink color.

Rwenzori double-collared sunbirds
Cinnyris stuhlmanni

Regal sunbird
Cinnyris regia

Bushbaby
The bushbaby is more closely related to the Madagascan lemurs than the monkeys of continental Africa. It uses its large, round eyes and ears to hunt insects and other prey at night. During the day it sleeps in tree-hollow nests.

Giant lobelia
Lobelia rhynchopetalum

Purple breasted sunbird
Nectarinia purpureiventris

CHAMELEONS

This family of lizards is best known for the ability to change color. While commonly considered a camouflage strategy, the color variation actually results from physiological changes and may be a means of communication. The upper and lower lids on a chameleon's eyes are fused, leaving it only a pinhole to see through. It grips prey—usually large insects—using suction cups on its tongue.

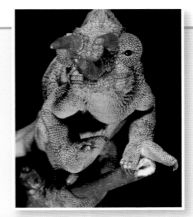

Johnston's chameleon
Endemic to the Albertine Rift, the male Johnston's chameleon resembles a mini triceratops. It uses its horns when fighting for a mate.

Strange-horned chameleon
A popular pet, famed for the bump on its nose, this over-collected chameleon is now endangered and lives only in the Rwenzori Mountains.

The Miombo Woodlands

This vast habitat spans much of south-central Africa, from southern Tanzania through Malawi, Zambia, Zimbabwe, and west to Angola through the southern part of the Democratic Republic of Congo. The Miombo woodlands covers more than 1.1 million square miles (3 million km²), which is 10 percent of the African continent, and takes its name from the Bantu word for the dominant tree genus, *Brachystegia*. The Miombo is characterized by a single, long wet season, when 30 to 39 inches (760–1000 mm) of rain falls, in contrast to the two rainy seasons of the savanna. Plant diversity is high, with more than 8,500 species, and the Miombo's suite of animals includes less common but specialized ungulates, such as Lichtenstein's hartebeest, eland, sable antelope, and black rhino. The region supports a high number of primates, including red colobus, and yellow and chacma baboons, but is perhaps best known as the home of the Gombe Stream Game Reserve, where Jane Goodall conducted her chimpanzee study.

Horned Creatures

The ungulates of the Miombo woodlands are adorned with some of the most spectacular horns of any of the African hoofed animals. Horns, which unlike antlers are not shed, serve a dual function—to protect the animals from predators and as weapons in combat between males for access to females. As a result males usually have larger, more elaborated horns than females.

Greater kudu
The corkscrew horns of the greater kudu indicate rank among males. Males interlock their horns when fighting, in an attempt to push each other off balance.

Sable antelope
Male sable antelope drop to their knees when in battle and fight with their horns, which can reach up to 40 inches (1 m) in length. They have been known to successfully defend themselves against lions.

Oryx
Supremely adapted to dry conditions, oryx occur in large herds and can survive for long periods without water. Their straight horns are extremely sharp, and can fend off lions.

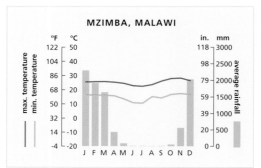

MZIMBA, MALAWI

⚡ CONSERVATION WATCH

The black rhinoceros is critically endangered—only around 4,000 remain in the wild. These rhinoceros have been heavily hunted, particularly for their horns, which are used in traditional medicine. Long, prehensile lips assist the black rhinoceros as it browses for leaves and twigs.

Animals of the woodlands

The animals of the Miombo woodlands must deal with a long, dry season each year. During the long rainy season, when water is plentiful, wildlife densities are low, and animals spread out across the landscape. When water dries up, animals congregate at high densities around the few permanent waterholes. Elephants, the dominant animal by weight, are also critical to excavating waterholes, allowing other animals access to water.

Northern carmine bee-eater
The striking carmine bee-eater catches bees on the wing and hits them against hard surfaces to remove their stings. It nests in or near riverbanks in large colonies, where the multiple nesting tunnels resemble high-rise apartments.

Dung beetle
The dung beetle serves an important function by improving soil composition and nutrient cycling. It locates dung using its keen sense of smell, rolls it into a ball, and buries it. Females lay their eggs inside the balls, which nourish the developing larvae.

Puff adder
Short and wide, the puff adder produces an extremely toxic venom and is one of the deadliest snakes in Africa. It lies in wait to ambush prey, such as small mammals and birds. When disturbed, the adder inflates its head and makes a loud hiss.

Ground pangolin
Pangolins are covered with large plate-like scales. When threatened, they curl up into a ball and the scales form a protective armor. Pangolins do not have teeth; instead, they rely on their specialized tongues to feed on ants.

Woodland home
The Miombo woodlands are home to some of Africa's most iconic predators, including leopards, wild dogs, cheetahs, hyenas, and lions. Recent studies have shown a sharp decline in the number of lions, once common across Africa, because of loss of habitat and direct persecution.

Rhinoceros defense
Rhinoceros have two forms of defense—their great bulk and long horn. Males use their horn when competing for females, and females use their horn to defend their young from predators. This critical function was demonstrated when rhinoceros were dehorned in Namibia to deter poachers. Juvenile mortality rose as a result.

Nile crocodile
An aggressive and feared predator, the Nile crocodile consumes a variety of mammals, ranging from the sitatunga to the wildebeest. Unlike most reptiles, it buries its eggs. Both parents diligently guard them and the mother continues to care for the hatchlings. Nile crocodiles have been known to live for up to 100 years.

THE OKAVANGO DELTA

The Okavango Delta, in the heart of southern Africa, is one of the largest water systems in the world that does not flow to an ocean. With its headwaters in the Cubango River, in Angola, the Okavango River runs through Namibia and terminates in a vast floodplain in northern Botswana. About 10,000 years ago, the waters fed the vast inland Lake Makgadikgadi, but earthquakes and faulting have since destroyed the lake. The delta experiences an annual cycle of flooding and retreat. Rains in Angola, beginning in October, swell the Okavango River and flood the delta. By April, dry conditions have returned, and the delta, which may then cover 6,200 square miles (16,000 km²), shrinks to nearly half that area. The lack of industry or agriculture along the river has kept its waters exceptionally pure, but proposed dams, increased human settlement, and agricultural irrigation threaten its quality and flow. The delta supports a wealth of wildlife—300 species of plants, 450 bird species, and 20 ungulate species.

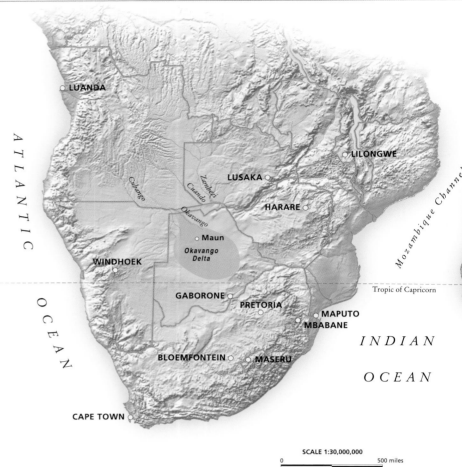

SCALE 1:30,000,000

THE HIPPOPOTAMUS

Hippopotamuses generally live in small groups, or pods, usually containing one male, several females, and their young. Sensitive to sunlight, they spend much of the day in water, venturing on to land at dusk to feed on grasses. Hippopotamus are hunted for their meat and ivory teeth. When threatened, they express their aggression by opening their mouths wide.

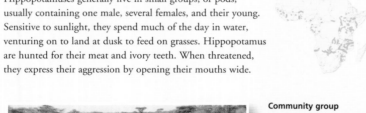

Community group
Hippopotamus pods are led by a bull, which strongly defends its territory and harem from other males. Congregations of up to 100 individuals have been observed; in some rivers hippopotamus densities are high.

Skin protection
The skin of the hippopotamus is sensitive to the harsh African sun. It secretes a red-tinted fluid that protects it against ultraviolet rays and may also have antibiotic properties.

Swamp society

The hippopotamus, widespread across Africa, commonly grazes on dry land at night. But in delta swamps it plays a critical role in maintaining pathways through thick vegetation—water lilies, papyrus, and water cabbage. These hippopotamus channels often connect lakes in the permanent swamps where waterbirds, such as the hammerkop and wattled crane, and the Cape clawless otter make their living.

Hammerhead stork
Scopus umbretta

Hippopotamus
Hippopotamus amphibius

MAUN, BOTSWANA

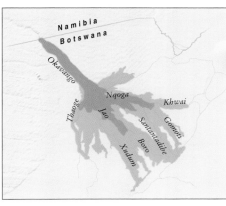

Waters of the delta

The floodplains of the Okavango Delta expand and retreat seasonally, but there are areas of permanent swamp.

- Seasonal floodplains
- Permanent swamp
- Channels

Red lechwe

The red lechwe, a medium-sized antelope, is an important food source for lions in the delta but is skilled at evading capture. Its hind quarters are longer than its forelimbs, giving it superior leaping abilities. When threatened, members of a lechwe herd disperse in different directions, effectively confusing potential predators.

Sitatunga

Sitatunga are well adapted to swamp life. Strong swimmers with water-resistant coats, they can submerge all but their nostrils and use their splayed hooves to negotiate boggy marshes. However, sitatunga are hunted for their meat and fall victim to snares set on swampy trails.

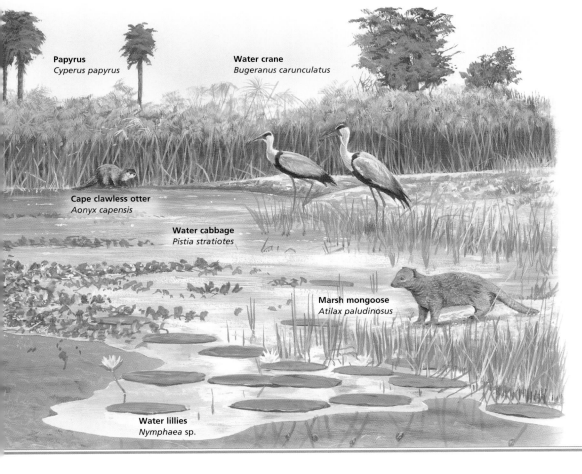

Papyrus
Cyperus papyrus

Water crane
Bugeranus carunculatus

Cape clawless otter
Aonyx capensis

Water cabbage
Pistia stratiotes

Marsh mongoose
Atilax paludinosus

Water lillies
Nymphaea sp.

AFRICA
BIG CARNIVORES

The plains and forests of Africa still support a spectacular group of large carnivores that survive by eating animals much larger than themselves. Carnivorous cats and rarer canids, similar to those still found in Africa, once prowled North America, Asia, and Europe, but were mostly exterminated 10,000 years ago. Lions, hyenas, cheetahs, leopards, and wild dogs are among the widest-ranging species found in Africa, however their pattern of vast movement puts them in direct conflict with an ever-growing human population. As available habitat is reduced, these animals begin competing with one another for food and a defined hierarchy operates, governed by those species that can successfully steal a kill from the others. The lion remains the undisputed king of beasts; hyenas trump wild dogs and cheetah; almost all species are capable of stealing from leopards, which drag their prey into trees in an effort to avoid such theft; and cheetahs employ their unsurpassed speed and cunning to outpace the competition.

AFRICAN CARNIVORE	TOP SPEED IN MILES PER HOUR (KM/H)	GROUP SIZE	LITTER SIZE
Cheetah	70 (112)	1–4	3–5
Lion	50 (80)	5–15	3–5
African wild dog	45 (72)	3–25	5–17
Hyena	40 (60)	2–90	1–2
Leopard	40 (60)	1	2–3

Spotted hyena
Spotted hyenas are among the most effective hunters on the African plains. They kill most of their own food and hunt in packs, chasing down weak or young animals. They efficiently crush bones using their massive teeth and strong jaw muscles, ingesting and digesting body parts that many other predators leave behind. Females are the dominant sex and possess sexual organs that are masculine in appearance. An alpha or dominant female leads each complex hyena clan, which may number up to 80 individuals.

Leopard
The leopard is an opportunistic, solitary hunter that prefers mid-sized antelope. Graceful and elegant, it silently stalks its prey. Like the cheetah and wild dog, the leopard hunts in areas and at times not favored by lions and hyenas, caching fresh kills in trees. Males have large ranges that encompass several female home ranges, but leopards are almost never seen in groups.

Cheetah
The cheetah is best known for its speed and has been clocked at up to 70 miles per hour (112 km/h). It can achieve such speed because of its streamlined body and enlarged heart and lungs. Cheetahs range over large areas and are threatened by habitat loss.

CHEETAH POPULATION

Kenya
Somalia
Tanzania
Angola Zambia
Namibia Zimbabwe
Botswana
South Africa

☐ Cheetah population circa 1900

Cheetah population circa 2000

☐ Low population density

☐ Medium population density

☐ High population density

● Protected area

LIONS

Once found across Africa, southern Europe, and western Asia, lions are now restricted to the savannas and grasslands of eastern and southern Africa. The largest of the African carnivores, they live in prides consisting of five to 10 related females and a coalition of two to three males. Loss of habitat forces them into conflict with humans and livestock, and populations have recently plummeted.

Mane
Only male lions have manes. The mane size and color indicates male quality, but not without a cost. The dark manes preferred by females raise a male's body temperature, demanding more energy use, and make the male more conspicuous.

Cubs
A lioness gives birth to a litter of up to four cubs, which are introduced to the pride at six weeks. Females may synchronize the timing of births and often nurse each others' offspring.

⚡ **CONSERVATION WATCH**

Once found across Africa in every habitat except true rain forest, the African wild dog has been exterminated from 32 African countries and fewer than 5,000 remain. Disease contracted from domestic dogs, habitat fragmentation, roads, snaring, and direct persecution have all contributed to the wild dog's decline. However, recent conservation efforts appear to be helping the species recover. Wild dogs hunt in packs of up to 20 adults and communally rear a single litter of puppies born to the dominant female.

Hunting
Females are the hunters of the pride, chasing down prey as a unit. They kill by strangulation or delivering a bite to the neck or head. Males may feed first, despite contributing little to the kill.

LIFE IN THE KALAHARI

The Kalahari describes a vast plateau in southern Africa. It includes both a large desert of about 200,000 square miles (518,000 km²) that covers part of Botswana, South Africa, and Namibia; and a much larger basin measuring some 400,000 square miles (1.03 million km²) that extends north into Angola and Zambia. This basin skirts the western edge of Zimbabwe and includes the whole Okavango River and delta system. At an altitude of approximately 3,000 feet (915 m), the Kalahari is not a true desert but a semi-desert, where stationary sand dunes are covered by grasslands, acacia woodlands, and acacia scrub. The flush of grass that follows annual rain supports some of the most significant wildlife populations in the region, including species once common across Africa, such as the giraffe, elephant, rhinoceros, and lion. Parks in the region include the Central Kalahari Game Reserve, the world's second largest protected area, and the Kgalagadi Transfrontier Park. San Bushmen have long wandered this landscape, living nomadically in the Kalahari for the past 20,000 years.

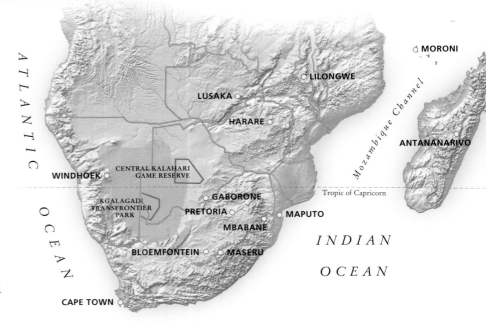

SCALE 1:35,000,000

0 ———— 500 miles
0 ———— 500 kilometers

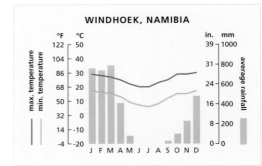

DESERT ADAPTATIONS

Wildlife in the Kalahari have adapted to the harsh environment primarily by living at low densities, being active at night, and traveling vast distances. Water, not food, is the key limiting resource. During the wet season, animals fan out across the Kalahari; they survive the drier periods by retreating to the seasonal riverbeds. Elephants—which excavate water holes in the rivers—are critical to the survival of many other species.

Elephant memory
The desert-dwelling elephants of Namibia are smaller than other elephants and can endure many days without water. Like others of their kind, they have a fine memory and may travel more than 45 miles (70 km) to reach water holes and feeding grounds they recall previously visiting.

Lion economies
The lions of the desert have lighter fur and black manes as an adaptation to the extreme daytime temperatures. They travel in smaller groups, over larger ranges, and hunt smaller mammals than lions living elsewhere.

Cape fox
The Cape fox is nocturnal and avoids the heat of the day by resting in burrows underground. It enjoys a varied diet of small mammals, insects, and reptiles, and may cache, or hide, its food.

Aardwolf
Despite being a member of the hyena family, the nocturnal aardwolf subsists on a diet of ants, consuming as many as 200,000 a night. It extracts them from mounds using its sticky tongue and is capable of detoxifying soldier ants. The aardwolf defends itself by secreting a substance similar to that of a skunk.

Springbok
The springbok is named for its tendency to "pronk," or repeatedly leap up to 13 feet (4 m), when escaping predators. During the pronk, a fold of skin with a crest of white fur is exposed on the rump. The springbok can survive for extended periods without water and tends to feed before dawn, when vegetation is most succulent, and at night, when dew has settled on plants.

Gemsbok
The gemsbok, or oryx, relies mainly on water contained within grass for moisture. It has a distinctive black pattern on its white face, with black stripes extending down its back and belly. Oryx have graceful horns that can reach 30 inches (76 cm), with the female growing taller and thinner horns than those of her male counterpart.

Aardvark
Powerful legs, special claws, a long snout and sticky tongue enable the aardvark to dig through termite mounds and ant nests (right), its thick skin wards off bites from prey. Aardvarks regularly dig themselves new burrows (above), which allows other mammals to use their abandoned shelters.

Meerkats

Meerkats, an iconic Kalahari species, live in clans of up to 50 individuals, dominated by a single breeding pair. Family members excavate burrows, help raise pups, and watch out for predators. Meerkats mostly eat insects, excavated using their non-retractable claws. While foraging, at least one clan member serves as sentry, scanning for predators. Meerkats often stand in the morning sun to warm their belly skin.

MADAGASCAR

More than 100 million years ago, Madagascar broke off from the African continent and for much of its history has been completely isolated. It is the world's fourth largest island, with an area of 226,000 square miles (587,000 km²). Its isolation, as well as the variety of habitats on the island, has contributed to the unusual diversity of wildlife that is found in Madagascar and nowhere else on Earth. The western and southern regions of the island are dominated by dry forests and thorny deserts and they harbor animals adapted to dry conditions. Along the eastern side of the island habitats are wetter and some of the most diverse tropical forests are found here. Overall, Madagascar is home to an astonishing 5 percent of the world's species, and 80 percent of them are endemic. Best known are the lemurs—a group of approximately 70 primate species. Despite the island being densely populated by humans and poor by global standards, the Madagascan government is making huge efforts to save the island's natural heritage.

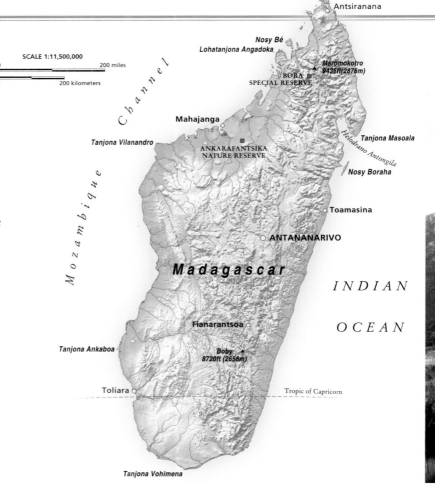

SCALE 1:11,500,000

0 — 200 miles
0 — 200 kilometers

Tanjona Bobaomby
Antsiranana
Nosy Bé
Lohatanjona Angadoka
Maromokotro 9436ft (2876m)
BORA SPECIAL RESERVE
Mahajanga
Tanjona Vilanandro
ANKARAFANTSIKA NATURE RESERVE
Tanjona Masoala
Helodrano Antongila
Nosy Boraha
Toamasina
ANTANANARIVO
Madagascar
Fianarantsoa
Tanjona Ankaboa
Boby 8720ft (2658m)
Toliara
Tropic of Capricorn
Tanjona Vohimena
Mozambique Channel
INDIAN OCEAN

SMALL FOREST CREATURES

With more than 400 species of reptiles and 300 species of frogs, Madagascar hosts a wide diversity of reptiles and amphibians. Half of the world's chameleon species exist only in Madagascar. Some evolutionary affinities are unexpected: pythons do not occur here but an endemic boa constrictor has its closest relatives in South America.

Panther chameleon
Found throughout Madagascar's tropical forest, the male panther chameleon is nearly twice the size of the female, and more vibrantly colored. Chameleons' coloration and patterns are social signals.

Giant leaf-tailed gecko
A master of camouflage, the giant leaf-tailed gecko spends much of its day resting while hanging upside down by its tail. If disturbed, it will stand with head and tail erect and emit a loud hiss.

Tomato frog
Despite its bright red color, the tomato frog sits quietly as it waits to ambush its insect prey. Its coloration acts as a warning to predators; if attacked it puffs up its body and gives off a toxic sticky substance.

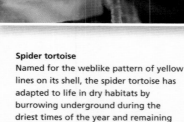

Spider tortoise
Named for the weblike pattern of yellow lines on its shell, the spider tortoise has adapted to life in dry habitats by burrowing underground during the driest times of the year and remaining buried until the rainy season begins.

Fossa
The fossa is the dominant and largest predator on Madagascar. More than 50 percent of its diet is made up of lemurs. Closely related to the mongoose, it is agile both on the ground and in trees. Widely distributed, it is always found at low densities, which makes it vulnerable to extinction.

ANTANANARIVO, MADAGASCAR

°F	°C		in.	mm
122	50		118	3000
104	40		98	2500
86	30		79	2000
68	20		59	1500
50	10		39	1000
32	0		20	500
14	-10		0	0
-4	-20			

max. temperature / min. temperature / average rainfall

J F M A M J J A S O N D

Lemur diversity

The sifakas, wooly lemurs, and the indri, all in the Indriidae family, are the largest lemurs: indris may weigh up to 22 pounds (10 kg). The world's smallest primate, the gray mouse lemur, weighs one to two ounces (40–60 grams). Mid-sized lemurs, such as the red-bellied lemur, weigh about 3 pounds (1.4 kg). The ruffed lemurs are the only primates to produce young in litters.

Gray mouse lemur
Microcebus murinus

Indri
Indri indri

🔴 **Red-ruffed lemur**
Varecia variegata rubra

Red-bellied lemur
Eulemur rubriventer

Island landscape
The weathering of rocky outcrops in the south of Madagascar has created some spectacular landforms. Also found here is a unique habitat, characterized by tall, spiny vegetation. Baobabs, aloes, and cactus-like euphorbia are common, but the most distinctive plants are the endemic Dideraceae trees, inlcuding the octopus tree.

Ring-tailed lemur
The ring-tailed lemur is the most terrestrial of the lemurs and is often found "sunbathing" in an upright stance. Like most lemurs, females are dominant. Aggressive interactions often include "stink fights," which involve flicking tails coated with a scent from glands in the wrist.

Malagasy civet
Found throughout Madagascar, the Malagasy civet, which looks like a small fox, typically lives in pairs that share a territory. Its diet is made up of small animals—rodents, birds, reptiles, and frogs. To cope with times of food shortage the fat stored in its tail may comprise up to 25 percent of its body weight.

⚡ **CONSERVATION WATCH**

The striking Coquerel's sifaka, a lemur, has never been numerous. It is found at low densities and only in the dry deciduous forests of northwestern Madagascar at altitudes of less than 300 feet (90 m). The loss of these forests to agriculture, and habitat degradation, are the main threats to the species, which is found only in two small, protected areas, the Ankarafantsika Nature Reserve and the Bora Special Reserve.

AYE-AYE

Perhaps the most distinctive of the Malagasy primates, the nocturnal aye-aye was originally mistaken for a rodent. In part this is because of its strange appearance as well as its rodent-like incisors that continue to grow throughout its life. It is the largest nocturnal primate, with big eyes and large, sensitive ears. Some local traditions identify aye-ayes with bad luck, often leading to their persecution.

Claws
Pointed claws allow aye-ayes to hang from branches. The distinctive elongated middle finger is used to tap tree branches to find and extract insect grubs inside.

Mother and young
Aye-ayes live a primarily solitary life with the only long-term bond being the one between a mother and her young.

AFRICA'S CORAL REEFS

While corals fringe the African continent, true reefs are mostly found off the east coast, from the Red Sea south to Mozambique and across to Madagascar. West and Central Africa, on the Atlantic coast, also possess some diverse corals, particularly on the islands of Cape Verde, but a combination of high rainfall and strong Atlantic currents, with cold oceanic upwellings, largely inhibits reef formation. Coral reefs are biologically diverse, highly productive, and critical to local fisheries and subsistence fishermen. This is particularly true for the densely populated coasts of Kenya, Tanzania, Mozambique, and Madagascar. Industrial run-off and pollutants, untreated sewage, and increasing sediment flows in rivers all threaten these coastal ecosystems. But most serious of all are the threats posed by global climate change. Sea surface temperature increases—the result of climate change and a particularly severe El Niño in 1997–98—hit the Western Indian Ocean particularly hard, killing 90 percent of corals across a large expanse.

MORONI, COMOROS

SCALE 1:45,000,000

750 miles

750 kilometers

ORNAMENTAL SHELLS

Mollusk shells are multilayered. The mother-of-pearl layer is made up primarily of calcium carbonate and gives the shell its luster and distinctive pattern. Shells are a protective fortress for the soft-bodied mollusks living within, their color and patterns providing camouflage from a multitude of predators. Algae may live along the lips of clam shells, where they trap sunlight and deliver the clam an energy-rich supply of food.

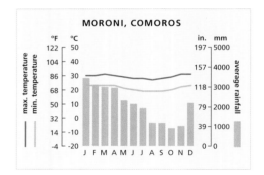

Cowrie
Cowries live under rocks and feed on algae at night. Their smooth, porcelain-like shells are wrapped in a mantle that is often brilliantly colored. In Africa, the shells were once used as currency and for decorating cloth and baskets.

Maxima clam
Clams are bivalves, having two shells to protect their soft bodies. The maxima clam lives in shallow waters near the top of the reef, where it attaches itself to the coral rubble or limestone surface and filters water to trap plankton.

Mantis shrimp
The stalked, compound eyes of the mantis shrimp are among the most complex of the animal kingdom. These active hunters use their robust claws to repeatedly smash prey, employing forces so strong that they have been known to crack glass.

Starfish
Starfish lack a centralized brain, but have two stomachs to digest their prey, and at least five arms, which they can regenerate if severed. A covering of spines prevents organisms from colonizing the skin of starfish, all of which can reproduce sexually and asexually.

Sweetlips
As its name suggests, the black-spotted sweetlip that lives in the Indian Ocean can be recognized by its lips and spots. Juveniles have six lines down their back, which later develop into spots. Sweetlips feed at night on invertebrates and can grow up to 18 inches (45 cm) in length.

Humphead wrasse
One of the largest fish inhabiting the coral reef, the humphead wrasse is distinguished by a large bulge on its head. Highly sedentary, it is active by day and rests in reef caves at night. A long lifespan—about 32 years—and slow breeding rate make the humphead wrasse vulnerable to over-fishing.

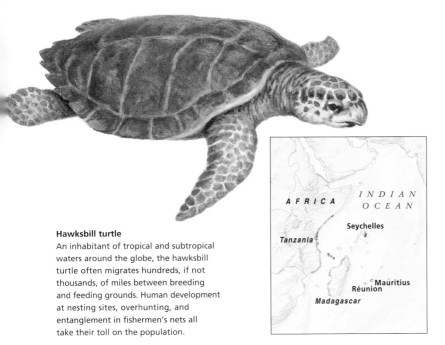

Hawksbill turtle
An inhabitant of tropical and subtropical waters around the globe, the hawksbill turtle often migrates hundreds, if not thousands, of miles between breeding and feeding grounds. Human development at nesting sites, overhunting, and entanglement in fishermen's nets all take their toll on the population.

AFRICA

INDIAN OCEAN

Seychelles

Tanzania

Mauritius

Réunion

Madagascar

ESTIMATED THREAT TO CORAL REEF

- Low
- Medium
- High

Potato grouper
Found in the Red Sea and Indo-West Pacific, the potato grouper is a large fish that feeds on other reef fish and crustaceans. It is highly territorial and known for its aggression, but its size makes the grouper susceptible to spear-fishing.

Frilled lizards are found in New Guinea and the tropical north and east coast of Australia. The capelike frill that lies over the lizard's shoulders flares up when it is frightened or angry, making it appear twice its actual size. The lizard opens its mouth wide, hisses loudly, and pushes up on its front legs to ward off predators.

AUSTRALASIA
& OCEANIA

AUSTRALASIA & OCEANIA

The biogeographic region of Australasia extends from the easternmost islands of the Indonesian archipelago to New Guinea and Australia. The region known as Oceania incorporates all the island groups in the southern Pacific Ocean, including New Zealand. Most of the land in these two regions consists of three remnants of what was once the ancient continent Gondwana; Australia and New Guinea being the largest, and New Zealand and New Caledonia the smaller fragments. The remaining island groups are mainly volcanic in origin or formed as coral atolls perched atop submerged volcanic remnants. The flora and fauna of Australasia and Oceania is rich in old endemic species that had ancestors in the forests of Gondwana. Foremost among the floral relicts are the Araucaria pines and southern beeches. Among the fauna, the large flightless ratite birds, monotremes, and marsupial mammals are also reminders of previous Gondwanan wildlife.

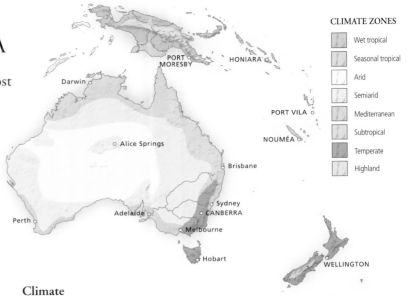

CLIMATE ZONES

Wet tropical
Seasonal tropical
Arid
Semiarid
Mediterranean
Subtropical
Temperate
Highland

Climate

Close proximity to the equator produces warm, humid conditions across much of Oceania. Hurricanes, known locally as cyclones, occur above 5 degrees south during the summer and extend to the northern latitudes of Australia. The middle latitudes are cooler, and moist onshore winds ensure regular rainfall in New Zealand and on Australia's east coast. However, the Australian interior is arid; less than 12 inches (300 mm) of rainfall is recorded each year across about half the continent.

New Guinea Highlands
The rain forests of the New Guinea highlands are home to many unique species of mammals and birds, including the tree kangaroos and birds-of-paradise.

The Tropical North
The "Top End" of Australia, with its iconic magnetic termite mounds, is home to many unique species adapted to the extremes of heavy summer rains and dry winters.

New Zealand
The kiwi is synonymous with New Zealand. It is one of the few survivors of an ancient line of flightless birds that once inhabited the great southern continent of Gondwana.

The Great Barrier Reef
Australia's Great Barrier Reef is the largest fringing coral reef in the world and its abundant coral and fish species make it an important global biodiversity hot spot.

The Australian Outback
The deserts of central Australia are home to arid-adapted species such as the bearded dragon, but oases in the form of artesian springs and ephemeral lakes occur here too.

Islands of the Southeast Pacific
Lord Howe Island is home to a host of seabirds that nest on its predator-free shores. Other islands are a sanctuary for endemic species including flightless birds.

Wildlife of Cape York
Cape York is both the bridge and the barrier between Australia and New Guinea, and its flora and fauna contain a fascinating mix of species from both major landmasses.

Temperate Southern Forests and Heathlands
Like the eucalyptus trees on which it feeds, Australia's iconic animal, the koala, is one of the most readily identified inhabitants of the temperate southern forests.

PROPORTIONS OF TOTAL LAND AREA

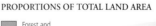

Forest and woodland
Arable land
Grazing
Other land

20.4%
23.6%
6.6%
49.4%

Land cover

Most of the Australian continent, as well as New Zealand, is suited to grazing, but in Australia livestock must roam widely to find sufficient food. Overall, one-quarter of Oceania is covered with forests. Arable land is scarce on many Pacific Islands, except where good rainfall and volcanic soils ensure agricultural productivity.

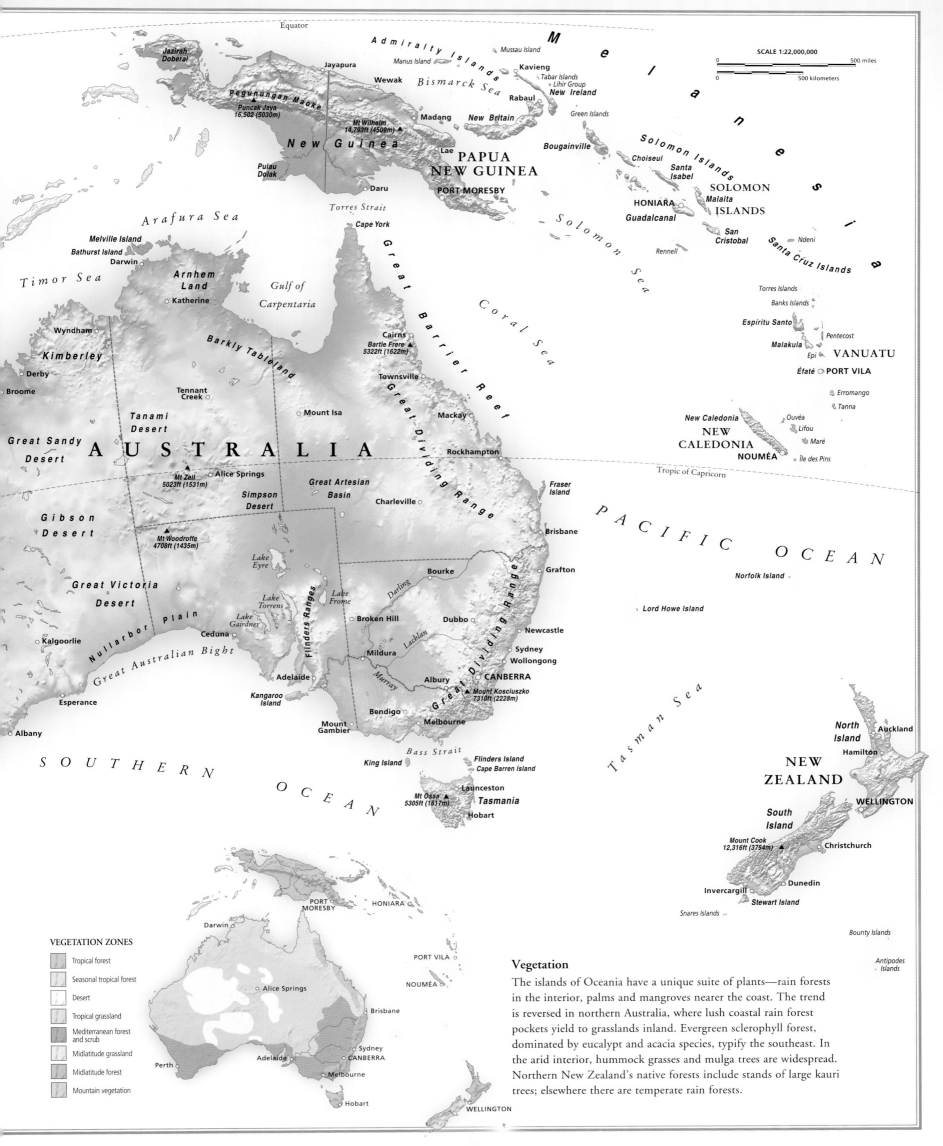

Equator

M e l a n e s i a

Jazirah
Doberai

Jayapura

Admiralty Islands

Mussau Island

Manus Island

Wewak

Bismarck Sea

Kavieng

Tabar Islands
Lihir Group

New Ireland

SCALE 1:22,000,000

0   500 miles

0   500 kilometers

Pegunungan Maoke
Puncak Jaya
16,502 (5030m)

Mt Wilhelm
14,793ft (4509m) ▲

Madang

Rabaul

New Britain

Green Islands

New Guinea

Lae

Pulau
Dolak

Daru

**PAPUA
NEW GUINEA**

PORT MORESBY

Bougainville

Solomon Islands

Choiseul

Santa
Isabel

**SOLOMON
ISLANDS**

HONIARA

Guadalcanal

Malaita

San
Cristobal

Ndeni

Solomon Sea

Rennell

Santa Cruz Islands

Arafura Sea

Torres Strait

Cape York

Torres Islands

Banks Islands

Espíritu Santo

Pentecost

Malakula

Epi

VANUATU

Melville Island

Bathurst Island

Darwin

Arnhem
Land

Katherine

*Gulf of
Carpentaria*

Cairns

Bartle Frere
5322ft (1622m)

Great Barrier Reef

Coral Sea

Éfaté **PORT VILA**

Timor Sea

Wyndham

Kimberley

Derby

Broome

Tennant
Creek

*Tanami
Desert*

Barkly Tableland

Townsville

Mackay

Erromango

Tanna

New Caledonia

Ouvéa

Lifou

**NEW
CALEDONIA**

Maré

*Great Sandy
Desert*

AUSTRALIA

Mt Zeil
5023ft (1531m) ▲

Alice Springs

*Simpson
Desert*

*Great Artesian
Basin*

Rockhampton

NOUMÉA

Île des Pins

Tropic of Capricorn

Mount Isa

Great Dividing Range

Charleville

Fraser
Island

*Gibson
Desert*

Mt Woodroffe
4708ft (1435m) ▲

Brisbane

Norfolk Island

*Great Victoria
Desert*

Lake
Eyre

Flinders Ranges

Lake
Torrens

Lake
Frome

Bourke

Darling

Grafton

Lord Howe Island

Kalgoorlie

Nullarbor Plain

Ceduna

Lake
Gairdner

Broken Hill

Dubbo

Lachlan

Newcastle

Esperance

Great Australian Bight

Adelaide

Mildura

Murray

Albury

Sydney

Wollongong

CANBERRA

Albany

Kangaroo
Island

Bendigo

Mount
Gambier

▲ Mount Kosciuszko
7310ft (2228m)

Melbourne

*North
Island*

Auckland

Hamilton

Bass Strait

King Island

Flinders Island

Cape Barren Island

Tasman Sea

**NEW
ZEALAND**

WELLINGTON

Mt Ossa ▲
5305ft (1617m)

Launceston

Tasmania

Hobart

*South
Island*

Mount Cook
12,316ft (3754m) ▲

Christchurch

S O U T H E R N   O C E A N

P A C I F I C   O C E A N

Invercargill

Dunedin

Stewart Island

Snares Islands

Bounty Islands

Antipodes
Islands

VEGETATION ZONES

Tropical forest

Seasonal tropical forest

Desert

Tropical grassland

Mediterranean forest
and scrub

Midlatitude grassland

Midlatitude forest

Mountain vegetation

PORT
MORESBY

HONIARA

Darwin

PORT VILA

NOUMÉA

Alice Springs

Brisbane

Sydney

CANBERRA

Perth

Adelaide

Melbourne

Hobart

WELLINGTON

Vegetation

The islands of Oceania have a unique suite of plants—rain forests
in the interior, palms and mangroves nearer the coast. The trend
is reversed in northern Australia, where lush coastal rain forest
pockets yield to grasslands inland. Evergreen sclerophyll forest,
dominated by eucalypt and acacia species, typify the southeast. In
the arid interior, hummock grasses and mulga trees are widespread.
Northern New Zealand's native forests include stands of large kauri
trees; elsewhere there are temperate rain forests.

MONOTREMES AND OTHER UNIQUE ANIMALS

Australia has unique remnants of the fauna that existed on the southern supercontinent, Gondwana, 200 million years ago. These include lungfish, ratites (large flightless birds), endemic turtles and frogs, and monotremes. Monotremes, or egg-laying mammals, are the only survivors of the early mammals that arose while dinosaurs dominated Earth. Fossil monotremes are found in South America and Australia, but the living species occur only in Australia and New Guinea. The surviving platypus species is found only in eastern Australia and the two echidna species, with short and long beaks, occur in Australia and New Guinea respectively. Until the Pleistocene period, 50,000 years ago, the long-beaked echidna's relatives also occurred in Australia. Monotremes have advanced mammalian characteristics, such as hair, mammary glands, although not teats, and a large cerebral cortex, but they retain some primitive reptilian features.

Short-beaked echidna
The short-beaked echidna is a spiky, rotund creature widely distributed throughout Australia and lowland New Guinea, where its preferred prey are plentiful. The echidna's diet consists of ants and termites, which it consumes in enormous quantities. It is frequently seen foraging by day, except during the hottest months of the year. When threatened, it can dig vertically into the soil, leaving only a few spines visible.

Claws and tongue
Echidnas use their powerful claws to excavate the nests and feeding tunnels of ants and termites. They then insert their long, sticky tongues into the galleries to lap up the insects.

Platypus
Platypus swim with their webbed front feet, using their hind feet to steer. When diving, they close their eyes and ears and search for food using electroreceptors within their beak, which detect the movement of prey. They are found in streams, rivers, and lakes in eastern Australia.

Monotremes
Monotremes lay eggs, which hatch after a short incubation period in either a nest or the mother's pouch. The young lap milk from the mother's mammary glands. In echidnas, the mammary glands lie within a pouch on the mother's belly. The highly specialized diet of the platypus includes freshwater crustaceans and insect larvae; the long-beaked echidna eats worms. All monotremes have a daily period of torpor (a deep sleep when the body temperature is lowered) and, in southern latitudes, the short-beaked echidna may hibernate in winter.

CURIOUS CREATURES

In addition to monotremes, Australia is home to many other unique animals. Among the most recognizable are the emu and cassowary, large flightless birds related to the ostrich of Africa and rheas of South America. Rarely seen inhabitants of inland waters, the lobe-finned lungfish and soft-shelled turtle also have relatives in Africa and South America. Ground frogs and toadlets, once considered part of an American family, are now recognized as uniquely Australian.

Pig-nosed turtle
Found only in Australia's far north, pig-nosed turtles are notable for their soft shells, which lack bony dermal plates. They live and breed in freshwater, flood-prone rivers, where the rising waters stimulate their eggs to hatch.

Australian lungfish
These air-breathing fish are restricted to two rivers in Queensland. Their lungs allow them to breathe air when caught in shallow pools but, unlike their African and American cousins, they cannot survive in mud alone.

Platypus young

The mother platypus incubates her eggs for two weeks in a nest near the end of a long burrow. She then suckles her young until they are old enough to forage, leaving them briefly to feed herself.

Burrow
The long nesting burrow ends in a small chamber lined with vegetation.

Entrance
Vegetation conceals the entrance, which is close to the water.

Corroboree frog
This colorful frog is restricted to sphagnum bogs above 3,500 feet (1,000 m) in the Australian Alps. It has a short breeding season and lays its large eggs in deep burrows.

Emu
Widespread over most of Australia, emus eat the leaves and flowers of a variety of native plants, as well as insects. The male incubates the eggs and cares for the young for at least six months. At maturity, emus can reach 8 feet (2.5 m) in height.

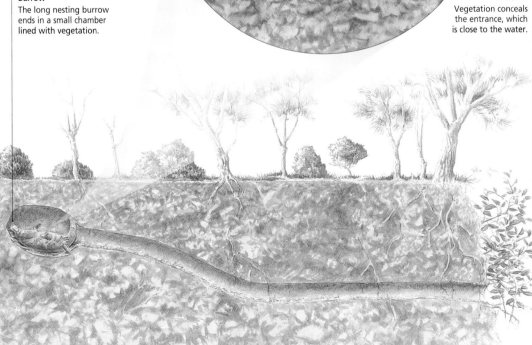

AUSTRALASIA & OCEANIA
AUSTRALIA'S MARSUPIALS

Marsupials evolved on the great southern continent of Gondwana around the time it was breaking up, and formed a major part of the early mammal fauna of both South America and Australia. In Australia they became the dominant mammals for much of the early Tertiary period, 65 million years ago. Marsupials have a more primitive brain and skeletal features, particularly the skull, than placental mammals. They deliver live young, but the young are born at an embryonic stage of development and newborns attach themselves to a teat, generally enclosed in a pouch on the mother's belly, where they are fed until they are fully furred and able to move around. Australia's living marsupials range in size from the tiny, three-inch (8 cm) planigale, which lives in grasslands, to the red kangaroo, which stands at 5 feet (1.5 m). However, the fossil record reveals more impressive marsupials of times gone by, such as giant wombats that reached the size of a modern-day rhinoceros.

Koala
The koala looks sleepy because it lives on a diet of highly toxic eucalypt leaves. It has the ability to detoxify the poisons but the effort required leaves little energy to spare. Koalas do not make nests but simply sleep in the fork of a tree.

Common wombat
The stout frame and limbs of the common wombat make it a formidable landscape architect, capable of excavating extensive burrow systems with nesting chambers and multiple entrances. A grazer, the wombat forages for food at night. Its large colon enables it to live, like a horse, on dry grasses.

Broad skull · Strong shoulders · Broad chest · Strong claws for digging

Southern brown bandicoot
Isoodon obesulus

Diverse habitats

Marsupials live in a variety of habitats. Trees provide shelter and food for possums, gliders, and the koala; rocky slopes are home to rock wallabies and wallaroos; and grassy nests hide the brown bandicoot. The elusive marsupial mole ploughs through soft sand without making a permanent burrow.

CONSERVATION WATCH

The Tasmanian devil, a carnivorous marsupial, is under severe threat from a virus that causes debilitating facial tumors. This contagious, fatal disease seems to be transferred between animals through biting. Efforts are continuing to establish a vaccine and an isolated, disease-free population. It is feared that the wild population could become extinct. Of Australia's 170 marsupial species, 10 are extinct, a further 34 are listed by the International Union for Conservation of Nature (IUCN) as threatened, and 26 are on the verge of threatened status.

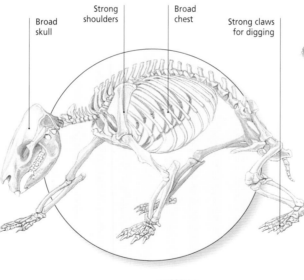

Sugar glider
Petaurus breviceps

Greater glider
Petauroides volans

Ringtail possum
Pseudocheirus peregrinus

Rock wallaby
Petrogale xanthopus

Spotted-tailed quoll
Dasyurus maculatus

Marsupial mole
Notoryctes typhlops

Protection
A half-grown joey spends many hours playing and hopping around but if hungry, tired, or threatened, it executes a quick somersault into its mother's protective pouch.

The joey pushes front feet and head into the pouch

It rolls forward into the pouch

It twists around to face outward

MARSUPIALS LARGE AND SMALL

Marsupials in Australia occur in all terrestrial habitats but are most numerous in wetter forested areas with more dense and diverse vegetation. Despite this, the majority of marsupials occupy select feeding niches. More than half are carnivores or insectivores/omnivores and most of the remainder are herbivores. The koala and greater glider can eat highly toxic eucalypt leaves. Termites, pollen and nectar, gums, resins, and fungi comprise other specialized marsupial diets.

Honey possum
Mouselike honey possums feast on pollen and nectar, reaching their brush-tipped tongues into the flowers of banksias and other heathland plants.

Brown antechinus
The brown antechinus, a small carnivorous marsupial, nests in hollow logs or in rock crevices, emerging at night to feed on beetles and spiders.

Red kangaroo
Widespread across Australia's inland, the red kangaroo browses on grasses and shrubs. It rests under trees by day, feeding mostly at dawn and dusk.

NEW GUINEA HIGHLANDS

The highlands of New Guinea are generally considered to include land over 3,000 feet (914 m). They consist of a central cordillera running east-west along the island, two large outliers on the Vogelkop and Huon peninsulas, and several smaller isolated mountain ranges. These highland areas amount to nearly 30 percent of New Guinea's total land area. The vegetation found here ranges from palm forests and rain forest in the wettest areas to tree-fern savannas and grasslands on the drier slopes. The extensive open grasslands characteristic of many highland valleys, known as kunai grasslands, may not be the result of human clearing but a natural vegetation type in areas of lower rainfall and soil fertility. Among the native mammal and bird species there is considerable variability in different regions. Subspecies or local variants might occur along the central range while related but distinct species are found on the peninsulas.

CONSERVATION WATCH

The long-beaked echidna was once a common resident of the rain forests above 2,000 feet (600 m) throughout New Guinea. It was, however, a delicacy for the Papuan peoples. Hunting, combined with a drastic loss of habitat, has resulted in it becoming endangered.

PORT MORESBY, PAPUA NEW GUINEA

SCALE 1:8,000,000

Remote landscapes

The rugged terrain of the New Guinea highlands and the small population, found mostly in scattered villages, has resulted in much of the densely forested country remaining undisturbed. The animal life found here—the cuscus, tree kangaroo, colorful Birds-of-Paradise, and the long-beaked echidna —are adapted to forest living. But, increasingly, human activities are causing habitat loss.

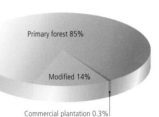

Primary forest 85%

Modified 14%

Commercial plantation 0.3%

Forests
The forests of New Guinea's highlands vary in nature according to altitude. On the lower slopes rain forests support flowering, fruit-bearing trees, which attract fruit bats, numerous birds, and some of the world's largest birdwing butterflies. On higher slopes the forest thins, gradually giving way to small subalpine trees and grasses.

Birdwing butterfly
The male Poseidon birdwing butterfly is often seen as a brilliant flash of iridescent green and yellow as it flits through the dappled light of the forest understory. Larvae of the birdwing feed on rain forest vines of the genus *Aristolochia*.

Goodfellow's tree kangaroo
Living in the rain forests of the Central Highlands, Goodfellow's tree kangaroo has suffered habitat loss because of forest-clearing for agriculture. However, it remains the most widespread species within the ornate tree kangaroo group.

Spotted cuscus
One of the most widespread mammals of New Guinea, the spotted cuscus occurs in all habitat types. It has long been a favorite food of the Papuan people, and has been transported to many of New Guinea's neighboring islands.

BIRDS-OF-PARADISE

Birds-of-paradise are synonymous with the island of New Guinea and the bright plumes the birds employ in their spectacular displays have been adopted by the local peoples in their equally colorful headdresses. The birds' range extends to Indonesia and subtropical Australia, but the center of diversity is in the New Guinea highlands. The bright, gaudy males perform elaborate acrobatic displays.

Raggiana bird-of-paradise
The Raggiana bird-of-paradise is the most common species in this family. Males gather in groups known as leks to perform their spectacular dance routines, which are accompanied by high-pitched calls.

King of Saxony
The male King of Saxony is unique, with its two long head plumes, but the female is easily mistaken for a drab honeyeater. Solitary males display from a dead limb high in the canopy.

Superb bird-of-paradise
The male superb bird-of-paradise is unmistakable, with electric-blue false wings on its chest and lustrous black erectile back feathers.

Huon astrapia
Huon astrapias are, like other astrapias, quiet birds of the middle to upper canopy. They fly in a characteristic flap-and-glide pattern, with their enormous tails trailing behind.

Blue bird-of-paradise
The male blue bird-of-paradise is solitary, unlike its close relative the Raggiana bird-of-paradise. It is also secretive, displaying in the treetops high on a hillside.

Manus Island

Bismarck Archipelago

New Ireland

Bismarck

Sea

Rabaul

New Britain

Huon Peninsula

Solomon

Sea

Kokoda

D'Entrecasteaux Islands

PORT MORESBY

Owen Stanley Ra.

GREAT BARRIER REEF

The Great Barrier Reef, a magnificent strand of coral reefs and islands set in clear, warm tropical waters, was one of Australia's first World Heritage nominations and was inscribed on the World Heritage List in 1981. Running parallel to the far northeast coast and spanning nearly 14 degrees of latitude the reef is the largest World Heritage Area. It covers some 134,286 square miles (347,800 km²) and The Great Barrier Reef Marine Park, which was declared in 1975 and which affords protection to the reef and its wildlife, contains most of the designated WHA. Despite its name, the reef is not one long barrier, but a series of 760 separate fringing reefs and more than 2,000 other reefs and cays inside the barrier, which range in size from less than 2.5 acres (1 ha) to more than 250,000 acres (100,000 ha). The shallow tropical water, with surface temperatures in the range of 75–86°F (24–30ºC), is an ideal environment for a wide variety of marine animals.

Marine life

The reef itself is composed of the skeletons of more than 300 species of hard corals and supports a highly diverse collection of marine life. It is home to more than 1,500 species of fish, 4,000 mollusk species, and over 400 species of sponge. Within its protected waters extensive seagrass beds provide food for dugongs and green turtles, and shelter for countless other creatures. The many small islands and coral cays support large numbers of nesting seabirds.

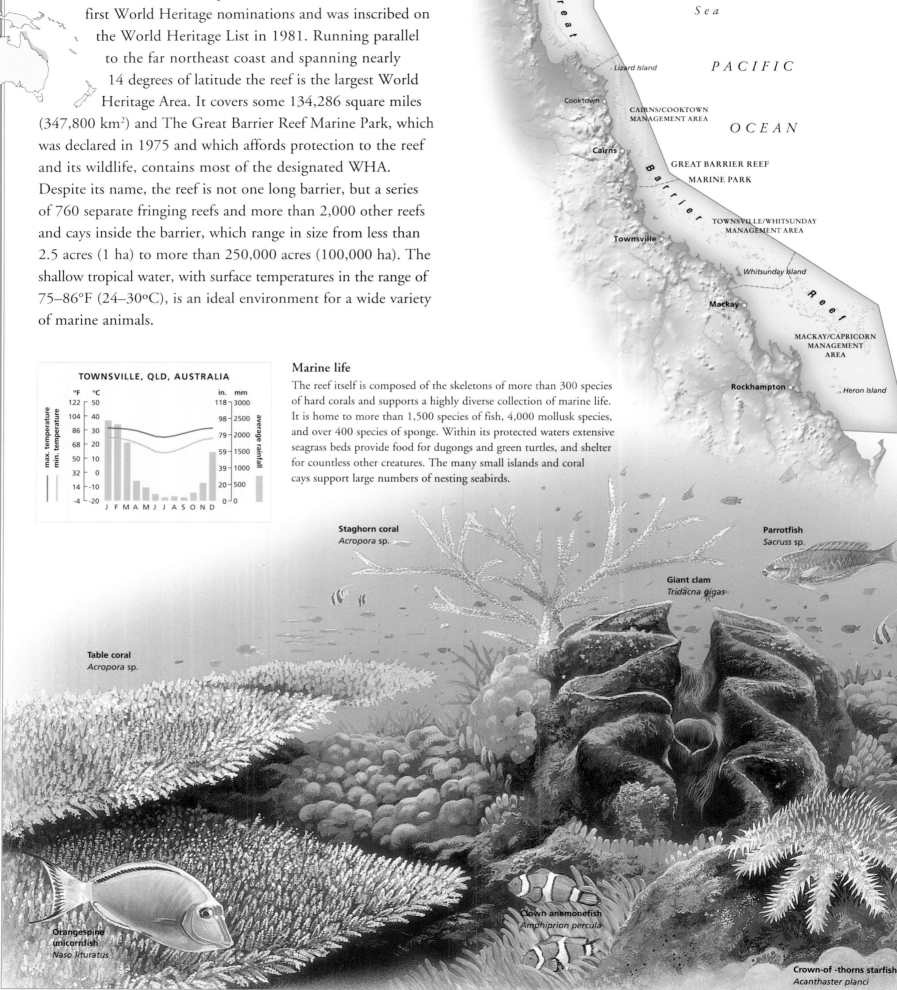

TOWNSVILLE, QLD, AUSTRALIA

SCALE 1:11,000,000
0 — 200 miles
0 — 200 kilometers

Cape York

Coral Sea

PACIFIC OCEAN

Great Barrier Reef

FAR NORTHERN MANAGEMENT AREA

Lizard Island

Cooktown

CAIRNS/COOKTOWN MANAGEMENT AREA

Cairns

GREAT BARRIER REEF MARINE PARK

TOWNSVILLE/WHITSUNDAY MANAGEMENT AREA

Townsville

Whitsunday Island

Mackay

MACKAY/CAPRICORN MANAGEMENT AREA

Rockhampton

Heron Island

Staghorn coral
Acropora sp.

Parrotfish
Sacruss sp.

Giant clam
Tridacna gigas

Table coral
Acropora sp.

Orangespine unicornfish
Naso lituratus

Clown anemonefish
Amphiprion percula

Crown-of-thorns starfish
Acanthaster planci

Minke whale

What was once referred to as the minke whale is now recognized as two species of small rorqual, one of which migrates to warmer waters during the southern winter. It is a frequent visitor to the coastal waters of the Great Barrier Reef, where it often swims close to divers, and the Western Australian coast.

Dugong

The dugong once inhabited extensive shallow waters around the Indian Ocean but now occurs only as small, remnant populations including the waters of northern Australia. Here seagrass beds provide food and shelter from predators.

Loggerhead turtle

The loggerhead turtle is one of several species of marine turtles that coexist in shallow tropical waters. Although sharing the same range they may have different diets. The loggerhead mainly eats mollusks and its powerful jaws are capable of crushing even large shells.

CONSERVATION WATCH

The greatest current threats to the Great Barrier Reef are from agricultural chemical runoff, coral predation by the crown-of-thorns starfish, and physical damage caused by the anchors of tourist vessels. Potential threats include oil spillage from large ships and the introduction of exotic marine organisms in their ballast, but rising sea levels is by far the greatest looming danger. Four plans of management contain strategies for dealing with these threats.

Sooty tern

Many small, inaccessible islands within the Great Barrier Reef provide a safe haven, free from the threat of terrestrial predators, for roosting and nesting seabirds. On such islands sooty tern colonies can nest safely on the sand.

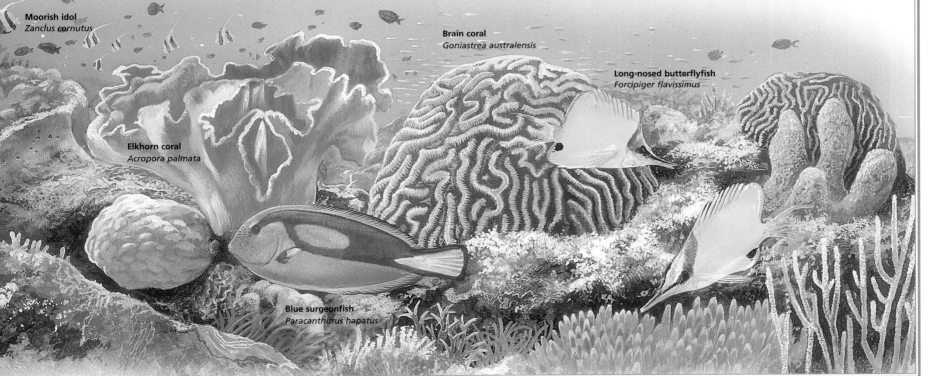

Moorish idol
Zanclus cornutus

Brain coral
Goniastrea australensis

Long-nosed butterflyfish
Forcipiger flavissimus

Elkhorn coral
Acropora palmata

Blue surgeonfish
Paracanthurus hapatus

WILDLIFE OF CAPE YORK

Cape York Peninsula is literally the northern finger of Australia pointing to the rest of the world. Torres Strait was not always water, and the flora, fauna, and peoples of this region bear witness to the close relationship between Australia and its nearest neighbor, the island of New Guinea. Cape York is significant because it demonstrates how recently the island of New Guinea became isolated from Australia. Many plants and animals have distributions that span the strait, such as the short-beaked echidna, striped possum, spotted cuscus, palm cockatoo, and birdwing butterfly. Many other groups have closely related, yet distinct species on either side of the strait, such as the tree kangaroos, pademelons, and dasyurids. Ancient rain forests once covered the entire area. As the continent of Australia entered a prolonged dry period its rain forests shrank. This coincided with the separation of Australia from New Guinea, which retained more of the ancient rain forest.

BRIDGE AND BARRIER – NEW GUINEA AND CAPE YORK	
TERRESTRIAL MAMMALS FOUND IN:	NUMBER OF SPECIES
New Guinea only	250
New Guinea and Cape York	19
New Guinea, Cape York, and elsewhere in Australia	14
Cape York only	16
Cape York and elsewhere in Australia	35
Australia-wide	240

Homecoming
Marine turtles are among the world's longest-lived animals, with green turtle females breeding for the first time in their 60th year. Studies have shown they consistently return, as adults, to breed at the beach where they scrambled into the sea as tiny hatchlings.

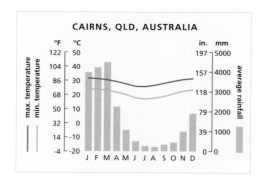

Striped possum
The striped possum of New Guinea and Cape York is Australasia's answer to the woodpecker. It uses its strong incisor teeth and elongated fourth finger to extract insect larvae from deep within tree branches, a characteristic it shares with the aye-aye, a Madagascan lemur.

Spectacled flying fox
Spectacled flying foxes are widely distributed in lowland New Guinea but in Cape York they roost in the rain forests and gallery forests at the tip of the cape and further to the south. Although they feed mainly on rain forest fruits, they have been persecuted by farmers for their habit of also raiding tropical fruit crops.

Common brushtail possum
A highly variable species, the common brushtail possum occurs as a pale slender form inhabiting tropical savannas, and a dark form living in the rain forests of Cape York and the Atherton Tableland of far north Queensland.

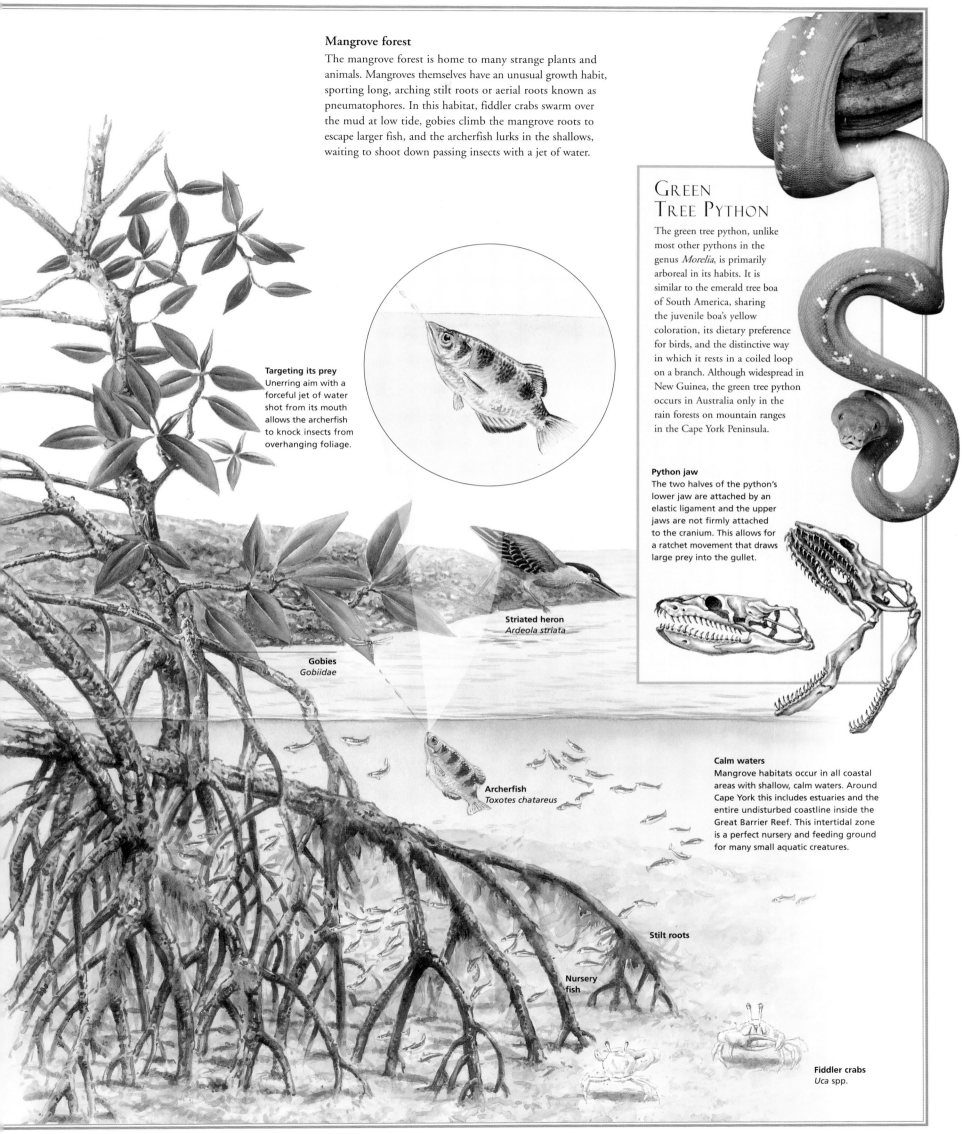

Mangrove forest

The mangrove forest is home to many strange plants and animals. Mangroves themselves have an unusual growth habit, sporting long, arching stilt roots or aerial roots known as pneumatophores. In this habitat, fiddler crabs swarm over the mud at low tide, gobies climb the mangrove roots to escape larger fish, and the archerfish lurks in the shallows, waiting to shoot down passing insects with a jet of water.

Targeting its prey
Unerring aim with a forceful jet of water shot from its mouth allows the archerfish to knock insects from overhanging foliage.

GREEN TREE PYTHON

The green tree python, unlike most other pythons in the genus *Morelia*, is primarily arboreal in its habits. It is similar to the emerald tree boa of South America, sharing the juvenile boa's yellow coloration, its dietary preference for birds, and the distinctive way in which it rests in a coiled loop on a branch. Although widespread in New Guinea, the green tree python occurs in Australia only in the rain forests on mountain ranges in the Cape York Peninsula.

Python jaw
The two halves of the python's lower jaw are attached by an elastic ligament and the upper jaws are not firmly attached to the cranium. This allows for a ratchet movement that draws large prey into the gullet.

Striated heron
Ardeola striata

Gobies
Gobiidae

Archerfish
Toxotes chatareus

Calm waters
Mangrove habitats occur in all coastal areas with shallow, calm waters. Around Cape York this includes estuaries and the entire undisturbed coastline inside the Great Barrier Reef. This intertidal zone is a perfect nursery and feeding ground for many small aquatic creatures.

Stilt roots

Nursery fish

Fiddler crabs
Uca spp.

WILDLIFE OF CAPE YORK
TROPICAL RAIN FORESTS

The Wet Tropics World Heritage Area (WTWHA) covers nearly 3,475 square miles (9,000 km²) of rich tropical rain forest that stretches from Townsville in the south to Cooktown in the north of northeastern Queensland. A verdant wonderland of rugged beauty, this region contains some of Australia's largest tracts of tropical rain forest. Most of the WTWHA, which was listed in 1988 on the basis that it met all four natural heritage criteria, is on public land and largely protected within a series of remote national parks. Where the rain forest extends to the coast it joins the Great Barrier Reef WHA. The rain forest ecosystems in the WTWHA contain more than 3,000 species of plants from more than 200 families, making this area one of the richest in botanical diversity in the world. The forests are home to several primitive forms of flowering plants and to many unique endemic species of animals, such as the musky rat-kangaroo.

Double-eyed fig parrot
The small but colorful double-eyed fig parrot is not often seen. It spends much of its time in the rain forest canopy where it enjoys a diet of native fig seeds. Its range also extends to New Guinea.

Musky rat-kangaroo
The musky rat-kangaroo is the smallest and most primitive member of the kangaroo group of families. It, alone, has retained the opposable first toe common to most other marsupial groups but absent in kangaroos. It forages during the day for fruits and fungi.

ENDEMIC SPECIES

CLASS	NO. OF SPECIES	EXAMPLE
Mammals	8	Herbert River ringtail possum
Birds	13	Tooth-billed catbird
Reptiles	18	Chameleon gecko
Amphibians (frogs)	20	Torrent frog
Fish	78	Cairns rainbowfish
Invertebrates	Thousands	Cairns birdwing butterfly

Lilly pilly
Acmena smithii

Tropical rain forest floor

The floor of a tropical rain forest is a rich field for fruit and insect eaters, and an ideal habitat for a wide range of invertebrates, including centipedes, snails, and beetles. Frogs and lizards find both food and shelter in the leaf litter or in decaying branches. The canopy of dense vegetation overhead prevents much light from reaching the forest floor. Emerging seedlings grow slowly but fungi thrive.

Green ringtail possum
These rain forest possums are solitary creatures that do not build a nest or retreat to tree hollows but, instead, spend their daylight hours curled up asleep on a branch. The green tint to their thick, woolly fur is the result of the individual hairs diffracting light.

Orange-thighed tree frog
Litoria xanthomera

Brush turkey
Alectura lathami

Rhinoceros beetle
Xylotrupes ulysses

Northern bettong
A small nocturnal member of the rat-kangaroo family, the northern bettong is found only in north Queensland. It has a long tail, a forward-facing pouch, and moves by hopping. Fungi forms a major part of its diet, which also includes grass stems, insects, and leaves.

Cassowary
The cassowary's natural habitat is rain forest although it sometimes ranges into gardens and orchards in search of fruit. Like the emu and ostrich, the male incubates the eggs and rears the chicks, which remain in its care for about nine months.

Fruit dispersal
Cassowaries play an important role in forest life by helping disperse the seeds of forest trees, including the quandong. They swallow the fruits whole and their digestive tract activates the seed, which is returned to the earth conveniently encased in fertilizer.

Chameleon gecko
Carpodactylus laevis

Scrub python
Morelia amethistina

Giant forest cricket
Papuaistis sp.

Centipede
Scolopendridae

THE TROPICAL NORTH

The far northwest regions of Australia share a different climatic pattern from that of Australia's east-coast tropics. Annual rainfall is high, averaging more than 47 inches (1,200 mm) in Darwin, but it falls during a short monsoonal wet season between November and April. The rest of the year the weather is dominated by hot, dry winds. This results in a different suite of ecosystems dominated by grassy woodlands and savannas. Palm forests and vine thickets grow in moister gullies but large areas of rain forest are absent. The landscape and topography also differ, and include extensive plateaus and tablelands dissected by spectacular gorges that are fringed by an escarpment of rugged sandstone cliffs. The area is home to the second largest national park in the world, Kakadu, which contains many of the tropical north's unique plants and animals.

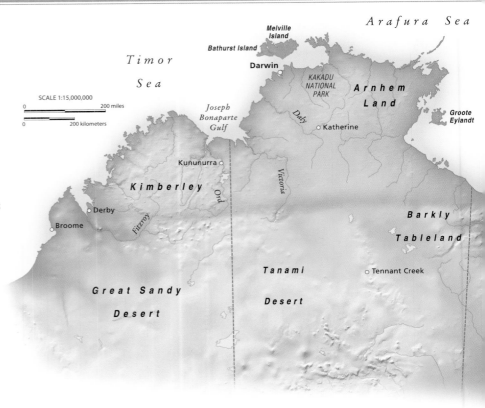

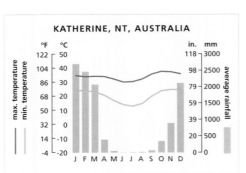

Gouldian finch
Found only in Australia's far north, the beautifully colored Gouldian finch is a seasonal visitor to the coast but breeds inland, nesting in tree hollows.

KAKADU NATIONAL PARK	
Land area	7,646 sq mi (1,980,400 ha)
No. of visitors per year	200,000
World Heritage listing	1981, extensions 1987, 1992
Mammals	62 species
Birds	280 species
Reptiles	123+ species
Amphibians (frogs)	25 species
Fish	51 freshwater species
Invertebrates	More than 10,000

TAIPAN

The taipan is one of Australia's largest and most venomous snakes. It is a "strike and wait" predator, biting its unsuspecting victim once or twice before retreating and waiting for it to die. It is particularly dangerous to humans because of its habit of lurking in long grass, where it waits to strike prey, such as a passing bandicoot, rat, small marsupial, or bird.

Saltwater crocodile
Rightly feared as ferocious predators, saltwater crocodiles are found in northern Australian seas, estuaries, large rivers and, during the wet season, coastal flood plains. The female crocodile builds a mound nest of rotting vegetation, which she guards while her eggs incubate.

Fang
The taipan's hollow fangs are fixed in the front of the upper jaw. A duct supplying venom leads from a gland in the back of the head.

Venom gland

NORTHERN QUOLL

Cane toads, introduced to Australia in 1935, are one of the tropical north's greatest threats. Poison from the toad's parotoid glands is highly toxic to most native animals. Although some species seem to have found ways to avoid or even consume toads, the northern quoll has proven particularly vulnerable. The toad's relentless movement across Arnhem Land and Kakadu has coincided with the deaths of large numbers of quolls. A major effort is being made to save the northern quoll by establishing populations on toad-free islands north of Darwin.

Cane toads
Cane toads have been in the western Gulf of Carpentaria for many years but have recently expanded their range to the west, reaching Darwin in 2005.

Soldier
Soldiers are armed either with huge jaws or, in the case of the spinifex termite, a snout capable of squirting a sticky, toxic fluid.

King
The king's main role is to fertilize the queen but when the colony is first founded the king also cares for the young.

Termite fortresses

Most termite species build insignificant nests, either underground or inside a tree or log. But the magnetic termite mound is characteristic of the tropical north landscape, as is the giant, up to 25 feet (7.6 m) high, mound of the spinifex termite.

Brolga
The brolga, one of two Australian crane species, is well known for its elaborate ritual dancing, which involves bouncing or leaping, bowing, and outstretched wing display. Once widespread it is now common only in the tropical north. Breeding pairs share nest duties and care for their young for up to a year.

Queen
Queen termites lose their wings once they find a male. Together they establish a temporary shelter, where the first brood is born. The queen may live for 50 years and lay up to 2,000 eggs per day.

Strong outer wall

Many small cavities and channels in inner section of mound

Special chamber for queen

High-rise mounds
Impressively tall termite mounds dot the grasslands and woodlands of Australia's far north. Their shape, often narrow at the top, and their careful alignment in relation to the sun's rays, helps to keep them as cool as possible. This reduces moisture loss and regulates the temperature within the mound.

Goannas often make their nest in the cool environment of a termite mound

AUSTRALIAN OUTBACK

The term outback generally refers to the semiarid and arid lands of Australia's interior. The name also conjures up images of Uluru and the splendid gorges of the MacDonnell Ranges, but most of the outback is actually flat or rolling land sparsely covered with grasslands or low woodlands, featuring stunted trees such as the mulga and mallee. These apparently bleak ecosystems actually support a rich variety of wildlife. Ants abound in the desert, feeding on the seeds of grasses in competition with small parrots and hopping mice. Termites devour the dead grasses. Lizards, birds, and small mammals feed in turn on the ants and other insects. Water is a major limiting factor in the desert and, paradoxically, it appears in many strange places in the outback. Places such as Lake Eyre, rocky gorges, and the myriad of mound springs scattered around the rim of the Great Artesian Basin, a vast aquifer, defy notions of a barren continent.

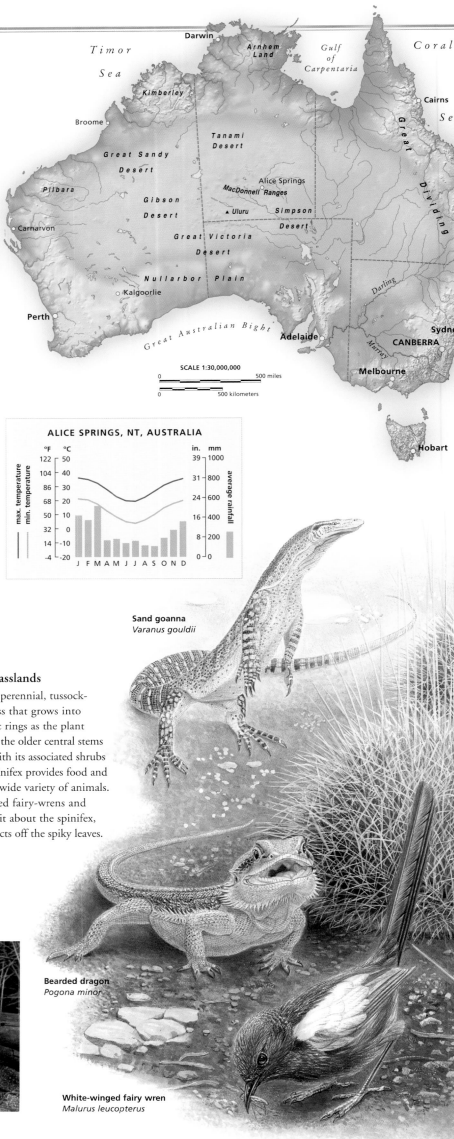

Sand goanna
Varanus gouldii

LANDMASS
Outback 69%
Rest of Australia 31%

POPULATION
Rest of Australia 97%
Outback population 3%

ALICE SPRINGS, NT, AUSTRALIA

Spinifex grasslands

Spinifex is a perennial, tussock-forming grass that grows into characteristic rings as the plant expands and the older central stems die. Along with its associated shrubs and trees, spinifex provides food and shelter for a wide variety of animals. White-winged fairy-wrens and grasswrens flit about the spinifex, gleaning insects off the spiky leaves.

Bearded dragon
Pogona minor

Thorny devil
The diminutive thorny devil's spiky skin provides protection from predators as it ranges the desert lapping up ants. Well-adapted to an arid climate, this lizard "drinks" moisture from dew on its scales.

CONSERVATION WATCH

The kowari is vulnerable in its range and populations have decreased dramatically over the past century. Its decline, and that of the greater bilby whose burrows it inhabits, appears to be linked to the loss of insect prey associated with the expansion of cattle grazing. A wide-ranging hunter, the kowari requires relatively large protected reserves for its future survival.

White-winged fairy wren
Malurus leucopterus

Bilby
Once widespread in the outback bilbies are now found in only a few refuges. These shy, nocturnal members of the bandicoot family, with ears and gait reminiscent of a rabbit, forage for fungi and insects. They spend the day in burrows to escape the inland heat.

Brisbane

Dingo
Members of the dog family, Canidae, dingoes occur widely in Australia from coastal to alpine regions, but they remain the quintessential symbol of the outback. They prey upon other mammals and birds, sometimes hunting in packs.

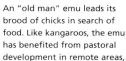

Spinifex tussock
Triodia sp.

Wedge-tailed eagle
The wedge-tailed eagle is Australia's largest bird of prey and is capable of taking a lamb or small kangaroo, but it feeds mainly on rabbits or carrion. Since the controlled decline of rabbits took effect, eagles have been forced to feed on roadkill and have fallen victim to vehicles themselves.

Emu
An "old man" emu leads its brood of chicks in search of food. Like kangaroos, the emu has benefited from pastoral development in remote areas, where dams and bores have assured these wide-ranging birds a reliable supply of water.

Mulgara
Dasycercus cristicauda

ROCKY GORGES

Flooding has carved outback gorges over millennia. During the wet season, rivers course through the gorges, filling waterholes in their deepest reaches. Plants such as figs and palms grow in the moist and sheltered sections, but most vegetation is adapted to the harsh dry season that follows, when wildlife relies on the gorges for survival. Prominent among these are the rock wallabies, which find shelter in the rocky gorge walls.

Black-flanked rock wallaby
At home in rocky gorges, rock wallabies are a familiar sight near water holes at many of Australia's most popular outback tourist sites, including Ormiston Gorge, in the West MacDonnell Ranges.

Sand-swimming skink
Lerista sp.

AUSTRALIAN OUTBACK
WATER IN THE DESERT

In many parts of the world, desert rivers such as Africa's Okavango or America's Colorado have their origins in adjacent high-rainfall regions. In Australia, the arid-zone rivers begin and end their journeys in the parched desert, where rainfall is a rare event. When it does rain, as a result of a massive frontal event or a cyclone penetrating far inland, the consequences are felt over vast areas and for many subsequent months. Rains falling on the inland plains of Australia's northeast, for example, make their slow way west into the Cooper and Diamantina systems. Rain further west swells the Finke River and all end up in the Lake Eyre Basin. These infrequent inundations provide the impetus for a massive, opportunistic breeding event, when all forms of life, from aquatic microorganisms to fish and birds, gather in vast numbers and multiply in the swelling lakes and billabongs.

Channel Country
The Diamantina River is a braided watercourse typical of the flat outback "Channel Country." The streambeds are often dry but, when rain does fall, can carry torrents of water to their ultimate destination, Lake Eyre. Vast areas of the surrounding flat country can be flooded for weeks after heavy rains.

Waiting for the rain
Long periods of drought in inland Australia make life impossible for frogs, which need to keep their skin moist. The water-holding frog has adapted to this harsh climate by burrowing into a chamber underground, shedding layers of skin to form a protective cocoon, and awaiting rain in a state of torpor. It then emerges to feed and mate.

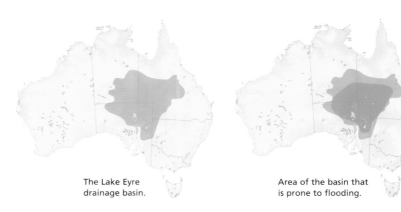

The Lake Eyre drainage basin.

Area of the basin that is prone to flooding.

Digging in
The frog digs itself a small burrow and prepares to wait for rains to return.

Inactive underground
Enclosed in its cocoon, the frog enters a state of torpor, which may last many months.

Rain arrives
When rainfall softens the soil the frog digs its way out to the surface.

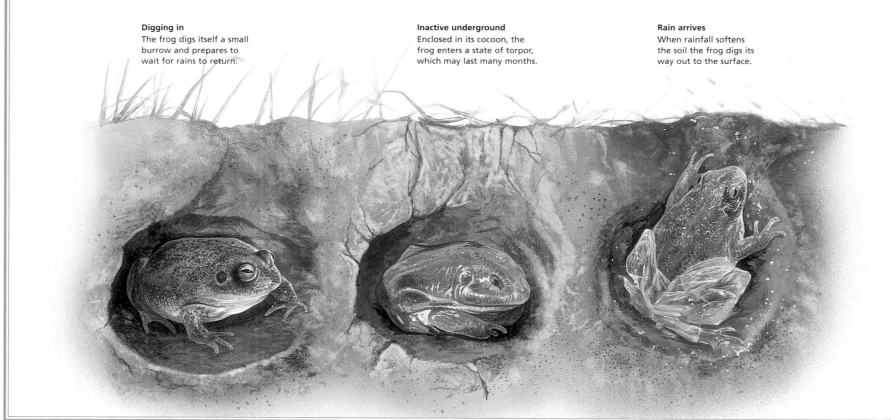

WATERBIRDS ON WETLANDS

The desert wetlands attract birds from all over Australia to the temporarily abundant feeding and breeding grounds. Ibis, egrets, spoonbills, and cormorants breed in trees fringing the rivers and billabongs. Pelicans, gulls, and terns nest on islands in the temporary lakes, and black swans, along with several duck species, nests in the reed beds fringing the wetlands.

Australian white ibis
Swamps are the favored feeding sites of the Australian white ibis, which dines on insects, crustaceans, fish, and frogs. While most birds breed in the Murray–Darling wetlands, some take advantage of ephemeral wetlands further inland on an opportunistic basis.

Royal spoonbill
The nomadic royal spoonbill, one of two species occurring in Australia, nests in small colonies scattered throughout northern and eastern Australia.

Pink-eared duck
The pink-eared duck is one of a group of nomadic species that takes advantage of the ephemeral waterways in the interior to breed when conditions are favorable. It retreats to coastal estuaries and lagoons when drought inevitably returns to the inland.

Australian pelican
Australian pelicans breed in several small breeding colonies around the continent's coastal fringe, but the major breeding site for vast numbers of pelicans is Lake Eyre. On the all-too-rare occasions when floodwaters reach the lake, it attracts many hundreds of birds.

Life in a billabong

Inland rivers may overflow their banks and flood surrounding plains after heavy rain, then shrink during drier times to form billabongs—isolated waterholes. The stagnant water in the billabong is an ideal habitat for smooth freshwater crayfish, or yabby, frogs, the long-necked tortoise, and myriad small fish and insects. Birds, including long-legged waders, are attracted to these rewarding feeding grounds.

Great egret
Ardea alba

Larvae of dragonfly

Yellowbelly
Macquaria ambigua

Snake-necked turtle
Chelodina longicollis

Yabby
Cherax sp.

Tadpoles

TEMPERATE FORESTS AND HEATHLANDS

Australia's southern forests and heathlands are dominated by two large plant families—the Myrtaceae, containing the iconic eucalypts commonly known as gum trees, melaleucas, and bottlebrushes; and the Proteaceae, whose banksias and grevilleas regenerate quickly after the fires that periodically raze the landscape. All have massive flowering events that attract nectar-feeding mammals, such as possums and fruit bats, birds such as honeyeaters and lorikeets, and insects, all of which pollinate the plants as they gorge themselves on the abundant nectar. Vegetation types vary according to the rock and soil types, and prevailing climate. Large trees, such as the karris of the far southwest and the mountain ash of the continent's southeast, occur in areas with higher rainfall and richer soils. Drier areas with poorer soils support gnarled angophoras, ghostly scribbly gums, and heathlands of stunted trees and shrubs.

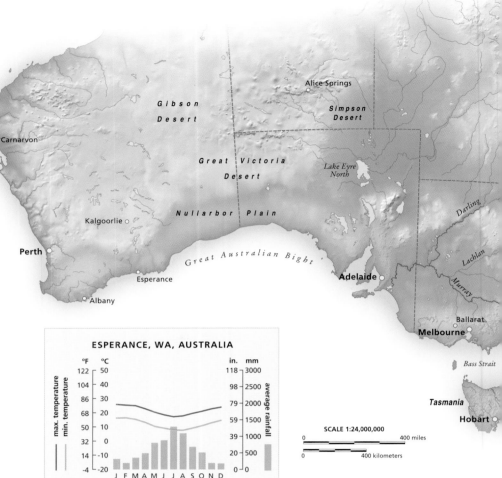

ESPERANCE, WA, AUSTRALIA

SCALE 1:24,000,000

New Holland honeyeater
This familiar resident of coastal woodlands and heath in the southeast and southwest of Australia is a frequent visitor to city parks and gardens. Often gathering in large flocks, it feeds on the nectar of shrubs and regards banksias and grevilleas among its favorites.

OTHER SPECIES IN THIS HABITAT	
COMMON NAME	SPECIAL FEATURE
Rock warbler	An endemic bird
Velvet worm	The link between worms and arthropods
Bristlebird	One of the oldest songbirds
Gilbert's potoroo	Endangered species, once considered extinct
Southern brown bandicoot	Numbers increasing in Sydney region
Brush turkey	Numbers increasing in Sydney region

Satin bowerbird
When the male satin bowerbird inherits or acquires a territory it changes into its deep blue–black plumage and builds a bower, which it lines with any blue objects it can find. The bird then hovers around the bower, burbling and calling to attract a mate.

Numbat
The numbat, a marsupial with a bushy tail and a pointed face, is exclusively a termite-eater. Its long tongue is a key player in its search for food as it explores feeding galleries of termites under the soil or in logs.

Forest fires
Many of the forests in the southern half of Australia are dependent on fire for their regeneration. Mature trees produce vast quantities of seed that cannot germinate until a massive fire burns off the old plants and simultaneously activates the seed.

Superb lyrebird
The superb lyrebird, named for the shape of its tail, is one of the oldest members of the songbird group that evolved in Australia before spreading to the rest of the world. The male lyrebird is an amazing mimic, capable of imitating almost any sound it hears.

⚡ **CONSERVATION WATCH**

The mountain pygmy possum is a true living fossil. It was first described from Pleistocene cave deposits, before living animals were discovered in 1966. Restricted to high alpine heathlands, it is highly endangered because of the threats of fire and global warming.

Winter warmth
During wintrer months the mountain pygmy possum survives in tunnels beneath the snow cover that forms an insulating barrier from the cold. Any reduction in the blanket of snow cover puts this tiny creature at risk.

Summer feast
During a time of plenty the mountain pygmy possum feasts on bogong moths, which come in their thousands to the possum's alpine habitat. Rich in fat, the moth is an ideal food for an animal that is about to enter a lean period.

Kookaburra
The kookaburra is one of Australia's most familiar birds. A dry-land kingfisher, it preys on lizards, snakes, worms, and cicadas and is a highly efficient hunter. Its raucous laughing call, often heard pre-dawn, is a familiar sound in the Australian bush.

Red-necked wallaby
The red-necked wallaby, generally solitary, is one of the most common members of the kangaroo family and the only one to live in high alpine areas. Its thick winter fur was highly prized by Aboriginal people for making warm winter capes.

COCKATOOS AND PARROTS

Parrots are characteristic of the three southern continents and southern Asia, with only a few species invading the northern tropics. Australia's parrot population is richly diverse and these colorful birds are a familiar sight in most parts of the country. Despite Australia having relatively few parrot species, 15 percent of the world's total, it has slightly more than its share of genera, 30 percent. Since the mid-19th century, when land clearing and urban development in Australia increased, many parrots have proven their adaptability. Several species of cockatoo are now more widespread than previously recorded and the distributions of other species have changed dramatically. Crimson rosellas are now resident year-round in lowland Sydney, where once they were only winter visitors. In many urban and suburban areas, the number of parrots has increased recently and, as forest areas decline, urban street trees have become popular roosting sites.

Turquoise parrot
A male turquoise parrot displays its beautiful wing and tail feathers as it prepares to land on a tree. The parrot occurs mostly in the eastern ranges, where it nests in tree hollows.

King parrot
The king parrot, distinguished by its brilliant red breast and head, is a large, forest-dwelling parrot. It feeds on the seeds of acacias and other understory shrubs and trees.

Black cockatoo
The handsome red-tailed black cockatoo feeds mostly on eucalypt seeds. In heavily timbered areas it feeds in the canopy but in more open country it is often seen on the ground.

Major Mitchell cockatoo
The pink or Major Mitchell cockatoo commonly travels in pairs or small groups. It inhabits ephemeral watercourses and remote billabongs, feeding in the nearby grasslands and dunes.

BILL TYPES

Parrots' bills, along with their bright plumage, are one of their most noticeable features. The upper bill is always downcurved but it varies in length from species to species. Some are long, ideal for digging into soft wood for insects or for cutting into ripe fruit. Others are short and strong, for breaking open cones or other tough seed cases.

Corella
The corella's long, narrow bill allows it to extract seeds from hard-coned plants and to dig up bulbs.

Double-eyed fig parrot
This parrot eats the seeds of soft-textured figs, slicing the fruit open neatly with the edge of its sharp bill.

Palm cockatoo
A huge bill and powerful jaw muscles allow the palm cockatoo to break open seed cases and unripe fruit.

Gang-gang cockatoo
The gang-gang cockatoo holds hard-cased fruit in one foot and cracks it open with its strong beak.

Rainbow lorikeet
Instead of using its bill, this lorikeet use its enlarged, hairy tongue to collect nectar and pollen from flowers.

Budgerigar
Sociable budgerigars create colorful spectacles in outback Australia. Frenetic flocks containing thousands of birds suddenly erupt from a waterhole and wheel around, only to alight briefly and take flight again.

Rainbow lorikeet
The rainbow lorikeet is found in the suburbs of most Australian cities with huge flocks roosting in gardens and dispersing during the day to feed on nectar-producing trees and shrubs.

Eastern rosella
Platycercus eximius

A VARIETY OF NESTS

The nests made by Australian parrots vary according to their range and the availability of safe sites. Hollows in tree trunks or branches are widely used as convenient nesting sites but parrots are found in a variety of habitats so nests may be on the ground, in grass, under rocks, or even in fence posts.

Ground nest
The ground parrot lives in grassy heathland and makes its nest on the ground, concealed by low-hanging foliage.

Tree nest
In common with many species of parrot, the Australian king parrot makes its nest in a deep hollow in a tree trunk.

Rock nest
Rock parrots, which live close to the coast, make their nest in a shallow depression protected by an overhanging rock.

Communal nest
Budgerigars nest in tree hollows but, unusually, they often nest communally, with several nests in one tree.

Termite nest
The golden-shouldered parrot makes its nest inside a termite mound at the end of a tunnel.

NEW ZEALAND

New Zealand's flora and fauna is a mixture of early Gondwanan elements, such as the Araucaria pines, tree ferns, moas, and kiwis, and species that have made the journey across the Tasman Sea or Pacific Ocean unaided. Most other native birds in New Zealand are close relatives of Australian species. However, the native bats are most closely related to a family of South American bats, and the four native frogs have even closer relatives living in Pacific coastal forests from British Columbia to California. New Zealand has 10 species of native mammals, three bats and seven pinnipeds, but it has 35 species of introduced mammals. Of these, the kiore and dog were introduced by the Maori and the rest, including a hedgehog, the rabbit, three rodents, and 16 ungulates, were brought by Europeans. Over the past 200 years these interlopers have had a devastating effect on native fauna and flora.

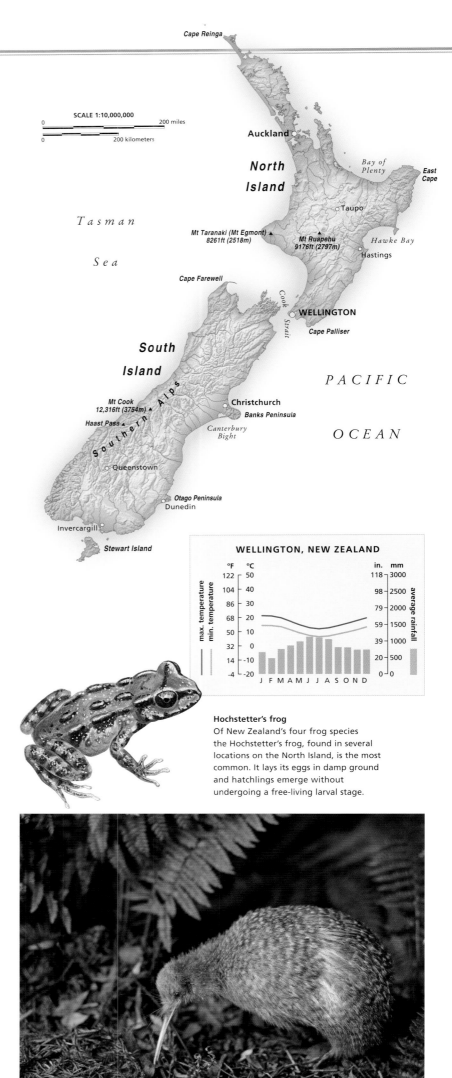

SCALE 1:10,000,000

WELLINGTON, NEW ZEALAND

Hochstetter's frog
Of New Zealand's four frog species the Hochstetter's frog, found in several locations on the North Island, is the most common. It lays its eggs in damp ground and hatchlings emerge without undergoing a free-living larval stage.

Kea
The kea is the alpine and subalpine parrot familiar to most visitors to New Zealand's Haast Pass, where it vandalizes the windscreen wipers of parked cars. It is also notorious for attacking sheep. Its numbers are declining.

Great spotted kiwi
The great spotted kiwi is the largest of the four kiwi species but, like the other three, its numbers are declining and it requires conservation. It is threatened by predation from domestic dogs and cats, as well as stoats.

Tuatara

Two species of tuatara survive on islands off New Zealand's coast. Despite their lizard-like appearance they are not lizards but belong to an ancient reptile order that predates the dinosaurs. They are now known only in New Zealand where half the population of the common species (*Sphenodon punctatus*) lives on Stephens Island in Cook Strait. They also occur on several other offshore islands.

Cave weta
About 70 species of weta, forest and cave-dwelling crickets, are found in New Zealand in all habitats from coastal scrubs to alpine areas.

Moa

The moa was a medium to large bird, now considered more closely related to the emu and cassowaries of Australia and New Guinea than to surviving kiwis. The two largest species, the South Island giant moa and the North Island giant moa, grew to about 12 feet (3.6 m) in height and they weighed about 550 pounds (250 kg). These giant birds browsed on trees and shrubs and, before the arrival of the Maori in the 10th century AD, their only predator was the Haast's eagle. By 1400 AD the Maori had exterminated the two large moas.

⚡ CONSERVATION WATCH

The kakapo, considered the world's heaviest parrot, was once widespread throughout New Zealand. The clearing of forests and predation have forced it onto a handful of islands. Flightless and nocturnal, it lives on fruits and other plant parts, and breeds only every three to five years.

INTRODUCED BIRDS

Of 335 bird species recorded in New Zealand, 40 have been introduced in the past 200 years. Many have contributed to the decline of endemic species, mostly through competition for food and nesting sites, but threatened species are benefiting from captive breeding programs.

Black tomtit
This tomtit, a subspecies found only on Snares Island, and the black robin are the only black species of the three Australasian robins living in New Zealand and its neighboring islands.

Tomtit
The tomtit, a common bird in New Zealand, is found in forested areas where it pursues the insects that form its diet. It also occasionally eats fruit.

ISLANDS OF THE SOUTHWEST PACIFIC

The islands of the tropical southwest Pacific Ocean have two separate origins. New Caledonia is a remnant of the ancient supercontinent Gondwana, and the rest, from the Solomon Islands to Vanuatu, are volcanic uplifted blocks along the Pacific Rim of Fire. New Caledonia is home to many ancient plants that demonstrate its affinity with Australia, but there are many endemic plant families, indeed more than 75 percent of its plant species occur nowhere else. Vegetation on the volcanic islands shows greater affinity with New Guinea and the Bismarck Archipelago. The larger islands have a high percentage of endemic land birds, including the kagu of New Caledonia. The smaller, more isolated islands frequently host large breeding colonies of pelagic seabirds. Prominent among these are Norfolk and Lord Howe islands and their satellites, such as Balls Pyramid, to Lord Howe's southeast.

Coral Sea

PACIFIC

New Caledonia
NOUMEA

Brisbane

Norfolk Island

Port Macquarie

Lord Howe Island

OCEAN

Sydney

Tasman Sea

New Zealan

SCALE 1:43,000,000

0   400 miles

0   400 kilometers

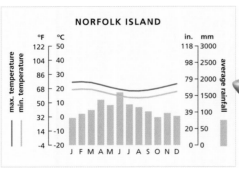

NORFOLK ISLAND

°F	°C		in.	mm
122	50		118	3000
104	40		98	2500
86	30		79	2000
68	20		59	1500
50	10		39	100
32	0		20	50
14	-10		0	0
-4	-20			

max. temperature
min. temperature
average rainfall

J F M A M J J A S O N D

Land snail
A large ground-dwelling snail, endemic to Lord Howe Island, is known to reach more than three inches (8 cm) in length at maturity. It is at risk of predation by rats.

Purple swamphen
The purple swamphen, or pukako, is one of the most successful colonizers of islands throughout the South Pacific. As long as it has access to reed beds for nesting, it can live in any moist environment.

Sooty tern
The large breeding colony of sooty terns on Lord Howe Island's Mount Eliza is one of the island's major natural attractions. Bird breeding colonies are normally found on inaccessible islands, but here the birds gather in large numbers and are readily observed.

PROVIDENCE PETREL

The Providence petrel is a pelagic species with an unusually narrow distribution, occurring mainly in the warmer waters of the southwest Pacific Ocean. During the non-breeding season some individuals migrate to the North Pacific but during the breeding season dense colonies gather on Lord Howe Island. The birds nest in burrows, the parents taking turns to incubate the egg.

Hatching
The Providence petrel parents share the duty of incubating their egg in a small underground nesting chamber at the end of a burrow.

Nestling
The nestling, which is often alone while the parents fly far out to sea to seek feed, is in danger of predation by rats or other birds.

⚡ CONSERVATION WATCH

Species of rail tend to evolve into flightless forms after they invade remote islands, of which the Lord Howe Island woodhen is one example. It was widespread and common on the island until feral cats and pigs decimated its population. By 1973 only a few individuals survived on Mount Gower and Mount Lidgbird. A safe breeding colony was established and, by the mid-1980s, 85 captive-bred individuals were reintroduced into the wild. The current population is around 200 birds.

🔶 Stick insect
The Lord Howe Island phasmid, stick insect, population on the main island was wiped out by introduced rats but survivors were discovered in 2001 on an outlying island. A small captive colony was established and their progeny will be reintroduced following a planned rat eradication program.

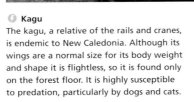

🔶 Kagu
The kagu, a relative of the rails and cranes, is endemic to New Caledonia. Although its wings are a normal size for its body weight and shape it is flightless, so it is found only on the forest floor. It is highly susceptible to predation, particularly by dogs and cats.

Red-crowned parakeet
The red-crowned parakeet's range once extended across New Zealand's main islands but is now restricted to a few offshore islands. The bird has a distinctive red crown and red band across its cheek and eye. It feeds mainly on seeds, fruit, and berries.

Emperor penguins live in Antarctica and are one of the few animals
to stay during winter. When penguin chicks are about six weeks old,
they collect in a group, or crèche, and are looked after by a single
adult. This allows other adult penguins to leave the colony and catch
food—emperor penguins feed their own chicks for about nine months

THE POLES

THE POLES

Polar regions at the ends of Earth are similar in their intense cold and seasonality, but different in their basic geography. The Arctic centers about a vast sea basin: a visitor to the north geographic pole stands on sea ice in the middle of a cold, deep ocean. The Antarctic centers on a high continent: a visitor to the south geographic pole stands on an icecap 9,301 feet (2,835 m) above sea level. Latitude for latitude the high continent makes the Antarctic region much colder than the Arctic. The geographical boundaries of these regions are the polar circles, located at

66° 33' N and S, each of 1,619 miles (2,606 km) radius and enclosing about 8 percent of Earth's surface. The Arctic region adjoins the temperate lands of the northern continents, and is constantly recruiting plants and animals overland from the south. Antarctica, an isolated continent, receives only the few plants and animals that can swim, fly, or be blown there. It also has fewer habitable areas to offer, hence its relative poverty of species. A small Arctic island may support as 90 species of flowering plant: the whole Antarctic continent supports only two.

The Arctic
The Arctic region is home to many land animals, although even the heavily furred polar bear must spend winter in a snow den.

SCALE 1:35,000,000

0   500 miles

0   500 kilometers

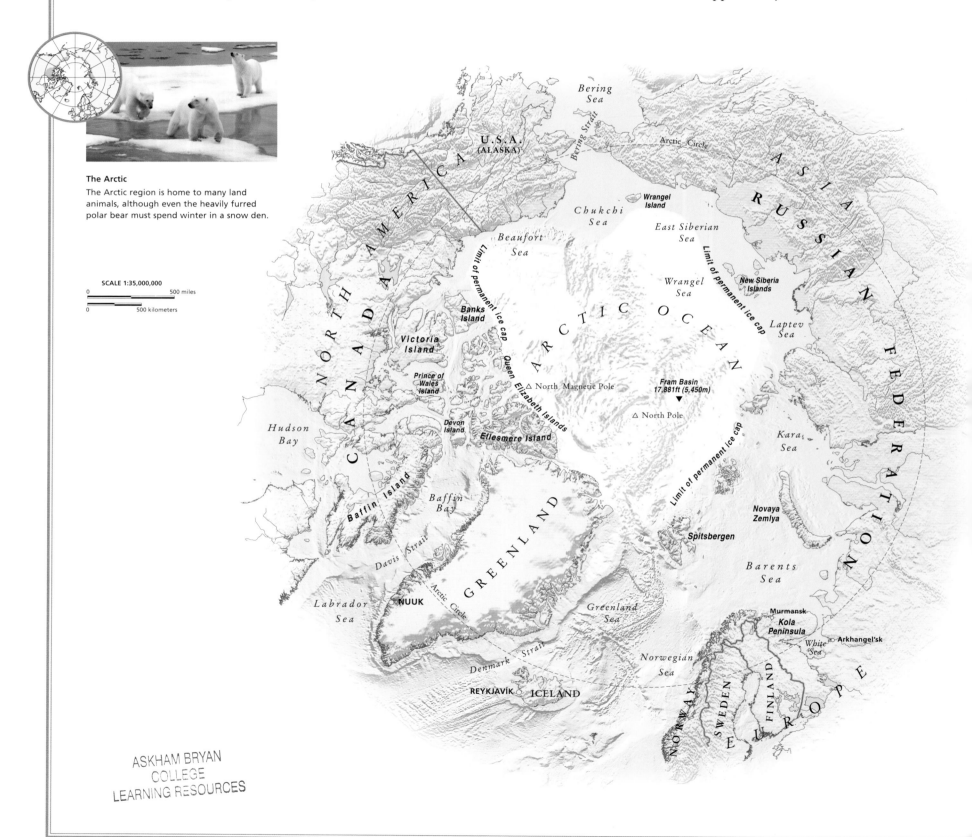

ASKHAM BRYAN
COLLEGE
LEARNING RESOURCES

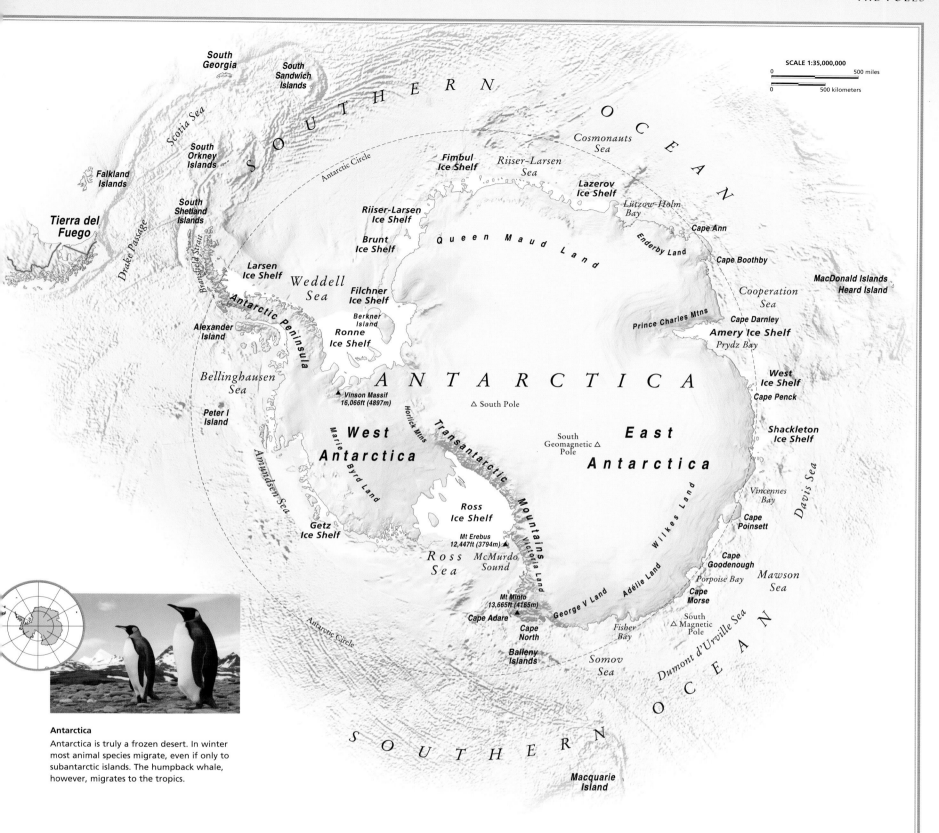

SCALE 1:35,000,000

South
Georgia

South
Sandwich
Islands

Falkland
Islands

Scotia Sea

South
Orkney
Islands

SOUTHERN

OCEAN

*Cosmonauts
Sea*

Fimbul
Ice Shelf

*Riiser-Larsen
Sea*

Lazerov
Ice Shelf

Antarctic Circle

*Lützow-Holm
Bay*

Cape Ann

Riiser-Larsen
Ice Shelf

Tierra del
Fuego

South
Shetland
Islands

Drake Passage

Bransfield Strait

Antarctic Peninsula

Brunt
Ice Shelf

Queen Maud Land

Enderby Land

Cape Boothby

Larsen
Ice Shelf

*Weddell
Sea*

Filchner
Ice Shelf

*Cooperation
Sea*

MacDonald Islands
Heard Island

Alexander
Island

Berkner
Island

Ronne
Ice Shelf

Prince Charles Mtns

Cape Darnley

Amery Ice Shelf

Prydz Bay

*Bellinghausen
Sea*

A N T A R C T I C A

West
Ice Shelf

Cape Penck

△ Vinson Massif
16,066ft (4897m)

△ South Pole

Peter I
Island

Shackleton
Ice Shelf

West
Antarctica

Horlick Mtns

Transantarctic Mountains

South
Geomagnetic △
Pole

East
Antarctica

Marie Byrd Land

Amundsen Sea

Victoria Land

Wilkes Land

*Vincennes
Bay*

Davis Sea

Getz
Ice Shelf

Ross
Ice Shelf

Cape
Poinsett

Mt Erebus
12,447ft (3794m) ▲

Cape
Goodenough

Porpoise Bay

*Mawson
Sea*

*Ross
Sea*

McMurdo
Sound

Cape
Morse

Mt Minto
13,665ft (4165m) ▲

George V Land

Adélie Land

South
△ Magnetic
Pole

Antarctic Circle

Cape Adare

Cape
North

*Fisher
Bay*

Dumont d'Urville Sea

Balleny
Islands

*Somov
Sea*

SOUTHERN

OCEAN

Macquarie
Island

Antarctica

Antarctica is truly a frozen desert. In winter
most animal species migrate, even if only to
subantarctic islands. The humpback whale,
however, migrates to the tropics.

THE ARCTIC

Climate

In the sunless winter, strong anticyclones form over the central core of pack
ice, North America, Greenland, and Siberia, bringing mean temperatures of
around -22°F (-30°C) to the central basin, -58°F (-50°C) over land. Through
the rest of the year eastward-moving cyclones bring rain, snow, and winds.
Mean monthly temperatures rise above freezing point from May to September.

Natural Resources

Marine life is limited in the Arctic Ocean but the more open oceans of the
Barents, Greenland, and Bering seas support rich fisheries. Native peoples
have long relied on sealing, whaling, and fur-trading. Seals are still hunted
commercially on pack ice off Newfoundland and the White Sea: whaling is
strictly limited for local communities. In northern Siberia and Alaska, huge
reserves of oil, coal, and gas have been tapped.

THE ANTARCTIC

Climate

A persistent winter anticyclone over the continent makes the highest points
of the plateau some of Earth's coldest places. The Russian station, Vostok,
recorded a world record low temperature of -126.9°F (-88.3°C) in August 1960.
Summer monthly mean temperatures rise to around -22°F (-30°C). Coastal
stations and the Antarctic Peninsula are much warmer.

Natural Resources

Stocks of the Southern Ocean's whales and seals were hunted almost to
extinction during the 19th and 20th centuries. They have recovered in recent
years, especially since the International Whaling Commission declared most
of the Southern Ocean a whale sanctuary in 1994. Of greater concern now is
illegal fishing, which is steadily depleting stocks of Antarctic cod, finfish, and
toothfish. Mining is banned under the Antarctic Treaty.

ARCTIC TUNDRA

Tundra is the rolling, treeless plains lying north of the boreal forests. Snow-covered in winter, it thaws in spring to reveal stony, wind-swept uplands and greener lowlands dotted with lakes, bogs, and marshes. Though underlain by permafrost, summer tundra supports mosses, grasses, rushes, and knee-high shrubs, brightened by patches of pink, white, blue, and yellow flowering plants. There is a brief fall of brown leaves, seeds, and bright red berries, before white winter sets in. Along its southern border tundra is fringed by a narrow zone of stunted trees and shrubs that merge with the forest itself. In the harsher north it thins gradually to near-sterile Arctic desert. Humans brought up in temperate conditions find tundra hostile, and wonder how plants and animals can survive there. Yet hundreds of kinds of living creatures, including humans, make their homes on tundra, either year-round or as summer migrants.

INSECTS

Insects disappear in winter, but emerge when the snow melts and the ground warms in spring. Moths, butterflies, hoverflies, and bumblebees search the flowers for nectar and pollen; blowflies breed on carcasses; damselflies, dragonflies, and caddisflies hover above the ponds; and swarms of midges, mosquitoes, and botflies plague the grazing caribou.

Bumblebee
Bumblebee queens spend winter deep in the soil, emerging in spring to warm up and find nesting holes near the surface. They collect pollen and nectar, and lay eggs to start their colonies.

Banded demoiselle
Damselflies spend years as larvae in ponds, feeding on other insects and growing slowly. When mature they climb out and fly for only a few days, long enough to mate and lay eggs.

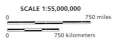

SCALE 1:55,000,000

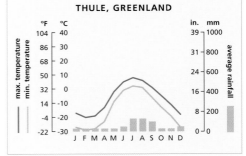

THULE, GREENLAND

Musk oxen
Musk oxen live in small wandering herds, feeding throughout the year on sedges, dwarf willows, and grasses. In fall they fatten and grow a dense, woolly coat. In winter they live only where the snow lies thin, so they can continue to find food.

Arctic fox
Gray or white in winter, brown or brown-and-white in summer, Arctic foxes live in well-drained hillside burrows, hunting constantly for ground squirrels, lemmings, and nesting birds. In winter many go out onto the sea ice, hunting for seal pups and scavenging after polar bears.

Life on the tundra

In winter much of the tundra lies blanketed in snow. Small animals, such as this ground squirrel, mice, and lemmings can continue living under cover—the ground is still warm and the blanket of snow protects them from the worst of the weather outside. Bigger animals cannot do this. Some, such as the caribou, migrate south to the shelter of forests. Others, such as musk oxen, fatten and grow massive coats to see them through winter.

Caribou

Thousands of caribou move north over the tundra in spring, giving birth to their fawns on the way. Shifting constantly, fattening on the new vegetation, they graze through the long summer days. In fall they mate, then turn south when the weather chills to spend winter in the forests.

Snowy owl

Snowy owls live year-round on the tundra, generally favoring areas where snow is thin. They perch on rocks or low bushes from which they can watch for prey, then swoop silently and almost invisibly on hares, lemmings, mice, ducks, and other small mammals and birds.

Lemming

A snowy owl may take up to 1,600 lemmings in a year. In good years when the snow melts early and lemmings are easy to catch, snowy owls can raise ten or more chicks. In bad years they may lay only three or four eggs and lose them all.

KEEPING WARM

To stay active, warm-blooded animals such as mammals and birds must feed to maintain their body temperature around 99°F (37°C). Big animals like this grizzly bear carry thick fat and dense fur insulation, but cannot find enough food in winter to keep their temperature up. So they find a sheltered den and hibernate, chill down and sleep the winter away.

THE ARCTIC
SUMMER BLOOM

Arctic land plants survive winter under tightly-packed snow, blanketed from harsh winds and extremely low temperatures. So do many insects, mice, lemmings, and other small animals. In spring, as the snow melts, the sun's rays penetrate to stimulate plant growth. Ponds and lakes thaw; algae, pondweeds, mosses, grasses, and flowering plants grow rapidly. As the air warms, insects by the million emerge, and birds and mammals that have wintered over begin to fatten. Now thousands of migrant birds fly north, some from as far as Africa, South America, and the southern USA, to feed and breed among the spring and summer abundance. Swans, divers, and ducks dabble in the streams and lakes. Geese browse the grasses and waders find insects among the grasses and shallow soils. Caribou and reindeer also move north, and porcupines, foxes, and brown and black bears emerge from the forests to hunt and scavenge.

Flowers that bloom in summer
For months this meadow in an Arctic corner of Newfoundland has been under snow. As winter ends the snow melts, lengthening days of sunshine warm the earth and vegetation, and the tundra springs to life. Arctic poppies and other quick-growing annuals appear first, providing a splash of color among the more sober perennial grasses.

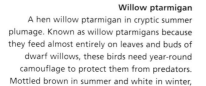

Red fox
The common red fox of Eurasia and North America ranges up into the Arctic but not generally as far north as Arctic foxes. Unlike Arctic foxes, red foxes stay the same color throughout the year, though with a much denser coat in winter.

Willow ptarmigan
Winter plumage

Willow ptarmigan
A hen willow ptarmigan in cryptic summer plumage. Known as willow ptarmigans because they feed almost entirely on leaves and buds of dwarf willows, these birds need year-round camouflage to protect them from predators. Mottled brown in summer and white in winter, they simply disappear into their background.

Willow ptarmigan
Summer plumage

Poppies and bearberry
The tundra turns brilliant red in fall as the dwarf shrubs prepare to shed their leaves. Red berries appear, too, rich in nutrients for bears and other animals. Among them grow lacy reindeer moss—a lichen that is half fungus, half alga, which reindeer and caribou like to eat.

Caribou
Caribou are wild deer of Arctic North America; reindeer are the wild and domesticated herds of Europe and Asia. They migrate north in spring, south in fall across the tundra. Calves are born during the spring migration.

Daylight hours
As spring advances, hours of daylight increase rapidly; the further north the longer the days. After the fall equinox days grow shorter than nights. For every extra hour of summer daylight, there is an extra hour of darkness in winter.

	Jan	Feb	Mar	Apr	May	Jun	Jul	Aug	Sept	Oct	Nov	Dec
80°N	0	2.3	13.6	24	24	24	24	24	13.1	0.8	0	0
70°N	2.5	8.3	12.5	17.1	24	24	24	17.2	12.6	8.2	2.4	0
60°N	7.1	9.8	12.3	15.1	17.6	18.9	17.7	15.1	12.4	9.7	7.1	5.9

Grizzly Bear
Grizzlies are big bears, always hungry and ready to eat any kind of food they can find. In summer they snap up lemmings, ground squirrels, nesting birds, eggs, or sick or injured caribou. They also eat grasses, shoots, and berries. In winter they hibernate.

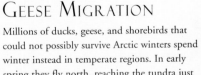

Barnacle geese
Branta leucopsis

GEESE MIGRATION

Millions of ducks, geese, and shorebirds that could not possibly survive Arctic winters spend winter instead in temperate regions. In early spring they fly north, reaching the tundra just as the snow is disappearing, the ponds are thawing, and the grass is beginning to grow. The summers here are short, so these seasonal migrants are always in a hurry to start nesting and laying their clutches of eggs.

Barnacle goose
Barnacle geese that nest in Svalbard winter in Britain: those that breed in the eastern Siberian Arctic spend their winters in the Netherlands. If spring comes late and the snow stays on the ground, they may not be able to breed at all.

THE ARCTIC
HUNTERS AND HUNTED

The basic tundra foods are grasses, lichens, shrubs, roots, seeds, and berries. These are eaten year-round by lemmings, mice, ground squirrels, hares, musk oxen, ptarmigan, overwintering finches, and ground insects. In summer migrant reindeer, caribou, and geese arrive to feed on the fresh growth. These plant-eating mammals, birds, and insects are preyed on by foxes, wolves, weasels, owls, falcons, ravens, and skuas. Birds and small mammals fall prey to smaller hunters: wolves take the big musk oxen and caribou, leaving skin and bones to be picked over by foxes and scavenging birds. Summer-visiting shorebirds (waders) feed mainly on ground-living insects. In streams, ponds, and lakes, ducks dabble for weeds and aquatic insects or dive deeper for fish. Grizzly and polar bears feed on anything from berries to dead caribou, and polar bears and Arctic foxes go out onto the sea ice to feed on seals.

Ground squirrel
These little animals feed for only three to four months of the year—the summer months in which grasses and other new shoots are richest in nutrients and most plentiful. At the end of summer they accumulate fat, then sleep away the winter in nests underground.

TERRESTRIAL ANIMALS		MARINE ANIMALS
CARNIVORES & OMNIVORES	HERBIVORES & INSECTIVORES	CARNIVORES & OMNIVORES
Foxes	Lemmings	Orcas
Wolves	Mice	Seals
Weasels	Squirrels	Walrus
Falcons	Reindeer	Sharks
Owls	Caribou	Gulls
Bears	Birds	Ducks and other birds

Glaucous gull
These elegant gulls forage along the seashore for plankton washed up by the tide, and patrol the cliffs and beaches where other seabirds nest, watching for unattended eggs and chicks.

FEEDING AT SEA

The basic sea food is plankton—tiny plant cells and shrimplike crustaceans that proliferate when the sea ice melts in spring. Animals from small fish to big whales feed on plankton, and the fish in turn are eaten by most seals, dolphins, small whales, and seabirds. Bearded seals and walrus eat clams, which live on the seabed and feed on debris that falls from above.

Puffin
Puffins, sometimes called sea parrots, spend their summers in clifftop burrows, often in colonies numbering many thousands. They feed at sea, catching small fish that they carry home to their nestlings.

Orca
Also called killer whales, orcas are found all over the world including the Arctic. They hunt in packs for seals and other whales. An orca can eat seven seals in one meal.

Arctic fox
Like stoats, Arctic foxes hunt birds and small mammals, so need to change color from summer to winter. This one, in summer coat, is jumping on a mouse or lemming. In winter many move out onto the sea ice, scavenging on seals killed by polar bears.

Arctic wolf
Arctic wolves hunt in packs of a dozen or more, often following migrating caribou or musk oxen and killing the calves and older animals that cannot keep up with the herds. They feed also on birds and small mammals, but large mammals are their main prey.

Great gray owl
Great gray owls live in the northern forests and along the forest–tundra edge. Like snowy owls they hunt for voles, mice, and small lemmings, watching and listening for movement, then swooping and pouncing to carry off their catch. Males bring most of the food to the nests.

Stoat
In summer the stoat is brown; in winter it turns white, with a black tip to its tail, and is called an ermine. A fierce hunter of small mammals and birds, it stalks quietly and pounces without being seen. This one has found a deep-frozen Arctic hare to feed on.

Char
Some char live in lakes, others in streams and rivers, where they feed mainly on insects and smaller fish. Despite spending part of their lives in the sea, river char can also be found far up mountain streams where they feast on salmon eggs.

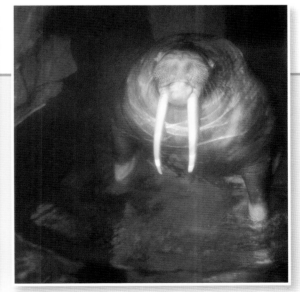

Harp seal
Harp seals live out on the sea ice, feeding on capelin, cod, and other shoaling fish. Pups are silky white for their first 12 days, then molt into harsher gray fur for swimming.

Greenland shark
The only sharks known in Arctic waters, these sluggish, bottom-living fish feed on seals and smaller fish. They are hunted for their oil and their sandpaper skin.

Walrus
Walruses look and swim like seals. They live on coastal sea ice and along Arctic shores, feeding by diving to the seabed, which they rake with their tusks for clams.

THE POLAR BEAR

Polar bears live around the Arctic Ocean and neighboring seas. Males weigh up to 1,322 pounds (600 kg), females are lighter, up to 550 pounds (250 kg): standing upright they are taller than a man. Unlike brown and grizzly bears, polar bears spend much of their lives on sea ice that, in winter, spreads along the coasts and covers the ocean. They live mainly on seals, which feed on fish and clams below the ice, but come up through cracks and holes to rest and produce their pups. As year-round residents in the Arctic, polar bears have to survive subzero temperatures. Their dense white fur, up to 12 inches (30 cm) thick, protects them from the worst polar weather. The fur is waterproof too, so bears can swim for hours in icy seas. In summer, when the ice softens and melts, they forage on land, eating grasses, berries, birds' eggs, and nestlings. In autumn they fatten on fish, particularly salmon and char, that they scoop from freshwater streams.

Defending their ground
Living where food is seldom plentiful, polar bears usually walk on their own. Two or three together are most likely to be a mother with cubs. When lone males meet they growl, roar, and even wrestle until one is driven away.

In search of food
Despite their weight and bulk, polar bears are agile. They leap from floe to floe and wander many miles every day in search of food. The ability to leave land and travel over sea ice gives them access to breeding seals—their main food in early spring.

Family group
Cubs stay with their mother for up to two years, until almost fully grown. It is a hard life, especially in winter, and one or more in each family may die. Those cubs that survive wander off independently, then the mother is ready to find another mate.

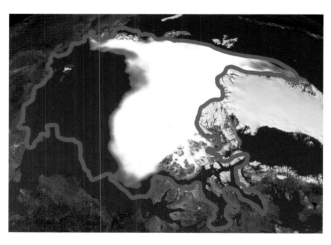

Lone hunter
Polar bears are lone animals that live by their wits, always hungry and very strong—powerful enough to break into houses and food stores. Though still hunted in small numbers, they are protected by international agreement throughout the Arctic.

Sea ice changes

Areas of both permanent and annually-renewed Arctic sea ice grow smaller year by year and have lost 38 percent of their area over the past 30 years. Numbers of both seals and polar bears are likely to fall; they may disappear altogether from some areas. Climates are always changing: the Arctic has been both warmer and cooler in the past, and seals and bears have survived the changes before.

HUNTING TO SURVIVE

Polar bears spend part of their time on land, but more on sea ice in coastal channels and bays. Females give birth on land, but take their cubs onto the sea ice where food is easier to find. Food is never plentiful so, after mating, males and females go their separate ways. Mothers hunt and bring up the cubs on their own.

Seal meat
On the sea ice bears hunt for seals, which in spring are raising pups among the floes. The adult female knows how to find and kill the seals, providing a meal for herself and her cubs.

Whale carcass
Polar bears are always ready to eat whatever they can find. Here, a mother and her grown cubs have followed the scent to a dead whale, washed up on a Svalbard shore.

Ringed seal
Ringed seals live close inshore among the pack ice, where they produce their pups in spring, often in hidden dens among the floes. Polar bears hunt by scent for both adults and pups.

Protecting young cubs
Mother and cubs break out of their winter den in spring and move toward the sea ice. The cubs stay close to their mother because there are hungry predators about—foxes, wolves, even other polar bears—ready to kill and eat them. Females guard their cubs fiercely.

Winter in the den
Polar bears mate in summer. In autumn the pregnant females dig dens for themselves in snowbanks, where they sleep throughout winter. Around December each gives birth to one, two, or sometimes three rabbit-sized cubs, which feed on the mother's rich milk. Between feeds, mothers and cubs save energy by sleeping. By March or April the cubs are large enough to leave the den.

ANTARCTIC DESERT

Antarctica is truly a desert, the largest and driest on Earth, yet it contains 70 percent of the world's fresh water and 90 percent of its ice. Much of the Antarctic ice sheet is 2.5 miles (4 km) high and almost 3 miles (5 km) thick in places. It is also cold. A record low of –129.3° (–89.5°C) was recorded in 1983. Little rain falls but what does fall can remain frozen for up to one million years preserving an excellent record of climate changes. Deep within the ice there are vast lakes, kept above freezing temperature by Earth's heat. Life is rare on the ice sheet and restricted to the margins near the "warm" ocean. Water temperatures drop to a minimum of 28.7°F (–1.8°C) in winter beneath sea ice. At the margins of the continent, dark rocks absorb sunlight and heat, leading to the growth of algae and lichens on their warm surface.

Adélie penguins
Adélie penguins are a symbol of the Antarctic. They occur abundantly around the Antarctic margin, gathering in large rookeries to bear their young in summer. But much of their life is spent at sea where they hunt for fish and krill.

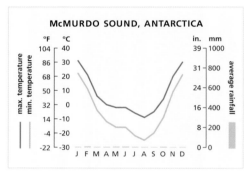

Blackfin icefish
The extreme cold of Antarctic waters is too severe an environment for most fish species. Some, however, have adapted to life here. The Antarctic icefish, such as the blackfin icefish, do not have hemoglobin in their blood, but have developed an "anti-freeze" capability.

SCALE 1:70,000,000

0 — 1500 miles
0 — 1500 kilometers

McMURDO SOUND, ANTARCTICA

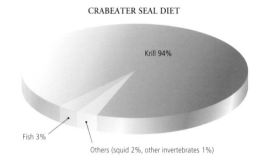

CRABEATER SEAL DIET

Krill 94%
Fish 3%
Others (squid 2%, other invertebrates 1%)

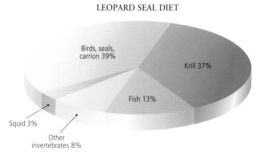

LEOPARD SEAL DIET

Birds, seals, carrion 39%
Krill 37%
Fish 13%
Squid 3%
Other invertebrates 8%

Leopard seal
Leopard seals have a disproportionately large head and wide-opening, strong jaws. Their varied diet includes large catches such as penguins and young crabeater seals but they also filter seawater for krill. They are occasionally seen ashore on subantarctic islands.

Taylor Valley
This is one of the "Dry Valleys" in the McMurdo Sound region. These valleys, which receive almost no precipitation, are deserts of the most extreme type. They are largely ice-free, except for some permanently frozen lakes. Life here is limited to species such as mosses and algae.

Ross seal
The Ross seal's range encircles the Antarctic continent but it is most likely to be found in the Ross Sea. It feeds mainly on squid but also takes some fish and krill. Young are born on pack ice in early summer and are suckled by their mother for about four weeks. This is the rarest of the Antarctic seals.

Crabeater seal
The crabeater seal is the most abundant seal species on Earth. It inhabits Antarctic pack ice and its population is estimated at 11 to 12 million. This seal has characteristic tri-lobed teeth, allowing it to filter krill-rich water. Krill are its major food.

Southern fur seal
These seals, which belong to the group known as eared seals, occur on islands close to the Antarctic continent but they do not breed on the ice. They spend most of the winter at sea, pursuing their diet of fish, krill, rock lobsters, and penguins.

FEEDING GROUNDS

A crustacean central to the Antarctic food chain, krill lives near the margin of Antarctic sea ice and is the main food source of baleen whales, many seals, and penguins. The total mass of krill is more than 100 million tons making it the target of the world's largest single-species fishery. A krill's diet comprises microplankton such as diatoms.

Swarms
Krill are usually widely dispersed in the water, but periodically they come together in dense swarms, covering many square miles. These swarms, which color the sea red, provide a convenient food concentration for whales.

Food
A form of plankton, the krill uses its front legs to filter food and pass it forward to its mouth. Krill has high potential for human use as food and for biochemicals.

ASKHAM BRYAN
COLLEGE
LEARNING RESOURCES

THE ANTARCTIC
LONG-DISTANCE MIGRANTS

Seasonal migration by wildlife is common in the natural world, allowing animals to move between distant environments to mate, bear young, and feed. Migration from the severe climatic conditions of polar regions is vital for many animals; food is plentiful in summer but in winter few animal species can survive. The emperor penguin is the only animal that is a year-round resident on the Antarctic ice. Others migrate, many of them long distances. Baleen whales, such as the humpback, migrate in both hemispheres along well-marked routes to the tropics during the polar winters. The northern and southern right whales, which have more restricted distributions and migration paths, also spend winter in warmer waters. The gray whale migrates from the northern Pacific Ocean to winter offshore from Mexico, a round trip of some 12,500 miles (20,000 km). Many bird and seal species also make long seasonal migrations from the high-latitude regions in winter.

Migration paths

Most aquatic migrating animals remain in their home hemisphere, even though they may travel long distances, but birds have no such limits and may migrate from one pole to the other. Whales migrate from polar regions, where they feed in summer, to the tropics where they mate and have their young. Seals migrate to bear their young on islands or other coasts in lower, subpolar latitudes.

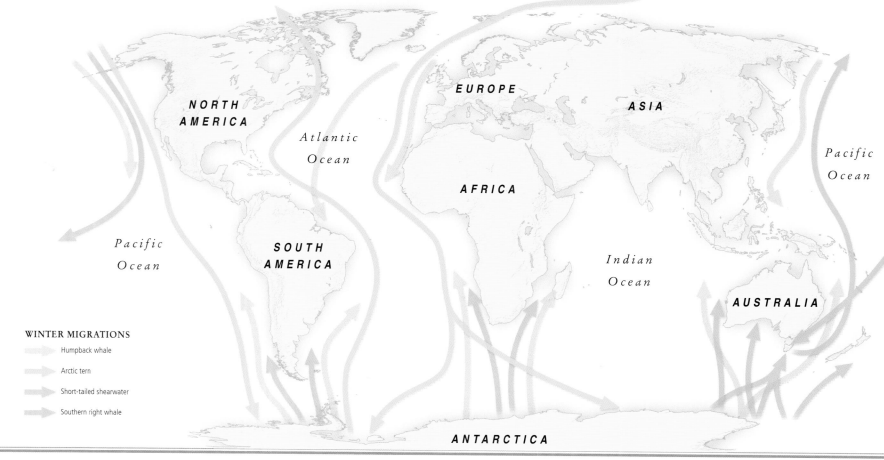

NORTH AMERICA

EUROPE

ASIA

Atlantic Ocean

Pacific Ocean

AFRICA

Pacific Ocean

SOUTH AMERICA

Indian Ocean

AUSTRALIA

WINTER MIGRATIONS

Humpback whale

Arctic tern

Short-tailed shearwater

Southern right whale

ANTARCTICA

Humpback whale

Humpback whales feed on swarms of krill in Antarctic waters (above). They gulp massive mouthfuls of krill and water, which are then filtered through their baleen "sieve" allowing them to retain and eat the krill. In the Arctic, humpback pods work cooperatively to form curtains of bubbles that concentrate krill in a restricted area. The humpback ends its migration in tropical waters, such as those off Tonga (left). Breaching may be a signal to others in the pod or elsewhere.

CONSERVATION WATCH

The Antarctic fin whale is second only to the blue whale in size. It is the fastest of the rorquals and cruises at 15 to 20 miles per hour (24–32 km/h). Its large size made it a desirable catch during the 20th-century whaling period and numbers have suffered.

Southern elephant seals
These juvenile elephant seals have migrated from the Antarctic winter and are resting in tussock grass on a subantarctic island. Elephant seals grow rapidly on their mother's rich milk and, weaned at about three weeks, can fend for themselves, feeding at sea.

Southern right whale
A southern right whale displays the unique callosities on its head and back. The species was named "the right whale" by whalers because it is slow, and therefore easier to catch, has a high oil content, and floats when dead.

MIGRATORY BIRDS

Birds that remain in the south polar regions year-round experience the maximum contrast between polar winters and summers. The Antarctic tern and several penguin species remain in the region; others, such as the albatross and the Arctic tern, travel vast distances.

Arctic tern
Arctic terns are renowned as great migrators—from their Arctic breeding grounds to the Antarctic. They can hover while observing small fish near the water's surface, then dive on their catch.

Arctic tern chick
Arctic tern chicks bred in the Arctic weigh only a few ounces. They migrate to the Antarctic for the southern summer.

Short-tailed shearwater
Short-tailed shearwaters breed in southeastern Australia and have two forms of migration—the traditional clockwise journey around the Pacific Ocean and a spring–summer round trip to Antarctic waters, gathering food for their young.

THE ANTARCTIC
ANTARCTIC BIRDS

The Southern Ocean, circling Antarctica and covering almost 5 percent of the planet's surface, is home to a large and diverse seabird community including albatrosses, petrels, gulls, terns, and cormorants. It is also a destination for northern hemisphere migrants, such as Arctic terns during the southern summer. Early sailors dubbed the Southern Ocean winds the "Roaring '40s," the "Furious '50s," and the "Screaming '60s." These winds provide excellent flying conditions for albatrosses and petrels that use the energy from the wind for flight—their wingspans reach more than 12 feet (3.5 m). Small oceanic islands in the Southern Ocean serve as nesting sites for millions of seabirds, which seek prey in the surrounding seas. Their aerodynamically streamlined bodies reduce the energy required for flight, and enable them to forage far from land. Seabirds use a variety of methods to capture prey, including surface seizing and diving.

South polar skua
South polar skuas are closely associated with breeding colonies of penguins. These predatory scavengers take eggs and small penguin chicks for food, but are aggressive in defense of their own breeding territories. The hook at the tip of their bill is used to rip flesh.

Snow petrel
Year-round residents of the Antarctic, snow petrels feed in open water among the ice. They are agile fliers and can survive winter storms. Snow petrels nest on the ground, laying one egg on bare rock in early summer.

Subantarctic skua
These skuas are found on subantarctic islands and some temperate islands south of New Zealand. They nest on the ground using vegetation, if present, for their nest. Two eggs are laid, but typically only one chick survives.

SNOWY SHEATHBILL

Snowy sheathbills are found on the Antarctic Peninsula and on islands in the South Atlantic Ocean. Their breeding distribution is closely associated with penguins, other species of seabirds, and fur seal colonies. During the summer months they scavenge from these colonies, taking eggs, chicks, and carrion.

South Atlantic and back
Fights made seasonally by the snowy sheathbill.

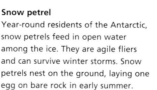

Migratory flights
These birds are capable of flying from the Antarctic region to wintering sites in Patagonia, Tierra del Fuego, and the Falkland Islands. Flights may exceed 2000 miles (3200 km) in each direction.

Seasonal residents
Snowy, or pale-faced, sheathbills are named for the sheath, or shield, that is present around their bill. They lay up to four eggs in a nest constructed on the ground in a sheltered cavity.

Wandering albatross on the wing

Albatrosses are perhaps the most efficient fliers on the planet. Their long wings generate enormous lift but prevent them from flapping the wings too rapidly. As a result, they are gliders, flying for long periods without flapping their wings. In light wind conditions they may rest on the water surface to conserve energy and await the next windy period. To take off from the water, they run into the wind with their wings outstretched.

Male display

Breeding males advertise themselves by bringing their wings to full stretch, raising their heads, and calling to prospective partners. Interested females approach and courtship rituals continue. The birds also use these behaviors to re-establish a bond between a pair that has bred before.

Air flow

Uplift

Aerodynamic design

A bird's wing is shaped so that air passes more quickly across the top, curved, surface than the bottom, providing essential lift.

Courtship rituals

Albatrosses use various courtship behaviors and vocalizations to establish the pair bond for the first time and, like many species of seabirds, they mate for life. A well-bonded pair has a greater chance of breeding successfully than first-time breeders.

Albatross chick

Perched on a nest made from vegetation and mud, this light-mantled sooty albatross chick waits for its next meal. Albatrosses lay just one egg and some species breed only every second year. Each season requires a coordinated effort by the parents to ensure their chick fledges.

Migratory path

Albatrosses make use of weather systems as they circumnavigate the globe. Strong and persistent westerlies are present over much of the southern hemisphere, and these winds provide the energy for the birds' long-distance flights. These flights are undertaken by non-breeding and juvenile birds, and by breeding adults that are restoring body reserves following a breeding season.

Pacific Ocean

SOUTH AMERICA

AFRICA

Indian Ocean

AUSTRALIA

ANTARCTICA

THE ANTARCTIC
PENGUIN PARADE

Of the 17 species of penguins, just four species are considered Antarctic: emperor, Adélie, chinstrap, and macaroni penguins. The remaining species are found on subantarctic and temperate islands as far north as the Galàpagos Islands at the equator, but all are confined to the southern hemisphere. Despite evolving from flighted ancestors, penguins are flightless but they "fly" through the water in order to feed. A variety of anatomical, physiological, and behavioral adaptations allow penguins to breed, feed, and survive. Their feathers are denser than those of any other bird, providing a streamlined and well-insulated body, and they have a thick layer of fat under the skin, providing further insulation and energy reserves for periods when they cannot feed. Up to 25 percent of a penguin's mass is in the breast muscles that power their flippers, which are used for swimming and for tobogganing over ice and snow.

Chinstrap penguin
Chinstrap penguins are so named because of the distinctive thin black line under their bills and on their cheeks. Their breeding colonies are found throughout the Antarctic Peninsula and on islands in the South Atlantic Ocean. A small breeding population is also found on the Balleny Islands, south of New Zealand.

Life on the ice
Penguins' feathers are highly adapted structures that form a dense layer to keep their body dry. They have strong feet with toes that provide a firm grip on ice and wet rocks.

Long toenails to grip onto ice

Feather layering

Nesting and feeding

Most penguin species nest close to the ocean. Diving underwater to feed, they seek prey concentrations such as krill swarms or schools of fish. All four species of Antarctic penguins breed around the Antarctic continent but the Adélie, chinstrap, and macaroni penguins choose only the coastal ice-free areas. Most colonies of emperor penguins, however, are found on the winter sea ice.

Distribution
Penguins are found along the coasts of all southern hemisphere continents, the Antarctic Peninsula, and on the small oceanic islands in the Southern Ocean.

Emperor penguins
Emperor penguins are the largest and heaviest penguins, with some individuals weighing more than 100 pounds (45 kg). They are capable of deep dives—the deepest recorded dive exceeded 1,600 feet (500 m) and took almost 20 minutes.

Penguin variety
Penguins are not just black and white, they are adorned with colorful crests, washes of rich oranges and yellows, and unique feather spots. Each species has a different shaped bill.

Emperor penguin
Aptenodytes forsteri

King penguin
Aptenodytes patagonicus

Chinstrap penguin
Pygoscelis antarctica

Adélie penguin
Pygoscelis adeliae

Yellow eyed penguin
Megadyptes antipodes

Magellanic penguin
Spheniscus magellanicus

Fiordland penguin
Eudyptes pachyrhynchus

Little penguin
Eudyptula minor

Adélie penguin

Adélie penguins are among the iconic species of penguin in the Antarctic and are the most widely distributed. Their diet is primarily crustaceans and fish, and they are capable of diving to 660 feet (200 m) to search for prey. Between dives, they rest on the surface or on ice floes to avoid predators such as leopard seals.

King penguin

King penguin colonies can number more than 100,000 pairs—so large the colonies are visible in satellite images. They are found on many of the subantarctic islands in the Southern Ocean where the maritime climate contrasts with the cold and dry climate of the Antarctic.

REARING OFFSPRING

Penguin chicks in the Antarctic face numerous threats from the moment they hatch. Temperatures can be extreme—as low as –40 degrees (–40°C) in midwinter when emperor penguins eggs hatch. Keeping the chicks warm is a full-time job for penguin parents as the newly hatched chicks are unable to keep themselves warm.

Protection

Until the chicks are quite large, almost half grown, they need their parents to protect them from the elements. Their own downy feathers do not protect them from low air temperatures.

Nest site

A rocky nest, built by the male, provides a home for the eggs and chicks. It is elevated above the surrounding terrain so that when the snow and ice melts during the summer it will not be flooded.

Bringing food

King penguins take more than a year to raise their chicks and, during winter months, a chick may wait weeks for its next meal. The parents forage over vast distances to provide their large chick with enough food.

Bottlenose dolphins live in the warm waters of the world. These social, active, and intelligent dolphins communicate with each other using a complex system of whistles, squeaks, and touch. They can travel at speeds of up to 18 miles an hour (30 km/h). All dolphins are cetaceans—a group that includes orcas and beluga whales.

THE OCEANS

THE OCEANS

Our Earth, the Blue Planet, is dominated by water. Some 70 percent of Earth's surface is covered by water, and life could not exist without it. About 200 million years ago, Earth was covered by one huge ocean with a single continent called Pangaea. Over the millennia, Pangaea broke up to form drifting continents, carried by great plates of Earth's crust. Today's five oceans—Pacific, Atlantic, Indian, Arctic, and Southern—were formed as continents drifted apart. The oceans comprise a vast three-dimensional space, where conditions at one spot on Earth can vary from bright, tropical warmth at the surface to perpetually dark, polar cold only a couple of miles below. Marine ecosystems can range from highly productive, brackish marshes, rocky coasts, and coral reefs to sterile mid-ocean regions bereft of nutrients. In this cornucopia of habitats, an extraordinary diversity of organisms has evolved with a wide array of adaptations to life in the sea.

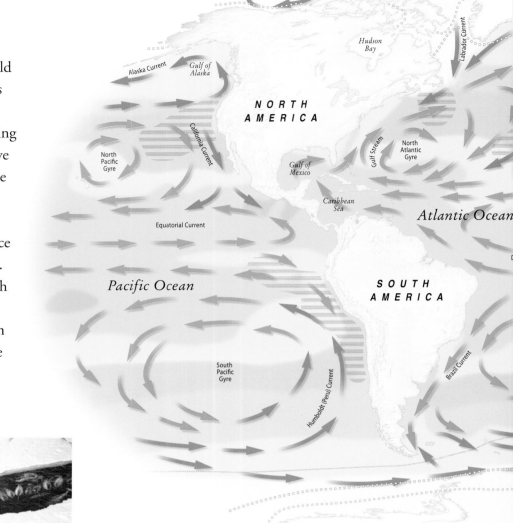

Pacific Ocean
The Pacific is the oldest and largest ocean. The coral reefs, stretching from Indonesia to the Great Barrier Reef off eastern Australia, harbor the most diverse marine fauna on Earth.

Arctic Ocean
The Arctic Ocean is essentially landlocked, and typified for aeons by permanent sea ice. Recent global warming is causing summer melting and threatens Arctic ecosystems.

Atlantic Ocean
The Atlantic formed 150 million years ago when the continents of Europe and North America broke apart, and Africa and South America separated along a submarine seam.

Southern Ocean
The nutrient-rich Southern Ocean, which flows around Antarctica, supports high plankton production. Great whales gather there in summer to gorge on shrimplike krill.

Indian Ocean
The Indian Ocean shares much of its tropical marine fauna with the western Pacific, with which it is connected. Currents move freely around the Indonesian islands and Australia.

KNOWN SPECIES

Land species 84%

Marine species 16%

MARINE SPECIES

Benthic species 98%

Open-water species 2%

CHLOROPHYLL CONCENTRATION

Lowest Very low Low Medium High Very high Highest

Ocean productivity
Scientists use satellite measurements of chlorophyll concentration at the sea surface to estimate the production of phytoplankton around the world. The oceans' productivity is highest at higher latitudes, and in upwelling areas near the equator and along the western sides of continents. The most productive fisheries are found in these same high-nutrient areas.

Marine species
Marine organisms make up only 16 percent of all known species. However, it is much easier to observe and collect plants and animals on land than in the oceans. A recent expedition to collect deepwater bottom animals off Antarctica discovered hundreds of new species.

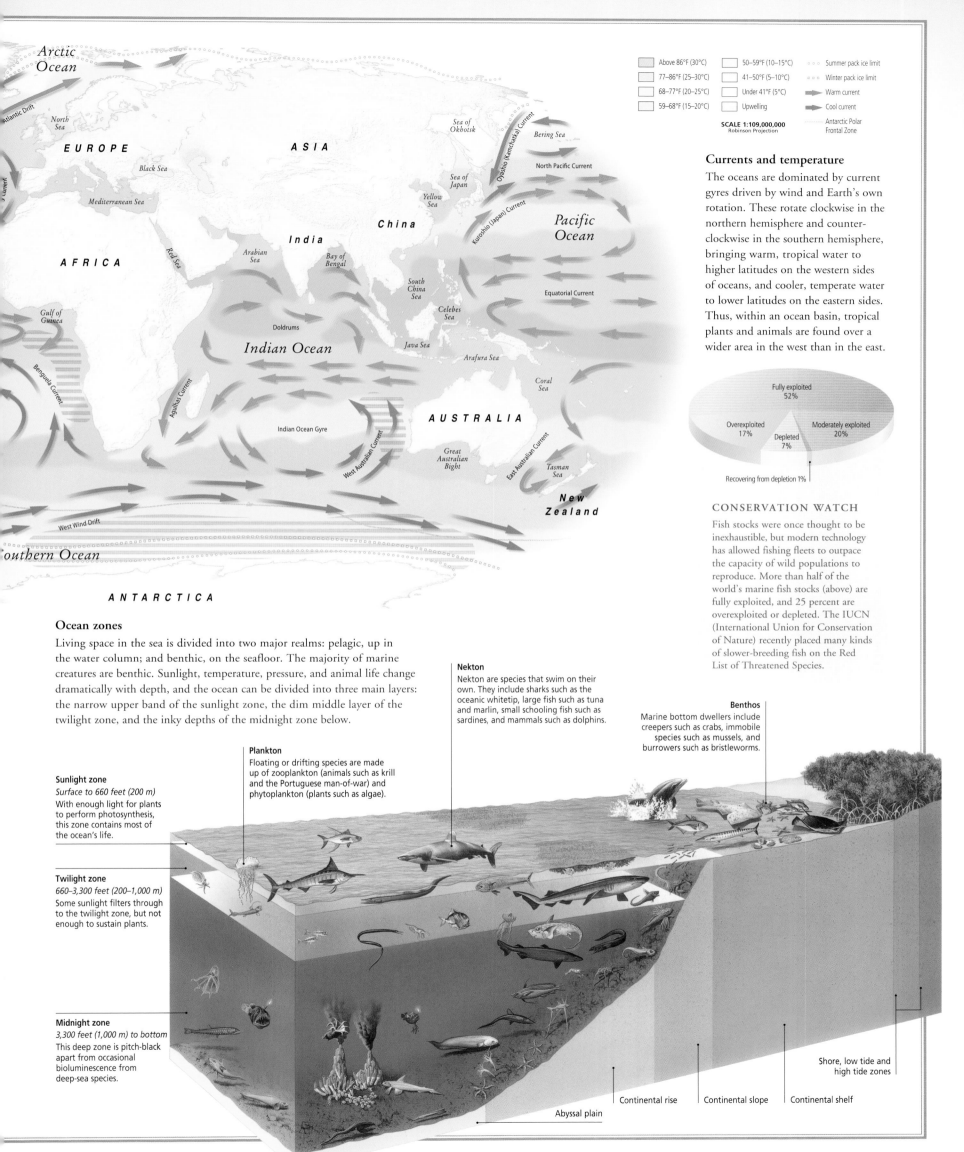

Above 86°F (30°C) 50–59°F (10–15°C) Summer pack ice limit
77–86°F (25–30°C) 41–50°F (5–10°C) Winter pack ice limit
68–77°F (20–25°C) Under 41°F (5°C) Warm current
59–68°F (15–20°C) Upwelling Cool current

SCALE 1:109,000,000 Antarctic Polar
Robinson Projection Frontal Zone

Arctic Ocean

EUROPE ASIA

North Sea *Sea of Okhotsk* *Bering Sea*
Black Sea *Sea of Japan* North Pacific Current
Atlantic Drift *Mediterranean Sea* *Yellow Sea*
Oyashio (Kamchatka) Current

India *China* *Pacific Ocean*
AFRICA *Red Sea* *Arabian Sea* *Bay of Bengal* *Kuroshio (Japan) Current*
Gulf of Guinea *South China Sea*
Celebes Sea Equatorial Current
Doldrums *Java Sea*
Indian Ocean *Arafura Sea*
Benguela Current *Agulhas Current* AUSTRALIA *Coral Sea*
Indian Ocean Gyre *Great Australian Bight* *East Australian Current* *Tasman Sea*
West Australian Current *New Zealand*
West Wind Drift
Southern Ocean
ANTARCTICA

Currents and temperature

The oceans are dominated by current gyres driven by wind and Earth's own rotation. These rotate clockwise in the northern hemisphere and counter-clockwise in the southern hemisphere, bringing warm, tropical water to higher latitudes on the western sides of oceans, and cooler, temperate water to lower latitudes on the eastern sides. Thus, within an ocean basin, tropical plants and animals are found over a wider area in the west than in the east.

Fully exploited 52%
Moderately exploited 20%
Depleted 7%
Overexploited 17%
Recovering from depletion 1%

CONSERVATION WATCH

Fish stocks were once thought to be inexhaustible, but modern technology has allowed fishing fleets to outpace the capacity of wild populations to reproduce. More than half of the world's marine fish stocks (above) are fully exploited, and 25 percent are overexploited or depleted. The IUCN (International Union for Conservation of Nature) recently placed many kinds of slower-breeding fish on the Red List of Threatened Species.

Ocean zones

Living space in the sea is divided into two major realms: pelagic, up in the water column; and benthic, on the seafloor. The majority of marine creatures are benthic. Sunlight, temperature, pressure, and animal life change dramatically with depth, and the ocean can be divided into three main layers: the narrow upper band of the sunlight zone, the dim middle layer of the twilight zone, and the inky depths of the midnight zone below.

Nekton
Nekton are species that swim on their own. They include sharks such as the oceanic whitetip, large fish such as tuna and marlin, small schooling fish such as sardines, and mammals such as dolphins.

Benthos
Marine bottom dwellers include creepers such as crabs, immobile species such as mussels, and burrowers such as bristleworms.

Plankton
Floating or drifting species are made up of zooplankton (animals such as krill and the Portuguese man-of-war) and phytoplankton (plants such as algae).

Sunlight zone
Surface to 660 feet (200 m)
With enough light for plants to perform photosynthesis, this zone contains most of the ocean's life.

Twilight zone
660–3,300 feet (200–1,000 m)
Some sunlight filters through to the twilight zone, but not enough to sustain plants.

Midnight zone
3,300 feet (1,000 m) to bottom
This deep zone is pitch-black apart from occasional bioluminescence from deep-sea species.

Shore, low tide and high tide zones
Continental shelf
Continental slope
Continental rise
Abyssal plain

THE PACIFIC OCEAN

The sea's richest biodiversity and biological productivity occurs in the Pacific Ocean. This vast body of water acts as a great thermostat that cools passing air masses in summer and warms them in winter. Because the size of the Pacific has moderated its marine climate, many fewer species extinctions occurred there during glaciations and other periods of extreme global climate change. The relatively stable ocean environment has allowed complex ecosystems to evolve. Coral reef communities of the Indo-Australian archipelago have the greatest diversity of tropical marine species, while the rocky coasts and kelp forests of the eastern North Pacific are home to the greatest temperate biodiversity. The Pacific has some of the highest oceanic nutrient levels and heaviest marine plankton blooms. The Bering Sea, where plankton production soars during the long summer days, and the Humboldt Current off northern South America, support two of the most productive fisheries on Earth.

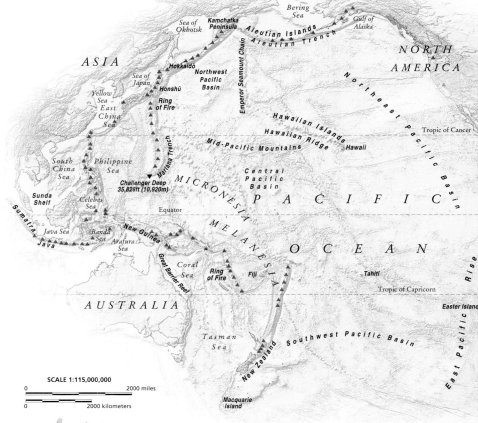

The dynamic Pacific
The central Pacific is marked by a long mountain ridge system from which Earth's crust arises and creeps west and east to collide with the continents. This violent tectonic activity—announced by earthquakes—causes mountain ranges and volcanoes to rise. Thus the perimeter of the Pacific is called The Ring of Fire.

OCEAN SHARE

Pacific Ocean
60.1 million sq miles
(155.6 million km²)
46%

All other oceans

Clown anemonefish
Amphiprion ocellaris

THE FACTS	
Area	60.1 million square miles (155.6 million km²)
Average depth	13,127 feet (4,001 m)
Maximum depth	35,840 feet (10,924 m)
Maximum width	11,200 miles (18,000 km)
Maximum length	8,600 miles (13,900 km)
Coastline length	84,297 miles (135,663 km)

Boobies and anchovies

Boobies are the avian torpedoes of the sea, folding their wings and dropping like darts out of the sky to skewer their anchovy prey in a trail of bubbles. Boobies congregate in rich ocean areas, where plankton abounds to support productive ocean food webs and large shoals of forage fish, such as anchovies. During most years, upwelling off Peru brings cold, nutrient-rich water to the surface to boost a flourishing ecosystem including plankton, fish, and seabirds such as Peruvian boobies.

EL NINO

In Spanish El Niño means "The Christ Child," a name bestowed because this oceanographic phenomenon often begins around Christmas off Peru. Warm nutrient-poor water from the central Pacific spreads eastward, and upwelling that normally dominates the region stops. During La Niña, the opposite conditions prevail. Scientists call the event the El Niño/Southern Oscillation, or ENSO, and it has profound influences on global weather patterns.

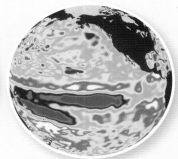

El Niño
The warm water caused by El Niño can raise sea levels by up to 8 inches (20 cm). The white patch shows El Niño moving eastward along the equator across the Pacific in March 1997.

La Niña
Lower than average sea levels, caused by cooler water, are shown in purple, during a La Niña event in July 1998. El Niño and La Niña events occur in the Pacific Ocean in no fixed cycles.

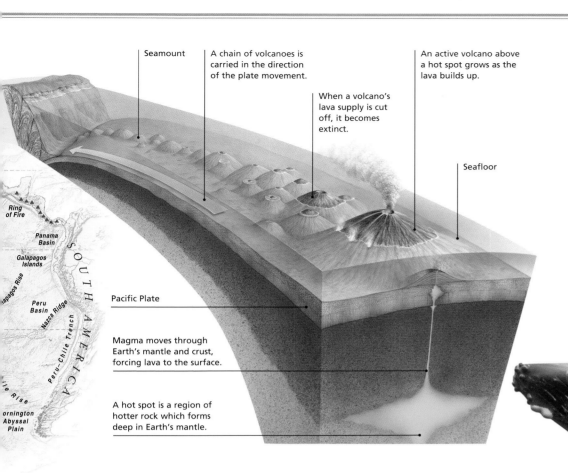

Seamount

A chain of volcanoes is carried in the direction of the plate movement.

When a volcano's lava supply is cut off, it becomes extinct.

An active volcano above a hot spot grows as the lava builds up.

Seafloor

Ring of Fire

Panama Basin

Galapagos Islands

SOUTH AMERICA

ápagos Rise

Nazca Ridge

Peru Basin

Peru–Chile Trench

le Rise

ornington Abyssal Plain

Pacific Plate

Magma moves through Earth's mantle and crust, forcing lava to the surface.

A hot spot is a region of hotter rock which forms deep in Earth's mantle.

The Hawaiian hot spot

Most volcanic islands exist for only 10 million to 30 million years before eroding back beneath the sea. The Hawaiian archipelago, however, has been forming continuously over a volcanic hot spot in the Pacific Plate for at least 70 million years. The Big Island of Hawaii is still active and growing. Other islands formed over the same hot spot and were carried northwest on the plate.

Unique species
When a single hot spot gradually produces a series of new islands, shallow-water species can island-hop along the chain and unique species have time to evolve. Of the 600 or so species of shorefish in Hawaii, 25 percent are endemic (found nowhere else). They include the Hawaiian turkeyfish, a reef fish with venomous spines.

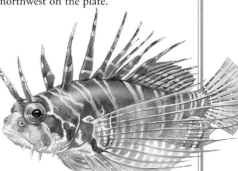

Kelp forest

Kelp are giant brown algae that may grow to 160 feet (50 m) or more in length. They require cool coastal temperatures and a rocky bottom upon which to attach. Kelp forests in the northeast Pacific provide a complex ecosystem that supports a wide variety of marine fish, such as these blacksmiths. Blacksmiths hover in the kelp and make forays into open water to feed on plankton.

Humpback whale
Large groups of black-and-white humpback whales gather to feed in summer in the plankton-rich waters off Alaska. In winter they swim halfway across the Pacific to warm subtropical haunts off Hawaii where their calves are born. Humpbacks are the most acrobatic of all the large whales, and often breach clear of the sea surface, falling with a giant splash.

⚡ CONSERVATION WATCH

The warm-blooded leatherback turtle can reach 1 ton (910 kg) in weight, and can dive more than 3,000 feet (914 m) to feast on jellyfish. Tens of thousands of leatherbacks once nested on the Pacific beaches of Central America, but no longer. Pacific leatherback populations have been decimated by capture in high-seas fisheries, and more frequent El Niño events are hampering their recovery.

THE ATLANTIC OCEAN

SCALE 1:125,000,000

The North Atlantic Ocean appeared some 160 million years ago when North America began to pull away from Eurasia after the breakup of the supercontinent Pangaea. The South Atlantic formed later, after South America separated from Africa. Consequently, the Atlantic is a newer, smaller ocean than the Pacific. Climatic variations in the Atlantic Ocean have been more extreme, and species diversity is much lower because of periodic extinctions. Both the Mediterranean and the Caribbean seas were once tropical arms of the Atlantic. When glaciers covered much of Europe and North America 10,000 years ago, only the tropical species in the Caribbean survived. Even so, the Caribbean today has only about half as many species of reef fish as we see in the western Pacific. The Atlantic does include some of the world's richest fishing areas, and these were a major impetus to colonization of the New World.

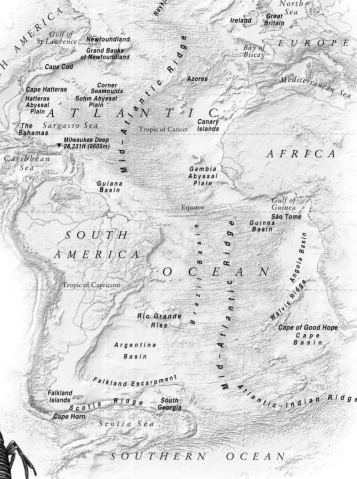

OCEAN SHARE

All other oceans

Atlantic Ocean
29.7 million sq miles
(76.8 million km²)
23%

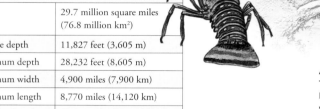

Caribbean spiny lobster
Panulirus argus

THE FACTS	
Area	29.7 million square miles (76.8 million km²)
Average depth	11,827 feet (3,605 m)
Maximum depth	28,232 feet (8,605 m)
Maximum width	4,900 miles (7,900 km)
Maximum length	8,770 miles (14,120 km)
Coastline length	69,510 miles (111,866 km)

Atlantic Ocean features
The Atlantic Ocean is characterized by a northern rim ringed by landmasses and rich fishing banks, high tropical diversity in the west, cool temperate waters in the east, and a vast stretch of open ocean with productive converging water masses in the south.

Atlantic puffin
The Atlantic puffin is a streamlined diver with stubby wings and a colorful bill it uses to capture sand eels and other small fish. Puffins congregate to feed at productive North Atlantic fishing banks, and nest high on isolated island cliffs where they are safe from most predators.

Blue marlin
The blue marlin lives in tropical and subtropical seas around the world. Its long bill and streamlined shape make the marlin perfectly suited for the rapid acceleration needed to disable and capture mahimahi, tuna, and other fast-swimming prey.

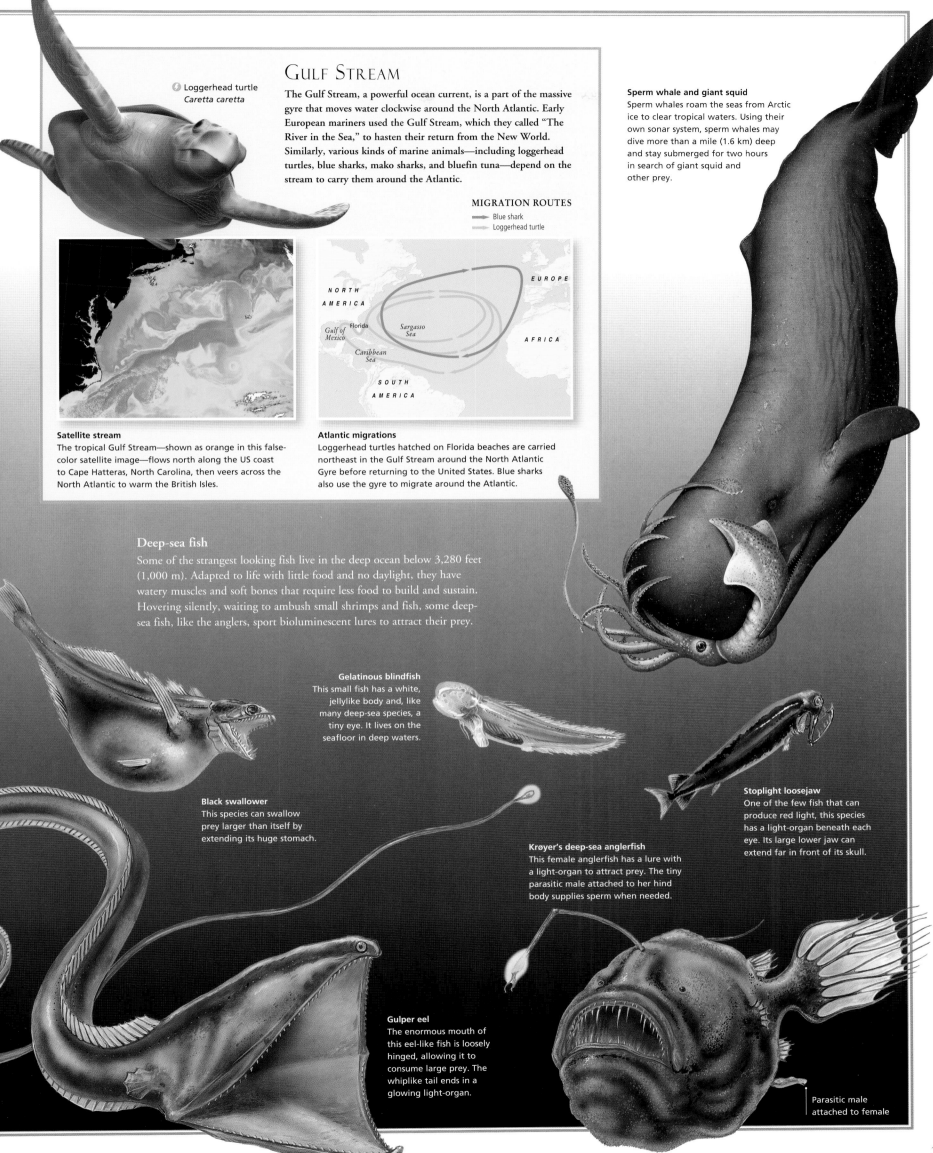

Loggerhead turtle
Caretta caretta

GULF STREAM

The Gulf Stream, a powerful ocean current, is a part of the massive gyre that moves water clockwise around the North Atlantic. Early European mariners used the Gulf Stream, which they called "The River in the Sea," to hasten their return from the New World. Similarly, various kinds of marine animals—including loggerhead turtles, blue sharks, mako sharks, and bluefin tuna—depend on the stream to carry them around the Atlantic.

MIGRATION ROUTES
➤ Blue shark
➤ Loggerhead turtle

Sperm whale and giant squid
Sperm whales roam the seas from Arctic ice to clear tropical waters. Using their own sonar system, sperm whales may dive more than a mile (1.6 km) deep and stay submerged for two hours in search of giant squid and other prey.

NORTH AMERICA

EUROPE

Gulf of Mexico

Florida

Sargasso Sea

AFRICA

Caribbean Sea

SOUTH AMERICA

Satellite stream
The tropical Gulf Stream—shown as orange in this false-color satellite image—flows north along the US coast to Cape Hatteras, North Carolina, then veers across the North Atlantic to warm the British Isles.

Atlantic migrations
Loggerhead turtles hatched on Florida beaches are carried northeast in the Gulf Stream around the North Atlantic Gyre before returning to the United States. Blue sharks also use the gyre to migrate around the Atlantic.

Deep-sea fish

Some of the strangest looking fish live in the deep ocean below 3,280 feet (1,000 m). Adapted to life with little food and no daylight, they have watery muscles and soft bones that require less food to build and sustain. Hovering silently, waiting to ambush small shrimps and fish, some deep-sea fish, like the anglers, sport bioluminescent lures to attract their prey.

Gelatinous blindfish
This small fish has a white, jellylike body and, like many deep-sea species, a tiny eye. It lives on the seafloor in deep waters.

Stoplight loosejaw
One of the few fish that can produce red light, this species has a light-organ beneath each eye. Its large lower jaw can extend far in front of its skull.

Black swallower
This species can swallow prey larger than itself by extending its huge stomach.

Krøyer's deep-sea anglerfish
This female anglerfish has a lure with a light-organ to attract prey. The tiny parasitic male attached to her hind body supplies sperm when needed.

Gulper eel
The enormous mouth of this eel-like fish is loosely hinged, allowing it to consume large prey. The whiplike tail ends in a glowing light-organ.

Parasitic male attached to female

THE INDIAN OCEAN

The Indian Ocean has a rich tropical shore fauna that stretches from South Africa, north to the Red Sea, east around the Indian subcontinent, and south through the Indo-Malayan archipelago to Western Australia. Coral reefs abound in the east and west, and sandy and muddy mangrove habitats dominate the Indian coast. Animal life of the Indian Ocean is closely related to that of the western Pacific, with many tropical shorefish species ranging from South Africa to the islands of the South Pacific. The Indian Ocean is home to a particularly wide variety of sharks, from small, bottom-grubbing catsharks to large, camouflaged wobbegongs and sleek requiem sharks. Olive ridley sea turtles gather to nest each year on Indian beaches. Productive upwelling across the central Indian Ocean supports tuna populations and the fisheries that pursue them.

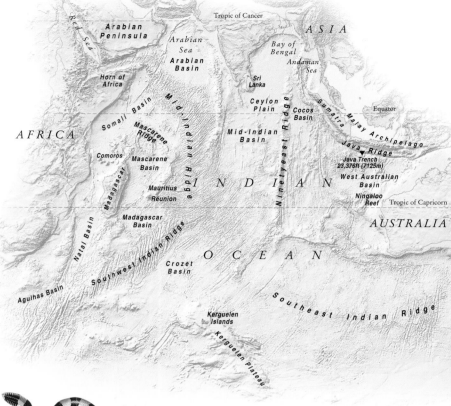

OCEAN SHARE

Indian Ocean
26.5 million sq miles
(68.6 million km²)
21%

All other oceans

THE FACTS	
Area	26.5 million square miles (68.6 million km²)
Average depth	12,644 feet (3,854 m)
Maximum depth	24,459 feet (7,455 m)
Maximum width	6,300 miles (10,200 km)
Maximum length	5,800 miles (9,400 km)
Coastline length	41,337 miles (66,526 km)

Yellow-lipped sea krait
Laticauda colubrina

SCALE 1:105,000,000

0   2000 miles

0   2000 kilometers

Indian Ocean formation
More than 100 million years ago, India, Australia, and Antarctica, together with Africa and South America, were joined in a southern supercontinent called Gondwana. India and Australia broke away and drifted slowly north and east to open the Indian Ocean basin.

COELACANTH

Coelacanths, primitive cousins of early fish that evolved into land vertebrates, were thought to have become extinct 65 million years ago. Then, in 1938, a trawler fishing off Mozambique dragged up a dark, bulky, rough-scaled monster of the deep. The creature was a coelacanth, in effect a living fossil. Today, remnant coelacanth populations have been found off East and South Africa, the Comoros Islands, Madagascar, and the Indonesian island of Sulawesi.

⚡ Living fossil
The discovery of a living coelacanth rocked the halls of science. Coelacanths frequent undersea volcanic slopes, hiding in caves by day and foraging at night as they drift with the currents.

Dolphins and baitball
Dolphins and several species of sharks follow migrating shoals of sardines, traveling south along the South African coast in summer and north in winter. Sardines and other schooling fish often form tight, spherical schools, called baitballs, when threatened by predators.

GREAT WHITE SHARK MIGRATION

Great white sharks were thought to be coastal denizens until recent satellite tracking experiments showed that they can migrate thousands of miles across the open ocean. A mature female great white tagged off South Africa swam all the way across the Indian Ocean to Western Australia, then returned within the year. The reasons for such sojourns remain obscure, but breeding is a prime candidate.

Coral communities

The Indian Ocean hosts a cornucopia of corals. Regions with little freshwater input and very clear water, such as the Red Sea (below), have particularly rich coral communities. Reef corals can occur deeper there because enough sunlight penetrates to allow photosynthesis by the algae that help nourish corals. Global warming and high sea temperatures cause potentially fatal coral bleaching.

Whale shark
Whale sharks (left and below) are the largest living fish, reaching 45 feet (13.5 m) in length, yet they are harmless plankton feeders. Large numbers gather each year to feast on billions of tiny eggs spawned by corals in places such as Ningaloo Reef off Western Australia.

Giant manta
Manta rays fly through tropical seas with flapping wings and mouths agape, filtering plankton as they go. The largest of all rays, they may reach 22 feet (6.5 m) in width. Mantas sometimes propel their huge bodies completely out of the water, landing with a thunderous splash.

THE ARCTIC OCEAN

Although the Arctic is the smallest ocean, its marine life is not well known because permanent sea ice and a harsh climate have made biological exploration difficult. Regardless, relatively few species inhabit the Arctic, a result of fluctuating climate during recent geological time. Sea ice has been a potent force in shaping the evolution of the creatures that do live there. The edges of the ice pack melt and shrink in spring and summer, providing a rich transition zone that supports lush phytoplankton growth. This primary production is the basis for most Arctic marine food webs. Several species of seals rest and pup on the ice surface while trying to avoid their polar bear predators. Beneath the ice, juvenile Arctic cod pursue tiny crustacean prey and hide from the seals and sleeper sharks that see them as potential meals. Great whales patrol the ice edge, engulfing tons of tiny zooplankton.

OCEAN SHARE

All other oceans

Arctic Ocean
5.4 million sq miles
(14.1 million km²)
4%

SCALE 1:45,000,000

THE FACTS	
Area	5.4 million square miles (14.1 million km²)
Average depth	4,690 feet (1,430 m)
Maximum depth	18,455 feet (5,625 m)
Maximum width	2,000 miles (3,200 km)
Maximum length	3,100 miles (5,000 km)
Coastline length	28,203 miles (45,389 km)

Common feather star
Florometra serratissima

Arctic Ocean features
Surrounded by land, the Arctic Ocean has been subject to extreme climatic fluctuations and species extinctions over time. Today, most families of animals in the Arctic Ocean have evolved from North Pacific groups that entered through periodic openings of the Bering Strait.

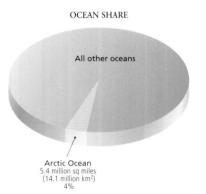

Arctic cod
Juvenile Arctic cod find shelter in crevices under the polar ice. Although members of the cod family are abundant and important in Arctic ecosystems, cods are the only fish family of Atlantic origin. All the other families, such as the sculpins, blennies, and flatfishes, came from the Pacific.

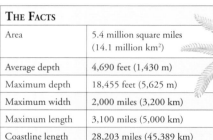

Sleeper shark
The huge Greenland shark and its close relative, the Pacific sleeper, are the apex predators in Arctic ecosystems—the marine equivalents of the polar bear. Curiously, the eyes of both species are commonly infected with a copepod parasite that may cause blindness but no other apparent health effects.

Whale species

There are two major types of whales: toothed species that feed on active fish and squid, and baleen whales that use long sheets of hairlike baleen to sieve out zooplankton and small fish from the water. Arctic residents include two toothed whales—the beluga and narwhal—and one baleen whale—the bowhead. Other baleen whales, such as the fin, minke, and North Atlantic right, arrive in summer to graze on zooplankton.

Minke whale
The minke whale is the smallest baleen whale in the Arctic.

Narwhal
The male narwhal has a single spiral tusk, like a unicorn's horn.

Fin whale
Fin whales often lunge-feed through clouds of krill.

Habitat zones

The Arctic summer brings birds to nest on the tundra and feed in the rich ocean waters. Explosive blooms of phytoplankton called diatoms support tiny grazing copepods and amphipods, both in the water and the pores of the ice. These in turn are consumed by small fish, such as capelin and herring, as well as by large whales. On the bottom, bristleworms, brittle stars, and clams abound.

ARCTIC JELLYFISH

Jelly animals are important predators in pelagic Arctic ecosystems. They include the 150 or so species of true jellyfish, or hydromedusae, and the eight species of colonial siphonophores. Both groups paralyze their prey with long, sticky, stinging tentacles, and eat fish, squid, shrimps, and even other jellyfish. A small number of harmless comb jellies have also been found in the Arctic Ocean.

Giant jelly
The Arctic lion's mane is the largest jellyfish in the world, with a bell-shaped body up to 7.5 feet (2.3 m) wide and tentacles 120 feet (36.5 m) long. Its venomous sting could kill a human.

Hula skirt stinger
The hula skirt siphonophore grows to about 16 inches (41 cm) and, despite its small size, packs a powerful sting like its tropical cousin, the Portuguese man-of-war.

Beluga
Belugas are gray at birth but turn white by the time they are five years old.

Bowhead
The bowhead is hunted by Inuit people and is an important part of their culture.

North Atlantic right whale
With fewer than 350 individuals left, this species is near extinction.

THE SOUTHERN OCEAN

The Southern Ocean flows around the frigid continent of Antarctica. Thirty million years ago this cold circumpolar current did not exist because Antarctica was connected to the tip of South America, and the region was warmed by currents from the north. When the connection parted, the circumpolar current was born, sea temperatures dropped, warm-adapted animals became extinct, and the cold-adapted survivors evolved into a unique fauna. The Southern Ocean has provided a stable polar climate where cold-water animals have had time to evolve and diversify. Perhaps the greatest symbol of the Antarctic is the penguin, with its insulating feathers and torpedo-shaped body, efficient at conserving heat and swimming. The 90 species of notothenioid fish, which fill many ecological niches, are no less remarkable. They have special molecules in their blood called glycoproteins that act like antifreeze.

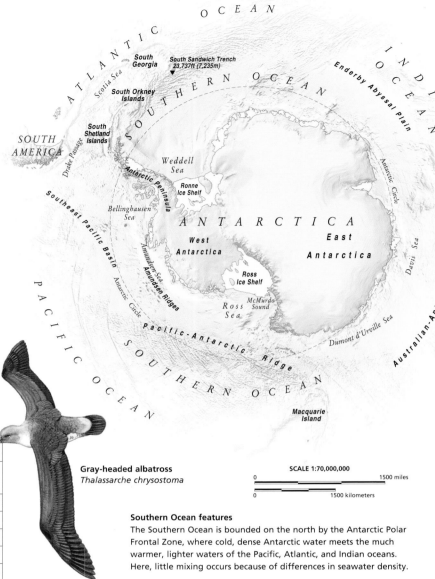

OCEAN SHARE

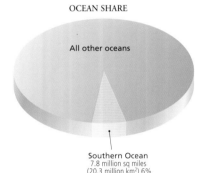

All other oceans

Southern Ocean
7.8 million sq miles
(20.3 million km²) 6%

THE FACTS	
Area	7.8 million square miles (20.3 million km²)
Average depth	14,750 feet (4,500 m)
Maximum depth	24,032 feet (7,235 m)
Maximum width	1,700 miles (2,700 km)
Maximum length	13,400 miles (21,500 km)
Coastline length	11,165 miles (17,968 km)

Gray-headed albatross
Thalassarche chrysostoma

SCALE 1:70,000,000

0   1500 miles

0   1500 kilometers

Southern Ocean features
The Southern Ocean is bounded on the north by the Antarctic Polar Frontal Zone, where cold, dense Antarctic water meets the much warmer, lighter waters of the Pacific, Atlantic, and Indian oceans. Here, little mixing occurs because of differences in seawater density.

Orcas spyhopping
Many kinds of whales visit the edge of the Antarctic ice in summer in search of food. Orcas often spyhop in the ice pack, poking their heads above the surface in search of resting seals or other prey that may be captured and consumed.

Naked dragonfish
The naked dragonfish, a common Antarctic bottom dweller, sits quietly waiting to ambush passing prey. This sit-and-wait strategy has reached its apex in closely related crocodile icefishes, which lack hemoglobin and take up all the oxygen they need from the frigid, oxygen-rich Antarctic water.

BOTTOM DWELLERS

Antarctic bottom communities are much more diverse than those of the Arctic. More than 90 percent of the invertebrates on the continental shelf originated in the Antarctic and occur nowhere else. Southern Ocean currents bring suspended zooplankton, phytoplankton, bacteria, and other microorganisms to bottom communities dominated by sponges, sea squirts, feather stars, and other filter feeders. In the deep Southern Ocean, hundreds of new species of worms and other tiny bottom creatures have recently been discovered.

Sea star
Sea stars are common members of Antarctic bottom communities. They prey on clams and other mollusks.

Anemone
Anemones are closely related to jellyfish. They prey on fish and other creatures that venture too close to their stinging tentacles.

Sea urchin
The Antarctic sea urchin grazes on algae, and camouflages itself with bits of shell and other debris to avoid predators.

KEYSTONE KRILL

Krill are small—1½ to 2½ inches (4–6 cm)—shrimplike creatures that swim in the Southern Ocean in swarms as dense as 13,000 per cubic yard (10,000 per m³). Living as long as five years, these small animals are the keystone food source upon which many species of fish, squid, penguins, seals, and whales depend for survival.

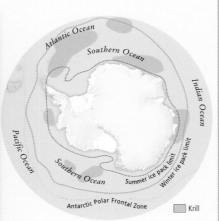

Commercial harvest
A ready source of protein, krill have attracted the interest of industrial fisheries. Large-scale harvest of krill has prompted concern that Antarctic food webs could be disrupted.

Southern distribution
Krill live in cold, productive seas at both ends of Earth, but reach their greatest concentrations in the Southern Ocean, where their phytoplankton food is at its most abundant.

⚡ CONSERVATION WATCH

The blue whale is the largest creature that ever lived on Earth, measuring up to 108 feet (33 m) in length, and weighing as much as 176 tons (160 t). Blue whales congregate in the Southern Ocean in summer to gorge on clouds of krill. In winter they head to more hospitable tropical climes to rest and have their calves.

King penguin
Unlike the five other species of Antarctic penguins that nest on the continent or the tip of the Antarctic Peninsula, king penguins prefer the more hospitable Southern Ocean islands, such as Macquarie Island. There they may be joined by a host of breeding seabirds, such as petrels, prions, and albatrosses.

Antarctic seals

The Antarctic is home to six species of seals, of which four—the Ross, Weddell, crabeater, and leopard seals—pup on the sea ice in spring. The Antarctic fur seal and the elephant seal breed in large colonies on beaches north of the pack ice. Most Antarctic seals include fish, squid, and krill in their diets, but the leopard seal also eats penguins and young seals.

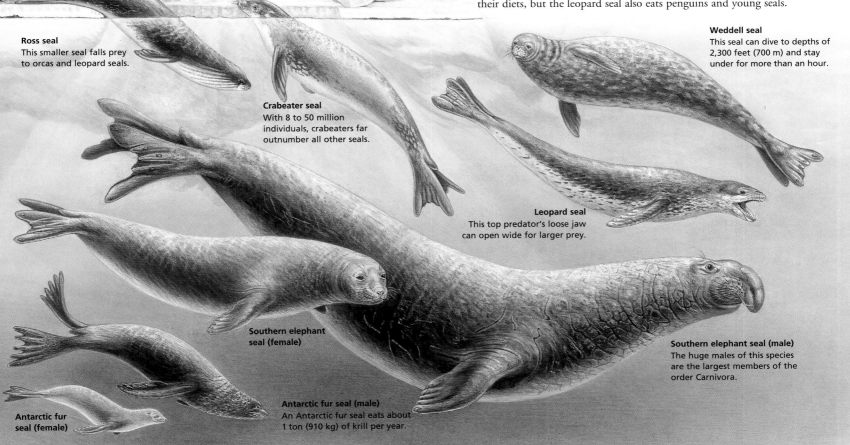

Ross seal
This smaller seal falls prey to orcas and leopard seals.

Crabeater seal
With 8 to 50 million individuals, crabeaters far outnumber all other seals.

Weddell seal
This seal can dive to depths of 2,300 feet (700 m) and stay under for more than an hour.

Leopard seal
This top predator's loose jaw can open wide for larger prey.

Southern elephant seal (female)

Antarctic fur seal (male)
An Antarctic fur seal eats about 1 ton (910 kg) of krill per year.

Antarctic fur seal (female)

Southern elephant seal (male)
The huge males of this species are the largest members of the order Carnivora.

This parrot snake is in Soberania National Park, Panama, Central America. It is eating a clutch of red-eyed tree frog tadpoles as they hatch from their eggs. All snakes are carnivorous and the parrot snake eats frogs, birds, lizards, and insects. Many snakes can lower their metabolic rate by 70 percent and eat only a few times a year.

FACTS ABOUT ANIMALS

Scientists have described and named at least 1.7 million species of plants, animals, and microorganisms, but new species are discovered almost every day and the total number of lifeforms is estimated at between 10 million and 30 million. The discipline of taxonomy provides a unique name for each organism and sorts organisms into hierarchies of increasingly exclusive groups, or taxa, based on their evolutionary relationships. The basic category is the species. Species are populations of organisms that share one or more similarities not found in related organisms, and can usually reproduce sexually only with each other. Each species is assigned a two-part scientific name. The first part, the generic name, gives the genus, the group of closely related organisms to which the species belongs. The second part, the specific name, is unique to that species within the genus. Animals are known by various common names around the world, so the scientific name is Latinized to avoid confusion. All taxa above the species level are meant to comprise an ancestral species and all it descendants. Recent genetic techniques have allowed comparison of organisms' DNA, forcing scientists to rethink the classification of many animals.

FACTFILE CONTENTS	
Mammals	p259
Birds	p268
Reptiles	p274
Amphibians	p275
Fish	p276
Invertebrates	p278

HOW TO USE THIS FACTFILE

Scientific name of order → **ORDER FALCONIFORMES**
Common name of order → **BIRDS OF PREY**
Total number of living species in order → **302 species**

Map showing distribution of order

Scientific name of family within the order

Common name of family → **Family Accipitridae**
Total number of living species in family → Hawks, eagles, kites, harriers & Old World vultures
234 species

Sharp-shinned hawk
Accipiter striatus
Common name of species (alternative common name also listed where relevant)
Scientific name of species
- ⊕ North & South America
- ⋀ Usually breeds in coniferous forest; various habitats in winter
- ↧ 9.5–13 in (24–34 cm)
- ↦ 17–22 in (43–56 cm)
- ⚖ 3.1–7.7 oz (87–218 g)
- ✿ Small birds, also large insects, small mammals
- ⚡ Least concern

Facts entry for every species captioned in this atlas. Species are arranged by taxonomic group, then alphabetically by scientific name within each group. To find a species by its common name, refer to the index, where Factfile entries are indicated by square brackets.

Wedge-tailed eagle
Aquila audax
Species' location: distribution and habitat
- ⊕ Australia, New Guinea
- ⋀ All terrestrial habitats
- ↧ Up to 43 in (110 cm)
- ↦ 9 ft (2.7 m)
Species' diet
- ⚖ 8.8 lb (4 kg)
- ✿ Medium-sized mammals, lizards, birds, carrion (especially roadkill)
IUCN Red List status (with extra notes as relevant)
- ⚡ Least concern (Tasmanian subspecies endangered)

Species' size: body length, tail length, wingspan, weight (as relevant)

KINGDOMS OF LIFE

All life on Earth can be classified into the six broad taxa known as kingdoms. These kingdoms are sometimes grouped into three higher domains: Bacteria (Eubacteria), Archaea (Archaebacteria), and Eukarya (Protista, Fungi, Plantae, and Animalia).

EUBACTERIA
Most known prokaryotes
10,000 species

These microorganisms were the only known prokaryotes, single-celled forms without a nucleus, until the discovery of archaebacteria in the 1970s. Eubacteria recycle nutrients in all Earth's habitats.

ARCHAEBACTERIA
Prokaryotes of extremes
18–23 phyla

Found in or around deep-sea vents, hot springs, and extremely salty water, these ancient lifeforms do not rely on oxygen. They are prokaryotes, but are very different genetically from other bacteria.

PROTISTA
Protists
250,000 species

Like fungi, plants, and animals, protists are eukaryotes, organisms with a cell nucleus. Protists are single-celled, or multicellular without specialized tissues. They include algae, cilia, and slime molds.

FUNGI
Fungi
100,000 species

Fungi include mushrooms, molds, and yeasts. They perform a vital ecological role in decomposing organic matter and recycling nutrients. Unlike plants, fungi cannot make their own food.

PLANTAE
Plants
350,000 species

The vast majority of plants create their own food through the process of photosynthesis and are the primary producers in ecosystems. They include flowering plants, mosses, and ferns.

ANIMALIA
Animals
1,350,000+ species

Animals make up the largest kingdom. It has about 30 phyla of invertebrates. A single phylum, Chordata, includes all the vertebrates—mammals, birds, reptiles, amphibians, and fish.

Animal classification
All lifeforms can be classified according to the Linnaean system. Each nested category contains organisms with progressively similar characteristics. This bobcat belongs to kingdom Animalia (all animals); phylum Chordata (animals with a centralized nerve cord); class Mammalia (all mammals); order Carnivora (with specialized teeth for eating meat); family Felidae (all cats); and genus *Lynx* (all lynxes). Finally, no other organism shares the scientific name of this species, *Lynx rufus.*

SPECIES
Lynx rufus
Bobcat

GENUS
Lynx
Bobcat, Eurasian lynx, Canadian lynx

FAMILY
Felidae
Bobcat, domestic cat, lion, leopard, jaguar

ORDER
Carnivora
Bobcat, seal, wolf, bear, skunk, meerkat

CLASS
Mammalia
Bobcat, kangaroo, human, dolphin, woolly mammoth

PHYLUM
Chordata
Bobcat, shark, salamander, dinosaur, albatross

KINGDOM
Animalia
Bobcat, stick insect, sea urchin, parrot, crocodile

MAMMALS

Mammals occupy all continents and almost all habitats. They nurse their young with milk from mammary glands, usually have body hair, and have a lower jaw bone that attaches directly to the skull. The 28 orders of the class Mammalia are divided into three major groups based on the structure of the reproductive tract. The most primitive are the egg-laying mammals, classified in a single order, the monotremes. Marsupials, which give birth to young in a very early stage of development, are now considered to consist of seven orders. The other 20 orders are made up of placental mammals. Recent DNA evidence indicates that there have been three major radiations of placentals in Africa, South America, and the northern hemisphere.

Icon key

⊕	Distribution	⊢	Tail length	✪	Diet
⋀	Habitat	⋌	Wingspan	⚡	Status
⊢	Length	⋋	Weight	♀♂	Female/male

PHYLUM CHORDATA
CHORDATES
53,000+ species

CLASS MAMMALIA
MAMMALS
4,791 species

EGG-LAYING MAMMALS
4 SPECIES IN 1 ORDER

ORDER MONOTREMATA
MONOTREMES
4 species

Platypus
Ornithorhynchus anatinus
- ⊕ Eastern Australia, Kangaroo Island, King Island
- ⋀ Freshwater streams, lakes, dams
- ⊢ Up to 16 in (40.5 cm)
- ⊢ 6 in (15 cm)
- ⋋ Up to 5 lb (2 kg)
- ✪ Aquatic invertebrates
- ⚡ Least concern

Short-beaked echidna
Tachyglossus aculeatus
- ⊕ Australia, New Guinea
- ⋀ All terrestrial habitats
- ⊢ Up to 14 in (35.5 cm)
- ⊢ 3 in (7.5 cm)
- ⋋ Up to 16 lb (7 kg)
- ✪ Ants, termites
- ⚡ Least concern

Long-beaked echidna
Zaglossus bruijni
- ⊕ New Guinea
- ⋀ Rain forest
- ⊢ Up to 25 in (63.5 cm)
- ⋋ Up to 22 lb (10 kg)
- ✪ Worms
- ⚡ Endangered

MARSUPIALS
298 SPECIES IN 7 ORDERS

ORDER DIDELPHIMORPHIA
AMERICAN OPOSSUMS
70+ species

Brown-eared woolly opossum
Caluromys lanatus
- ⊕ South America
- ⋀ Tropical forest
- ⊢ 11 in (27.5 cm)
- ⊢ 16 in (40.5 cm)
- ⋋ 1.1 lb (500 g)
- ✪ Fruit & nectar of flowering trees, seeds, leaves, soft vegetables, small invertebrates, carrion
- ⚡ Near threatened

Common opossum
Didelphis marsupialis
- ⊕ Mexico to Argentina
- ⋀ Forest, plantations
- ⊢ Up to 14 in (35.5 cm)
- ⊢ Up to 18 in (45.5 cm)
- ⋋ ♂ 3.3 lb (1.5 kg)
- ✪ Fruits, small animals
- ⚡ Least concern

Virginia opossum
Didelphis virginiana
- ⊕ Eastern & central USA, Mexico, northern Costa Rica
- ⋀ Deciduous forest, urban areas
- ⊢ 22.5–31.5 in (57–80 cm)
- ⊢ 7–12 in (18–30.5 cm)
- ⋋ 2.5–11.5 lb (1–5 kg)
- ✪ Fruits, nuts, grain, earthworms, insects, small vertebrates, carrion
- ⚡ Least concern

ORDER PAUCITUBERCULATA
SHREW OPOSSUMS
6 species

ORDER MICROBIOTHERIA
MONITO DEL MONTE
1 species

ORDER DASYUROMORPHIA
QUOLLS, DUNNARTS, NUMBAT & ALLIES
71 species

Brown antechinus
Antechinus stuartii
- ⊕ Eastern Australia
- ⋀ Forest, prefers wet sclerophyll forest
- ⊢ ♂ 6–10 in (15–25 cm), ♀ 5.5–8.5 in (14–22 cm)
- ⊢ Almost as long as body length
- ⋋ ♂ 1–2.5 oz (29–71 g), ♀ 0.6–1.3 oz (17–36 g)
- ✪ Beetles, spiders, cockroaches, other invertebrates, mice, plants, pollen
- ⚡ Least concern

Northern quoll
Dasyurus hallucatus
- ⊕ Restricted areas in northern Australia
- ⋀ Rocky habitats, savanna, coastal eucalypt forest
- ⊢ 9.4–13.8 in (24–35 cm)
- ⊢ 8.3–12.2 in (21–31 cm)
- ⋋ 10.5–31.5 oz (300–900 g)
- ✪ Small mammals, reptiles, beetles, ants, termites, grasshoppers, other invertebrates, figs, other soft fruits
- ⚡ Near threatened

Numbat
Myrmecobius fasciatus
- ⊕ Southwest Australia
- ⋀ Rain forest
- ⊢ Up to 11 in (28 cm)
- ⊢ 4 in (10 cm)
- ⋋ Up to 1.6 lb (725 g)
- ✪ Termites
- ⚡ Vulnerable

Tasmanian devil
Sarcophilus harrisii
- ⊕ Tasmania
- ⋀ Forest
- ⊢ Up to 25 in (63.5 cm)
- ⊢ 10 in (25.5 cm)
- ⋋ Up to 20 lb (9 kg)
- ✪ Carrion
- ⚡ Endangered

ORDER PERAMELEMORPHIA
BANDICOOTS
24 species

Bilby
Macrotis lagotis
- ⊕ Central Australia
- ⋀ Acacia scrub, hummock grassland
- ⊢ Up to 18 in (45.5 cm)
- ⊢ 11 in (28 cm)
- ⋋ Up to 5 lb (2.3 kg)
- ✪ Arthropods, tubers, fungi
- ⚡ Vulnerable

ORDER NOTORYCTEMORPHIA
MARSUPIAL MOLES
2 species

ORDER DIPROTODONTIA
POSSUMS, KANGAROOS, KOALAS, WOMBATS & ALLIES
125 species

Suborder Vombatiformes
Koala & wombats
4 species

Koala
Phascolarctos cinereus
- ⊕ South & east Australia
- ⋀ Woodland, forest
- ⊢ Up to 32 in (81 cm)
- ⋋ Up to 22 lb (10 kg)
- ✪ Leaves, shoots
- ⚡ Near threatened

Common wombat
Vombatus ursinus
- ⊕ Australia
- ⋀ Open forest, grassland
- ⊢ Up to 50 in (127 cm)
- ⊢ 2 in (5 cm)
- ⋋ Up to 80 lb (36 kg)
- ✪ Leaves, grass
- ⚡ Least concern

Suborder Phalangeriformes
Possums
64 species

Mountain pygmy possum
Burramys parvus
- ⊕ Australian Alps
- ⋀ Alpine rock scree above treeline
- ⊢ Up to 4.5 in (11.5 cm)
- ⊢ 6 in (15 cm)
- ⋋ Up to 3 oz (85 g)
- ✪ Insects, seeds, fruits
- ⚡ Endangered

Striped possum
Dactylopsila trivirgata
- ⊕ Australia, New Guinea, Pacific islands
- ⋀ Forest, savanna
- ⊢ Up to 11 in (28 cm)
- ⊢ 14 in (35.5 cm)
- ⋋ Up to 1.3 lb (600 g)
- ✪ Insects, fruits, honey
- ⚡ Least concern

Green ringtail possum
Pseudochirops archeri
- ⊕ Northeast Australia
- ⋀ Rain forest
- ⊢ 14.5 in (37 cm)
- ⊢ 14.5 in (37 cm)
- ⋋ 2.2 lb (1 kg)
- ✪ Leaves of fig trees
- ⚡ Near threatened

Spotted cuscus
Spilocuscus maculatus
- ⊕ Northern Australia, New Guinea, Pacific islands
- ⋀ All forest types
- ⊢ Up to 22 in (56 cm)
- ⊢ 22 in (56 cm)
- ⋋ Up to 13 lb (5.9 kg)
- ✪ Leaves, shoots, fruit
- ⚡ Least concern

Honey possum
Tarsipes rostratus
- ⊕ Western Australia
- ⋀ Coastal heath
- ⊢ Up to 4 in (10 cm)
- ⊢ 4 in (10 cm)
- ⋋ Up to 0.4 oz (10 g)
- ✪ Nectar, pollen
- ⚡ Least concern

Bilby
Macrotis lagotis

Common brushtail possum
Trichosurus vulpecula
- ⊕ Southeast Australia
- ⋀ Forest, suburban gardens
- ⊢ Up to 20 in (51 cm)
- ⊢ 16 in (40.5 cm)
- ⋋ Up to 9 lb (4.1 kg)
- ✪ Leaves, flowers, fruits
- ⚡ Least concern

Suborder Macropodiformes
Kangaroos, wallabies & allies
57 species

Northern bettong
Bettongia tropica
- ⊕ Small range in tropical northeast Australia
- ⋀ Dry, open eucalypt woodland
- ⊢ 12 in (30 cm)
- ⊢ 11.5–14 in (29–36 cm)
- ⋋ 2.2–3.3 lb (1–1.5 kg)
- ✪ Underground fungi, insects, leaves, stems
- ⚡ Endangered

Goodfellow's tree kangaroo
Dendrolagus goodfellowi
- ⊕ New Guinea
- ⋀ Rain forest
- ⊢ Up to 25 in (63.5 cm)
- ⊢ 30 in (76 cm)
- ⋋ Up to 15 lb (6.8 kg)
- ✪ Leaves, shoots
- ⚡ Endangered

Musky rat-kangaroo
Hypsiprymnodon moschatus
- ⊕ Far northwest Australia
- ⋀ Tropical rain forest
- ⊢ 8 in (20 cm)
- ⊢ 4.7–6.3 in (12–16 cm)
- ⋋ 1.1 lb (500 g)
- ✪ Fruits, roots, stems, seeds, fungi
- ⚡ Least concern

Red-necked wallaby
Macropus rufogriseus
- ⊕ Eastern Australia
- ⋀ Forest, heathland, coastal scrub
- ⊢ Up to 36 in (91.5 cm)
- ⊢ 35 in (89 cm)
- ⋋ Up to 60 lb (27 kg)
- ✪ Leaves, shoots
- ⚡ Least concern

Red kangaroo
Macropus rufus
- ⊕ Australia
- ⋀ Grassland, desert
- ⊢ ♂ up to 4.6 ft (1.4 m); ♀ up to 3.6 ft (1.1 m)
- ⊢ 3–3.3 ft (0.9–1 m)
- ⋋ ♂ up to 187 lb (85 kg), ♀ up to 77 lb (35 kg)
- ✪ Grasses, herbs
- ⚡ Least concern

Black-flanked rock wallaby, Black-footed rock wallaby
Petrogale lateralis
- ⊕ South & west Australia
- ⋀ Rocky gorges & hills
- ⊢ Up to 23 in (58.5 cm)
- ⊢ 20 in (51 cm)
- ⋋ Up to 18 lb (8.2 kg)
- ✪ Grasses, herbs
- ⚡ Vulnerable

Red kangaroo
Macropus rufus

PLACENTAL MAMMALS
4,489 SPECIES IN 20 ORDERS

ORDER CINGULATA
ARMADILLOS
20 species

Nine-banded armadillo
Dasypus novemcinctus
- ⊕ Southern USA through to northern Argentina & Uruguay
- ⋀ Grassland, forest
- ▦ 30 in (76 cm)
- ᚓ 13.5 in (34 cm)
- ✘ 13 lb (5.9 kg)
- ✿ Mostly insects, also worms, snails, eggs, small amphibians, berries
- ⚡ Least concern

Three-banded armadillo
Tolypeutes tricinctus
- ⊕ Brazil
- ⋀ Tropical forests on chalky grounds
- ▦ 8–10 in (20.5–25.5 cm)
- ᚓ 3 in (7.5 cm)
- ✘ 4.4 lb (2 kg)
- ✿ Beetle larvae, ants, termites
- ⚡ Vulnerable

ORDER PILOSA
ANTEATERS & SLOTHS
9 species

Brown throated three-toed sloth
Bradypus variegatus
- ⊕ Central & South America
- ⋀ Rain forest
- ▦ 23 in (58.5 cm)
- ᚓ 2.3 in (6 cm)
- ✘ 11 lb (5 kg)
- ✿ Leaves, shoots, foliage
- ⚡ Least concern

Giant anteater
Myrmecophaga tridactyla
- ⊕ Central & South America
- ⋀ Grassland, deciduous forest, rain forest
- ▦ 6.6 ft (2 m)
- ᚓ 35 in (89 cm)
- ✘ 140 lb (63.5 kg)
- ✿ Ants, termites
- ⚡ Vulnerable

ORDER PHOLIDOTA
PANGOLINS
7 species

Ground pangolin
Manis temminckii
- ⊕ East & southern Africa
- ⋀ Woodland, savanna, grassland
- ▦ 14–24 in (35.5–61 cm)
- ᚓ 12–20 in (30.5–51 cm)
- ✘ 15–40 lb (6.8–18.1 kg)
- ✿ Ants
- ⚡ Near threatened

ORDER SORICOMORPHA
SHREWS, MOLES & SOLENODONS
370 species

Star-nosed mole
Condylura cristata
- ⊕ Southeast Canada, northeast USA to Georgia
- ⋀ Moist fields, meadows, woods, marshes
- ▦ 5–9 in (12.5–23 cm)
- ᚓ 2–4 in (5–10 cm)
- ✘ 1.4–3 oz (40–85 g)
- ✿ Worms, insects, insect larvae; also small crustaceans, mollusks, fish
- ⚡ Least concern

Water shrew
Neomys fodiens
- ⊕ Northern Eurasia
- ⋀ Pond, marsh
- ▦ Up to 4 in (10 cm)
- ᚓ Up to 2.8 in (7 cm)
- ✘ Up to 1.6 oz (45 g)
- ✿ Worms, crustaceans, fish
- ⚡ Least concern

Solenodon
Solenodon cubanus
- ⊕ East Cuba
- ⋀ Wooded or brushy areas
- ▦ 11 in (28 cm)
- ᚓ 21 in (53.5 cm)
- ✘ 2.2 lb (1 kg)
- ✿ Arthropods, worms, snails, small reptiles; also roots, fruits, foliage
- ⚡ Endangered

ORDER AFROSORICIDA
TENRECS & GOLDEN MOLES
47 species

ORDER ERINACEOMORPHA
HEDGEHOGS & GYMNURES
21 species

ORDER DERMOPTERA
FLYING LEMURS
2 species

ORDER SCANDENTIA
TREE SHREWS
17 species

ORDER CHIROPTERA
BATS
993 species

Golden-capped fruit bat
Acerodon jubatus
- ⊕ Philippines
- ⋀ Primary & secondary forests from sea level to 3,600 ft (1,100 m)
- ⊰ 5–5.6 ft (1.5–1.7 m)
- ✘ Up to 2.6 lb (1.2 kg)
- ✿ Figs
- ⚡ Endangered

Common fruit bat
Artibeus jamaicensis
- ⊕ Central & South America
- ⋀ Rain forest, scrub forest
- ▦ 4 in (10 cm)
- ⊰ 16 in (40 cm)
- ✘ 1.6 oz (45 g)
- ✿ Nectar, pollen, flower parts, insects
- ⚡ Least concern

Honduran white bat
Ectophylla alba
- ⊕ Central America, Caribbean
- ⋀ Rain forest
- ▦ 1.5 in (4 cm)
- ⊰ 4 in (10 cm)
- ✘ 0.18 oz (5 g)
- ✿ Fruits, seeds, flowers, pollen, insects
- ⚡ Near threatened

Southern long-nosed bat
Leptonycteris curasoae
- ⊕ Southern Arizona to Mexico & northern South America
- ⋀ Arid scrub, arid grassland, oak forest, tropical dry forest
- ▦ 3–3.3 in (7.5–8.5 cm)
- ⊰ 14–16 in (36–40 cm)
- ✘ 0.5–0.9 oz (15–25 g)
- ✿ Nectar & pollen of saguaro, other cacti, agaves, silk trees
- ⚡ Vulnerable

Spectacled flying fox
Pteropus conspicillatus
- ⊕ Northeast Australia, New Guinea, Pacific islands
- ⋀ Rain forest, gallery forest, paperbark forest, mangroves
- ▦ Up to 11 in (28 cm)
- ⊰ 5 ft (1.5 m)
- ✘ Up to 2 lb (905 g)
- ✿ Fruits, nectar
- ⚡ Least concern

Mediterranean horseshoe bat
Rhinolophus euryale
- ⊕ Southern Europe, northern Africa
- ⋀ Caves
- ▦ Up to 3.5 in (9 cm)
- ⊰ Up to 12.5 in (32 cm)
- ✘ Up to 0.6 oz (15 g)
- ✿ Moths, insects
- ⚡ Vulnerable

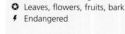

Mediterranean horseshoe bat
Rhinolophus euryale

ORDER PRIMATES
PRIMATES
291 species

Suborder Strepsirhini
Prosimians
63 species

Aye-aye
Daubentonia madagascariensis
- ⊕ East Madagascar
- ⋀ Rain forest, deciduous forest
- ▦ 16 in (40.5 cm)
- ᚓ 16 in (40.5 cm)
- ✘ 6 lb (2.7 kg)
- ✿ Invertebrates, seeds, fruit, nectar
- ⚡ Endangered

Indri
Indri indri
- ⊕ East Madagascar
- ⋀ Montane forest
- ▦ 24 in (61 cm)
- ᚓ 20 in (51 cm)
- ✘ 13–25 lb (6–11 kg)
- ✿ Leaves, fruits, seeds
- ⚡ Endangered

Ring-tailed lemur
Lemur catta
- ⊕ South Madagascar
- ⋀ Deciduous forest, dry scrubland
- ▦ 17 in (43 cm)
- ᚓ 23 in (60 cm)
- ✘ 5 lb (2.2 kg)
- ✿ Fruits, leaves
- ⚡ Vulnerable

Gray mouse lemur
Microcebus murinus
- ⊕ West Madagascar
- ⋀ Secondary forest, spiny desert
- ▦ 5 in (12.5 cm)
- ᚓ 6 in (15 cm)
- ✘ 3.9 oz (110 g)
- ✿ Fruits, invertebrates, flowers
- ⚡ Least concern

Slow loris
Nycticebus coucang
- ⊕ Southeast Asia
- ⋀ Rain-forest canopy
- ▦ 12–15 in (30–38 cm)
- ✘ Up to 4.4 lb (2 kg)
- ✿ Fruits, leaves, insects, bird eggs, young birds
- ⚡ Least concern

Greater bushbaby
Otolemur crassicaudatus
- ⊕ East & southern Africa
- ⋀ Gallery forest, savanna woodland, montane forest
- ▦ 12 in (30.5 cm)
- ᚓ 16 in (40.5 cm)
- ✘ 2.4 lb (1.1 kg)
- ✿ Gum, fruits, insects
- ⚡ Least concern

Coquerel's sifaka
Propithecus coquereli
- ⊕ Northwest Madagascar
- ⋀ Dry deciduous forest
- ▦ 17 in (43 cm)
- ᚓ 23 in (58.5 cm)
- ✘ 8–9 lb (3.6–4.1 kg)
- ✿ Leaves, flowers, fruits, bark
- ⚡ Endangered

Tarsier
Tarsius syrichta
- ⊕ Southeastern Philippines
- ⋀ Primary & secondary forests
- ▦ 4–6 in (10–15 cm)
- ᚓ About twice its body length
- ✘ ♂ 5 oz (140 g), ♀ 4 oz (115 g)
- ✿ Insects, spiders, small lizards, birds
- ⚡ Data deficient

Red-ruffed lemur
Varecia rubra
- ⊕ East Madagascar
- ⋀ Rain forest
- ▦ 20 in (51 cm)
- ᚓ 24 in (61 cm)
- ✘ 8 lb (3.6 kg)
- ✿ Fruits, seeds, leaves
- ⚡ Endangered

Suborder Haplorhini
Monkeys & apes
228 species

Family Cebidae
Marmosets & allies
58 species

Pygmy marmoset
Callithrix pygmaea
- ⊕ West Amazon Basin in South America
- ⋀ Rain forest
- ▦ 5 in (12.5 cm)
- ᚓ 6 in (15 cm)
- ✘ 4.2 oz (120 g)
- ✿ Fruits, leaves, insects
- ⚡ Least concern

White-faced capuchin
Cebus capucinus
- ⊕ Central America, northwest South America
- ⋀ Forest, mangroves
- ▦ 35 in (89 cm)
- ᚓ 18 in (45.5 cm)
- ✘ 11 lb (5 kg)
- ✿ Fruits, insects
- ⚡ Least concern

Pied tamarin
Saguinus bicolor
- ⊕ Small region north of Amazon River in Brazil
- ⋀ Rain forest
- ▦ 11 in (28 cm)
- ᚓ 16 in (40.5 cm)
- ✘ 15 oz (425 g)
- ✿ Fruits, flowers, invertebrates
- ⚡ Critically endangered

Emperor tamarin
Saguinus imperator
- ⊕ Southwest Amazon Basin
- ⋀ Tropical forest
- ▦ 10 in (25 cm)
- ᚓ 13 in (33 cm)
- ✘ 14 oz (495 g)
- ✿ Fruits, nectar, plant sap, frogs, snails
- ⚡ Least concern

Family Aotidae
Night monkeys
8 species

Family Pitheciidae
Titis, sakis & uakaris
40 species

Family Atelidae
Howler, spider & woolly monkeys
24 species

Red howler monkey
Alouatta belzebul
- ⊕ Venezuela to upper Amazon Basin
- ⋀ Forest canopy
- ▦ 28 in (71 cm)
- ᚓ 29 in (73.5 cm)
- ✘ 15 lb (6.8 kg)
- ✿ Fruits, leaves, flowers, small birds, reptiles, mammals
- ⚡ Least concern

Gelada baboon
Theropithecus gelada

Mantled howler monkey
Alouatta palliate
- ⊕ Central & South America
- ⋏ Rain forest
- ▭ 6 ft (1.8 m)
- ▭ 35 in (89 cm)
- ✕ 19 lb (8.6 kg)
- ✿ Fruits, leaves and flowers
- ⚡ Endangered

Family Cercopithecidae
Old World monkeys
81 species

Owl-faced monkey, Hamlyn's monkey
Cercopithecus hamlyni
- ⊕ Albertine Rift in east Africa
- ⋏ Bamboo, rain forest
- ▭ 16–26 in (40.5–66 cm)
- ▭ 20–26 in (51–66 cm)
- ✕ ♂ 10–22 lb (4.5–10 kg)
- ✿ Fruits, leaves
- ⚡ Near threatened

Golden monkey
Cercopithecus kandti
- ⊕ Albertine Rift in east Africa
- ⋏ Montane, bamboo forest
- ▭ ♂ 19–26 in (48–67 cm), ♀ 18–21 in (46–53 cm)
- ✕ 10–25 lb (4.5–11.3 kg), ♀ 7.7–10 lb (3.5–4.5 kg)
- ✿ Leaves, bamboo, fruits
- ⚡ Endangered

Blue monkey
Cercopithecus mitis
- ⊕ East & central Africa
- ⋏ Evergreen forest
- ▭ 17–27 in (43–68.5 cm)
- ▭ 21–43 in (53.5–109 cm)
- ✕ 11–15 lb (5–6.8 kg)
- ✿ Fruits, leaves
- ⚡ Least concern

Black and white colobus
Colobus guereza
- ⊕ East & central Africa
- ⋏ Primary & secondary forest, riverine forest, wooded grassland
- ▭ 19–29 in (48–73.5 cm)
- ▭ 26–35 in (66–89 cm)
- ✕ 25–51 lb (11.5–23 kg)
- ✿ Leaves, fruits
- ⚡ Least concern

Japanese macaque
Macaca fuscata
- ⊕ Japan
- ⋏ Subtropical to subalpine evergreen & deciduous forest
- ▭ Up to 31–37 in (79–95 cm)
- ▭ Up to 4 in (10 cm)
- ✕ ♂ 22–31 lb (10–14 kg), ♀ 12 lb (5.5 kg)
- ✿ Fruits; also seeds, young leaves & flowers, tree bark, insects
- ⚡ Data deficient

Barbary macaque
Macaca sylvanus
- ⊕ Northern Morocco, northern Algeria, introduced to Gibraltar
- ⋏ Mixed oak, cedar forest
- ▭ Up to 30 in (76 cm)
- ▭ Up to 1 in (2.5 cm)
- ✕ Up to 29 lb (13.1 kg)
- ✿ Leaves, fruits, insects
- ⚡ Vulnerable

Drill
Mandrillus leucophaeus
- ⊕ West Cameroon, Nigeria, Equatorial Guinea
- ⋏ Gallery & lowland rain forest, montane forest
- ▭ 24–29 in (61–73.5 cm)
- ▭ 2–3 in (5–7.5 cm)
- ✕ ♂ 55 lb (25 kg), ♀ 25 lb (11.5 kg)
- ✿ Fruits, seeds, invertebrates
- ⚡ Endangered

Mandrill
Mandrillus sphinx
- ⊕ Cameroon, Gabon, Congo
- ⋏ Primary evergreen forest
- ▭ 22–32 in (56–81 cm)
- ▭ 3 in (7.5 cm)
- ✕ 24–59 lb (11–27 kg)
- ✿ Fruits, seeds
- ⚡ Vulnerable

Proboscis monkey
Nasalis larvatus
- ⊕ Lowland Borneo
- ⋏ Mangrove swamps, riparian forest, rain forest
- ▭ 28 in (71 cm)
- ▭ 29.5 in (75 cm)
- ✕ ♂ 53 lb (24 kg), ♀ 26 lb (12 kg)
- ✿ Seeds, leaves, mangrove shoots, unripe fruit
- ⚡ Endangered

Olive baboon
Papio anubis
- ⊕ East Africa
- ⋏ Woodland, savanna near rock outcrops
- ▭ ♂ 27.5 in (70 cm)
- ▭ 16 in (40 cm)
- ✕ ♂ up to 53 lb (24 kg), ♀ up to 31 lb (14 kg)
- ✿ Roots, fruits, flowers, leaves, insects, bird eggs, small mammals
- ⚡ Least concern

Miss Waldron's red colobus
Piliocolobus badius waldronae
- ⊕ West Africa (possibly Côte d'Ivoire)
- ⋏ Rain-forest canopy
- ▭ 3 ft (1 m)
- ✿ Fruits, seeds, foliage
- ⚡ Critically endangered (declared extinct in 2000)

Red-shanked douc monkey
Pygathrix nemaeus
- ⊕ Cambodia, China, Vietnam, Laos
- ⋏ Tropical forest
- ▭ 24–30 in (61–76 cm)
- ▭ 22–30 in (56–76 cm)
- ✕ ♂ up to 15 lb (7 kg), ♀ up to 11 lb (5 kg)
- ✿ Leaves high in fiber
- ⚡ Endangered

Golden monkey
Rhinopithecus roxellana
- ⊕ Central & southwest China
- ⋏ Temperate montane forests
- ▭ ♂ 23–27 in (58–68 cm), ♀ 19–20.5 in (47.5–52 cm)
- ▭ Same as body length
- ✕ ♂ 44 lb (19.8 kg), ♀ 27 lb (12.4 kg)
- ✿ Lichens, trees, shrubs, vines, insects
- ⚡ Vulnerable

Crested langur
Semnopithecus cristatus
- ⊕ Myanmar, Indochina, Borneo
- ⋏ Coastal, mangroves, riverine forest
- ▭ 18–20 in (46–51 cm)
- ▭ ♂ 26–30 in (67–75 cm), ♀ 20–23 in (50–58 cm)
- ✕ 12.5 lb (5.7 kg)
- ✿ Fruits, leaves, shoots
- ⚡ Least concern

Common langur
Semnopithecus entellus
- ⊕ India, Pakistan
- ⋏ Subtropical or tropical dry forest, scrubland
- ▭ ♂ 20–31 in (51–78 cm), ♀ 16–27 in (40–68 cm)
- ▭ 27–40 in (69–101 cm)
- ✕ ♂ 40 lb (18 kg), ♀ 24.5 lb (11.2 kg)
- ✿ Fruits, buds, fruits, flowers, supplemented with insects
- ⚡ Near threatened

Gelada baboon
Theropithecus gelada
- ⊕ Ethiopia
- ⋏ Montane grassland
- ▭ ♂ 27–29 in (68.5–74 cm), ♀ 19–25 in (48–63.5 cm)
- ▭ ♂ 18–21 in (45.5–53.5 cm), ♀ 12–20 in (30.5–51 cm)
- ✕ ♂ 44 lb (20 kg), ♀ 28 lb (12.7 kg)
- ✿ Leaves, grasses
- ⚡ Near threatened

Family Hylobatidae
Gibbons (Lesser apes)
11 species

White-handed gibbon, Lar gibbon
Hylobates lar
- ⊕ China, Indonesia, Malaysia, Myanmar, north Sumatra, Thailand
- ⋏ Rain-forest canopy
- ▭ Up to 23 in (58.5 cm)
- ✕ 12.5–15.5 lb (5.7–7 kg), ♀ 11.5 lb (5.3 kg)
- ✿ Fruits, also tender leaves, flowers, shoots, insects, snails, bird eggs
- ⚡ Near threatened

Capped gibbon
Hylobates pileatus
- ⊕ Southeast Thailand, Cambodia
- ⋏ Rain forest
- ▭ 16–26 in (40–65 cm)
- ✕ 9–18 lb (4–8 kg)
- ✿ Leaves, fruits, flowers, buds, insects, bird eggs, small birds
- ⚡ Vulnerable

Family Hominidae
Great apes
6 species

Mountain gorilla
Gorilla beringei
- ⊕ Uganda, Rwanda, Democratic Republic of Congo
- ⋏ Montane & bamboo forest
- ▭ ♂ 4.6–6 ft (1.4–1.8 m), ♀ 4.3–5 ft (1.3–1.5 m)
- ✕ ♂ 350 lb (159 kg), ♀ 216 lb (98 kg)
- ✿ Leaves, shoots, stems
- ⚡ Endangered

Western gorilla
Gorilla gorilla
- ⊕ West & central Africa
- ⋏ Primary & secondary forest, lowland swamp, montane forest
- ▭ ♂ 5.6 ft (1.7 m), ♀ 5 ft (1.5 m)
- ✕ ♂ 374 lb (170 kg), ♀ 158 lb (72 kg)
- ✿ Fruits, leaves, shoots, stems
- ⚡ Critically endangered

Bonobo
Pan paniscus
- ⊕ Democratic Republic of Congo
- ⋏ Tropical rain forest
- ▭ ♂ 28–34 in (71–87 cm), ♀ 28–29 in (71–74 cm)
- ✕ ♂ 86 lb (39 kg), ♀ 68 lb (31 kg)
- ✿ Fruits, leaves, terrestrial herbs
- ⚡ Endangered

Chimpanzee
Pan troglodytes
- ⊕ West, central & east Africa
- ⋏ Rain forest, dry woodland savanna, grassland
- ▭ 32 in (81 cm)
- ✕ ♂ 88–132 lb (40–60 kg), ♀ 70–103 lb (32–47 kg)
- ✿ Fruits, leaves, terrestrial herbs, flowers, insects, small vertebrates
- ⚡ Endangered

Sumatran orangutan
Pongo abelii
- ⊕ Sumatra
- ⋏ Tropical rain forest
- ▭ ♂ up to 4.6 ft (1.4 m), ♀ 3 ft (0.9 m)
- ✕ ♂ up to 200 lb (90 kg), ♀ up to 100 lb (45 kg)
- ✿ Fruits, insects, bird eggs, small vertebrates
- ⚡ Critically endangered

Bornean orangutan
Pongo pygmaeus
- ⊕ Borneo
- ⋏ Tropical rain forest
- ▭ ♂ up to 5 ft (1.5 m), ♀ up to 3.5 ft (1 m)
- ✕ ♂ up to 245 lb (110 kg), ♀ up to 135 lb (60 kg)
- ✿ Fruits, also young leaves, shoots, seeds, bark, insects, bird eggs
- ⚡ Endangered

ORDER CARNIVORA
CARNIVORES
275 species

Family Canidae
Dogs & foxes
34 species

Coyote
Canis latrans
- ⊕ North America to Central America
- ⋏ Desert, grassland, forest, farmland, suburbs, cities
- ▭ 30–39 in (75–100 cm)
- ▭ 10–16 in (25.5–40.5 cm)
- ✕ ♂ 17–44 lb (8–20 kg), ♀ 15–40 lb (7–18 kg)
- ✿ Mammals from mice to deer, birds, snakes, plant material, carrion
- ⚡ Least concern

Gray wolf
Canis lupus
- ⊕ Northern North America, parts of Eurasia
- ⋏ Coniferous & deciduous forest, tundra, plains
- ▭ 34–51 in (87–130 cm)
- ▭ 14–20 in (35–51 cm)
- ✕ ♂ 66–176 lb (30–80 kg), ♀ 51–121 lb (23–55 kg)
- ✿ Deer, hares, other mammals
- ⚡ Least concern

Dingo
Canis lupus dingo
- ⊕ Mainland Australia
- ⋏ Most Australian habitats, from desert to rain forest
- ▭ Up to 39.5 in (100 cm)
- ▭ Up to 14 in (36 cm)
- ✕ Up to 53 lb (24 kg)
- ✿ Kangaroos, wallabies, small mammals, birds, fruits
- ⚡ Vulnerable

European wolf
Canis lupus lupus
- ⊕ Europe, Asia
- ⋏ Forest
- ▭ Up to 5.3 ft (1.6 m)
- ▭ Up to 22 in (56 cm)
- ✕ Up to 130 lb (59 kg)
- ✿ Carnivorous
- ⚡ Least concern

Arctic fox
Vulpes lagopus

Ethiopian wolf
Canis simensis
- ⊕ Ethiopia
- ⋏ Montane grassland
- ▭ 35–39 in (90–100 cm)
- ▭ 10–14 in (25–35 cm)
- ✕ 26–39 lb (11.5–18 kg)
- ✿ Rodents & other small mammals
- ⚡ Endangered

Maned wolf
Chrysocyon brachyurus
- ⊕ South America
- ⋏ Grassland, scrub forest
- ▭ 35 in (90 cm)
- ▭ 17.5 in (44.5 cm)
- ✕ 50 lb (22.5 kg)
- ✿ Rodents, hares, birds, fish, fruits, sugarcane, tubers
- ⚡ Near threatened

Andean red fox, Culpeo
Lycalopex culpaeus
- ⊕ South America
- ⋏ Forest, prairie
- ▭ 44 in (112 cm)
- ▭ 13 in (33 cm)
- ✕ 13 lb (6 kg)
- ✿ Mammals, ungulates, vertebrates, poultry, livestock
- ⚡ Least concern

African wild dog
Lycaon pictus
- ⊕ Scattered in sub-Saharan Africa
- ⋏ Woodland, savanna, grassland
- ▭ 29–44 in (74–112 cm)
- ▭ 12–16 in (30–41 cm)
- ✕ 39–79 lb (18–36 kg)
- ✿ Small to medium mammals such as antelopes
- ⚡ Endangered

Raccoon dog
Nyctereutes procyonoides
- ⊕ East Asia
- ⋏ Deciduous woodland, mixed forest
- ▭ Up to 24 in (61 cm)
- ▭ Up to 7 in (18 cm)
- ✕ Up to 22 lb (10 kg)
- ✿ Invertebrates, frogs, lizards, rodents, birds, crabs, seeds, berries
- ⚡ Least concern

Patagonian gray fox
Pseudalopex griseus
- ⊕ Chile, Patagonia, Argentina
- ⋏ Areas with lots of brush or woods
- ▭ 39 in (100 cm)
- ▭ 17 in (43 cm)
- ✕ 10 lb (4.5 kg)
- ✿ Hares, rodents, also berries, bird eggs, insects
- ⚡ Least concern

Cape fox
Vulpes chama
- ⊕ South Africa
- ⋏ Grassland, steppe, semidesert scrub
- ▭ 24–24 in (54–61 cm)
- ▭ 11–16 in (28–40 cm)
- ✕ 5.5–7.7 lb (2.5–3.5 kg)
- ✿ Invertebrates, small vertebrates such as mice
- ⚡ Least concern

Arctic fox
Vulpes lagopus
- ⊕ Arctic tundra & forests
- ⋏ Tundra, moorland
- ▭ Up to 27.5 in (70 cm)
- ▭ Up to 16 in (40 cm)
- ✕ Up to 18 lb (8 kg)
- ✿ Insects, small mammals, birds, carrion
- ⚡ Least concern

Red fox
Vulpes vulpes
- North America, Europe, northern & central Asia, northern Africa, Arabia, introduced in Australia
- Deciduous woodland, mixed forest
- Up to 32 in (81 cm)
- Up to 16 in (41 cm)
- Up to 15 lb (6.8 kg)
- Invertebrates such as insects & mollusks, small vertebrates such as rodents & birds, bird eggs, fruits
- Least concern

Fennec fox
Vulpes zerda
- Central Sahara
- Desert, steppe
- 15–16 in (38–41 cm)
- 7–8 in (18–21 cm)
- 1.8–3.3 lb (0.8–1.5 kg)
- Desert grasshoppers, other invertebrates, fruits
- Data deficient

Family Ursidae
Bears & panda
9 species

Giant panda
Ailuropoda melanoleuca
- Southwest China (Gansu, Shaanxi & Sichuan provinces)
- Bamboo & coniferous forests
- Up to 5 ft (1.5 m)
- 154–275 lb (70–125 kg)
- Bamboo leaves & shoots
- Endangered

Sun bear
Helarctos malayanus
- Southeast Asia
- Tropical rain forest
- 4 ft (1.2 m)
- 145 lb (65 kg)
- Fruits, insects
- Vulnerable

Spectacled bear
Tremarctos ornatus
- Tropical Andes
- Rain forest, cloud forest
- 6 ft (1.8 m)
- 3 in (7.5 cm)
- 180 lb (820 kg)
- Fruits, leaves, insects
- Vulnerable

American black bear
Ursus americanus
- Non-Arctic Canada & Alaska through USA to northern Mexico
- Diverse habitats from deciduous forest to desert, and subtropical forests to boreal forest & tundra
- 4–6.5 ft (1.2–2 m)
- 3–5.5 in (8–14 cm)
- ♂ 103–900 lb (47–409 kg), ♀ 86–520 lb (39–236 kg)
- Fruits, nuts, vegetation; also meat, insects
- Least concern

Brown bear, Grizzly bear
Ursus arctos
- Northwest North America, Europe south to Spain, north & central Asia
- Arctic tundra, boreal forest, open plains, edges of deserts
- 3–9 ft (0.9–2.7 m)
- 2.5–8 in (6.5–20 cm)
- 175–1,300 lb (80–590 kg) or more
- Plants, fungi, insects, birds, mammals, carrion
- Least concern (though some subspecies are endangered)

European brown bear
Ursus arctos arctos
- Pockets in northwest North America, Wyoming, western & northern Europe, Himalaya, Japan
- Mountain, forest
- Up to 9.2 ft (2.8 m)
- Up to 5 in (12.7 cm)
- Up to 460 lb (205 kg)
- Berries, fish, mammals
- Least concern

Siberian brown bear
Ursus arctos collaris
- Siberia, Mongolia, eastern Kazakhstan
- Taiga forest
- Up to 9 ft (2.8 m)
- Up to 5 in (12.7 cm)
- 220–1,500 lb (100–680 kg)
- Berries, roots, fungi, sprouts, insects, fish, small mammals
- Least concern

Polar bear
Ursus maritimus
- Arctic coastal areas
- Tundra, sea ice
- Up to 8 ft (2.5 m)
- 4 in (10 cm)
- ♂ up to 800 lb (360 kg), ♀ 200 lb (550 kg)
- Seals, fish, birds, eggs, carrion, berries
- Vulnerable

Asiatic black bear
Ursus thibetanus
- Afghanistan, Pakistan to China, Korea, Japan
- Forest (lowlands to hilly areas)
- 4.5–6.5 ft (1.4–2 m)
- Up to 4 in (10 cm)
- ♂ 220–480 lb (100–218 kg), ♀ 110–275 lb (50–125 kg)
- Plant matter such as acorns, nuts, bamboo & berries, insects, carrion, smaller vertebrates
- Vulnerable

Family Mustelidae
Mustelids
56 species

Tayra
Eira barbara
- Central America, South America, Trinidad
- Rain forest
- Up to 28 in (70 cm)
- 16 in (40 cm)
- Up to 13 lb (5.8 kg)
- Fruits, invertebrates, reptiles
- Least concern

Wolverine
Gulo gulo
- Northern North America, Europe, Asia
- Boreal forest, Arctic tundra
- 25.5–41 in (65–104 cm)
- 6.6–10.2 in (17–26 cm)
- ♂ 28–31 lb (12.7–14 kg), ♀ 18.3–21.8 lb (8.3–9.9 kg)
- Carrion of moose & caribou, ground squirrels, ptarmigan, snowshoe hares
- Vulnerable

Northern river otter
Lontra canadensis
- Canada & USA except southwest deserts & high Arctic
- Lakes, rivers, streams, swamps, marshes, estuaries
- 35–51 in (89–130 cm)
- 12–20 in (30–51 cm)
- 11–31 lb (5–14 kg)
- Fish, frogs, crayfish, turtles, birds, eggs, muskrats
- Least concern

Eurasian otter
Lutra lutra
- Europe, Asia, Africa
- River, wetlands
- Up to 43 in (110 cm)
- Up to 22 in (55 cm)
- Up to 26 lb (12 kg)
- Fish, crustaceans
- Near threatened

Pine marten
Martes martes
- Northern Europe
- Forest
- Up to 21 in (53 cm)
- Up to 10 in (25 cm)
- Up to 3.5 lb (1.6 kg)
- Small mammals, birds, frogs
- Least concern

Sable
Martes zibellina
- Siberia, northern Mongolia, China, Japan (Hokkaido)
- Forest
- 15–22 in (38–56 cm)
- 3.5–5 in (9–12 cm)
- 1.9–4 lb (0.9–1.8 kg)
- Small mammals, birds, fish
- Least concern

European badger
Meles meles
- Britain & western Europe to China, Korea & Japan
- Woodland, fields
- Up to 35.4 in (90 cm)
- Up to 8 in (20.5 cm)
- Up to 35 lb (16 kg)
- Earthworms, beetles, small mammals, reptiles, amphibians, eggs, fruits, roots, other plants
- Least concern

Stoat
Mustela erminea
- Arctic
- Tundra, moors, fields, marshes, boreal forest, woodland
- 10 in (25 cm)
- 4 in (10 cm)
- ♂ 7–16 oz (200–440 g), ♀ 5–10 oz (140–280 g)
- Insects, small amphibians, reptiles, birds, mammals, carrion
- Least concern

Black-footed ferret
Mustela nigripes
- Formerly, interior North America from southern Canada to northern Mexico
- Grassland, semidesert, desert
- 19–23.6 in (48–60 cm)
- 4.2–5.5 in (10.5–14 cm)
- ♂ 2–2.5 lb (905–1,125 g), ♀ 1.4–1.9 lb (635–860 g)
- Prairie dogs
- Critically endangered (was extinct in the wild; zoo-bred animals have been reintroduced)

Least weasel
Mustela nivalis
- North America, Europe, Asia
- Meadows, marshes, grassy fields
- Up to 10 in (26 cm)
- Up to 3 in (7.5 cm)
- Up to 9 oz (250 g)
- Mice, voles, small rodents
- Least concern

Polecat
Mustela putorius
- Europe
- Wetlands, forest
- Up to 18 in (46 cm)
- Up to 9 in (23 cm)
- Up to 3.8 lb (1.7 kg)
- Rodents, birds, frogs
- Least concern

Giant river otter
Pteronura brasiliensis
- Southern Venezuela & Colombia to northern Argentina
- Amazon rain forest
- 6.5 ft (2 m)
- 3.3 ft (1 m)
- 75 lb (34 kg)
- Fish, crabs
- Endangered

American badger
Taxidea taxus
- Southwest Canada, USA, Mexico
- From alpine meadows to prairie, marshes & desert
- 23.5–31 in (60–79 cm)
- 4–5 in (10–13 cm)
- 9–26 lb (4–12 kg)
- Rodents (especially squirrels), birds, reptiles, insects
- Least concern

Family Mephitidae
Skunks
13 species

Striped skunk
Mephitis mephitis
- Southern Canada (except Pacific coast), USA, northern Mexico
- All habitat types except extremely arid ones
- 22.5–31.5 in (58–80 cm)
- 6.8–12 in (17–30 cm)
- 2.5–11.5 lb (1.1–5.2 kg)
- Insects, small rodents, rabbits, birds, eggs, carrion, fruits, vegetation
- Least concern

Family Ailuridae
Red panda
1 species

Red panda
Ailurus fulgens
- China, India, Bhutan, Laos, Nepal, Myanmar
- Mountain forest with coniferous & deciduous trees
- 16–24 in (40–60 cm)
- 12–24 in (30–60 cm)
- 6.5–13 lb (3–6 kg)
- Bamboo, berries, fruits, mushrooms, roots, acorns, lichen, grasses, also birds, fish, eggs, rodents, insects
- Endangered

Family Phocidae
True seals
19 species

Leopard seal
Hydrurga leptonyx
- Southern Ocean
- Antarctic pack ice, subantarctic islands
- ♂ 8–11 ft (2.4–3.3 m)
- ♂ 440–990 lb (200–449 kg), ♀ 485–1,250 lb (220–565 kg)
- Krill, penguins, fish, squid, young crabeater seals
- Least concern

Weddell seal
Leptonychotes weddellii
- Southern Ocean
- Fast ice & sea around Antarctica
- ♂ up to 9.5 ft (2.9 m), ♀ up to 11.5 ft (3.5 m)
- 880–1,320 lb (400–600 kg)
- Fish, squid, crustaceans
- Least concern

Crabeater seal
Lobodon carcinophagus
- Southern Ocean
- Pack ice, ice floes at pack-ice edge
- 8.5 ft (2.6 m)
- 750 lb (340 kg)
- Mainly krill, also squid, fish
- Least concern

Southern elephant seal
Mirounga leonina
- Argentina, New Zealand, subantarctic islands
- Subantarctic regions
- ♂ 16.3 ft (5 m), ♀ 9.8 ft (3 m)
- ♂ 19 in (48 cm), ♀ 11 in (28 cm)
- ♂ 4 tons (3.6 t), ♀ 0.8 tons (0.7 t)
- Cephalopods such as squid & cuttlefish, large fish such as sharks
- Vulnerable

Monk seal
Monachus monachus
- Coastal west Africa, Aegean Sea
- Coastal & island waters, sea caves for breeding
- Up to 7.8 ft (2.4 m)
- Up to 705 lb (320 kg)
- Fish, mollusks, octopus
- Critically endangered

Ross seal
Ommatophoca rossii
- Southern Ocean
- Pack ice
- 10 ft (3 m)
- 470 lb (214 kg)
- Squid, fish, krill
- Vulnerable

Harp seal
Phoca groenlandica
- Gulf of St Lawrence & Newfoundland, White Sea, Greenland Sea, ice-strewn seas further north in summer
- Arctic seas, pack ice
- 6–7 ft (1.8–2 m)
- 260–300 lb (118–135 kg)
- Capelin, Arctic cod
- Least concern

European badger
Meles meles

Ringed seal
Phoca hispida
- ⊕ Arctic coasts & oceans, lakes in Russia & Finland
- ▲ Inshore fast ice, pack ice
- ↹ 4 ft (1.25 m)
- ⚖ 150 lb (65 kg)
- ✿ Planktonic crustaceans, fish, squid
- ⚡ Least concern

European harbor seal
Phoca vitulina vitulina
- ⊕ North Atlantic, North Pacific
- ▲ Coastal, marine
- ↹ Up to 6.2 ft (1.9 m)
- ⚖ Up to 375 lb (170 kg)
- ✿ Crustaceans, squid, fish
- ⚡ Least concern

Family Otariidae
Sea lions & fur seals
14 species

Southern fur seal, Antarctic fur seal
Arctocephalus gazella
- ⊕ Southern Ocean
- ▲ Rocks, beaches & tussock grass thickets on subantarctic islands & particularly around Antarctic Peninsula
- ↹ ♂ 5.5–6.5 ft (1.7–2 m), ♀ 3.3–4.3 ft (1–1.3 m)
- ⚖ ♂ 275–440 lb (125–200 kg), ♀ 55–88 lb (25–40 kg)
- ✿ Krill, fish, squid
- ⚡ Least concern

California sea lion
Zalophus californianus
- ⊕ West coast of North America
- ▲ Coastal waters
- ↹ 8 ft (2.4 m)
- ⚖ 660 lb (300 kg)
- ✿ Squid, fish
- ⚡ Least concern

Galápagos sea lion
Zalophus californianus wollebaecki
- ⊕ Galápagos Islands
- ▲ Shallow coastal waters
- ↹ 6.5 ft (2 m)
- ↹ 11 in (28 cm)
- ⚖ 880 lb (400 kg)
- ✿ Sardines
- ⚡ Vulnerable

Family Odobenidae
Walrus
1 species

Walrus
Odobenus rosmarus
- ⊕ Circumarctic coasts (separate North Atlantic & North Pacific subspecies)
- ▲ Shallow coastal seas
- ↹ ♂ up to 16 ft (4.3 m), ♀ up to 8 ft (2.4 m)
- ⚖ Up to 1.8 tons (1.6 t)
- ✿ Bottom-dwelling bivalve mollusks
- ⚡ Least concern

Southern fur seal
Arctocephalus gazella

Family Procyonidae
Raccoons
19 species

Ringtail
Bassariscus astutus
- ⊕ Southwest USA, Mexico, Baja Peninsula
- ▲ Rocky & mountainous terrain, arid shrubland, woodland
- ↹ 24–32 in (62–81 cm)
- ↹ 12–17 in (31–44 cm)
- ⚖ 2–3 lb (0.9–1.3 kg)
- ✿ Plants, small mammals, insects, fruits, acorns, lizards, birds, eggs
- ⚡ Least concern

Kinkajou
Potos flavus
- ⊕ Southern Mexico to Bolivia & Brazil
- ▲ Rain forest
- ↹ 22 in (56 cm)
- ↹ 22 in (56 cm)
- ⚖ 7 lb (3.2 kg)
- ✿ Fruits, nectar from flowers
- ⚡ Least concern

Northern raccoon
Procyon lotor
- ⊕ North & Central America, introduced to Europe
- ▲ All habitat types where there is water, including urban areas
- ↹ 23.7–37.5 in (60–95 cm)
- ↹ 7.5–16 in (19–40.5 cm)
- ⚖ 4–23 lb (1.8–10.4 kg)
- ✿ Insects, fish, crustaceans, mollusks, small rodents, birds, eggs, carrion, fruits, seeds
- ⚡ Least concern

Family Hyaenidae
Hyenas & aardwolf
4 species

Spotted hyena
Crocuta crocuta
- ⊕ Sub-Saharan Africa
- ▲ Savanna, grassland
- ↹ 3.3–6 ft (1–1.8 m)
- ↹ 10–14 in (25–36 cm)
- ⚖ 88–198 lb (40–90 kg)
- ✿ Small to large mammals, carrion
- ⚡ Least concern

Striped hyena
Hyaena hyaena
- ⊕ North & northeast Africa
- ▲ Arid steppe, scrub, savanna
- ↹ 39–47 in (100–120 cm)
- ↹ 11–14 in (25–35 cm)
- ⚖ 55–121 lb (25–55 kg)
- ✿ Carrion, small mammals
- ⚡ Near threatened

Aardwolf
Proteles cristata
- ⊕ East & south Africa
- ▲ Grassland, savanna
- ↹ 21–31 in (55–80 cm)
- ↹ 8–12 in (20–30 cm)
- ⚖ 17–26 lb (8–12 kg)
- ✿ Termites
- ⚡ Least concern

Family Viverridae
Civets, genets & linsangs
35 species

Fossa
Cryptoprocta ferox
- ⊕ Madagascar
- ▲ Rain forest
- ↹ 23–30 in (58–76 cm)
- ↹ 22–28 in (55–70 cm)
- ⚖ 15–26 lb (7–12 kg)
- ✿ Small to medium vertebrates such as lemurs
- ⚡ Endangered

Malagasy civet
Fossa fossana
- ⊕ Madagascar
- ▲ Primary forest
- ↹ 16–18 in (40–45 cm)
- ↹ 8–10 in (21–25 cm)
- ⚖ 3.3–4.4 lb (1.5–2 kg)
- ✿ Small mammals such as rodents
- ⚡ Vulnerable

Family Herpestidae
Mongooses
34 species

Indian gray mongoose
Herpestes edwardsii
- ⊕ Indian subcontinent, eastern Arabian peninsula, Sri Lanka, southeastern China
- ▲ Open forest, scrubland, farmland
- ↹ 14–17 in (35–43 cm)
- ↹ 17 in (43 cm)
- ⚖ 2–4 lb (0.9–1.8 kg)
- ✿ Birds, reptiles, small mammals, insects
- ⚡ Least concern

Meerkat
Suricata suricata
- ⊕ Southern Africa
- ▲ Bushland, scrub
- ↹ 10–12 in (25–30 cm)
- ↹ 7–9 in (18–24 cm)
- ⚖ 21–34 oz (590–955 g)
- ✿ Insects
- ⚡ Least concern

Family Felidae
Cats
36 species

Cheetah
Acinonyx jubatus heckii
- ⊕ Northern Africa
- ▲ Woodland, savanna, grassland
- ↹ 3–5 ft (1–1.5 m)
- ↹ 26–35 in (65–90 cm)
- ⚖ 77–143 lb (35–65 kg)
- ✿ Small to medium mammals such as antelopes & gazelles
- ⚡ Endangered

Geoffroy's cat
Felis geoffroyi

Geoffroy's cat
Felis geoffroyi
- ⊕ Southern Bolivia & Paraguay to Argentina & Chile
- ▲ Scrubby woodland
- ↹ 36 in (90 cm)
- ↹ 16 in (40 cm)
- ⚖ 7 lb (3 kg)
- ✿ Small lizards, insects, rodents, frogs, fish
- ⚡ Near threatened

Wildcat
Felis silvestris
- ⊕ Africa, Europe to western China & northwestern India
- ▲ Mountain, forest
- ↹ Up to 28 in (71 cm)
- ↹ Up to 12 in (30 cm)
- ⚖ Up to 30 lb (13.6 kg)
- ✿ Rodents, birds
- ⚡ Least concern

Margay
Leopardus wiedii
- ⊕ Central & South America
- ▲ Rain forest
- ↹ 42 in (107 cm) including tail
- ↹ 18 in (46 cm)
- ⚖ 20 lb (9 kg)
- ✿ Arboreal animals, birds, reptiles, insects
- ⚡ Vulnerable

Canada lynx
Lynx canadensis
- ⊕ Most of Canada & Alaska, south to northern Rocky Mountains
- ▲ Boreal forest
- ↹ 26–42 in (67–107 cm)
- ↹ 2–5 in (5–13 cm)
- ⚖ 9–38 lb (4.5–17.3 kg)
- ✿ Snowshoe hares, other small mammals, deer, birds
- ⚡ Least concern

Eurasian lynx
Lynx lynx
- ⊕ France, Balkans, Iraq, Scandinavia to China
- ▲ Mountain, forest
- ↹ Up to 4.3 ft (1.3 m)
- ↹ Up to 10 in (25 cm)
- ⚖ Up to 66 lb (30 kg)
- ✿ Deer, small mammals, rodents
- ⚡ Near threatened

Iberian lynx
Lynx pardinus
- ⊕ Formerly Spain & Portugal, now restricted to southern Spain
- ▲ Grassland, woodland
- ↹ 33–43 in (85–110 cm)
- ↹ 5–12 in (12–30 cm)
- ⚖ ♂ 30–57 lb (13–26 kg), ♀ 20 lb (9 kg)
- ✿ Rabbits, small mammals, other vertebrates
- ⚡ Critically endangered

Bobcat
Lynx rufus
- ⊕ Most of USA, southern Canada, Mexico
- ▲ Nearly all habitats from mountains to swamps & deserts
- ↹ 2–4 ft (60–120 cm)
- ↹ 3.5–8 in (9–20 cm)
- ⚖ ♂ 16–68 lb (7.2–31 kg), ♀ 8–53 lb (3.6–24 kg)
- ✿ Mammals from mice to deer fawns, especially rabbits; birds, reptiles, amphibians, insects
- ⚡ Least concern

Clouded leopard
Neofelis nebulosa
- ⊕ Southern China, Southeast Asia, eastern Himalaya, northeast India
- ▲ Subtropical & tropical moist forests
- ↹ 24–36 in (61–92 cm)
- ↹ Up to 35.5 in (90 cm)
- ⚖ 33–51 lb (15–23 kg)
- ✿ Deer, pigs, primates, birds
- ⚡ Vulnerable

Lion
Panthera leo
- ⊕ Sub-Saharan Africa
- ▲ Savanna, grassland
- ↹ ♂ Up to 8 ft (2.4 m), ♀ 6 ft (1.8 m)
- ↹ 23–39 in (60–100 cm)
- ⚖ ♂ 330–573 lb (150–260 kg), ♀ 269–401 lb (122–182 kg)
- ✿ Medium to large mammals
- ⚡ Vulnerable

Asiatic lion
Panthera leo persica
- ⊕ Gir Forest in state of Gujarat, India
- ▲ Forest
- ↹ ♂ 5.5–7 ft (1.7–2 m), ♀ 4.5–5.5 ft (1.3–1.7 m)
- ↹ Up to 39.5 in (1 m)
- ⚖ ♂ 330–500 lb (150–225 kg), ♀ 220–330 lb (100–150 kg)
- ✿ Small mammals, deer, muntjac, sambar, wild boar, nilgai, cattle
- ⚡ Critically endangered

Jaguar
Panthera onca
- ⊕ Mexico to Argentina
- ▲ Forest, grassland, pasture, ranches
- ↹ 8.8 ft (2.7 m)
- ↹ 30 in (76 cm)
- ⚖ 350 lb (159 kg)
- ✿ Meat, mammals, reptiles, fish
- ⚡ Near threatened

Leopard
Panthera pardus
- ⊕ Sub-Saharan Africa
- ▲ Woodland, savanna, grassland
- ↹ ♂ 4.9–6.3 ft (1.5–1.9 m), ♀ 3.3–4.6 ft (1–1.4 m)
- ↹ 23–43 in (68–110 cm)
- ⚖ ♂ 77–198 lb (35–90 kg), ♀ 61–154 lb (28–70 kg)
- ✿ Small to medium mammals
- ⚡ Least concern

Sri Lankan leopard
Panthera pardus kotiya
- ⊕ Sri Lanka
- ▲ Dry monsoon forest, tropical rain forest, montane forest
- ↹ 3–7.8 ft (0.9–2.4 m)
- ↹ 23–39 in (58–99 cm)
- ⚖ ♂ 125 lb (56 kg), ♀ 64 lb (30 kg)
- ✿ Small mammals, deer, muntjac, sambar, wild boar, monkeys, domestic dogs, cattle
- ⚡ Endangered

Tiger
Panthera tigris
- ⊕ India to Vietnam, Siberia to Indonesia
- ▲ Forest
- ↹ 9 ft (2.7 m)
- ↹ 3 ft (1 m)
- ⚖ Up to 795 lb (360 kg)
- ✿ Deer, wild pigs, cattle
- ⚡ Endangered

Siberian tiger
Panthera tigris altaica
- ⊕ Far eastern Russia, northeastern China, North Korea
- ▲ Taiga
- ↹ 6.3–8 ft (1.9–2.5 m)
- ↹ 3 ft (1 m)
- ⚖ ♂ up to 700 lb (320 kg), ♀ up to 400 lb (181 kg)
- ✿ Deer, goat antelopes, small mammals
- ⚡ Endangered

Bengal tiger
Panthera tigris tigris
- ⊕ India, Bhutan, Nepal, Bangladesh, Myanmar
- ⋀ Dry monsoon forest, mangrove swamp forest
- ⬓ ♂ 8.8–10 ft (2.7–3 m), ♀ 7.8–8.5 ft (2.4–2.6 m)
- ⬗ 33–37 in (84–94 cm)
- ⚖ ♂ 400–570 lb (180–258 kg), ♀ 220–350 lb (100–160 kg)
- ❂ Deer, muntjac, sambar, wild boar, monkeys, wild cattle, livestock, serpents, birds
- ⚡ Endangered

Mountain lion, Puma, Cougar
Puma concolor
- ⊕ North & South America
- ⋀ Nearly all habitats except agricultural land & barren desert
- ⬓ ♂ 3–6 ft (0.9–1.8 m), ♀ 3–5 ft (0.9–1.5 m)
- ⬗ 21–36 in (53–91 cm)
- ⚖ ♂ 120–165 lb (55–75 kg), ♀ 77–110 lb (35–50 kg)
- ❂ Mammals, including deer & other large hoofed species
- ⚡ Near threatened

Snow leopard
Unica unica
- ⊕ Mountains of central Asia (including the Himalaya), Afghanistan, northern Pakistan, eastern Tibet
- ⋀ Mountainous meadows, high rocky regions
- ⬓ 39–51 in (99–130 cm)
- ⬗ 32–39 in (81–99 cm)
- ⚖ 77–121 lb (35–55 kg)
- ❂ Wild goats, deer, small mammals, wild boar
- ⚡ Endangered

ORDER PROBOSCIDEA
ELEPHANTS
2 species (living)

Asian elephant
Elephas maximus
- ⊕ India, Nepal, Bangladesh, Bhutan, Sri Lanka, China, Thailand, Laos, Cambodia, Malaysia, Indonesia
- ⋀ Evergreen & dry deciduous forest, swamps, grassland
- ⬓ Up to 24.5 ft (7.5 m)
- ⬗ 3.25–5 ft (1–1.5 m)
- ⚖ 3.3–5.5 tons (3–5 t)
- ❂ Grasses, leaves, bark, fruit
- ⚡ Endangered

African elephant
Loxodonta africana
- ⊕ Sub-Saharan Africa
- ⋀ Forest to semidesert
- ⬓ 29.6 ft (9 m)
- ⬗ 3 ft (1 m)
- ⚖ ♂ 4.4–6.9 tons (4–6.3 t), ♀ 2.4–3.9 tons (2.2–3.5 t)
- ❂ Grasses, woody plants
- ⚡ Vulnerable

Woolly mammoth
Mammuthus primigenius
- ⊕ North America, Eurasia, Siberia
- ⋀ Dry cold grassland & steppe
- ⬓ 11.5 ft (3.5 m); tusks to up 16 ft (4.8 m) long
- ⚖ 5.6–13 tons (5–12 t)
- ❂ Grasses, sagebrush
- ⚡ Extinct c. 1,700 BC

Indian rhinoceros
Rhinoceros unicornis

ORDER SIRENIA
DUGONG & MANATEES
5 species

Family Trichechidae
Manatees
3 species

West Indian manatee
Trichechus manatus
- ⊕ Georgia & Florida to Brazil, Orinoco River
- ⋀ Shallow rivers, bays, estuaries, coastal waters
- ⬓ 12 ft (3.6 m)
- ⬗ 27 in (68.5 cm)
- ⚖ 1,600 lb (725 kg)
- ❂ Grasses, turtle grass, algae, mangrove leaves, water hyacinths
- ⚡ Vulnerable

Family Dugongidae
Dugong
2 species

Dugong
Dugong dugon
- ⊕ Red Sea to southwest Pacific islands
- ⋀ Shallow coastal waters
- ⬓ Up to 4.5 ft (1.4 m)
- ⚖ Up to 900 lb (408 kg)
- ❂ Seagrasses
- ⚡ Vulnerable

Steller's sea cow
Hydrodamalis gigas
- ⊕ Bering Sea
- ⋀ Cold coastal waters
- ⬓ Up to 29.5 ft (9 m)
- ⬗ 5 in (13 cm)
- ⚖ More than 3.3 tons (3 t)
- ❂ Kelp
- ⚡ Extinct 1768

ORDER PERISSODACTYLA
ODD-TOED UNGULATES
18 species

Family Equidae
Horses, zebras & asses
9 species

Wild horse
Equus caballus
- ⊕ USA, some Atlantic coastal islands
- ⋀ Shrubby sagebrush plains & mountains, juniper woodland
- ⬓ 9.5 ft (2.9 m)
- ⬗ 35 in (90 cm)
- ⚖ 770–1,545 lb (350–700 kg)
- ❂ Grasses, forbs, shrubs
- ⚡ Feral domestic invasive in North America

Grevy's zebra
Equus grevyi
- ⊕ Ethiopia, Kenya
- ⋀ Grassland
- ⬓ 8.1–9.6 ft (2.5–3 m)
- ⬗ 16–29 in (40–74 cm)
- ⚖ ♂ 948 lb (430 kg), ♀ 849 lb (385 kg)
- ❂ Grasses
- ⚡ Endangered

Sumatran rhinoceros
Dicerorhinus sumatrensis

Indian wild ass, Khur, Onager
Equus hemionus
- ⊕ Gujarat Province (India)
- ⋀ Saline desert, grassland in arid zone, shrubland
- ⬓ Up to 8.5 ft (2.6 m)
- ⚖ 550 lb (250 kg)
- ❂ Grasses, leaves, fruits
- ⚡ Data deficient

Przewalski's horse
Equus przewalskii
- ⊕ Mongolia
- ⋀ Semidesert steppe
- ⬓ 6.9 ft (2.1 m)
- ⬗ 2.9 ft (90 cm)
- ⚖ 660 lb (300 kg)
- ❂ Grasses
- ⚡ Critically endangered

Plains zebra
Equus quagga
- ⊕ East & southern Africa
- ⋀ Savanna, woodland
- ⬓ 7.2–8.2 ft (2.2–2.5 m)
- ⬗ 18–22 in (45–57 cm)
- ⚖ ♂ 485–710 lb (220–322 kg), ♀ 385–552 lb (175–250 kg)
- ❂ Grasses
- ⚡ Least concern

Family Tapiridae
Tapirs
4 species

Baird's tapir
Tapirus bairdii
- ⊕ Central America
- ⋀ Tropical forests
- ⬓ 6.5 ft (2 m)
- ⬗ 5 in (13 cm)
- ⚖ Up to 880 lb (400 kg)
- ❂ Plants, fallen fruits
- ⚡ Endangered

Brazilian tapir
Tapirus pinchaque
- ⊕ Tropical South America east of Andes
- ⋀ Tropical forest
- ⬓ 7 ft (2.1 m)
- ⬗ 3 in (8 cm)
- ⚖ 500 lb (227 kg)
- ❂ Ferns, horsetails, fruits, leaves
- ⚡ Endangered

Family Rhinocerotidae
Rhinoceroses
5 species

White rhinoceros
Ceratotherium simum
- ⊕ Central & southern Africa
- ⋀ Grassland
- ⬓ 11.8–13.7 ft (3.6–4.2 m)
- ⬗ 31–39 in (80–100 cm)
- ⚖ ♂ 2.2–4 tons (2–3.6 t), ♀ 1.5–2.2 tons (1.4–2 t)
- ❂ Grasses
- ⚡ Near threatened

Black rhinoceros
Diceros bicornis

White rhinoceros
Ceratotherium simum

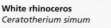

Sumatran rhinoceros
Dicerorhinus sumatrensis
- ⊕ Malaysia, Sumatra, Sabah, Borneo
- ⋀ Rain forest, swamps, cloud forest
- ⬓ 8.3 ft (2.5 m)
- ⬗ 20 in (50 cm)
- ⚖ 1,100–1,700 lb (500–800 kg)
- ❂ Grasses, leaves, some fruit
- ⚡ Critically endangered

Black rhinoceros
Diceros bicornis
- ⊕ Southern Africa (also some central & eastern Africa)
- ⋀ Savanna, grassland, shrubland
- ⬓ 9.6–12.2 ft (2.9–3.7 m)
- ⬗ 23–27 in (68–68 cm)
- ⚖ 0.8–1.5 tons (0.7–1.4 t)
- ❂ Leaves, twigs, branches
- ⚡ Critically endangered

Indian rhinoceros
Rhinoceros unicornis
- ⊕ Nepal, Bhutan, Assam (India)
- ⋀ Tall grassland & forest in Himalayan foothills
- ⬓ 13.2 ft (4 m)
- ⬗ 2.3 ft (70 cm)
- ⚖ ♂ 2.4–3.3 tons (2.2–3 t), ♀ 1.8 tons (1.6 t)
- ❂ Grasses, leaves
- ⚡ Endangered

ORDER HYRACOIDEA
HYRAXES
Hyraxes
7 species

Rock hyrax
Procavia capensis
- ⊕ Throughout Africa
- ⋀ Mountain cliffs, rocky outcrops
- ⬓ 15–23 in (38–58 cm)
- ⚖ 4–12 lb (1.8–5.4 kg)
- ❂ Grasses, herbs
- ⚡ Least concern

ORDER TUBULIDENTATA
AARDVARK
1 species

Aardvark
Orycteropus afer
- ⊕ Sub-Saharan Africa
- ⋀ Savanna, grassland, woodland, scrub
- ⬓ 3.3–5.2 ft (1–1.6 m)
- ⬗ 17–25 in (43–63 cm)
- ⚖ 88–180 lb (40–82 kg)
- ❂ Termites, ants, larvae
- ⚡ Least concern

ORDER ARTIODACTYLA
EVEN-TOED UNGULATES
218 species
* DNA evidence shows that even-toed ungulates are more closely related to whales than to any other group.

Family Bovidae
Cattle, antelopes & sheep
136 species

Subfamily Bovinae
Cattle & spiral-horned antelopes
26 species

Bison, American bison
Bison bison
- ⊕ North-central Canada, throughout USA except coasts, northern Mexico
- ⋀ Midgrass & shortgrass prairies, forest meadows
- ⬓ 7–12.5 ft (2.1–3.8 m)
- ⬗ 17–35 in (43–90 cm)
- ⚖ ♂ 1,015–2,000 lb (460–907 kg), ♀ 790–1,110 lb (358–504 kg)
- ❂ Mixed grasses
- ⚡ Near threatened

Gaur
Bos frontalis
- ⊕ India, Bangladesh, Bhutan, Laos, Cambodia, peninsular Malaysia, Borneo, Nepal, Thailand, Vietnam, Myanmar
- ⋀ Tropical woodland, grassland
- ⬓ 8.2–12 ft (2.5–3.6 m)
- ⚖ ♂ 1.1–1.7 tons (1–1.5 t), ♀ 0.8–1.1 tons (0.7–1 t)
- ❂ Grasses, shoots, fruits
- ⚡ Vulnerable

Yak
Bos grunniens
- ⊕ Himalayan region of south-central Asia, Quinghai–Tibetan Plateau, Mongolia
- ⋀ Treeless uplands, mountains, plateaus
- ⬓ 10–11 ft (3–3.4 m)
- ⚖ Up to 1.3 tons (1.2 t)
- ❂ Grasses, lichens, other vegetation
- ⚡ Vulnerable

Nilgai
Boselaphus tragocamelus
- ⊕ Peninsular India
- ⋀ Grassland, scrubland, forest woodland
- ⬓ 6–6.5 ft (1.8–2 m)
- ⚖ 265–530 lb (120–240 kg)
- ❂ Grasses, leaves, buds, fruits
- ⚡ Least concern

Tamaraw
Bubalus mindorensis
- ⊕ Mindoro island in the Philippines
- ⋀ Tropical highland forest, prefers thick brush near open glade areas
- ⬓ 7.2 ft (2.2 m)
- ⬗ 24 in (60 cm)
- ⚖ ♀ 440–660 lb (200–300 kg)
- ❂ Grasses, young bamboo shoots
- ⚡ Critically endangered

African buffalo
Syncerus caffer
- ⊕ Sub-Saharan Africa
- ⋀ Grassland
- ⬓ 5.5–11 ft (1.7–3.4 m)
- ⬗ 20–31 in (50–80 cm)
- ⚖ 551–1,874 lb (250–850 kg)
- ❂ Grasses
- ⚡ Least concern

Mountain nyala
Tragelaphus buxtoni
- ⊕ Ethiopia
- ⋀ Montane woodland, grassland
- ⬓ 6.2–8.2 ft (1.9–2.5 m)
- ⬗ 8–10 in (20–25 cm)
- ⚖ 440–660 lb (200–300 kg)
- ❂ Herbs, shrubs, grasses
- ⚡ Endangered

Bongo
Tragelaphus euryceros
- ⊕ West & central Africa
- ⋀ Rain forest with dense undergrowth
- ⬓ 5.5–8.2 ft (1.7–2.5 m)
- ⬗ 9–25 in (23–64 cm)
- ⚖ ♂ 529–893 lb (240–405 kg), ♀ 462–557 lb (210–253 kg)
- ❂ Leaves, shrubs, herbs

Greater kudu
Tragelaphus strepsiceros

Sitatunga, Marshbuck
Tragelaphus spekii
- ⊕ Central Africa
- ⋀ Swampland
- ⬛ ♂ 4.9–5.6 ft (1.5–1.7 m), ♀ 3.8–5.1 ft (1.1–1.6 m)
- ⬛ 7–12 in (18–30 cm)
- ✖ ♂ 176–286 lb (80–130 kg), ♀ 88–187 lb (40–85 kg)
- ✿ Shrubs, herbs, grasses
- ⚡ Least concern

Greater kudu
Tragelaphus strepsiceros
- ⊕ East & southern Africa
- ⋀ Woodland, evergreen forest
- ⬛ ♂ 6.3–8 ft (1.9–2.4 m), ♀ 6–7.7 ft (1.8–2.3 m)
- ⬛ 12–22 in (30–55 cm)
- ✖ ♂ 420–695 lb (190–315 kg), ♀ 265–475 lb (120–215 kg)
- ✿ Leaves, herbs, grasses
- ⚡ Least concern

Subfamily Cephalophinae
Duikers
19 species

Blue duiker
Philantomba monticola
- ⊕ Central Africa
- ⋀ Lowland & montane rain forest
- ⬛ 22–35 in (55–90 cm)
- ⬛ 3–5 in (7–13 cm)
- ✖ 8–20 lb (3.5–9 kg)
- ✿ Fruits, leaves
- ⚡ Least concern

Subfamily Hippotraginae
Grazing antelopes
6 species

Addax, Screwhorn antelope
Addax nasomaculatus
- ⊕ Niger, possibly Chad; formerly northern Africa
- ⋀ Desert
- ⬛ 4–6 ft (1.2–1.8 m)
- ⬛ 11–14 in (27–35 cm)
- ✖ ♂ 220–298 lb (100–135 kg), ♀ 132–198 lb (60–90 kg)
- ✿ Desert grasses
- ⚡ Critically endangered

Sable antelope
Hippotragus niger
- ⊕ East & southern Africa
- ⋀ Miombo woodland
- ⬛ 6.2–8.3 ft (1.9–2.5 m)
- ⬛ 16–30 in (40–75 cm)
- ✖ ♂ 440–595 lb (200–270 kg), ♀ 418–507 lb (190–230 kg)
- ✿ Grasses
- ⚡ Least concern

Scimitar-horned oryx
Oryx dammah
- ⊕ Formerly North Africa
- ⋀ Semidesert, grassland
- ⬛ 6.2–7.2 ft (1.9–2.2 m)
- ⬛ 18–24 in (45–60 cm)
- ✖ 298–308 lb (135–140 kg)
- ✿ Grasses, herbs, shrubs
- ⚡ Extinct in the wild

Gemsbok
Oryx gazella
- ⊕ Southwest Africa
- ⋀ Woodland, grassland
- ⬛ 6–6.4 ft (1.8–1.95 m)
- ⬛ 16–19 in (40–48 cm)
- ✖ ♂ 396–529 lb (180–240 kg), ♀ 396–496 lb (180–225 kg)
- ✿ Grasses, herbs
- ⚡ Least concern

Arabian oryx
Oryx leucoryx
- ⊕ Arabian peninsula
- ⋀ Desert
- ⬛ 5–7.9 ft (1.5–2.4 m)
- ⬛ 154 lb (70 kg)
- ✿ Grasses, vegetation
- ⚡ Endangered (extinct in the wild 1972, reintroduced after captive-breeding programs)

Subfamily Antilopinae
Gazelles, dwarf antelopes & saiga
34 species

Springbok
Antidorcas marsupialis
- ⊕ Southwest Africa
- ⋀ Savanna, shrubland
- ⬛ 3.9–4.9 ft (1.2–1.5 m)
- ⬛ 5–11 in (13–28 cm)
- ✖ ♂ 66–130 lb (30–59 kg), ♀ 44–95 lb (20–43 kg)
- ✿ Grasses, shrubs
- ⚡ Least concern

Thomson's gazelle
Eudorcas thomsoni
- ⊕ East Africa
- ⋀ Grassland, savanna
- ⬛ 23–35 in (58–90 cm)
- ⬛ 9–14 in (23–36 cm)
- ✖ 29–49 lb (13–22 kg)
- ✿ Grasses, herbs, shrubs
- ⚡ Least concern

Dorcas gazelle
Gazella dorcas
- ⊕ North Africa
- ⋀ Semidesert
- ⬛ 35–43 in (90–110 cm)
- ⬛ 6–8 in (15–20 cm)
- ✖ 33–44 lb (15–20 kg)
- ✿ Herbs, shrubs, grasses
- ⚡ Vulnerable

Gerenuk
Litocranius walleri
- ⊕ East Africa
- ⋀ Semiarid bushland
- ⬛ 4.6–5.2 ft (1.4–1.6 m)
- ⬛ 9–14 in (23–36 cm)
- ✖ 62–115 lb (28–52 kg)
- ✿ Tree leaves
- ⚡ Near threatened

Saiga antelope
Saiga tatarica
- ⊕ Kalmykia (Russia), eastern Mongolia, Kazakhstan
- ⋀ Semidesert steppe
- ⬛ 3.6–4.7 ft (1.1–1.46 m)
- ⬛ 2.4–5.2 in (6–13 cm)
- ✖ 80–139 lb (36–63 kg)
- ✿ Grasses
- ⚡ Critically endangered

Subfamily Caprinae
Sheep & goats
33 species

Takin
Budorcas taxicolor
- ⊕ Eastern Himalaya, including China & Bhutan
- ⋀ High bamboo forests
- ⬛ ♂ 7.2 ft (2.2 m), ♀ 5.6 ft (1.7 m)
- ✖ Up to 770 lb (350 kg)
- ✿ Grasses, buds, leaves
- ⚡ Vulnerable

Markhor
Capra falconeri
- ⊕ Northern Pakistan, Turkmenistan, Afghanistan
- ⋀ Rugged, sparsely wooded hills & mountain slopes
- ⬛ 4.3–6 ft (1.3–1.8 m)
- ⬛ 4–8 in (10–20 cm)
- ✖ 90–240 lb (40–110 kg)
- ✿ Grasses, shrubs, trees
- ⚡ Endangered

Ibex, Alpine ibex
Capra ibex
- ⊕ Alps & other mountains in Europe
- ⋀ Protected mountainsides
- ⬛ Up to 5.6 ft (1.7 m)
- ⬛ Up to 12 in (30 cm)
- ✖ Up to 264 lb (120 kg)
- ✿ Grasses, leaves, twigs
- ⚡ Least concern

Walia ibex
Capra walie
- ⊕ Ethiopia
- ⋀ Steep rocky areas at altitudes of 8,200–14,800 ft (2,500–4,500 m)
- ⬛ Height: 27–43 in (68–109 cm)
- ✖ 180–280 lb (80–125 kg)
- ✿ Bushes, herbs, lichens, shrubs, grasses
- ⚡ Critically endangered

Himalayan tahr
Hemitragus jemlahicus
- ⊕ Northern Himalayan region, Tibet
- ⋀ Rugged wooded hills, mountain slopes
- ⬛ 3.9–5.6 ft (1.2–1.7 m)
- ✖ 286–397 lb (135–180 kg)
- ✿ Grasses, shrubs, trees
- ⚡ Vulnerable

Red goral
Naemorhedus baileyi
- ⊕ China, India, Myanmar
- ⋀ Tropical & subtropical dry forests & grasslands
- ⬛ 3 ft (1 m)
- ✖ 44–66 lb (20–30 kg)
- ✿ Lichens, grasses, weeds, tender stems, leaves, twigs
- ⚡ Vulnerable

Mountain goat
Oreamnos americanus
- ⊕ Western North America
- ⋀ Cliffs & alpine meadows in high mountains, at or above treeline
- ⬛ 4.3–6 ft (1.3–1.8 m)
- ⬛ 3.3–5.5 in (8–14 cm)
- ✖ ♂ 100–300 lb (46–136 kg), ♀ 100–185 lb (46–84 kg)
- ✿ Grasses, herbs, ferns, lichens, twigs
- ⚡ Least concern

Musk ox
Ovibos moschatus
- ⊕ Arctic Canada, Greenland, Svalbard
- ⋀ Arctic tundra
- ⬛ 7 ft (2 m)
- ⬛ 4 in (10 cm)
- ✖ 660 lb (300 kg)
- ✿ Grasses, sedges, willow
- ⚡ Least concern

Bighorn sheep
Ovis canadensis
- ⊕ Rocky Mountains, desert southwest; once more widespread
- ⋀ Open, treeless mountain habitats with cliffs or steep terrain
- ⬛ 5–6.2 ft (1.5–1.9 m)
- ⬛ 2.7–4.7 in (7–12 cm)
- ✖ ♂ 165–298 lb (75–135 kg), ♀ 106–187 lb (48–85 kg)
- ✿ Grasses, forbs
- ⚡ Least concern

Cyprus mouflon
Ovis orientalis ophion
- ⊕ Cyprus
- ⋀ Mountain
- ⬛ Up to 5 ft (1.5 m)
- ⬛ Up to 4 in (10 cm)
- ✖ Up to 120 lb (54.4 kg)
- ✿ Short grasses, shrubs
- ⚡ Vulnerable

Chamois
Rupicapra rupicapra
- ⊕ Europe, introduced to New Zealand
- ⋀ Mountains
- ⬛ Up to 4.3 ft (1.3 m)
- ⬛ Up to 6 in (15 cm)
- ✖ Up to 136 lb (62 kg)
- ✿ Grasses, leaves, fungi
- ⚡ Least concern

Subfamily Reduncinae
Reedbucks & lechwe
8 species

White-eared kob
Kobus kob
- ⊕ Sudan, Ethiopia
- ⋀ Grassland
- ⬛ 5.2–6 ft (1.6–1.8 m)
- ⬛ 4–6 in (10–15 cm)
- ✖ ♂ 187–267 lb (85–121 kg), ♀ 132–170 lb (60–77 kg)
- ✿ Grasses
- ⚡ Least concern

Red lechwe
Kobus leche
- ⊕ Southern Africa
- ⋀ Swampland
- ⬛ ♂ 5.2–6 ft (1.6–1.8 m), ♀ 4.3–5.6 ft (1.3–1.7 m)
- ⬛ 12–18 in (30–46 cm)
- ✖ ♂ 187–287 lb (85–130 kg), ♀ 132–209 lb (60–95 kg)
- ✿ Grasses
- ⚡ Least concern

Subfamily Aepycerotinae
Impala
1 species

Subfamily Peleinae
Rhebok
1 species

Subfamily Alcelaphinae
Wildebeest & topi
7 species

Wildebeest, Blue wildebeest
Connochaetes taurinus
- ⊕ Southern & east Africa
- ⋀ Grassland
- ⬛ 5.5–7.8 ft (1.7–2.4 m)
- ⬛ 24–39 in (60–100 cm)
- ✖ ♂ 364–639 lb (165–290 kg), ♀ 309–573 lb (140–260 kg)
- ✿ Grasses
- ⚡ Least concern

Subfamily Pantholopinae
Chiru
1 species

Chiru antelope
Pantholops hodgsonii
- ⊕ Tibetan plateau
- ⋀ Semiarid grassland, alpine steppe
- ⬛ 3.9–4.3 ft (1.2–1.3 m)
- ⬛ 7–12 in (18–30 cm)
- ✖ 57–88 lb (26–40 kg)
- ✿ Grasses, forbs
- ⚡ Endangered

Family Cervidae
Deer

44 species

Moose, Elk
Alces alces
- ⊕ Northern North America, Eurasia
- ⋀ Boreal & deciduous forest near lakes
- ⬛ 7.9–10.5 ft (2.4–3.2 m)
- ⬛ 3–5 in (8–13 cm)
- ✖ 595–1,320 lb (270–600 kg)
- ✿ Leaves, twigs, aquatic plants
- ⚡ Least concern

Visayan spotted deer
Cervus alfredi
- ⊕ Panay island in central Philippines
- ⋀ Forests
- ⬛ Up to 4.3 ft (1.3 m)
- ✖ 55–176 lb (25–80 kg)
- ✿ Grasses, leaves
- ⚡ Endangered

Red deer
Cervus elaphus
- ⊕ Europe, North America
- ⋀ Forest
- ⬛ Up to 8 ft (2.4 m)
- ⬛ Up to 8 in (20 cm)
- ✖ Up to 650 lb (295 kg)
- ✿ Grasses
- ⚡ Least concern

Sardinian red deer
Cervus elaphus corsicanus
- ⊕ Sardinia
- ⋀ Mountain, forest
- ⬛ Up to 8.7 ft (2.7 m)
- ⬛ Up to 11 in (27 cm)
- ✖ Up to 750 lb (340 kg)
- ✿ Short grasses, shrubs
- ⚡ Vulnerable

Eld's deer
Cervus eldii
- ⊕ India, Myanmar, Thailand, Cambodia, China, Vietnam, Laos
- ⋀ Open forest near rivers & marshland
- ⬛ 5–6 ft (1.5–1.8 m), ♂ antlers up to 6.6 ft (2 m)
- ⬛ 8–12 in (20–30 cm)
- ✖ Up to 330 lb (150 kg)
- ✿ Grasses, herbaceous plants, shoots
- ⚡ Vulnerable

Fallow deer
Dama dama
- ⊕ Mediterranean to southwest Asia
- ⋀ Deciduous woodland, meadow
- ⬛ Up to 5.3 ft (1.6 m)
- ⬛ Up to 9 in (23 cm)
- ✖ Up to 187 lb (85 kg)
- ✿ Grasses, herbs, leaves
- ⚡ Least concern

Taruca, North Andean deer
Hippocamelus antisensis
- ⊕ Northern Andes (South America)
- ⋀ Rugged hills, mountain slopes, alpine grassland
- ⬛ 5.6 ft (1.7 m)
- ⬛ 5 in (13 cm)
- ✖ 143 lb (65 kg)
- ✿ Lichens, mosses, herbs, grasses
- ⚡ Data deficient

Indian muntjac
Muntiacus muntjak
- ⊕ Indian subcontinent, Sri Lanka, Southeast Asia
- ⋀ Dry monsoon forest, tropical rain forest, montane forest, scrubland
- ⬛ 35–53 in (90–135 cm)
- ⬛ 5.2–9 in (13–23 cm)
- ✖ 33–44 lb (15–20 kg)
- ✿ Grasses, leaves, fruits, tender shoots, seeds
- ⚡ Least concern

Mule deer
Odocoileus hemionus
- ⊕ Western North America into north & central Mexico
- ⋀ Mountains, forest, desert, brushland
- ⬛ 4.1–5.5 ft (1.25–1.7 m)
- ⬛ 4.5–8.5 in (11–21 cm)
- ✖ ♂ 88–265 lb (40–120 kg), ♀ 66–176 lb (30–80 kg)
- ✿ Plants including grasses, forbs, new twigs of trees & shrubs, acorns
- ⚡ Least concern

White-tailed deer
Odocoileus virginianus
- ⊕ Southern Canada, USA, northern South America
- ▲ Diverse wooded habitats: northern temperate to semiarid to rain forest
- ▭ 2.8–7.8 ft (0.85–2.4 m)
- ▭ 7–12 in (17–30 cm)
- ✶ 48–300 lb (22–137 kg)
- ✿ Green leaves, twigs, shoots, acorns, berries, seeds, grasses
- ⚡ Least concern

Northern pudu
Pudu puda
- ⊕ Southern Chile to southwest Argentina
- ▲ Rain forest
- ▭ 23–33 in (58–84 cm)
- ▭ 3 in (8 cm)
- ✶ 22 lb (10 kg)
- ✿ Twigs, bark, fruits, leaves, seeds
- ⚡ Vulnerable

Caribou, Reindeer
Rangifer tarandus
- ⊕ Northern North America, northern Eurasia
- ▲ Boreal forest, Arctic tundra
- ▭ 4.6–6.9 ft (1.4–2.1 m)
- ▭ 4.3–7.9 in (11–20 cm)
- ✶ 179–337 lb (81–153 kg), ♀ 139–207 lb (63–94 kg)
- ✿ Leaves of shrubs & plants in summer, lichen in winter
- ⚡ Least concern

Family Tragulidae
Chevrotains
4 species

Family Moschidae
Musk deer
4 species

Family Antilocapridae
Pronghorn
1 species

Pronghorn
Antilocapra americana
- ⊕ Mostly in lower 48 US states
- ▲ Flat, rolling expanses from hot deserts to alpine plateaus without deep snow cover in winter
- ▭ 4.3–4.9 ft (1.3–1.5 m)
- ▭ 4–5.7 in (10–14.5 cm)
- ✶ ♂ 93–130 lb (42–59 kg), ♀ 90–110 lb (41–50 kg)
- ✿ Variety of plants, especially forbs & shrubs
- ⚡ Least concern

Family Giraffidae
Giraffe & okapi
2 species

Giraffe
Giraffa camelopardalis
- ⊕ East & southern Africa; formerly throughout the northern, eastern & southern savannas
- ▲ Acacia woodland, savanna
- ▭ 11.5–15.7 ft (3.5–4.8 m)
- ▭ 30–43 in (76–110 cm)
- ✶ ♂ 2–2.1 tons (1.8–1.9 t), ♀ 0.5–1.3 tons (0.45–1.2 t)
- ✿ Tree leaves, shrubs
- ⚡ Least concern

Okapi
Okapia johnstoni
- ⊕ Democratic Republic of Congo
- ▲ Rain forest
- ▭ 6.2–6.9 ft (1.9–2.1 m)
- ▭ 12–16.5 in (30–42 cm)
- ✶ 460–550 lb (210–250 kg)
- ✿ Leaves, fruits, ferns, fungus
- ⚡ Near threatened

Family Camelidae
Camels & llamas
6 species

Bactrian camel
Camelus bactrianus
- ⊕ Northwest China, Mongolia
- ▲ Rocky desert, steppe grassland
- ▭ 10 ft (3 m)
- ✶ 1,800 lb (815 kg)
- ✿ Grasses, leaves of shrubs
- ⚡ Critically endangered

Llama
Lama glama
- ⊕ From southern Peru to northwest Argentina
- ▲ Puna, high Andes, paramo
- ▭ 6.5 ft (2 m)
- ▭ 9 in (23 cm)
- ✶ 265 lb (120 kg)
- ✿ Grasses, halophytes
- ⚡ Domesticated

Guanaco
Lama guanicoe
- ⊕ Southern Peru to eastern Argentina & Tierra del Fuego
- ▲ Puna, high Andes, paramo, Patagonian grassland
- ▭ 6.5 ft (2 cm)
- ▭ 9 in (23 cm)
- ✶ 330 lb (150 kg)
- ✿ Shrubs, lichens, fungi
- ⚡ Least concern

Alpaca
Vicugna pacos
- ⊕ Andes of Ecuador, southern Peru, northern Bolivia & northern Chile
- ▲ Puna, high Andes, paramo
- ▭ 7.2 ft (2.2 m)
- ▭ 8 in (20 cm)
- ✶ 99–174 lb (45–79 kg)
- ✿ Grasses, halophytes
- ⚡ Domesticated

Vicuña
Vicugna vicugna
- ⊕ Andes of southern Peru, western Bolivia, northwestern Argentina & northern Chile
- ▲ Windswept, cold, semiarid plains or puna, high Andes
- ▭ 4.9 ft (1.5 m)
- ▭ 9 in (23 cm)
- ✶ 110 lb (50 kg)
- ✿ Grasses, small forbs, lichens, water daily
- ⚡ Least concern

Vicuña
Vicugna vicugna

Family Suidae
Pigs
14 species

Red river hog
Potamochoerus porcus
- ⊕ West & central Africa
- ▲ Rain forest, swamp forest
- ▭ 3.3–5 ft (1–1.5 m)
- ▭ 12–18 in (30–45 cm)
- ✶ 99–254 lb (45–115 kg)
- ✿ Roots, tubers, fruits
- ⚡ Least concern

Wild boar
Sus scrofa
- ⊕ Eurasia & northern Africa
- ▲ River valley, forest
- ▭ Up to 6 ft (1.8 m)
- ▭ Up to 12 in (30 cm)
- ✶ Up to 440 lb (200 kg)
- ✿ Grasses, nuts, berries, carrion, roots, tubers, insects, small reptiles
- ⚡ Least concern

Family Tayassuidae
Peccaries
3 species

Chacoan peccary
Catagonus wagneri
- ⊕ Paraguay, Bolivia, Brazil, Argentina
- ▲ Dry briars or thorny bushes
- ▭ 38–46 in (96–117 cm)
- ▭ 1.2–4 in (3–10 cm)
- ✶ 66–95 lb (30–43 kg)
- ✿ Cacti, roots, seedpods
- ⚡ Endangered

Family Hippopotamidae
Hippopotamuses
4 species

Pygmy hippopotamus
Hexaprotodon liberiensis
- ⊕ Guinean forests of West Africa, Liberia
- ▲ Rivers
- ▭ 6.5 ft (2 m)
- ✶ Up to 605 lb (275 kg)
- ✿ Riparian forest plants
- ⚡ Endangered

Hippopotamus
Hippopotamus amphibius
- ⊕ Sub-Saharan Africa
- ▲ Grassland with permanent water
- ▭ 9–11.5 ft (2.8–3.5 m)
- ▭ 14–20 in (35–50 cm)
- ✶ ♂ 0.7–3.5 tons (0.65–3.2 t), ♀ 0.6–2.8 tons (0.5–2.5 t)
- ✿ Grasses
- ⚡ Vulnerable

Hippopotamus
Hippopotamus amphibius

ORDER CETACEA
CETACEANS
81 species

Suborder Odontoceti
Toothed whales
68 species

Beluga
Delphinapterus leucas
- ⊕ Arctic & subarctic waters
- ▲ Inlets, fjords, channels, bays, shallows, river mouths
- ▭ Up to 16.5 ft (5 m)
- ✶ Up to 1.7 tons (1.5 t)
- ✿ Octopuses, squid, fish, crabs, snails
- ⚡ Vulnerable

Common dolphin
Delphinus delphis
- ⊕ Temperate to tropical oceans
- ▲ Coastal waters
- ▭ Up to 6.5 ft (2 m)
- ✶ Up to 440 lb (200 kg)
- ✿ Sardines, anchovies, squid
- ⚡ Least concern

Pink river dolphin, Amazon dolphin
Inia geoffrensis
- ⊕ Amazon River, Orinoco River
- ▲ Main rivers, small channels, lakes
- ▭ 9.8 ft (3 m)
- ▭ 20 in (50 cm)
- ✶ 198 lb (90 kg)
- ✿ Crustaceans, catfish, small freshwater fish
- ⚡ Vulnerable

Baiji, Yangtze river dolphin
Lipotes vexillifer
- ⊕ Yangtze valley (China)
- ▲ Rivers, lakes
- ▭ Up to 8 ft (2.5 m)
- ✶ 300–510 lb (135–230 kg)
- ✿ Fish
- ⚡ Critically endangered

Narwhal
Monodon monocerus
- ⊕ Arctic seas
- ▲ Deep water near loose pack ice
- ▭ Up to 20 ft (6 m) without tusk
- ✶ Up to 1.8 tons (1.6 t)
- ✿ Cod, squid, shrimps, some fish
- ⚡ Data deficient

Orca
Orcinus orca
- ⊕ Worldwide, especially polar seas
- ▲ Coastal waters
- ▭ Up to 32 ft (9.8 m)
- ✶ Up to 11 tons (10 t)
- ✿ Fish, squid, sea lions, seals, penguins
- ⚡ Data deficient

Sperm whale
Physeter catodon
- ⊕ Circumglobal, tropics to pack ice
- ▲ Deep to surface waters
- ▭ Up to 61 ft (18.5 m)
- ✶ Up to 77 tons (70 t)
- ✿ Giant squid, octopus, deepwater fish, sharks, skates
- ⚡ Vulnerable

Atlantic spotted dolphin
Stenella frontalis
- ⊕ Warm temperate to tropical Atlantic
- ▲ Continental shelf, shallows
- ▭ 7.5 ft (2.3 m)
- ✶ ♂ 310 lb (140 kg), ♀ 285 lb (130 kg)
- ✿ Fish, squid
- ⚡ Data deficient

Beluga
Delphinapterus leucas

Suborder Mysticeti
Baleen whales
13 species

Bowhead
Balaena mysticetus
- ⊕ Arctic & subarctic waters
- ▲ Follow receding ice drifts; bays & estuaries in summer
- ▭ 49–59 ft (15–18 m)
- ✶ Up to 110 tons (100 t)
- ✿ Plankton, krill, small fish
- ⚡ Least concern

Minke whale
Balaenoptera acutorostrata
- ⊕ Northern hemisphere oceans from Arctic to tropics
- ▲ Usually coastal waters
- ▭ Up to 36 ft (11 m)
- ✶ Up to 11 tons (10 t)
- ✿ Plankton, krill, small fish
- ⚡ Near threatened

Blue whale
Balaenoptera musculus
- ⊕ All oceans except high Arctic
- ▲ Open ocean
- ▭ Up to 110 ft (33.5 m)
- ✶ Up to 209 tons (190 t)
- ✿ Plankton, krill, small fish
- ⚡ Endangered

Fin whale
Balaenoptera physalus
- ⊕ Circumglobal oceans, pack ice to subtropics
- ▲ Open ocean, coastal waters
- ▭ Up to 82 ft (25 m)
- ✶ Up to 88 tons (80 t)
- ✿ Plankton, krill, small fish
- ⚡ Endangered

Southern right whale
Eubalaena australis
- ⊕ Southern Ocean (summer), New Zealand, Australia, Argentina, Brazil, Chile, Mozambique, South Africa
- ▲ Polar waters to feed; shallow continental shelves to bear young
- ▭ 50 ft (15 m)
- ✶ 60 tons (65 t)
- ✿ Plankton, krill, small fish
- ⚡ Least concern

North Atlantic right whale
Eubalaena glacialis
- ⊕ Subarctic to cold-temperate North Atlantic Ocean
- ▲ Shallow coastal waters, deep basins
- ▭ Up to 59 ft (18 m)
- ✶ Up to 99 tons (90 t)
- ✿ Plankton, krill, small fish
- ⚡ Endangered

Humpback whale
Megaptera novaeangliae
- ⊕ Circumglobal oceans, ice edge to tropics
- ▲ Open ocean, coastal waters
- ▭ Up to 49 ft (15 m)
- ✶ Up to 71.5 tons (65 t)
- ✿ Plankton, krill, small fish
- ⚡ Vulnerable

ORDER RODENTIA
RODENTS
2,015 species

Suborder Sciurognathi
Squirrel-like rodents, mouselike rodents & gundis
1,797 species

SQUIRREL-LIKE RODENTS
383 SPECIES IN 8 FAMILIES

American beaver
Castor canadensis
- ⊕ North America except desert & tundra regions
- ⋀ Lakes, ponds, streams
- 🐾 39–47 in (100–120 cm)
- 🐾 9–13 in (23–33 cm)
- ✗ 35–66 lb (16–30 kg)
- ✿ Land & aquatic plants, tree leaves, inner bark, wood
- ⚡ Least concern

European beaver
Castor fiber
- ⊕ Western Europe to eastern Siberia
- ⋀ Rivers, marshes
- 🐾 Up to 4.3 ft (1.3 m)
- 🐾 Up to 12 in (30 cm)
- ✗ Up to 75 lb (34 kg)
- ✿ Plants, bark, leaves
- ⚡ Near threatened

Black-tailed prairie dog
Cynomys ludovicianus
- ⊕ Great Plains of North America
- ⋀ Shortgrass & midgrass prairie
- 🐾 13–17 in (34–42 cm)
- 🐾 2.4–3.7 in (6–9.5 cm)
- ✗ ♂ 20–53 oz (575–1,490 g), ♀ 27–36 oz (765–1,030 g)
- ✿ Grasses, herbs, seeds
- ⚡ Near threatened

Merriam's kangaroo rat
Dipodomys merriami
- ⊕ Southwest USA, northern Mexico, Baja Peninsula
- ⋀ Various dry habitats
- 🐾 7.6–11 in (20–28 cm)
- 🐾 4.7–7 in (12–18 cm)
- ✗ 1.8–1.8 oz (33–53 g)
- ✿ Seeds, green vegetation, insects
- ⚡ Least concern

Northern flying squirrel
Glaucomys sabrinus
- ⊕ Northern North America, southern Appalachians
- ⋀ Conifer, mixed & deciduous forests
- 🐾 11–13 in (28–34 cm)
- 🐾 5–6 in (13–15 cm)
- ✗ 2.6–5 oz (75–140 g)
- ✿ Mushrooms, other fungi, fruits, nuts, seeds, insects, bird eggs, flesh of small mammals & birds
- ⚡ Least concern (but Appalachian subspecies endangered)

Northern flying squirrel
Glaucomys sabrinus

Marmot
Marmota marmota

Gray squirrel
Sciurus carolinensis

Marmot
Marmota marmota
- ⊕ Mountainous areas in Europe, northern Canada, USA
- ⋀ Mountain
- 🐾 Up to 21 in (54 cm)
- 🐾 Up to 6 in (16 cm)
- ✗ Up to 17.5 lb (8 kg)
- ✿ Grasses, herbs, insects
- ⚡ Least concern

Gray squirrel
Sciurus carolinensis
- ⊕ Eastern & central North America, introduced to Europe
- ⋀ Forest, now urban parks
- 🐾 9–10 in (23–25 cm)
- 🐾 6–10 in (15–25 cm)
- ✗ 19 oz (540 g)
- ✿ Seeds, nuts, bark
- ⚡ Least concern

Red squirrel
Sciurus vulgaris
- ⊕ Western Europe to eastern Russia, Korea, northern Japan
- ⋀ Deciduous woodland, mixed forest
- 🐾 Up to 9.5 in (24 cm)
- 🐾 Up to 8 in (20 cm)
- ✗ Up to 12 oz (350 g)
- ✿ Seeds, nuts, flowers
- ⚡ Near threatened

Arctic ground squirrel
Spermophilus parryii
- ⊕ Siberia, Alaska, Canada
- ⋀ Arctic tundra, open meadows
- 🐾 14 in (35 cm)
- 🐾 6 in (15 cm)
- ✗ 32 oz (900 g)
- ✿ Grasses, herbs, berries, seeds, horsetails
- ⚡ Least concern

Eastern chipmunk
Tamias striatus
- ⊕ Eastern USA except southeast coast, southeastern Canada
- ⋀ Deciduous & boreal forest, suburban areas, cities
- 🐾 8.5–11.5 in (22–29 cm)
- 🐾 3–4.5 in (8–12 cm)
- ✗ 2.8–5.2 oz (80–150 g)
- ✿ Nuts, small seeds, some vegetation, fungi, animal matter
- ⚡ Least concern

Red squirrel
Sciurus vulgaris

MOUSE-LIKE RODENTS
1,409 SPECIES IN 3 FAMILIES

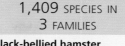

Black-bellied hamster
Cricetus cricetus
- ⊕ Europe
- ⋀ Low-lying farmland
- 🐾 ♂ 10.5–12.5 in (27–32 cm), ♀ 8.7–9.8 in (22–25 cm)
- ✗ ♂ 16 oz (450 g), ♀ 12.5 oz (350 g)
- ✿ Grains, fruits, roots, plants
- ⚡ Least concern

Long-eared jerboa
Euchoreutes naso
- ⊕ China, Mongolia (Gobi desert)
- ⋀ Desert, semidesert
- 🐾 Up to 3.5 in (9 cm)
- 🐾 Up to 6.4 in (16 cm)
- ✗ 0.8–1.3 oz (23–38 g)
- ✿ Insects
- ⚡ Endangered

Desert jerboa
Jaculus jaculus
- ⊕ North Africa
- ⋀ Desert
- 🐾 7–13 in (17–32 cm)
- 🐾 6–9 in (14–22 cm)
- ✗ 1.8–2.5 oz (50–70 g)
- ✿ Seeds, stems, roots
- ⚡ Least concern

Steppe lemming
Lagurus lagurus
- ⊕ Russia, Ukraine
- ⋀ Steppe
- 🐾 3–5.5 in (8–14 cm)
- 🐾 0.3–0.8 in (0.7–2 cm)
- ✗ 0.9–1.2 oz (25–35 g)
- ✿ Shoots, leaves, seeds
- ⚡ Least concern

Snow vole
Microtus nivalis
- ⊕ Europe
- ⋀ Mountain
- 🐾 Up to 7 in (18 cm)
- 🐾 Up to 4 in (10 cm)
- ✗ Up to 1.5 oz (43 g)
- ✿ Grasses, plants
- ⚡ Least concern

Dormouse
Muscardinus avellanarius
- ⊕ Europe
- ⋀ Rocky areas, forest
- 🐾 Up to 7.5 in (19 cm)
- 🐾 Up to 6.5 in (16.5 cm)
- ✗ Up to 7 oz (200 g)
- ✿ Plants, seeds, insects
- ⚡ Near threatened

Desert woodrat
Neotoma lepida
- ⊕ Southwest USA, Baja Peninsula
- ⋀ Desert scrubland, coastal sage scrub
- 🐾 9–15 in (23–38 cm)
- 🐾 3.7–7.5 in (9.5–19 cm)
- ✗ 4.5–5.7 oz (128–162 g)
- ✿ Leafy vegetation, especially succulents
- ⚡ Least concern

Muskrat
Odontra zibethicus
- ⊕ North America from Alaska to southern USA
- ⋀ Brackish & freshwater lakes, ponds, streams, rivers, marshes
- 🐾 16–24 in (41–62 cm)
- 🐾 7–12 in (18–30 cm)
- ✗ 1.5–4 lb (0.7–1.8 kg)
- ✿ Aquatic plants such as cattails, fish, crustaceans, snails
- ⚡ Least concern

Patagonian mara
Dolichotis patagonum

Southern grasshopper mouse
Onychomys torridus
- ⊕ Mexico, southwest USA
- ⋀ Desert scrub
- 🐾 Up to 5 in (13 cm)
- 🐾 2.4 in (6 cm)
- ✗ 0.8 oz (22 g)
- ✿ Mice, scorpions, beetles
- ⚡ Least concern

Cloud rat
Phloeomys pallidus
- ⊕ Philippines
- ⋀ Tropical forest, nests in hollow trees
- 🐾 12–20 in (30–50 cm)
- ✗ Up to 5.5 lb (2.5 kg)
- ✿ Young leaves
- ⚡ Near threatened

Family Ctenodactylidae
Gundis
5 species

Suborder Hystricognathi
Cavy-like rodents
218 species

Patagonian mara
Dolichotis patagonum
- ⊕ Central & southern Argentina
- ⋀ Brushy areas with sandy soil, foothills, open grassland
- 🐾 29 in (73.5 cm)
- 🐾 2 in (5 cm)
- ✗ 36 lb (16.3 kg)
- ✿ Leaves, grasses, herbs, fruits, cacti, seeds
- ⚡ Near threatened

North American porcupine
Erethizon dorsatum
- ⊕ Southern Canada, Alaska, western USA
- ⋀ Boreal forest, tundra, desert, chaparral, rangelands
- 🐾 24–51 in (60–130 cm)
- 🐾 7–10 in (18–25 cm)
- ✗ 11–40 lb (5–18 kg)
- ✿ Bark, cambium, phloem tissue of coniferous trees
- ⚡ Least concern

Capybara
Hydrochaeris hydrochaeris
- ⊕ Panama to northeast Argentina
- ⋀ Ponds, rivers & lakes in habitats from savanna to rain forest
- 🐾 24 in (61 cm)
- 🐾 2 in (5 cm)
- ✗ Up to 100 lb (45 kg)
- ✿ Grasses, aquatic vegetation
- ⚡ Least concern

Southern viscacha
Lagidium viscacia
- ⊕ Argentina, Bolivia, Chile, Peru
- ⋀ Rocky mountainous country
- 🐾 Up to 16 in (40 cm)
- 🐾 5 in (13 cm)
- ✗ Up to 6.6 lb (3 kg)
- ✿ Grasses, mosses, lichens
- ⚡ Data deficient

Giant mole rat
Tachorcytes macrocephalus
- ⊕ Ethiopia
- ⋀ Shrubland, grassland
- 🐾 6–11 in (15–28 cm)
- 🐾 0.4–3 in (1–8 cm)
- ✗ 5.6–21 oz (160–600 g)
- ✿ Grasses, herbs
- ⚡ Vulnerable

ORDER LAGOMORPHA
HARES, RABBITS & PIKAS
82 species

Snowshoe hare
Lepus americanus
- ⊕ Canada, Alaska, western & northeast USA
- ⋀ Boreal forest
- 🐾 14–20 in (36–51 cm)
- 🐾 1–2.3 in (2.5–6 cm)
- ✗ ♂ 2–3.7 lb (0.9–1.7 kg), ♀ 2–5 lb (0.9–2.3 kg)
- ✿ Green vegetation, twigs, shoots, bark, buds, leaves
- ⚡ Least concern

Black-tailed jackrabbit
Lepus californicus
- ⊕ Western USA, northern Mexico
- ⋀ Desert, prairie, chaparral, farmland
- 🐾 18–25 in (46–64 cm)
- 🐾 2–4 in (5–11 cm)
- ✗ 2.8–7.3 lb (1.3–3.3 kg)
- ✿ Forbs, grasses, shrubs
- ⚡ Least concern

Alpine hare
Lepus timidus
- ⊕ Eurasia
- ⋀ Mountains
- 🐾 Up to 24 in (60 cm)
- 🐾 Up to 8 in (20 cm)
- ✗ Up to 10.4 lb (4.7 kg)
- ✿ Leaves, twigs
- ⚡ Least concern

European rabbit
Oryctolagus cuniculus
- ⊕ Europe, introduced worldwide
- ⋀ Forest edges, fields
- 🐾 Up to 18 in (46 cm)
- ✗ Up to 5 lb (2.2 kg)
- ✿ Grasses, other plants
- ⚡ Least concern

Amami rabbit
Pentalagus furnessi
- ⊕ Ryukyu Islands (Japan)
- ⋀ Dense old-growth forests, Japanese pampas grassland at forest edge
- 🐾 17–20 in (43–51 cm)
- ✗ 4.4–6.6 lb (2–3 kg)
- ✿ Bamboo shoots, berries, leaves & stems of sweet potato
- ⚡ Endangered

ORDER MACROSCELIDEA
ELEPHANT SHREWS
15 species

Snowshoe hare
Lepus americanus

Birds

Birds may be the most mobile of all the animals. They descended from reptiles that developed the ability to fly, and although some bird species have lost their flying ability, they all retain feathers. The American ornithologist Alexander Wetmore devised a classification of the orders and families of birds in the 1930s, basing it on structural similarities in limbs, skeletons, and feathers. Since then, DNA and other molecular studies have shown that many structural traits traditionally used for classifying birds are unreliable because of convergent evolution. The bird classification used here takes account of many of these changes.

Icon key

⊕	Distribution	✈	Tail length	★	Diet
⋀	Habitat	✈	Wingspan	⚡	Status
⇲	Length	✖	Weight	♀♂	Female/male

PHYLUM CHORDATA
CHORDATES
53,000+ species

CLASS AVES
BIRDS
9,743 species

ORDER TINAMIFORMES
TINAMOUS

74 species

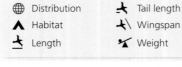

ORDER STRUTHIONIFORMES
OSTRICH

1 species

Ostrich
Struthio camelus
- ⊕ East & southern Africa
- ⋀ Savanna, desert
- ⇲ Height: 8.2 ft (2.5 m)
- ✈ 79 in (2 m)
- ✖ ♂ 220–286 lb (100–130 kg), ♀ 198–242 lb (90–110 kg)
- ★ Grasses, seeds, leaves
- ⚡ Least concern

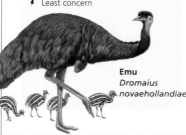

Emu
Dromaius novaehollandiae

ORDER RHEIFORMES
RHEAS

2 species

Rhea, Ñandú
Rhea americana
- ⊕ East, southeast & central-west South America
- ⋀ Tall grassland, savanna, scrub forest, chaparral, desert
- ⇲ 5 ft (1.5 m)
- ✈ 22 in (56 cm)
- ✖ 55 lb (25 kg)
- ★ Leaves, seeds, fruits, flowers, invertebrates, small vertebrates
- ⚡ Near threatened

ORDER CASUARIIFORMES
CASSOWARIES & EMUS

4 species

Southern cassowary
Casuarius casuarius
- ⊕ Seram (Indonesian island), southern New Guinea, northeast Australia
- ⋀ Rain forest
- ⇲ Up to 6 ft (1.8 m)
- ✖ Up to 140 lb (63 kg)
- ★ Fruits
- ⚡ Vulnerable

Emu
Dromaius novaehollandiae
- ⊕ Australia
- ⋀ Open habitats including farmland
- ⇲ Up to 6.5 ft (2 m)
- ✖ 65–100 lb (30–45 kg)
- ★ Green leafy shoots, insects, fruits
- ⚡ Least concern

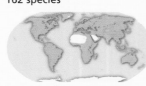

Indian peafowl
Pavo cristatus

ORDER APTERYGIFORMES
KIWIS

3 species

Great spotted kiwi
Apteryx haastii
- ⊕ South Island of New Zealand
- ⋀ Forest, wetlands, tussock grassland
- ⇲ Up to 18 in (46 cm)
- ✖ Up to 7 lb (3 kg)
- ★ Invertebrates, fallen fruits
- ⚡ Vulnerable

ORDER GALLIFORMES
GAMEBIRDS

290 species

Hazel grouse
Bonasa bonasia
- ⊕ Northern Eurasia, central & eastern Europe
- ⋀ Dense mixed coniferous woodland
- ⇲ 14–15 in (35–38 cm)
- ✈ 18–19 in (45–48 cm)
- ★ Plant matter, insects
- ⚡ Least concern

Greater sage grouse
Centrocercus urophasianus
- ⊕ Temperate North America
- ⋀ Foothills, plains, mountain slopes with sagebrush
- ⇲ 28–38 in (71–97 cm)
- ✈ 6–8 in (15–20 cm)
- ✖ 3–6.5 lb (1.4–3 kg)
- ★ Leaves, stems, flowers, fruits, insects
- ⚡ Near threatened

Willow ptarmigan, Willow grouse
Lagopus lagopus
- ⊕ Circumarctic Alaska, Canada, Eurasia, Greenland
- ⋀ Tundra, boreal (birch) forest
- ⇲ 15 in (38 cm)
- ✈ 24 in (61 cm)
- ★ Vegetation, insects
- ⚡ Least concern

Monal pheasant
Lophophorus impejanus
- ⊕ Himalaya, from eastern Afghanistan to western China
- ⋀ Mountainous regions at 7,900–14,800 ft (2,400–4,500 m)
- ⇲ 24 in (60 cm)
- ✖ 4–5.3 lb (1.8–2.4 kg)
- ★ Seeds, tubers, shoots, invertebrates
- ⚡ Least concern

Wild turkey
Meleagris gallopavo
- ⊕ Southern Canada to Mexico, Florida
- ⋀ Hardwood forest, swamps, grassland, ponderosa pine, chaparral
- ⇲ 3.5 ft (1.1 m)
- ✈ 3.9–5 ft (1.2–1.5 m)
- ✖ 5.5–24 lb (2.5–10.8 kg)
- ★ Nuts, seeds, fruits, insects, buds, salamanders
- ⚡ Least concern

Indian peafowl
Pavo cristatus
- ⊕ Indian subcontinent, Sri Lanka
- ⋀ Monsoon forest, scrubland, deciduous forest
- ⇲ ♂ 7.3 ft (2.2 m) in full breeding plumage, ♀ 34 in (86 cm)
- ✖ ♂ 11 lb (5 kg), ♀ 7.5 lb (3.4 kg)
- ★ Seeds, fruits, insects, reptiles, small mammals
- ⚡ Least concern

Black grouse
Tetrao tetrix
- ⊕ Northern Eurasia
- ⋀ Forest, forest edge
- ⇲ Up to 19 in (48 cm)
- ✈ Up to 28 in (72 cm)
- ✖ Up to 2.6 lb (1.2 kg)
- ★ Buds, shoots, berries
- ⚡ Least concern

Western tragopan
Tragopan melanocephalus
- ⊕ Himalaya, from Pakistan to India
- ⋀ Temperate forest, coniferous forest
- ⇲ 19–24 in (48–60 cm)
- ✖ ♂ up to 4.9 lb (2.2 kg), ♀ up to 3 lb (1.4 kg)
- ★ Leaves, shoots, seeds, invertebrates
- ⚡ Vulnerable

ORDER ANSERIFORMES
WATERFOWL

162 species

Mandarin duck
Aix galericulata
- ⊕ Eastern Russia, China, Japan
- ⋀ Shallow lakes, marshes, ponds
- ⇲ 16–19 in (41–49 cm)
- ✈ 26–30 in (65–75 cm)
- ✖ 15–24 oz (430–690 g)
- ★ Plants, seeds
- ⚡ Least concern

Wigeon, Eurasian wigeon
Anas penelope
- ⊕ Northern Eurasia
- ⋀ Marshes, lakes
- ⇲ Up to 19 in (48 cm)
- ✈ Up to 31.5 in (80 cm)
- ✖ Up to 28 oz (800 g)
- ★ Leaves, shoots
- ⚡ Least concern

Barnacle goose
Branta leucopsis
- ⊕ Eastern Greenland & North Atlantic islands (summer); Scotland & Netherlands (winter)
- ⋀ Tundra, cliffs, pasture
- ⇲ 24 in (60 cm)
- ✈ 4.5 ft (1.4 m)
- ✖ 4 lb (1.8 kg)
- ★ Grasses, low herbs
- ⚡ Least concern

Abyssinian blue-winged goose
Cyanochen cyanoptera
- ⊕ Ethiopia
- ⋀ Rivers, freshwater lakes, swamps
- ⇲ 24–30 in (60–76 cm)
- ✈ 4.3–5.6 ft (1.3–1.7 m)
- ✖ 3.3 lb (1.5 kg)
- ★ Grasses, herbs
- ⚡ Near threatened

Whooper swan
Cygnus cygnus
- ⊕ Northern Eurasia
- ⋀ Wetlands, forest
- ⇲ Up to 5.3 ft (1.6 m)
- ✈ Up to 7.8 ft (2.4 m)
- ✖ Up to 33 lb (15 kg)
- ★ Aquatic plants, grasses
- ⚡ Least concern

Pink-eared duck
Malacorhynchus membranaceus
- ⊕ Australia
- ⋀ All wetland types; highly nomadic
- ⇲ Up to 18 in (45 cm)
- ✈ 29 in (73 cm)
- ✖ 13 oz (370 g)
- ★ Aquatic invertebrates
- ⚡ Least concern

ORDER SPHENISCIFORMES
PENGUINS

17 species

Emperor penguin
Aptenodytes forsteri
- ⊕ Antarctica
- ⋀ Ocean, ice sheet
- ⇲ Up to 5 ft (1.5 m)
- ✖ 48–82 lb (22–37 kg)
- ★ Fish, crustaceans
- ⚡ Least concern

King penguin
Aptenodytes patagonicus
- ⊕ Antarctica
- ⋀ Islands, ocean
- ⇲ 35–40 in (90–100 cm)
- ✖ 20–38 lb (9–17 kg)
- ★ Fish, cephalopods
- ⚡ Least concern

Adélie penguin
Pygoscelis adeliae
- ⊕ Antarctica
- ⋀ Ocean, islands, ice
- ⇲ 28 in (70 cm)
- ✖ 8–17.5 lb (3.8–8 kg)
- ★ Crustaceans, fish, squid
- ⚡ Least concern

Chinstrap penguin
Pygoscelis antarcticus
- ⊕ Antarctica
- ⋀ Ocean, islands, ice
- ⇲ 28–30 in (70–76 cm)
- ✖ 7.5–12 lb (3.5–5.5 kg)
- ★ Crustaceans, fish, squid
- ⚡ Least concern

Magellanic penguin
Spheniscus magellanicus
- ⊕ Antarctica
- ⋀ Coastal areas, islands, remote continental regions
- ⇲ 28 in (70 cm)
- ✖ 11 lb (5 kg)
- ★ Cuttlefish, sardines, squid, krill, other crustaceans
- ⚡ Near threatened

ORDER GAVIIFORMES
DIVERS

5 species

Abyssinian blue-winged goose
Cyanochen cyanoptera

ORDER PODICIPEDIFORMES
GREBES
19 species

Eared grebe
Podiceps nigricollis
- 🌐 Western USA & Canada, southern Mexico, Europe, Asia, Africa
- ⋏ Freshwater lakes & ponds (breeding), salt water (winter)
- ⥮ 12–14 in (30–35 cm)
- ⥯ 20–22 in (51–55 cm)
- ⚖ 7–26 oz (200–735 g)
- ✪ Aquatic insects, spiders, brine shrimp
- ⚡ Least concern

ORDER PROCELLARIIFORMES
ALBATROSSES & PETRELS
112 species

Wandering albatross
Diomedea exulans
- 🌐 Southern Ocean, Australia
- ⋏ Ocean, islands
- ⥮ 3–4.5 ft (1–1.4 m)
- ⥯ 8–11.5 ft (2.5–3.5 m)
- ⚖ 15–25 lb (6.5–11.5 kg)
- ✪ Cephalopods, fish
- ⚡ Vulnerable

Snow petrel
Pagodroma nivea
- 🌐 Antarctic continent & peninsula, South Georgia
- ⋏ Islands, ice, ocean
- ⥮ 12–16 in (30–40 cm)
- ⥯ 30–38 in (75–96 cm)
- ⚖ 7–14 oz (200–400 g)
- ✪ Crustaceans, fish, cephalopods
- ⚡ Least concern

Providence petrel
Pterodroma solandri
- 🌐 Pacific Ocean, oceanic islands
- ⋏ Salt water, nests on islands
- ⥮ Up to 16 in (40 cm)
- ⥯ 40 in (100 cm)
- ⚖ 17.5 oz (500 g)
- ✪ Fish, cephalopods, crustaceans
- ⚡ Vulnerable

Short-tailed shearwater
Puffinus tenuirostris
- 🌐 South & southeast coasts of Australia, North Pacific
- ⋏ Islands around southeast Australia, New Zealand to breed
- ⥮ 16–17 in (41–43 cm)
- ⥯ 39 in (99 cm)
- ⚖ 7 oz (200 g)
- ✪ Fish, small krill
- ⚡ Least concern

Wandering albatross
Diomedea exulans

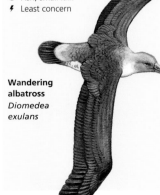

ORDER PHOENICOPTERIFORMES
FLAMINGOS
5 species

Lesser flamingo
Phoenicopterus minor
- 🌐 Eastern & southern Africa
- ⋏ Saline lakes
- ⥮ 31–36 in (78–91 cm)
- ⥯ 38 in (96 cm)
- ⚖ 24–32 oz (680–905 g)
- ✪ Algae, crustaceans
- ⚡ Near threatened

Greater flamingo
Phoenicopterus ruber roseus
- 🌐 South America, southern Europe to Indian subcontinent
- ⋏ Deltas, coastal lagoons
- ⥮ Up to 4.3 ft (1.3 m)
- ⥯ Up to 5.6 ft (1.7 m)
- ⚖ Up to 8 lb (3.6 kg)
- ✪ Crustaceans, algae
- ⚡ Least concern

ORDER CICONIIFORMES
HERONS & ALLIES
118 species

Roseate spoonbill
Ajaia ajaja
- 🌐 Southern USA to southern South America
- ⋏ Coastal mangroves, swamps
- ⥮ 32 in (80 cm)
- ⥯ 48 in (122 cm)
- ⚖ 2.6–4 lb (1.2–1.8 kg)
- ✪ Fish, frogs, crustaceans
- ⚡ Least concern

Great blue heron
Ardea herodias
- 🌐 Alaska & Canada south to northern South America
- ⋏ Calm seacoasts, freshwater lakes & rivers
- ⥮ 3.3– 4.6 ft (1–1.4 m)
- ⥯ 5.6–6.6 ft (1.7–2 m)
- ⚖ 4.6–5.5 lb (2.1–2.5 kg)
- ✪ Mostly fish but also invertebrates & small vertebrates
- ⚡ Least concern

Black stork
Ciconia nigra
- 🌐 Europe (summer); tropical Africa, China (winter)
- ⋏ Forest, wetlands
- ⥮ Up to 3.3 ft (1 m)
- ⥯ Up to 5 ft (1.5 m)
- ⚖ Up to 6.5 lb (3 kg)
- ✪ Fish, invertebrates
- ⚡ Least concern

Least bittern
Ixobrychus exilis
- 🌐 Southern Canada to northern Argentina
- ⋏ Freshwater or brackish marshes with tall emergent vegetation
- ⥮ 11–14 in (28–36 cm)
- ⥯ 16–18 in (41–46 cm)
- ⚖ 1.8–3.6 oz (50–100 g)
- ✪ Small fish, insects
- ⚡ Least concern

Yellow-crowned night heron
Nyctanassa violacea
- 🌐 USA to northeast South America
- ⋏ Swamps, marshes
- ⥮ 24 in (60 cm)
- ⥯ Up to 44 in (112 cm)
- ⚖ 22 oz (625 g)
- ✪ Crustaceans, mollusks, frogs, fish
- ⚡ Least concern

Common spoonbill
Platalea leucorodia
- 🌐 Breeds southern Eurasia, northern Africa; winters in tropics
- ⋏ Wetlands, estuaries
- ⥮ Up to 3 ft (0.9 m)
- ⥯ Up to 4.6 ft (1.4 m)
- ⚖ Up to 3.3 lb (1.5 kg)
- ✪ Fish, crabs, frogs
- ⚡ Least concern

Royal spoonbill
Platalea regia
- 🌐 Australia, New Zealand, Indonesia, Papua New Guinea, Pacific islands
- ⋏ Wetlands, estuaries
- ⥮ Up to 29.5 in (75 cm)
- ⥯ Up to 47 in (120 cm)
- ⚖ Up to 30 oz (850 g)
- ✪ Fish, crabs, frogs, aquatic invertebrates
- ⚡ Least concern

Glossy ibis
Plegadis falcinellus
- 🌐 North & South America, Eurasia, Africa, Australia
- ⋏ Wetlands, estuaries
- ⥮ Up to 26 in (65 cm)
- ⥯ Up to 41 in (105 cm)
- ⚖ Up to 29 oz (820 g)
- ✪ Crabs, insects, small snakes
- ⚡ Least concern

Australian white ibis
Threskiornis molucca
- 🌐 Eastern & northern Australia
- ⋏ Fresh & tidal wetlands
- ⥮ 25.5–29.5 in (65–75 cm)
- ⥯ 44–50 in (110–125 cm)
- ⚖ 3–5 lb (1.4–2.4 kg)
- ✪ Fish, aquatic invertebrates
- ⚡ Least concern

ORDER PELECANIFORMES
PELICANS & ALLIES
63 species

Australian pelican
Pelecanus conspicillatus
- 🌐 Australia, Papua New Guinea, western Indonesia
- ⋏ Rivers, estuaries, lakes, water
- ⥮ Up to 6.2 ft (1.9 m)
- ⥯ 8.5 ft (2.6 m)
- ⚖ Up to 29 lb (13 kg)
- ✪ Fish
- ⚡ Least concern

Dalmatian pelican
Pelecanus crispus
- 🌐 Breeds in southern Eurasia, winters to India
- ⋏ Swamps, shallow lakes
- ⥮ Up to 5.6 ft (1.7 m)
- ⥯ Up to 10 ft (3 m)
- ⚖ Up to 33 lb (15 kg)
- ✪ Fish
- ⚡ Vulnerable

Galápagos brown pelican
Pelecanus occidentalis urinator

Galápagos brown pelican
Pelecanus occidentalis urinator
- 🌐 Galápagos Islands
- ⋏ Bays, ocean, beaches, lagoons
- ⥮ 3.6–4.6 ft (1.1–1.4 m)
- ⥯ 6.5 ft (2 m)
- ⚖ 10 lb (4.5 kg)
- ✪ Fish
- ⚡ Least concern

Blue-footed booby
Sula nebouxii
- 🌐 Northwest Mexico to northern Peru, Galápagos Islands
- ⋏ Marine, tropical & subtropical islands
- ⥮ 32 in (81 cm)
- ⥯ 5 ft (1.5 m)
- ⚖ 3 lb (1.4 kg)
- ✪ Fish, squid, offal
- ⚡ Least concern

Peruvian booby
Sula variegata
- 🌐 Peru Current, Chile, Peru
- ⋏ Marine
- ⥮ 30 in (76 cm)
- ⥯ Up to 2.9 lb (1.3 kg)
- ⚖ Fish, squid, offal
- ⚡ Least concern

ORDER FALCONIFORMES
BIRDS OF PREY
302 species

Family Accipitridae
Hawks, eagles, kites, harriers & Old World vultures
234 species

Sharp-shinned hawk
Accipiter striatus
- 🌐 North & South America
- ⋏ Usually breeds in coniferous forest; various habitats in winter
- ⥮ 9.5–13 in (24–34 cm)
- ⥯ 17–22 in (43–56 cm)
- ⚖ 3.1–7.7 oz (87–218 g)
- ✪ Small birds, also large insects, small mammals
- ⚡ Least concern

Wedge-tailed eagle
Aquila audax
- 🌐 Australia, Papua New Guinea
- ⋏ All terrestrial habitats
- ⥮ Up to 43 in (110 cm)
- ⥯ 9 ft (2.7 m)
- ⚖ 8.8 lb (4 kg)
- ✪ Medium-sized mammals, lizards, birds, carrion (especially roadkill)
- ⚡ Least concern (Tasmanian subspecies endangered)

Golden eagle
Aquila chrysaetos
- 🌐 Northern Hemisphere
- ⋏ Forest, mountains
- ⥮ Up to 32 in (82 cm)
- ⥯ Up to 7 ft (2 m)
- ⚖ Up to 11.7 lb (5.3 kg)
- ✪ Mammals, birds
- ⚡ Least concern (rare in Europe)

Galápagos hawk
Buteo galapagoensis
- 🌐 Galápagos Islands
- ⋏ Tropical dry forest & shrubland
- ⥮ 21 in (54 cm)
- ⥯ 47 in (120 cm)
- ⚖ 24 oz (680 g)
- ✪ Lizards, snakes, rodents, birds, giant centipedes & other invertebrates, carrion
- ⚡ Vulnerable

Bearded vulture
Gypaetus barbatus

Red-tailed hawk
Buteo jamaicensis
- 🌐 North & Central America
- ⋏ Forest, desert, urban areas
- ⥮ 18–26 in (46–66 cm)
- ⥯ 3.6–5 ft (1.1–1.5 m)
- ⚖ ♂ up to 2.5 lb (1 kg), ♀ up to 3.5 lb (1.6 kg)
- ✪ Small mammals, birds, reptiles
- ⚡ Least concern

Northern harrier
Circus cyaneus
- 🌐 North & Central America, north & central Asia, north Africa
- ⋏ Open grassland, woods along streams, wetlands
- ⥮ 18–20 in (46–51 cm)
- ⥯ 40–46 in (102–117 cm)
- ⚖ 10.6–26.5 oz (300–750 g)
- ✪ Mice, small mammals, small birds
- ⚡ Least concern

Bearded vulture
Gypaetus barbatus
- 🌐 Europe, Africa, India, Tibet
- ⋏ Mountains, islands
- ⥮ Up to 9 ft (2.8 m)
- ⥯ Up to 9 ft (2.8 m)
- ⚖ Up to 15.5 lb (7 kg)
- ✪ Bones
- ⚡ Least concern

Bald eagle
Haliaeetus leucocephalus
- 🌐 North America
- ⋏ Lakes, rivers, seacoasts
- ⥮ Up to 30 in (76 cm)
- ⥯ 6.5 ft (2 m)
- ⚖ 6.5–14 lb (3–6.3 kg)
- ✪ Fish, waterfowl, mammals, carrion
- ⚡ Least concern

Harpy eagle
Harpia harpyja
- 🌐 Southern Mexico to northern Argentina
- ⋏ Tropical forest
- ⥮ 41 in (104 cm)
- ⥯ 7 ft (2.1 m)
- ⚖ 20 lb (9 kg)
- ✪ Sloths, monkeys, opossums, reptiles, birds
- ⚡ Near threatened

Red kite
Milvus milvus
- 🌐 Europe & northwest Africa
- ⋏ Mountain, forest
- ⥮ Up to 25 in (63.5 cm)
- ⥯ Up to 6.6 ft (2 m)
- ⚖ Up to 3 lb (1.4 kg)
- ✪ Small mammals, birds, carrion
- ⚡ Near threatened

Philippine eagle
Pithecophaga jefferyi
- 🌐 Philippine islands (Luzon, Mindanao)
- ⋏ Rain forest
- ⥮ ♀ 3 ft (1 m)
- ⥯ ♀ 6.5 ft (2 m)
- ⚖ ♂ 11 lb (5 kg), ♀ 15.5 lb (7 kg)
- ✪ Small arboreal mammals, reptiles
- ⚡ Critically endangered

Martial eagle
Polemaetus bellicosus
- 🌐 Sub-Saharan Africa
- ⋏ Semidesert, savanna
- ⥮ 30–35.5 in (76–90 cm)
- ⥯ 6.2–8.5 ft (1.9–2.6 m)
- ⚖ 11.5 lb (5.2 kg)
- ✪ Birds, small mammals
- ⚡ Least concern

Lappet-faced vulture
Torgos tracheliotus
- 🌐 East & southern Africa
- ⛰ Semiarid or desert areas
- ↥ 31–45 in (78–114 cm)
- ↤ 8 ft (2.5 m)
- ⚖ 15 lb (6.7 kg)
- ✿ Carrion, live prey
- ⚡ Vulnerable

Family Pandionidae
Osprey
1 species

Osprey
Pandion haliaetus
- 🌐 North & South America, Eurasia, Africa, Australia
- ⛰ River valley, coasts
- ↥ Up to 24 in (61 cm)
- ↤ Up to 6 ft (1.8 m)
- ⚖ Up to 4.4 lb (2 kg)
- ✿ Fish
- ⚡ Least concern

Family Falconidae
Falcons & caracaras
60 species

Lanner falcon
Falco biarmicus
- 🌐 Africa, southeast Europe, northwest Asia
- ⛰ Fields
- ↥ Up to 16.5 in (42 cm)
- ↤ Up to 40 in (100 cm)
- ⚖ Up to 26.5 oz (750 g)
- ✿ Small birds, insects, mammals
- ⚡ Least concern

Eleonora's falcon
Falco eleonorae
- 🌐 Breeds on European islands, winters in Madagascar
- ⛰ Scrub, cliffs
- ↥ Up to 15 in (38 cm)
- ↤ Up to 47 in (120 cm)
- ⚖ Up to 12 oz (340 g)
- ✿ Insects
- ⚡ Least concern

Lesser kestrel
Falco naumanni
- 🌐 Sub-Saharan Africa
- ⛰ Desert, grassland, steppe
- ↥ 11–13 in (28–33 cm)
- ↤ 25–28 in (64–72 cm)
- ⚖ 4.5–6 oz (130–170 g)
- ✿ Insects, such as grasshoppers & termites
- ⚡ Vulnerable

Peregrine falcon
Falco peregrinus
- 🌐 Worldwide except extreme polar regions & New Zealand
- ⛰ Mountain, river valley
- ↥ Up to 19 in (48 cm)
- ↤ Up to 43 in (110 cm)
- ⚖ Up to 3.5 lb (1.5 kg)
- ✿ Birds, mammals
- ⚡ Least concern

Gyrfalcon
Falco rusticolus
- 🌐 Arctic coasts & islands of North America & Eurasia
- ⛰ Tundra, mountains
- ↥ 19–26 in (48–66 cm)
- ↤ 3.6–5.2 ft (1.1–1.6 m)
- ⚖ ♂ up to 3 lb (1.4 kg), ♀ up to 4.6 lb (2.1 kg)
- ✿ Other birds such as grouse; mammals such as marmots & hares
- ⚡ Least concern

American kestrel
Falco sparverius
- 🌐 Canada, USA
- ⛰ Diverse open habitats from meadows & deserts to urban areas
- ↥ 9–12 in (23–30 cm)
- ↤ 20–24 in (51–60 cm)
- ⚖ 2.8–5.8 oz (80–165 g)
- ✿ Small vertebrates, large insects
- ⚡ Least concern

Family Sagittariidae
Secretary bird
1 species

Secretary bird
Sagittarius serpentarius
- 🌐 Sub-Saharan Africa
- ⛰ Grassland, savanna
- ↥ 4–5 ft (1.2–1.5 m)
- ↤ 6.8 ft (2 m)
- ⚖ 7 lb (3.3 kg)
- ✿ Small mammals, lizards, snakes, large insects, young birds reptiles, insects
- ⚡ Least concern

Family Cathartidae
New World vultures
7 species
Some schemes place this family into its own order, Cathartiformes.

Turkey vulture
Cathartes aura
- 🌐 North & South America
- ⛰ Forest to grassland & desert
- ↥ 26 in (66 cm)
- ↤ 5.6 ft (1.7 m)
- ⚖ 3 lb (1.4 kg)
- ✿ Scavenger, carrion
- ⚡ Least concern

American black vulture
Coragyps atratus
- 🌐 Southeastern USA to South America
- ⛰ Open land with wooded or brushy areas; many other lowland habitats
- ↥ 24–27 in (61–69 cm)
- ↤ 4.5–5 ft (1.3–1.5 m)
- ⚖ 3.5–5 lb (1.6–2.2 kg)
- ✿ Carrion
- ⚡ Least concern

Condor, Andean condor
Vultur gryphus
- 🌐 Andes (South America)
- ⛰ Open grassland, mountains
- ↥ Up to 4.3 ft (1.3 m)
- ↤ 10.8 ft (3.3 m)
- ⚖ Up to 33 lb (15 kg)
- ✿ Carrion from large & medium-sized mammals
- ⚡ Near threatened

ORDER GRUIFORMES
CRANES & ALLIES
212 species

Black-crowned crane
Balearica pavonina
- 🌐 Sub-Saharan Africa
- ⛰ Marshes, swamps
- ↥ 40 in (100 cm)
- ↤ 6.2 ft (1.9 m)
- ⚖ 8 lb (3.6 kg)
- ✿ Insects, reptiles, small mammals
- ⚡ Near threatened

Black-crowned crane
Balearica pavonina

Lord Howe Island woodhen
Gallirallus sylvestris
- 🌐 Lord Howe Island (Australia)
- ⛰ Rain forest
- ↥ Up to 18 in (46 cm)
- ↤ Up to 20.5 in (52 cm)
- ⚖ Up to 18.7 oz (530 g)
- ✿ Insects, mollusks, invertebrates
- ⚡ Endangered

Whooping crane
Grus americana
- 🌐 Breeds in northwest Canada, winters in Texas; introduced central Florida & Wisconsin, USA
- ⛰ Freshwater marshes, prairie, grain fields, shallow lakes, salt marshes
- ↥ 4.9 ft (1.5 m)
- ↤ 7.5 ft (2.3 m)
- ⚖ 13–17 lb (6–7.8 kg)
- ✿ Plants, grain, fish, frogs, mollusks, crustaceans, insects
- ⚡ Endangered

Common crane
Grus grus
- 🌐 Breeds in northern Eurasia, winters in Africa & southern Eurasia
- ⛰ Wetlands
- ↥ Up to 4.3 ft (1.3 m)
- ↤ Up to 7.8 ft (2.4 m)
- ⚖ Up to 13.2 lb (6 kg)
- ✿ Leaves, berries, insects, small birds, mammals
- ⚡ Least concern

Red-crowned crane
Grus leucogeranus
- 🌐 Breeds in Siberia, Japan; winters in Korea, Taiwan, China
- ⛰ Marshes, riverbanks, rice fields, other wet areas
- ↥ Height: 4.5 ft (1.4 m)
- ↤ Up to 8 ft (2.5 m)
- ⚖ 17–22 lb (7.7–10 kg)
- ✿ Amphibians, fish, aquatic invertebrates, aquatic plants
- ⚡ Critically endangered

Brolga
Grus rubicunda
- 🌐 Tropical & eastern Australia
- ⛰ Grassland, wetlands, farmland
- ↥ Up to 4.2 ft (1.3 m)
- ↤ Up to 9 ft (2.7 m)
- ⚖ 13 lb (6 kg)
- ✿ Invertebrates, small vertebrates, tubers, shoots
- ⚡ Least concern

Hoatzin
*Opisthocomus hoazin**
- 🌐 Orinoco delta & Amazon in South America
- ⛰ Tropical rain forest
- ↥ 26 in (66 cm)
- ↤ 40 in (100 cm)
- ⚖ 32 oz (900 g)
- ✿ Leaves, shoots of marsh plants
- ⚡ Least concern
Some schemes place the hoatzin into its own order, Opisthocomiformes.

Great bustard
Otis tarda
- 🌐 Central Eurasia
- ⛰ Open grassland
- ↥ 31.5–43 in (80–110 cm)
- ↤ 5.9–8.2 ft (1.8–2.5 m)
- ⚖ ♂ 22–35 lb (10–16 kg), ♀ 8–11 lb (3.5–5 kg)
- ✿ Seeds, insects, worms, frogs
- ⚡ Vulnerable

Purple swamphen
Porphyrio porphyrio
- 🌐 Europe, Africa, tropical Asia, Australasia
- ⛰ Wetlands, lakes, rivers, parks
- ↥ Up to 20 in (51 cm)
- ↤ Up to 40 in (100 cm)
- ⚖ Up to 2.2 lb (1 kg)
- ✿ Aquatic vegetation, small invertebrates & vertebrates
- ⚡ Least concern

Kagu
Rhynochetos jubatus
- 🌐 New Caledonia
- ⛰ Rain forest, montane forest
- ↥ Up to 22 in (56 cm)
- ↤ Up to 32 in (81 cm)
- ⚖ Up to 2.4 lb (1.1 kg)
- ✿ Mollusks, worms, arthropods, lizards
- ⚡ Endangered

Rouget's rail
Rougetius rougetii
- 🌐 Eritrea, Ethiopia
- ⛰ Marshy areas of montane grassland
- ↥ 5.5–20 in (14–51 cm)
- ✿ Seeds, aquatic insects, crustaceans
- ⚡ Near threatened

ORDER CHARADRIIFORMES
WADERS & SHOREBIRDS
351 species

Marbled murrelet
Brachyramphus marmoratus
- 🌐 Pacific coast of North America
- ⛰ Breeds in coastal old-growth coniferous forest; winters offshore
- ↥ 9–10 in (23–25.5 cm)
- ↤ 16 in (41 cm)
- ⚖ 9.1–12.6 oz (258–357 g)
- ✿ Small fish, shrimps, other crustaceans
- ⚡ Endangered

Subantarctic skua, Brown skua
Catharacta lonnbergi
- 🌐 Subantarctic, Antarctic
- ⛰ Nests on islands; disperses over ocean in non-breeding season
- ↥ 20–25 in (51–64 cm)
- ↤ 4–5 ft (1.25–1.6 m)
- ⚖ 3–5.5 lb (1.3–2.5 kg)
- ✿ Scavenges seabird eggs, chicks & adults, seal placentas & pups; predates burrowing petrels
- ⚡ Least concern

Piping plover
Charadrius melodus
- 🌐 Breeds in midwest Canada & USA, Great Lakes, Atlantic coast; winters along US Atlantic & Gulf coasts
- ⛰ Open sandy beaches, alkali flats
- ↥ 7 in (18 cm)
- ↤ 15 in (38 cm)
- ⚖ 1.5–2.2 oz (43–63 g)
- ✿ Insects, aquatic invertebrates
- ⚡ Near threatened

Dotterel
Charadrius morinellus
- 🌐 Northern Eurasia
- ⛰ Mountain, tundra, mudflat
- ↥ Up to 8 in (20 cm)
- ↤ Up to 23 in (59 cm)
- ⚖ Up to 3.8 oz (110 g)
- ✿ Insects, invertebrates
- ⚡ Least concern

Snowy sheathbill
Chionis albus
- 🌐 Breeds South Atlantic Ocean & Antarctic Peninsula; some winter in Falkland Islands
- ⛰ Rocky islands & coast
- ↥ 14–16 in (35–40 cm)
- ↤ 30–34 in (76–86 cm)
- ⚖ 16–28 oz (460–800 g)
- ✿ Scavenges carrion, eggs, placentas, feces, marine items
- ⚡ Least concern

Puffin, Atlantic puffin
Fratercula arctica
- 🌐 Breeds along North Atlantic coasts; winters in warmer seas
- ⛰ Rocky coast & islands
- ↥ 14 in (36 cm)
- ↤ 30 in (76 cm)
- ⚖ 18 oz (500 g)
- ✿ Small fish caught near surface
- ⚡ Least concern

Eurasian oystercatcher
Haematopus ostralegus
- 🌐 Western Europe, central Eurasia, eastern Asia
- ⛰ Coastal
- ↥ Up to 16.5 in (42 cm)
- ↤ Up to 33 in (83 cm)
- ⚖ Up to 19 oz (540 g)
- ✿ Mollusks, mussels, worms
- ⚡ Least concern

Little gull
Hydrocoloeus minutus
- 🌐 Breeds northern Eurasia, northern Canada; winters western Europe, northeast USA
- ⛰ Estuaries, coastal marshes
- ↥ Up to 10 in (25 cm)
- ↤ Up to 31 in (78 cm)
- ⚖ Up to 4.2 oz (120 g)
- ✿ Insects, fish, invertebrates
- ⚡ Least concern

Herring gull
Larus argentatus
- 🌐 North America, Eurasia
- ⛰ Coastal
- ⚖ Up to 24 in (60 cm)
- ↤ Up to 4.6 ft (1.4 m)
- ⚖ Up to 2.6 lb (1.2 kg)
- ✿ Omnivorous, scavenges food
- ⚡ Least concern

Laughing gull
Larus atricilla
- 🌐 US Atlantic & Gulf of Mexico coast
- ⛰ Ocean coasts
- ↥ 15–18 in (38–46 cm)
- ↤ 36–47 in (91–120 cm)
- ⚖ 7.8–13 oz (203–371 g)
- ✿ Aquatic & terrestrial invertebrates, fish, squid, garbage, berries
- ⚡ Least concern

Sooty tern
Onychoprion fuscatus
- 🌐 Tropical oceans
- ⛰ Ocean, islands
- ↥ Up to 18 in (46 cm)
- ↤ 36 in (91 cm)
- ⚖ Up to 10 oz (285 g)
- ✿ Fish
- ⚡ Least concern

Eurasian golden plover
Pluvialis apricaria
- 🌐 Breeds northern Eurasia; winters southern Europe, north Africa
- ⛰ Fields, tidal flats, tundra
- ↥ Up to 11 in (28 cm)
- ↤ Up to 28 in (72 cm)
- ⚖ Up to 7.7 oz (220 g)
- ✿ Insects, crustaceans, berries
- ⚡ Least concern

Arctic tern
Sterna paradisaea

Black skimmer
Rynchops niger
- 🌐 North & South America
- ⛰ Estuaries, coasts, ponds, lakes
- ⟷ 16–20 in (41–51 cm)
- ⤢ 44 in (112 cm)
- ⚖ 7.5–15.8 oz (212–447 g)
- ✿ Small fish
- ⚡ Least concern (threatened or endangered in some US states)

South polar skua
Stercorarius maccormicki
- 🌐 Antarctica
- ⛰ Breeds on ice-free areas, typically in association with penguin colonies
- ⟷ 20–22 in (51–56 cm)
- ⤢ 4.3–5.2 ft (1.3–1.6 m)
- ⚖ 1.3–3.5 lb (0.6–1.6 kg)
- ✿ Penguin eggs, chicks & adults, small fish
- ⚡ Least concern

Arctic tern
Sterna paradisaea
- 🌐 Circumpolar, breeds in the far north, winters in the far south
- ⛰ Hatches in the Arctic, migrates south to feed, returns north to breed
- ⟷ 14 in (36 cm)
- ⤢ 30–34 in (76–85 cm)
- ⚖ 3.4–4.2 oz (95–120 g)
- ✿ Small fish, crustaceans
- ⚡ Least concern

Northern lapwing
Vanellus vanellus
- 🌐 Temperate Eurasia
- ⛰ Fields, mudflats
- ⟷ Up to 12 in (31 cm)
- ⤢ Up to 28 in (72 cm)
- ⚖ Up to 7 oz (198 g)
- ✿ Insects, invertebrates
- ⚡ Least concern

ORDER PTEROCLIDIFORMES SANDGROUSE
16 species

Burchell's sandgrouse
Pterocles burchelli
- 🌐 Southern Africa
- ⛰ Desert, scrubland
- ⟷ 9–16 in (24–40 cm)
- ⚖ 5–23 oz (150–650 g)
- ✿ Seeds
- ⚡ Least concern

Sandgrouse, Pallas's sandgrouse
Syrrhaptes paradoxus
- 🌐 Central Asia
- ⛰ Dry steppe
- ⟷ 12–16 in (30–41 cm)
- ⤢ 27.5 in (70 cm)
- ⚖ 7–10.6 oz (200–300 g)
- ✿ Legume seeds, plant shoots
- ⚡ Least concern

ORDER COLUMBIFORMES PIGEONS
313 species

Passenger pigeon
Ectopistes migratorius
- 🌐 Eastern North America
- ⛰ Forest, prairie edge
- ⟷ 14 in (35 cm)
- ⤢ 8 in (20 cm)
- ✿ Seeds
- ⚡ Extinct

Dodo
Raphus cucullatus
- 🌐 Island of Mauritius
- ⛰ Forest
- ⟷ 40 in (100 cm)
- ⚖ 44 lb (20 kg)
- ✿ Fruits, seeds
- ⚡ Extinct

ORDER PSITTACIFORMES PARROTS
364 species

Australian king parrot
Alisterus scapularis
- 🌐 Eastern Australia
- ⛰ Rain forest, eucalypt forest, orchards, parks, gardens
- ⟷ Up to 18 in (46 cm) including tail
- ⚖ Up to 9.7 oz (275 g)
- ✿ Seeds, fruits
- ⚡ Least concern

Blue-fronted parrot
Amazona aestiva
- 🌐 Bolivia, Brazil, Paraguay, northern Argentina; introduced Stuttgart, Germany
- ⛰ Tropical forest, palm groves
- ⟷ 14 in (35 cm)
- ⤢ 8 in (20 cm)
- ⚖ 10 lb (4.5 kg)
- ✿ Avocado & other fruits, seeds
- ⚡ Least concern

Orange-winged parrot
Amazona amazonica
- 🌐 Tropical South America
- ⛰ Tropical forest
- ⟷ 14 in (35 cm)
- ⤢ 35 in (90 cm)
- ⚖ 12 oz (340 g)
- ✿ Seeds, fruits, berries, flowers, nuts
- ⚡ Least concern

Scarlet macaw
Ara macao
- 🌐 Central America to Amazonian Peru & Brazil
- ⛰ Tall deciduous trees of forests & rivers
- ⟷ Up to 36 in (91 cm) including tail
- ⤢ 45 in (114 cm)
- ⚖ Up to 2.5 lb (1 kg)
- ✿ Fruits, seeds, clay
- ⚡ Least concern

Major Mitchell cockatoo
Cacatua leadbeateri
- 🌐 Inland Australia
- ⛰ Mallee, mulga, timbered watercourses
- ⟷ Up to 16 in (41 cm)
- ⚖ Up to 17 oz (480 g)
- ✿ Fruits, seeds
- ⚡ Least concern

Red-tailed black cockatoo
Calyptorhynchus banksii
- 🌐 Australia, especially northern half
- ⛰ Rain forest, woodland, shrubland, grassland
- ⟷ Up to 4.6 ft (1.4 m)
- ⤢ 16 in (41 cm)
- ⚖ Up to 30.6 oz (870 g)
- ✿ Leaves, shoots
- ⚡ Least concern

Red-crowned parakeet
Cyanoramphus novaezelandiae
- 🌐 New Zealand offshore islands
- ⟷ 10.5 in (27 cm)
- ⚖ 1.8–3.9 oz (50–110 g)
- ✿ Seeds, fruit, berries
- ⚡ Vulnerable

Double-eyed fig parrot
Cyclopsitta diophthalma
- 🌐 New Guinea, tropical coast of Australia
- ⛰ Rain forest
- ⟷ Up to 6 in (16 cm)
- ✿ Fruits, fungi, lichens, insects
- ⚡ Least concern

Budgerigar
Melopsittacus undulatus
- 🌐 Drier parts of Australia
- ⛰ Scrubland, open woodland, grassland
- ⟷ 7 in (18 cm)
- ⚖ 1–1.4 oz (30–40 g)
- ✿ Grass seeds
- ⚡ Least concern

Orange-bellied parrot
Neophema chrysogaster
- 🌐 Southwest Tasmania, coastal Victoria
- ⛰ Salt marsh, grassland
- ⟷ 8 in (20 cm)
- ⚖ 1.6 oz (45 g)
- ✿ Seeds, berries, shrubs, grasses
- ⚡ Critically endangered

Turquoise parrot
Neophema pulchella
- 🌐 Eastern Australia
- ⛰ Grassland, open woodland
- ⟷ 8 in (20 cm)
- ⤢ 16 in (40 cm)
- ⚖ Up to 1.4 oz (40 g)
- ✿ Seeds
- ⚡ Least concern

Kea
Nestor notabilis
- 🌐 South Island of New Zealand
- ⛰ Alpine areas, subalpine forest
- ⟷ Up to 20 in (51 cm)
- ⤢ 40 in (100 cm)
- ⚖ Up to 2.2 lb (1 kg)
- ✿ Plants, beetle larvae, other birds, mammals including sheep
- ⚡ Vulnerable

African gray parrot
Psittacus erithacus
- 🌐 West & central Africa
- ⛰ Rain forest
- ⟷ 13–16 in (33–41 cm)
- ⤢ 18–20 in (46–51 cm)
- ⚖ 16 oz (450 g)
- ✿ Seeds, fruits
- ⚡ Near threatened

Kakapo
Strigops habroptila
- 🌐 New Zealand offshore islands
- ⛰ Forest
- ⟷ Up to 25 in (64 cm)
- ⤢ Up to 36 in (91 cm)
- ⚖ Up to 5 lb (2.5 kg)
- ✿ Fruits, leaves, stems, seeds
- ⚡ Critically endangered

Rainbow lorikeet
Trichoglossus haematodus
- 🌐 Australia, eastern Indonesia, Papua New Guinea, New Caledonia, Solomon Islands, Vanuatu
- ⛰ Rain forest, eucalypt forest, woodland, parks, gardens
- ⟷ Up to 13 in (33 cm)
- ⤢ 7 in (17 cm)
- ⚖ 4.5 oz (130 g)
- ✿ Fruits, nectar
- ⚡ Least concern

ORDER CUCULIFORMES CUCKOOS & TURACOS
162 species

Greater roadrunner
Geococcyx californianus
- 🌐 Southwest USA, Mexico
- ⛰ Desert, scrubland
- ⟷ 22 in (56 cm)
- ⤢ Up to 24 in (61 cm)
- ⚖ 10.5 oz (300 g)
- ✿ Insects, small reptiles, rodents
- ⚡ Least concern

Guira cuckoo
Guira guira
- 🌐 South America
- ⛰ Open scrubby areas
- ⟷ 16 in (40 cm)
- ⤢ 3.6–5 ft (1.1–1.5 m)
- ⚖ 3.7 oz (105 g)
- ✿ Spiders, frogs, small mammals, smaller birds
- ⚡ Least concern

Lady Ross's turaco
Musophaga rossae
- 🌐 Central & southern Africa
- ⛰ Rain forest
- ⟷ 15–18 in (38–46 cm)
- ⚖ 16 oz (450 g)
- ✿ Leaves, fruits
- ⚡ Least concern

ORDER STRIGIFORMES OWLS
195 species

Tengmalm's owl, Boreal owl
Aegolius funereus
- 🌐 Northern North America & Eurasia
- ⛰ Mountain, boreal forest
- ⟷ Up to 12 in (30 cm)
- ⤢ Up to 24 in (62 cm)
- ⚖ Up to 4 oz (114 g)
- ✿ Rodents
- ⚡ Least concern

Burrowing owl, Bolivian burrowing owl
Athene cunicularia
- 🌐 North & South America
- ⛰ Grassland, rangeland, desert
- ⟷ 10 in (25 cm)
- ⤢ 22 in (56 cm)
- ⚖ 6 oz (170 g)
- ✿ Large insects, small rodents, reptiles
- ⚡ Least concern

Orange-bellied parrot
Neophema chrysogaster

Eagle owl Eurasian eagle owl
Bubo bubo
- 🌐 Eurasia
- ⛰ Mountains, forest
- ⟷ Up to 28 in (71 cm)
- ⤢ Up to 7 ft (2 m)
- ⚖ Up to 9 lb (4 kg)
- ✿ Small mammals
- ⚡ Least concern

Snowy owl
Nyctea scandiaca
- 🌐 Arctic Alaska, Canada, Greenland & Eurasia
- ⛰ Tundra, boreal forest
- ⟷ Up to 28 in (70 cm)
- ⤢ 4.2–5 ft (1.3–1.5 m)
- ⚖ 4.4 lb (2 kg)
- ✿ Lemmings & other small mammals
- ⚡ Least concern

Spectacled owl
Pulsatrix perspicillata
- 🌐 Mexico, Central America, northern South America (not Andes)
- ⛰ Rain forest
- ⟷ Up to 18 in (46 cm)
- ⤢ 36 in (91 cm)
- ⚖ Up to 32 oz (900 g)
- ✿ Mice, skunk, insects, spiders, caterpillars, bats, birds, frogs
- ⚡ Least concern

Great gray owl
Strix nebulosa
- 🌐 Northern hemisphere
- ⛰ Forest
- ⟷ Up to 33 in (84 cm)
- ⤢ Up to 5 ft (1.5 m)
- ⚖ Up to 3.2 lb (1.5 kg)
- ✿ Rodents
- ⚡ Least concern

Ural owl
Strix uralensis
- 🌐 Scandinavia to Japan & Korea
- ⛰ Taiga forest
- ⟷ 20–23 in (51–59 cm)
- ⤢ 45–49 in (115–125 cm)
- ⚖ ♂ up to 24.6 oz (700 g), ♀ up to 2.5 lb (1.2 kg)
- ✿ Rodents, smaller birds
- ⚡ Least concern

ORDER CAPRIMULGIFORMES NIGHTJARS & ALLIES
118 species

White-winged nightjar
Eleothreptus candicans
- 🌐 Bolivia, Brazil, Paraguay
- ⛰ Dry lowland grassland
- ⟷ 8 in (20 cm)
- ⤢ 11 in (28 cm)
- ⚖ 1.8 oz (50 g)
- ✿ Beetles, moths
- ⚡ Endangered

Scarlet macaws
Ara macao

Order Apodiformes
Hummingbirds & swifts
429 species

Costa's hummingbird
Calypte costae
- 🌐 Southwestern USA & Mexico
- ⛰ Desert, semidesert
- ⚊ Up to 4 in (10 cm)
- ⚊ Up to 4 in (10 cm)
- ⚖ 0.1 oz (3 g)
- ❂ Flower nectar, tree sap, small insects
- ⚡ Least concern

Order Coliiformes
Mousebirds
6 species

Order Trogoniformes
Trogons
39 species

Resplendent quetzal
Pharomachrus mocinno
- 🌐 Central America
- ⛰ Montane cloud forest
- ⚊ 14 in (36 cm)
- ⚊ ♂ 25 in (64 cm) tail streamer
- ⚊ 16 in (40 cm)
- ⚖ 7.5 oz (210 g)
- ❂ Fruits, insects, frogs
- ⚡ Near threatened

Order Coraciiformes
Kingfishers & allies
209 species

Red-knobbed hornbill
Aceros cassidix
- 🌐 Indonesia
- ⛰ Tropical rain forest
- ⚊ 27–32 in (70–80 cm)
- ⚖ ♂ 5.3–5.5 lb (2.4–2.5 kg)
- ❂ Mainly figs, also insects, other fruits
- ⚡ Least concern

European kingfisher
Alcedo atthis
- 🌐 Eurasia, northern Africa
- ⛰ Rivers, marshes
- ⚊ Up to 6 in (16 cm)
- ⚊ Up to 10 in (25 cm)
- ⚖ Up to 1.4 oz (40 g)
- ❂ Freshwater fish, also aquatic invertebrates
- ⚡ Least concern

Northern flicker
Colaptes auratus

Laughing kookaburra
Dacelo novaeguineae

Southern ground hornbill
Bucorvus cafer
- 🌐 Sub-Saharan Africa
- ⛰ Savanna, woodland, grassland
- ⚊ 3–4.3 ft (0.9–1.3 m)
- ⚊ 3.9–5.9 ft (1.2–1.8 m)
- ⚖ 7–13.5 lb (3.2–6.2 kg)
- ❂ Small vertebrates, insects
- ⚡ Least concern

Laughing kookaburra
Dacelo novaeguineae
- 🌐 Eastern & southwestern Australia
- ⛰ Woods, open forest, gardens, parks
- ⚊ Up to 18 in (47 cm)
- ⚊ 25–26 in (64–66 cm)
- ⚖ 12 oz (340 g)
- ❂ Reptiles, frogs, invertebrates
- ⚡ Least concern

Northern carmine bee-eater
Merops nubicus
- 🌐 Sub-Saharan Africa
- ⛰ Savanna, woodland
- ⚊ 14 in (35 cm)
- ⚊ 12 in (30 cm)
- ⚊ 11–12.5 in (28–32 cm)
- ⚖ 1.4–2.1 oz (40–60 g)
- ❂ Bees & other flying insects
- ⚡ Least concern

Southern yellow-billed hornbill
Tockus leucomelas
- 🌐 Southern Africa
- ⛰ Woodland, grassland
- ⚊ 19–24 in (48–61 cm)
- ⚊ 5.9–7 ft (1.8–2 m)
- ⚖ 4–6 lb (1.8–2.7 kg)
- ❂ Seeds, insects
- ⚡ Least concern

Cuban tody
Todus multicolor
- 🌐 Cuba
- ⛰ Dry mountainous scrubland, tropical forest, mountainous evergreen forest, pine forest, seashore
- ⚊ 4 in (10 cm)
- ⚊ 4.3 (10.9 cm)
- ⚖ 0.2 oz (6 g)
- ❂ Small adult & larval insects, spiders, small lizards
- ⚡ Least concern

Order Piciformes
Woodpeckers & allies
398 species

Northern flicker
Colaptes auratus
- 🌐 North & Central America, West Indies
- ⛰ Open areas
- ⚊ 12 in (30 cm)
- ⚊ 20 in (50 cm)
- ⚖ 4.5 oz (130 g)
- ❂ Insects, especially ants
- ⚡ Least concern

Versicolor barbet
Eubucco versicolor
- 🌐 Bolivia, Peru
- ⛰ Tropical forest
- ⚊ 9 in (23 cm)
- ⚊ 27 in (68 cm)
- ⚖ 3.9 oz (110 g)
- ❂ Fruits, insects
- ⚡ Least concern

Gila woodpecker
Melanerpes uropygialis
- 🌐 Southwestern USA
- ⛰ Desert with saguaro & other large cacti for nesting; streamside woodland, dry forest
- ⚊ 9 in (23 cm)
- ⚊ 16 in (41 cm)
- ⚖ 1.8–2.8 oz (51–79 g)
- ❂ Insects, fruits, seeds, bird eggs, lizards
- ⚡ Least concern

Keel-billed toucan
Ramphastos sulfuratus
- 🌐 Southern Mexico to Venezuela & Colombia
- ⛰ Rain forest
- ⚊ 25 in (63 cm)
- ⚊ 16 in (41 cm)
- ⚖ 14 oz (400 g)
- ❂ Fruits, insects, bird eggs, tree frogs
- ⚡ Least concern

Toco toucan
Ramphastos toco
- 🌐 Central & eastern South America
- ⛰ Lowlands, swamps, savanna, canopy of tropical rain forest
- ⚊ Up to 25 in (64 cm); bill length up to 8 in (20 cm)
- ⚊ 24 in (61 cm)
- ⚖ 19 oz (540 g)
- ❂ Small fruits, berries
- ⚡ Least concern

Toucan barbet
Semnornis ramphastinus
- 🌐 South America
- ⛰ Tropical forest
- ⚊ 10 in (25 cm)
- ⚊ 25 in (63 cm)
- ⚖ 3.5 oz (100 g)
- ❂ Fruits, insects
- ⚡ Near threatened

Order Passeriformes
Passerines
5,754 species in 96 families, including the families listed below

Family Alaudidae
Larks
91 species

Horned lark, Shore lark
Eremophila alpestris
- 🌐 North America, northern Eurasia, mountains of southeast Europe
- ⛰ Shore, field, tundra
- ⚊ Up to 8.3 in (21 cm)
- ⚊ Up to 12.6 in (32 cm)
- ⚖ Up to 1.3 oz (37 g)
- ❂ Insects, seeds
- ⚡ Least concern

Family Cardinalidae
Cardinals
43 species

Rose-breasted grosbeak
Pheucticus ludovicianus
- 🌐 Breeds in Canada & eastern USA; winters from Mexico to northern South America & Caribbean
- ⛰ Woodland, orchards, parks, gardens
- ⚊ 7–8 in (18–20 cm)
- ⚊ 11–13 in (28–33 cm)
- ⚖ 1.4–1.7 oz (39–49 g)
- ❂ Insects, seeds, fruits, buds
- ⚡ Least concern

Family Corvidae
Crows, magpies & jays
120+ species

Western scrub jay
Aphelocoma californica
- 🌐 Western USA, Mexico
- ⛰ Lowland scrub, woodland, gardens
- ⚊ 12 in (30 cm)
- ⚊ 15 in (38 cm)
- ⚖ 2.8 oz (80 g)
- ❂ Arthropods, fruits, acorns, seeds
- ⚡ Least concern

Common raven
Corvus corax
- 🌐 Nearly worldwide
- ⛰ Open areas in diverse habitats including tundra, forest, prairie, desert, farmland, cities
- ⚊ 22–27 in (56–68 cm)
- ⚊ 46 in (117 cm)
- ⚖ 1.5–3.5 lb (0.7–1.6 kg)
- ❂ Small mammals & birds, bird eggs, insects, grain, fruit, refuse, carrion
- ⚡ Least concern

Blue jay
Cyanocitta cristata
- 🌐 Southern Canada, eastern USA to central Texas
- ⛰ Edges of deciduous, conifer & mixed forests; gardens
- ⚊ 10–12 in (25–30 cm)
- ⚊ 13–17 in (33–43 cm)
- ⚖ 2.5–3.5 oz (70–100 g)
- ❂ Insects, acorns, nuts, bird eggs, small mammals & birds
- ⚡ Least concern

Azure-winged magpie
Cyanopica cyana
- 🌐 China, Korea, Japan, Mongolia
- ⛰ Coniferous & broadleaf forests, gardens
- ⚊ 12–14 in (31–35 cm)
- ⚊ 6–8 in (16–20 cm)
- ❂ Acorns, pine nuts, insects, fruits, berries
- ⚡ Least concern

Spotted nutcracker
Nucifraga caryocatactes
- 🌐 Eurasia
- ⛰ Coniferous forest
- ⚊ Up to 13.8 in (35 cm)
- ⚊ Up to 21 in (53 cm)
- ⚖ Up to 6 oz (170 g)
- ❂ Nuts, seeds
- ⚡ Least concern

Siberian jay
Perisoreus infaustus
- 🌐 Northern Eurasia
- ⛰ Boreal forest
- ⚊ 12 in (30 cm)
- ❂ Insects, berries, bird eggs & nestlings, small mammals & birds
- ⚡ Least concern

Family Cotingidae
Cotingas
90 species

Andean cock-of-the-rock
Rupicola peruvianus
- 🌐 Venezuela, Colombia, Ecuador, Peru, Bolivia
- ⛰ Rain forest
- ⚊ 13 in (33 cm)
- ⚊ 14 in (35 cm)
- ⚖ 2.5 oz (70 g)
- ❂ Fruits
- ⚡ Least concern

Family Emberizidae
Buntings & American sparrows
400 species

Great pampas finch
Embernagra platensis
- 🌐 Argentina, Bolivia, Brazil, Paraguay, Uruguay
- ⛰ Tropical high-altitude shrubland, temperate grassland & swamps
- ⚊ 2.5 in (6.3 cm)
- ⚊ 2 in (5 cm)
- ⚖ 1 oz (28 g)
- ❂ Seeds, insects
- ⚡ Least concern

Brewer's sparrow
Spizella breweri
- 🌐 Breeds southwestern Canada, western USA; winters southwestern USA, Mexico
- ⛰ Dense stands of sagebrush amid grassy areas
- ⚊ 5.5 in (14 cm)
- ⚊ 8 in (20 cm)
- ⚖ 0.5 oz (14 g)
- ❂ Grasshoppers, beetles, other insects, seeds, some plant material
- ⚡ Near threatened

Family Estrildidae
Estrildid finches
130 species

Gouldian finch
Erythrura gouldiae
- 🌐 Northern Australia
- ⛰ Tropical woodland, spinifex grassland
- ⚊ 4.5–5.5 in (12–14 cm)
- ❂ Seeds, insects
- ⚡ Endangered

Family Icteridae
American blackbirds, New World orioles, grackles & cowbirds
88 species

Red-winged blackbird
Agelaius phoeniceus
- 🌐 North & Central America
- ⛰ Wetlands, grassy areas, open patches in woodland
- ⚊ 7–9 in (18–23 cm)
- ⚊ 12–16 in (30–41 cm)
- ⚖ 1.1–2.7 oz (31–76 g)
- ❂ Insects, seeds, grain
- ⚡ Least concern

Rusty blackbird
Euphagus carolinus
- 🌐 Breeds Alaska, Canada, New England; winters throughout eastern & central USA
- ⛰ Swampy boreal forest in summer; swamps & wet woodland in winter
- ⚊ 8–10 in (21–25 cm)
- ⚊ 15 in (37 cm)
- ⚖ 1.6–2.8 oz (45–79 g)
- ❂ Insects in summer; acorns, seeds, fruits in winter
- ⚡ Vulnerable

Brown-headed cowbird
Molothrus ater
- 🌐 Temperate to subtropical North America
- ⛰ Grassland, woodland edges, thickets, fields, prairie, pasture, orchards, suburban & urban areas
- ⚊ 7–9 in (18–23 cm)
- ⚊ 11–14 in (28–35 cm)
- ⚖ 1.3–1.8 oz (37–51 g)
- ❂ Seeds, spiders, insects
- ⚡ Least concern

Gouldian finch
Erythrura gouldiae

Family Meliphagidae
Honeyeaters
182 species

New Holland honeyeater
Phylidonyris novaehollandiae
- ⊕ Southern Australia
- ⋀ Forest & woodland, heath
- ⊀ 7 in (18 cm)
- ⊀ 0.7 oz (20 g)
- ✿ Nectar, insects
- ⚡ Least concern

Family Menuridae
Lyrebirds
2 species

Superb lyrebird
Menura novaehollandiae
- ⊕ Southeastern Australia
- ⋀ Rain forest, eucalypt forest, gullies
- ⊀ Up to 40 in (100 cm)
- ⊀ 2.2 lb (1 kg)
- ✿ Invertebrates, seeds
- ⚡ Least concern

Family Mimidae
Mockingbirds & thrashers
30+ species

Chalk-browed mockingbird
Mimus saturninus
- ⊕ Northeast Brazil, Bolivia, Paraguay, Uruguay, northern Argentina
- ⋀ Savanna, shrubland, degraded forest
- ⊀ 10 in (25 cm)
- ⊀ 12 in (30 cm)
- ⊀ 2.1 oz (59 g)
- ✿ Insects, worms
- ⚡ Least concern

Curve-billed thrasher
Toxostoma curvirostre
- ⊕ Southwestern USA, Mexico
- ⋀ Desert, semidesert, thorn scrub, shrubby areas, open brushland
- ⊀ 11 in (28 cm)
- ⊀ 13 in (33 cm)
- ⊀ 3 oz (85 g)
- ✿ Insects, seeds, berries
- ⚡ Least concern

Family Paradisaeidae
Birds of paradise
40+ species

Huon astrapia
Astrapia rothschildi
- ⊕ Huon Peninsula (Papua New Guinea)
- ⋀ Rain forest
- ⊀ Up to 27 in (68 cm)
- ✿ Fruits, insects
- ⚡ Least concern

Superb bird-of-paradise
Lophorina superba
- ⊕ New Guinea
- ⋀ Rain forest
- ⊀ Up to 10 in (23 cm)
- ⊀ Up to 3 oz (85 g)
- ✿ Fruits, insects
- ⚡ Least concern

Raggiana bird-of-paradise
Paradisaea raggiana
- ⊕ New Guinea
- ⋀ Tropical forest
- ⊀ Up to 13 in (33 cm)
- ⊀ ♂ 9.5 oz (270 g), ♀ 6.1 oz (173 g)
- ✿ Fruits, insects
- ⚡ Least concern

Blue bird-of-paradise
Paradisaea rudolphi
- ⊕ Southeastern New Guinea
- ⋀ Rain forest, gardens
- ⊀ Up to 12 in (30 cm)
- ⊀ Up to 6.2 oz (176 g)
- ✿ Fruits, insects
- ⚡ Vulnerable

King of Saxony bird-of-paradise
Pteridophora alberti
- ⊕ New Guinea
- ⋀ Rain forest
- ⊀ Up to 9 in (22 cm)
- ⊀ Up to 3 oz (87 g)
- ✿ Fruits, insects
- ⚡ Least concern

Family Paridae
Tits, chickadees & titmice
64 species

Blue tit
Parus caeruleus
- ⊕ Temperate & subarctic Europe & western Asia
- ⋀ Deciduous or mixed woodland
- ⊀ Up to 4.8 in (12 cm)
- ⊀ Up to 7 in (18 cm)
- ⊀ Up to 4 oz (113 g)
- ✿ Insects
- ⚡ Least concern

Family Parulidae
New World warblers
119 species

Black-throated blue warbler
Dendroica caerulescens
- ⊕ Breeds eastern North America; winters Caribbean & Central America
- ⋀ Breeds in deciduous & mixed woodland; winters in tropical forest
- ⊀ 4–5 in (10–13 cm)
- ⊀ 7–8 in (18–20 cm)
- ⊀ 0.3–0.4 oz (8–11 g)
- ✿ Insects, small fruits
- ⚡ Least concern

Yellow warbler
Dendroica petechia
- ⊕ Breeds in much of North America; winters in Caribbean, Central America & northern South America
- ⋀ Willows & other moist thickets, shrubland, fields, mangroves
- ⊀ 5 in (13 cm)
- ⊀ 6–8 in (16–20 cm)
- ⊀ 0.3–0.4 oz (9–11 g)
- ✿ Insects, spiders
- ⚡ Least concern

Cape May warbler
Dendroica tigrina
- ⊕ Breeds across Canadian boreal forest & south to northern USA; winters in Caribbean
- ⋀ Breeds in coniferous forest; winters in various habitats
- ⊀ 5 in (13 cm)
- ⊀ 7–9 in (19–22 cm)
- ⊀ 0.3–0.4 oz (9–12 g)
- ✿ Spruce budworms & other insects in summer; nectar & insects in winter
- ⚡ Least concern

American redstart
Setophaga ruticilla
- ⊕ Breeds southern Canada & eastern USA; winters Caribbean & from Mexico to northern South America
- ⋀ Moist, shrubby second-growth deciduous forest
- ⊀ 4–5 in (11–13 cm)
- ⊀ 6–7 in (16–19 cm)
- ⊀ 0.2–0.3 oz (6–9 g)
- ✿ Insects
- ⚡ Least concern

Family Passeridae
True sparrows
40 species

Cape sparrow
Passer melanurus
- ⊕ Southern Africa
- ⋀ Savanna, grassland
- ⊀ 6 in (16 cm)
- ⊀ 10 in (25 cm)
- ⊀ 1 oz (30 g)
- ✿ Seeds, insects
- ⚡ Least concern

Family Petroicidae
Australian robins
45 species

Tom tit
Petroica macrocephala
- ⊕ New Zealand
- ⋀ Forest, scrub
- ⊀ Up to 5 in (13 cm)
- ⊀ Up to 0.4 oz (11 g)
- ✿ Insects
- ⚡ Least concern

Black tomtit
Petroica macrocephala danefaerdi
- ⊕ New Zealand
- ⋀ Forest, scrub
- ⊀ Up to 5 in (13 cm)
- ⊀ Up to 0.4 oz (11 g)
- ✿ Insects
- ⚡ Not listed

Black robin
Petroica traversi
- ⊕ Chatham Islands (New Zealand)
- ⋀ Forested offshore islands
- ⊀ Up to 6 in (15 cm)
- ⊀ Up to 0.9 oz (25 g)
- ✿ Insects
- ⚡ Endangered

Family Ploceidae
Weavers
155 species

Slender-billed weaver bird
Ploceus pelzelni
- ⊕ Sub-Saharan Africa
- ⋀ Savanna
- ⊀ 0.6–0.7 in (14–19 mm)
- ⊀ 2–2.5 in (5–6.5 cm)
- ✿ Insects & other small invertebrates
- ⚡ Least concern

Family Ptilonorhynchidae
Bowerbirds
17 species

Satin bowerbird
Ptilonorhynchus violaceus
- ⊕ Eastern Australia
- ⋀ Rain forest, eucalypt forest, gardens
- ⊀ Up to 12 in (32 cm)
- ⊀ 7 oz (200 g)
- ✿ Leaves, fruits, insects
- ⚡ Least concern

Family Sturnidae
Starlings
107 species

Red-billed oxpecker
Buphagus erythrorhynchus
- ⊕ Sub-Saharan Africa
- ⋀ Open savanna
- ⊀ 8 in (20 cm)
- ⊀ 1.8 oz (50 g)
- ✿ Insects, ticks, ungulate blood
- ⚡ Least concern

European starling
Sturnus vulgaris
- ⊕ Europe & southwest Asia; introduced North America, South Africa, Australia, New Zealand
- ⋀ Gardens, fields
- ⊀ 8 in (20 cm)
- ⊀ 16 in (40 cm)
- ⊀ 2–3 oz (60–90 g)
- ✿ Insects
- ⚡ Least concern

Family Troglodytidae
Wrens
59 species

Cactus wren
Campylorhynchus brunneicapillus
- ⊕ Southwestern USA to central Mexico
- ⋀ Arid lowlands, mountain thorn scrub
- ⊀ 7–9 in (18–22 cm)
- ⊀ 5 in (12 cm)
- ⊀ 1–1.7 oz (30–50 g)
- ✿ Insects, spiders
- ⚡ Least concern

Family Turdidae
Thrushes & allies
305 species

American robin
Turdus migratorius
- ⊕ Throughout North America to Mexico
- ⋀ Forest, woodland, gardens
- ⊀ 8–11 in (20–28 cm)
- ⊀ 12–16 in (30–40 cm)
- ⊀ 2.7 oz (77 g)
- ✿ Insects, earthworms, fruits
- ⚡ Least concern

American robin
Turdus migratorius

BIRD SIZE COMPARISON

Gouldian finch
Erythrura gouldiae

Bee hummingbird
Mellisuga helenae

Hoopee
Upupa epops

Ostrich
Stuthio camelus

Greater flamingo
Phoenicopterus ruber roseus

King penguin
Aptenodytes patagonicus

King vulture
Sarcoramphus papa

Jungle fowl
Gallus gallus

Sulfur-breasted toucan
Ramphastos sulfuratus

Raggiana bird-of-paradise
Paradisaea raggiana

Satin bowerbird
Ptilonorhynchus violaceus

REPTILES

Reptiles were the first animals to conquer land. With their impermeable scaly skin, internal fertilization, and closed eggs, they were able to live independently of water. The class Reptilia—living reptiles—traditionally includes the four orders of turtles, crocodilians, tuatara, and squamates (which contains suborders of lizards, snakes, and worm lizards). With DNA evidence, many relationships in this class have become controversial. The traditional reptile groupings have been used here, but most are currently under revision. Crocodilians are in fact most closely related to birds, and turtles may belong in a separate class altogether. The suborders within Squamata are artificial, as limbless lizards, snakes, and worm lizards all evolved from lizards that lost their limbs. Only the status of the tuatara as an ancient order by itself is agreed upon.

Icon key

- 🌐 Distribution
- 🔺 Habitat
- 〰 Length
- ⤚ Tail length
- ✖ Weight
- ♀♂ Female/male
- ✪ Diet
- ⚡ Status

PHYLUM CHORDATA
CHORDATES
53,000+ species

CLASS REPTILIA
REPTILES
7,973 species

ORDER TESTUDINES
TORTOISES & TURTLES
293 species

Loggerhead turtle
Caretta caretta
- 🌐 Circumglobal, temperate to tropical oceans
- 🔺 Oceanic & coastal waters, nests on beaches
- 〰 30–40 in (76–100 cm)
- ✖ Up to 297 lb (135 kg)
- ✪ Mollusks, crustaceans, aquatic plants
- ⚡ Endangered

Pig-nosed turtle
Carettochelys insculpta
- 🌐 Australia, Indonesia, New Guinea
- 🔺 Tropical freshwater streams
- 〰 Up to 27 in (70 cm)
- ✖ Up to 45 lb (20 kg)
- ✪ Omnivorous
- ⚡ Vulnerable

Green turtle
Chelonia mydas
- 🌐 Circumtropical
- 🔺 Oceanic & coastal waters, nests on beaches
- 〰 5 ft (1.5 m)
- ✖ Up to 452 lb (205 kg)
- ⚡ Endangered

Painted turtle
Chrysemys picta
- 🌐 North America
- 🔺 Slow-moving shallow fresh water, ponds, lakes
- 〰 Up to 10 in (25 cm)
- ✖ 2 oz (57 g)
- ✪ Mollusks, crayfish, small fish, aquatic plants
- ⚡ Not listed

Leatherback turtle
Dermochelys coriacea
- 🌐 Circumglobal, cool temperate to tropics
- 🔺 Oceanic & coastal waters, nests on beaches
- 〰 6.5 ft (2 m)
- ✖ 550–1,984 lb (250–900 kg)
- ⚡ Critically endangered

Galápagos giant tortoise
Geochelone nigra (formerly *elephantopus*)
- 🌐 Galápagos Islands
- 🔺 Tropical grassland, dry forest
- 〰 4 ft (1.2 m)
- ✖ 660 lb (300 kg)
- ✪ Cactus, grasses, leaves, sedges, vines, fruits
- ⚡ Vulnerable

Desert tortoise
Gopherus agassizii
- 🌐 Parts of Nevada, California, Utah, Arizona & Mexico
- 🔺 Flat lands & rocky slopes in desert
- 〰 Up to 14.5 in (37 cm)
- ✖ 8–15 lb (3.5–6.8 kg)
- ✪ Green & dried plants, spring wildflowers, cactus pads
- ⚡ Vulnerable

Big-headed turtle
Platysternon megacephalum
- 🌐 Southeast Asia
- 🔺 Fast-moving streams & brooks
- 〰 Up to 16 in (40 cm)
- ✪ Fish, mollusks, worms
- ⚡ Endangered

Spider tortoise
Pyxis arachnoides
- 🌐 South coast of Madagascar
- 🔺 Woodland, bushland
- 〰 4 in (10 cm)
- ✪ Grasses, herbs
- ⚡ Vulnerable

ORDER CROCODILIA
CROCODILIANS
23 species

Philippine crocodile
Crocodylus mindorensis
- 🌐 Philippines
- 🔺 Freshwater lakes, ponds, tributaries, marshes; nests & basks on land
- 〰 Up to 10 ft (3 m)
- ✖ Up to 220 lb (100 kg)
- ✪ Aquatic invertebrates, small vertebrates
- ⚡ Critically endangered

Nile crocodile
Crocodylus niloticus
- 🌐 Sub-Saharan Africa
- 🔺 Freshwater marshes, mangrove swamps
- 〰 Up to 20 ft (6 m)
- ✖ Up to 1,609 lb (730 kg)
- ✪ Fish, mammals
- ⚡ Least concern

Saltwater crocodile
Crocodylus porosus
- 🌐 Southeast Asia, northern Australia
- 🔺 Coastal waters, rivers, billabongs
- 〰 Up to 24 ft (7 m)
- ✖ Up to 1.1 tons (1 t)
- ✪ Fish, waterfowl, mammals
- ⚡ Least concern

Siamese crocodile
Crocodylus siamensis
- 🌐 Thailand, Laos, Cambodia, Vietnam, Indonesia
- 🔺 Swamps, oxbow lakes, slow-moving sections of streams & rivers
- 〰 Up to 4 ft (3 m)
- ✪ Critically endangered

Gharial
Gavialis gangeticus
- 🌐 Northern South Asia from Pakistan to Burma
- 🔺 Larger rivers
- 〰 16 ft (5 m)
- ✖ 1,500 lb (680 kg)
- ✪ Fish
- ⚡ Critically endangered

Black caiman
Melanosuchus niger
- 🌐 Bolivia, Brazil, Colombia, Ecuador, French Guiana, Guyana, Peru
- 🔺 Slow-moving rivers, wetlands, flooded savannas
- 〰 20 ft (6 m)
- ⤚ 6.5 ft (2 m)
- ✖ 2,300 lb (1,043 kg)
- ✪ Fish, turtles, capybara, deer
- ⚡ Least concern

ORDER RHYNCOCEPHALIA
TUATARA
2 species

Tuatara
Sphenodon punctatus
- 🌐 New Zealand
- 🔺 Rodent-free offshore islands
- 〰 Up to 24 in (61 cm)
- ✖ 2.2 lb (1 kg)
- ✪ Invertebrates
- ⚡ Least concern (needs updating, threatened by habitat loss & introduction of Polynesian rat)

ORDER SQUAMATA
LIZARDS & SNAKES
7,655 species

Suborder Amphisbaenia
Worm lizards
140 species

Suborder Lacertilia
Lizards
4,560 species

Spiny-footed lizard
Acanthodactylus erythrurus
- 🌐 Algeria, Morocco, Portugal, Spain
- 🔺 Dry, sparsely vegetated habitats
- 〰 Up to 8 in (20 cm)
- ⤚ Up to 8 in (20 cm)
- ✪ Insects
- ⚡ Least concern

Marine iguana
Amblyrhynchus cristatus
- 🌐 Galápagos Islands
- 🔺 Shallow reefs, rocky coastlines
- 〰 18 in (46 cm)
- ⤚ 9 in (23 cm)
- ✖ 4.4 lb (2 kg)
- ✪ Red & green marine algae
- ⚡ Vulnerable

Fiji banded iguana
Brachylophus fasciatus
- 🌐 Fiji, Tonga
- 🔺 Arboreal
- 〰 Up to 32 in (81 cm) including tail
- ⤚ Up to 24 in (61 cm)
- ✖ 10.6 oz (300 g)
- ✪ Trees, shrubs, hibiscus flowers
- ⚡ Endangered

Strange-horned chameleon
Bradypodion xenorhinus
- 🌐 Albertine Rift (east Africa)
- 🔺 Montane forest
- ⤚ 11 in (28 cm)
- ✪ Insects
- ⚡ Not listed

Johnston's chameleon
Chamaeleo johnstoni
- 🌐 Albertine Rift (east Africa)
- 🔺 Montane forest
- 〰 12 in (30 cm)
- ✖ 3 oz (85 g)
- ✪ Crickets, worms
- ⚡ Not listed

Land iguana
Conolophus pallidus
- 🌐 Galápagos Islands
- 🔺 Arid lowlands
- 〰 39 in (100 cm)
- ⤚ 21 in (53 cm)
- ✖ 28 lb (13 kg)
- ✪ Low-growing plants & shrubs, such as cactus, fallen fruits, cactus pads
- ⚡ Vulnerable

Greater earless lizard
Cophosaurus texanus
- 🌐 Southernmost Arizona & Mexico (summer only), dry parts of Mexico to northern South America
- 🔺 Arid scrub & grassland, oak forest, tropical dry forest
- 〰 3.5 in (9 cm)
- ✖ 0.5–0.9 oz (15–25 g)
- ✪ Insects, spiders
- ⚡ Least concern

Panther chameleon
Furcifer pardalis
- 🌐 North Madagascar
- 🔺 Forest, scrubland
- ⤚ ♂ 18 in (46 cm), ♀ 9 in (23 cm)
- ✪ Insects
- ⚡ Not listed

Gila monster
Heloderma suspectum
- 🌐 Southwest USA to northern Mexico
- 🔺 Semiarid rocky regions of desert scrub & grassland
- 〰 Up to 22 in (56 cm)
- ⤚ 6 in (15 cm)
- ✖ 4 lb (1.8 kg)
- ✪ Small birds & mammals, eggs, lizards, frogs, insects, carrion
- ⚡ Near threatened

Sail-tailed water lizard
Hydrosaurus amboinensis
- 🌐 Southeast Asia, New Guinea
- 🔺 Rain forest near rivers
- 〰 Up to 40 in (100 cm)
- ✪ Plants, insects, rodents
- ⚡ Not listed

Thorny devil
Moloch horridus
- 🌐 Central Australia
- 🔺 Sandy arid & semiarid habitats
- 〰 Up to 4 in (10 cm)
- ⤚ 4 in (10 cm)
- ✖ 1–3 oz (30–90 g)
- ✪ Ants
- ⚡ Not listed

Greater short-horned lizard
Phrynosoma hernandesi
- 🌐 Southern Canada through central and western USA to northern Mexico
- 🔺 Shortgrass on the northern Great Plains, sagebrush in Great Basin
- 〰 2.5–6 in (6.4–15.2 cm)
- ✪ Invertebrates
- ⚡ Least concern

Italian wall lizard
Podarcis sicula
- 🌐 Western & central Europe; introduced USA
- 🔺 Forest, shrubland, grassland, beaches, farmland & urban areas
- 〰 Up to 8 in (20 cm)
- ⤚ Up to 5 in (13 cm)
- ✖ Up to 0.5 oz (15 g)
- ✪ Plants
- ⚡ Least concern

Green turtle
Chelonia mydas

Central bearded dragon
Pogona vitticeps
- 🌐 Central Australia
- 🔺 Rocky desert to dry woodland
- 📏 24 in (61 cm) including tail
- ⚖ 7 oz (200 g)
- ✴ Insects, mice, leaves, flowers
- ⚡ Not listed

Chuckwallah
Sauromalus obesus
- 🌐 Southwest USA to northern Mexico
- 🔺 Rocky desert, lava flows, hillsides, rocky outcrops
- 📏 Up to 9 in (23 cm) without tail
- 📏 Up to 9 in (23 cm)
- ⚖ 2 lb (900 g)
- ✴ Leaves, buds, flowers, fruits
- ⚡ Least concern

Desert spiny lizard
Sceloporus magister
- 🌐 Southwest USA
- 🔺 Arid to semiarid regions with rock piles & crevices for shelter
- 📏 10 in (25 cm)
- ✴ Insects, spiders, lizards, plant material
- ⚡ Least concern

Giant leaf–tailed gecko
Uroplatus fimbriatus
- 🌐 East Madagascar
- 🔺 Primary rain forest
- 📏 7 in (18 cm)
- ✴ Insects
- ⚡ Not listed

Gray monitor
Varanus griseus
- 🌐 North Africa, western Asia
- 🔺 Desert & semidesert habitats
- 📏 23 in (58 cm)
- 📏 Up to 34 in (87 cm)
- ⚖ Up to 6.3 lb (2.8 kg)
- ✴ Insects, other lizards, snakes, frogs, small mammals, bird & reptile eggs
- ⚡ Not listed

Komodo dragon
Varanus komodoensis
- 🌐 Lesser Sunda islands, Komodo, Flores, Gili, Montang, Padar
- 🔺 Arid forest & savanna on volcanic islands
- 📏 Up to 10 ft (3 m)
- ⚖ 200 lb (91 kg)
- ✴ Carrion, deer, pigs, water buffalo
- ⚡ Vulnerable

Suborder Serpentes
Snakes
2,955 species

Puff adder
Bitis arietans
- 🌐 Sub-Saharan Africa
- 🔺 Grassland, woodland, forest
- 📏 27–35 in (68–90 cm)
- ⚖ 13 lb (6 kg)
- ✴ Small mammals, birds, reptiles
- ⚡ Not listed

Sidewinding adder, Peringuey's desert adder
Bitis peringueyi
- 🌐 Southwest Africa
- 🔺 Desert
- 📏 Up to 12 in (32 cm)
- ✴ Lizards
- ⚡ Not listed

Boa constrictor
Boa constrictor
- 🌐 Central America, South America, Caribbean
- 🔺 Rain forest, savanna, semiarid areas
- 📏 Up to 13 ft (4 m)
- ⚖ 60 lb (27 kg)
- ✴ Meat, birds, monkeys, peccaries, rodents, iguanas, young crocodilians, lizards
- ⚡ Not listed

Luzon mangrove snake
Boiga dendrophila divergens
- 🌐 Philippines
- 🔺 Lowland rain forest, mangrove swamps
- 📏 6–8 ft (1.8–2.4 m)
- ✴ Small mammals, lizards, frogs, snakes, fish
- ⚡ Not listed (but common)

Western rattlesnake
Crotalus viridis
- 🌐 Most of western USA, northern Mexico, southwestern Canada
- 🔺 Open, dry habitats with rocky outcrops
- 📏 3–4 ft (90–120 cm)
- ✴ Small mammals, birds, reptiles
- ⚡ Least concern

Spotted harlequin snake
Homoroselaps lacteus
- 🌐 Southern Africa
- 🔺 Old termite mounds, grassland
- 📏 12–24 in (30–60 cm)
- ✴ Legless lizards, snakes
- ⚡ Not listed

Carpet python
Morelia spilota
- 🌐 Australia, New Guinea, Indonesia
- 🔺 Forest, woodland
- 📏 Up to 13 ft (4 m)
- ⚖ Up to 11 lb (5 kg)
- ✴ Small mammals, birds
- ⚡ Not listed

King cobra
Ophiophagus hannah
- 🌐 South & Southeast Asia
- 🔺 Dense forests
- 📏 Up to 18 ft (5.5 m)
- ⚖ 20 lb (9 kg)
- ✴ Other snakes
- ⚡ Not listed

Taipan
Oxyuranus scutellatus
- 🌐 Australia
- 🔺 Woodland, grassland
- 📏 Up to 10 ft (3 m)
- ✴ Small mammals, particularly rats & bandicoots
- ⚡ Not listed

Burmese python
Python molurus bivittatus
- 🌐 Myanmar, Thailand, Laos, Cambodia, Vietnam, Indonesia
- 🔺 Rain forest, grassland, marshes, swamps, rocky foothills, woodland, river valleys
- 📏 Up to 23 ft (7 m)
- ⚖ Up to 200 lb (91 kg)
- ✴ Birds, small and medium-sized mammals
- ⚡ Not listed (but uncommon)

Lataste's viper
Vipera latastei
- 🌐 Northern Morocco to northern Algeria, northwestern Tunisia
- 🔺 Coastal dune, rocky crevice
- 📏 Up to 23 in (60 cm)
- ✴ Reptiles, small mammals
- ⚡ Near threatened

Lebetine viper
Vipera lebetina
- 🌐 Subspecies distributed in northern Africa & central Asia
- 🔺 Desert & semidesert areas
- 📏 7 ft (2 m)
- ✴ Small mammals, lizards
- ⚡ Not listed

Lebetine viper
Vipera lebetina

AMPHIBIANS

Amphibians have smooth skin without scales. They lay eggs in water and metamorphose from a water-breathing juvenile to an air-breathing adult. The living amphibians evolved from the same common ancestor and are grouped into three orders: the frogs and toads (Anura), the salamanders and newts (Caudata), and the caecilians (Gymnophiona).

Icon key
- 🌐 Distribution
- 🔺 Habitat
- 📏 Length
- ⚖ Weight
- ✴ Diet
- ⚡ Status

PHYLUM CHORDATA
CHORDATES
53,000+ species

CLASS AMPHIBIA
AMPHIBIANS
5,558 species

ORDER CAUDATA
SALAMANDERS & NEWTS
472 species

Mudpuppy
Necturus maculosus

Spotted salamander
Ambystoma maculatum
- 🌐 Eastern USA, southern Canada
- 🔺 Deciduous forests with semi-permanent ponds
- 📏 6–10 in (15–25 cm)
- ✴ Mollusks, earthworms, centipedes, millipedes, spiders, insects
- ⚡ Least concern

Japanese giant salamander
Andrias japonicus
- 🌐 China, Japan
- 🔺 Brooks, ponds
- 📏 Up to 5 ft (1.5 m)
- ⚖ Up to 55 lb (25 kg)
- ✴ Fish, insects, crustaceans, worms
- ⚡ Near threatened

Mudpuppy
Necturus maculosus
- 🌐 Eastern & central North America
- 🔺 Ponds, streams, rivers
- 📏 Up to 19 in (48 cm)
- ✴ Crustaceans, fish, snails, insect larvae
- ⚡ Least concern

Red salamander
Pseudotriton ruber
- 🌐 Eastern USA
- 🔺 Deciduous forests, under fallen bark, logs, rocks; leaf litter of streams & brooks
- 📏 3–7 in (8–18 cm)
- ✴ Earthworms, insects, other salamanders
- ⚡ Least concern

European fire salamander
Salamandra salamandra
- 🌐 Western & southern Europe
- 🔺 Deciduous forest close to streams
- 📏 Up to 10 in (25 cm)
- ⚖ 0.7 oz (19 g)
- ✴ Insects, spiders, earthworms, slugs
- ⚡ Least concern

Alpine newt
Triturus alpestris
- 🌐 Europe from French Atlantic coastline east to the Ukrainian Carpathians, Romania, Bulgaria & the Balkans
- 🔺 Forest, ponds
- 📏 Up to 5 in (12 cm)
- ⚖ Up to 0.35 oz (10 g)
- ✴ Invertebrates
- ⚡ Least concern

ORDER GYMNOPHIONA
CAECILIANS
149 species

ORDER ANURA
FROGS & TOADS
4,937 species

Red-eyed tree frog
Agalychnis callidryas
- 🌐 Central America
- 🔺 Forest near rivers & ponds
- 📏 3 in (7.5 cm)
- ✴ Insects
- ⚡ Least concern

Oriental fire-bellied toad
Bombina orientalis
- 🌐 Korea, Japanese islands (Tsushima & Kyushu), northeast China, nearby parts of Russia
- 🔺 In or near ponds, lakes, swamps, slow-moving streams
- 📏 1.5–2 in (4–5 cm)
- ✴ Tadpoles eat algae, then insects; toadlets eat small invertebrates; adults eat beetles, ants, flies, other insects, worms, snails
- ⚡ Least concern

Cane toad
Bufo marinus
- 🌐 Rio Grande Valley of Texas south to central Amazon & southeastern Peru; widely introduced
- 🔺 Forested areas with semi-permanent water
- 📏 Up to 10 in (25 cm)
- ⚖ 4 oz (113 g)
- ✴ Insects, mollusks, lizards
- ⚡ Least concern

Golden toad
Bufo periglenes
- 🌐 Costa Rica
- 🔺 Rain forest, cloud forest
- 📏 2 in (5 cm)
- ⚖ 0.6 oz (20 g)
- ✴ Small invertebrates
- ⚡ Extinct

Water-holding frog
Cyclorana platycephala
- 🌐 Australia
- 🔺 Grassland, swamps, billabongs, claypans
- 📏 Up to 3 in (7.6 cm)
- ✴ Invertebrates
- ⚡ Least concern

Blue poison-dart frog
Dendrobates azureus
- 🌐 Suriname (South America)
- 🔺 Ponds & streams
- 📏 Up to 2 in (5 cm)
- ⚖ 0.11 oz (3 g)
- ✴ Insects
- ⚡ Vulnerable

Strawberry poison-dart frog
Dendrobates pumilio
- 🌐 Central America, especially Costa Rica
- 🔺 Rain forest
- 📏 Up to 1 in (2.5 cm)
- ✴ Tadpoles eat unfertilized eggs from mother, then algae & detritus; adults eat small invertebrates
- ⚡ Least concern

Tomato frog
Dyscophus antongilii
- 🌐 Northeast Madagascar
- 🔺 Primary rain forest, coastal forest, flooded areas
- 📏 3 in (7 cm)
- ✴ Insects
- ⚡ Near threatened

Hochstetter's frog
Leiopelma hochstetteri
- 🌐 New Zealand
- 🔺 Damp areas near streams
- 📏 Up to 1.8 in (4.5 cm)
- ✴ Insects
- ⚡ Vulnerable

Paradox frog
Pseudis paradoxa
- 🌐 South America
- 🔺 Marshes, permanent ponds in savanna, open forest in tropical lowlands
- 📏 2 in (5 cm)
- ✴ Larvae, small insects, tiny invertebrates
- ⚡ Least concern

Corroboree frog
Pseudophryne corroboree
- 🌐 Southeast Australia
- 🔺 Alpine sphagnum bogs
- 📏 Up to 1.4 in (3.5 cm)
- ✴ Insects
- ⚡ Critically endangered

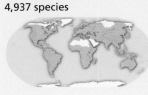

Corroboree frog
Pseudophryne corroboree

FISH

Fish are an immensely diverse array of animals, and most biologists regard the term "fish" as a convenient name, rather than a closely defined taxonomic entity, that describes aquatic vertebrates with gills and fins. There are various classification schemes for the fish but one of the most widely accepted recognizes five classes of living species grouped into two superclasses: the jawless fish of Agnatha, comprising hagfish and lampreys, and the jawed fish of Gnathostoma, comprising cartilaginous fish (sharks and rays), lobe-finned fish (lungfish and allies), and ray-finned fish (most bony fish).

Icon key

- ⊕ Distribution
- ⋏ Habitat
- ⬓ Length
- ⬗ Tail length
- ⬗ Weight
- ✪ Diet
- ⚡ Status

PHYLUM CHORDATA
CHORDATES
53,000+ species

SUPERCLASS AGNATHA
JAWLESS FISH
Lampreys & hagfish
105 species

SUPERCLASS GNATHOSTOMATA
JAWED FISH
c. 26,000 species

CARTILAGINOUS FISH

CLASS CHONDRICHTHYES
CARTILAGINOUS FISH
999 species

SUBCLASS ELASMOBRANCHII
SHARKS, RAYS & ALLIES
962 species

SUPERORDER SELACHIMORPHA SHARKS
415 species

Long-tailed thresher shark
Alopias vulpinus
- ⊕ Worldwide, cool to temperate oceans
- ⋏ Open ocean & coastal waters
- ⬓ Up to 25 ft (7.5 m)
- ⬗ Up to 770 lb (348 kg)
- ✪ Schooling fish, crustaceans, squid
- ⚡ Data deficient

Great white shark
Carcharodon carcharias
- ⊕ Worldwide, temperate to subtropical oceans
- ⋏ Open ocean & coastal waters
- ⬓ Up to 20 ft (6 m)
- ⬗ 2.1 tons (1.9 t)
- ✪ Fish, turtles, marine mammals
- ⚡ Vulnerable

Whale shark
Rhincodon typus
- ⊕ Circumtropical and warm-temperate seas
- ⋏ Open ocean, coastal waters
- ⬓ Up to 46 ft (14 m)
- ⬗ Up to 15 tons (13.6 t)
- ✪ Plankton
- ⚡ Vulnerable

Greenland shark
Somniosus microcephalus
- ⊕ Arctic Ocean to subtropical Atlantic Ocean
- ⋏ From beneath the ice in Arctic, to deep sea in subtropics
- ⬓ 24 ft (7.3 m)
- ⬗ 1.2 tons (1.1 t)
- ✪ Bony fish, squid, cuttlefish
- ⬓ Near threatened

Scalloped hammerhead shark
Sphyrna lewini
- ⊕ Tropical & warm-temperate oceans
- ⋏ Open ocean & coastal waters
- ⬓ Up to 14 ft (4.3 m)
- ⬗ Up to 330 lb (150 kg)
- ✪ Fish, cephalopods, crustaceans, other sharks
- ⚡ Near threatened

SUPERORDER BATOIDEA RAYS & ALLIES
547 species

Giant manta
Manta birostris
- ⊕ Circumtropical oceans
- ⋏ Open ocean
- ⬓ 30 ft (9.1 m)
- ⬗ 3.3 tons (3 t)
- ✪ Tiny animals filtered from plankton
- ⬓ Near threatened

Giant devil ray
Mobula mobular
- ⊕ Eastern Atlantic: off Ireland, Mediterranean Sea, Portugal to Senegal, possibly northwest Atlantic
- ⋏ Marine waters over continental shelves & near oceanic islands
- ⬓ Up to 16.5 ft (5 m)
- ⬗ Up to 77 lb (35 kg)
- ✪ Plankton, small fish
- ⚡ Endangered

Largetooth sawfish
Pristis microdon
- ⊕ Tropical Indian Ocean, Southeast Asia, New Guinea
- ⋏ Shallow coastal waters, river mouths, larger rivers
- ⬓ Up to 23 ft (7 m)
- ⬗ 1,322 lb (600 kg)
- ✪ Benthic animals
- ⚡ Critically endangered

SUBCLASS HOLOCEPHALI
CHIMAERAS
37 species

BONY FISH

CLASS SARCOPTERYGII
LOBE-FINNED FISH
11 species

Coelacanth
Latimeria chalumnae
- ⊕ South Africa to Kenya, Comoros Islands, Madagascar
- ⋏ Underwater volcanic slopes 490–2,300 ft (150–700 m) below surface
- ⬓ 6.5 ft (2 m)
- ⬗ 209 lb (95 kg)
- ✪ Cuttlefish, squid, octopus, fish
- ⚡ Critically endangered

Australian lungfish
Neoceratodus forsteri
- ⊕ Burnett & Mary rivers (Queensland, Australia)
- ⋏ Fresh water
- ⬓ Up to 5 ft (1.5 m)
- ⬗ Up to 90 lb (40 kg)
- ✪ Frogs, fish, invertebrates, some plants
- ⚡ Vulnerable

CLASS ACTINOPTERYGII
RAY-FINNED FISH
c. 25,000 species

SUBCLASS CHONDROSTEI
BICHIRS & ALLIES
52 species

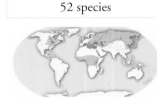

American paddlefish
Polyodon spathula
- ⊕ Mississippi River system, including Missouri River into Montana, Ohio River, major tributaries
- ⋏ Slow-flowing water of large rivers, usually deeper than 4 ft (1.2 m)
- ⬓ Up to 7 ft (2.2 m)
- ⬗ Up to 220 lb (100 kg)
- ✪ Zooplankton
- ⚡ Vulnerable

SUBCLASS NEOPTERYGII
NEOPTERYGIANS
24,615 species

INFRACLASS HOLOSTEI
BOWFINS & GARS
8 species

INFRACLASS TELEOSTEI
TELEOSTS
24,607 species

SUPERORDER OSTEOGLOSSOMORPHA
BONYTONGUES & ALLIES
221 species

Pirarucu
Arapaima gigas
- ⊕ Amazon River Basin, South America
- ⋏ Rain-forest rivers
- ⬓ Up to 15 ft (4.5 m)
- ⬗ Up to 440 lb (200 kg)
- ✪ Catfish, small birds
- ⚡ Data deficient

SUPERORDER ELOPOMORPHA
EELS & ALLIES
911 species

Gulper eel, Pelican eel
Eurypharynx pelecanoides
- ⊕ Worldwide, tropical to temperate oceans
- ⋏ Deep sea, at depths of 3,000–27,000 ft (900–8,000 m)
- ⬓ 24–40 in (60–100 cm), including long whiplike tail
- ✪ Other fish, shrimps, plankton
- ⚡ Not listed

SUPERORDER CLUPEOMORPHA
SARDINES & ALLIES
378 species

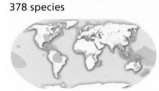

SUPERORDER OSTARIOPHYSI
CATFISH & ALLIES
7,023 species

Long-tailed thresher shark
Alopias vulpinus

Great white shark
Carcharodon carcharias

Giant manta
Manta birostris

Sockeye salmon
Oncorhynchus nerka

SUPERORDER PROTACANTHOPTERYGII SALMONS & ALLIES

502 species

Cutthroat trout
Oncorhynchus clarkii
- Freshwater rivers & streams in western North America; Pacific Coast ocean; widely introduced
- Relatively small streams, with gravel bottoms & gentle gradients; some live in ocean & spawn in streams
- 6–40 in (15–100 cm)
- Up to 42 lb (19 kg)
- Small fish, crustaceans, insects
- Not listed

Sockeye salmon
Oncorhynchus nerka
- Pacific coast of North America from Alaska to northern California; coastal northern Japan; Russian Far East north to Siberia
- Winters in open ocean; enters rivers in summer; spawns in lake tributaries
- Up to 33 in (84 cm)
- Average 5–8 lb (2.3–3.6 kg), but up to 15 lb (6.8 kg)
- Squid, small fish, plankton
- Not listed

SUPERORDER STENOPTERYGII DRAGONFISH & ALLIES

415 species

Stoplight loosejaw
Malacosteus niger
- Atlantic, Pacific & Indian oceans, South China Sea
- Deep sea
- 6–8 in (15–20 cm)
- Crustaceans
- Not listed

SUPERORDER CYCLOSQUAMATA LIZARDFISH & ALLIES

229 species

SUPERORDER SCOPELOMORPHA LANTERNFISH

251 species

SUPERORDER POLYMIXIOMORPHA BEARDFISH

10 species

SUPERORDER LAMPRIDIOMORPHA OPAHS & ALLIES

23 species

Oarfish
Regalecus glesne
- Temperate to tropical Pacific & Atlantic oceans
- Open ocean
- Up to 26 ft (8 m), with unconfirmed reports of fish twice that length
- 600 lb (270 kg)
- Crustaceans, jellyfish, squid
- Not listed

SUPERORDER PARACANTHOPTERYGII CODS, ANGLERFISH & ALLIES

1,382 species

Gelatinous blindfish
Aphyonus gelatinosus
- Eastern Atlantic, southwest Pacific, western Indian Ocean
- Deep sea, benthic
- 6 in (15 cm)
- Benthic organisms
- Not listed

Arctic cod
Boreogadus saida
- Arctic Ocean
- Under ice, water column
- 16 in (40 cm)
- Zooplankton, benthic animals
- Not listed

Krøyer's deep-sea anglerfish
Ceratias holboelli
- Circumglobal, tropical to temperate waters
- Deep sea
- 20–30 in (50–75 cm)
- Zooplankton, benthic animals
- Not listed

SUPERORDER ACANTHOPTERYGII SPINY-RAYED FISH

13,262 species

Humphead wrasse
Cheilinus undulatus
- Red Sea, Indian & Pacific oceans
- Coral reefs, mangroves, seagrass beds
- Up to 7.5 ft (2.3 m)
- Up to 421 lb (191 kg)
- Mollusks, fish, crustaceans
- Endangered

Black swallower
Chiasmodon niger
- Atlantic, Indian & Pacific oceans
- Tropical & subtropical waters
- 10 in (25 cm)
- Bony fish
- Not listed

Blacksmith
Chromis punctipinnis
- Temperate eastern Pacific
- Shore waters
- 10 in (25 cm)
- Planktonic invertebrates, benthic algae, weeds
- Not listed

Potato grouper
Epinephelus tukula
- Indian & western Pacific oceans
- Coral reefs
- Up to 6.5 ft (2 m)
- Up to 242 lb (110 kg)
- Fish, crustaceans
- Not listed

Naked dragonfish, Ploughfish
Gymnodraco acuticeps
- Southern Ocean
- Near bottom at depths of 0–1,800 ft (0–550 m)
- Up to 13.4 in (34 cm)
- Other fish, small crustaceans, bristleworms
- Not listed

Blue marlin
Makaira nigricans
- Tropical to warm temperate Atlantic
- Open ocean
- 16.5 ft (5 m)
- Up to 1,800 lb (820 kg)
- Dolphinfish, tuna, squid
- Not listed

Black-spotted sweetlips
Plectorhinchus gaterinus
- Indian Ocean
- Coral reefs
- Up to 18 in (46 cm)
- Crustaceans, mollusks
- Not listed

Hawaiian turkeyfish
Pterois sphex
- Hawaiian waters
- Coastal waters, benthic
- 9 in (23 cm)
- Crabs, shrimps, fish
- Not listed

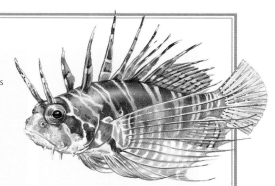

Hawaiian turkeyfish
Pterois sphex

Parrotfish, Stoplight parrotfish
Sparisoma viride
- Tropical western Atlantic, including Caribbean Sea
- Coral reefs
- Up to 22 in (55 cm)
- Up to 3.5 lb (1.6 kg)
- Coral polyps, algae growing on rocks
- Not listed

Great barracuda
Sphyraena barracuda
- Indian, Pacific & Atlantic oceans
- Warm seas
- 42 in (106 cm)
- 4 in (10 cm)
- 88 lb (40 kg)
- Other fish
- Not listed

Yellowtail scad
Trachurus novaezelandiae
- Australia, New Zealand
- Cool to temperate coastal waters
- Up to 20 in (50 cm)
- Crustaceans
- Not listed

FISH SIZE COMPARISON

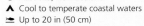

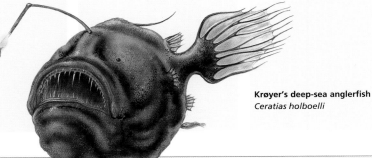

Whale shark
Rhincodon typus

Great white shark
Carcharodon carcharias

Black marlin
Makaira indica

Wels catfish
Silurus glanis

Great barracuda
Sphyraena barracuda

Green moray
Gymnothorax funebris

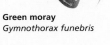

Footballer cod
Plectropomus laevis

Blackfin pacu
Colossoma macropomum

Red bigeye fish
Priacanthus macracanthus

Blue tang
Acanthurus coeruleus

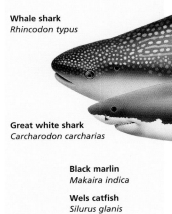

Gelatinous blindfish
Aphyonus gelatinosus

Stoplight loosejaw
Malacosteus niger

Krøyer's deep-sea anglerfish
Ceratias holboelli

INVERTEBRATES

More than 95 percent of animals are invertebrates. They are characterized by a structure that they all lack: a backbone or vertebral column. Invertebrates are divided into about 30 phyla, each displaying a distinct body form. Their evolutionary relationships can be inferred from their anatomy, their early development, and more recently from molecular analyses, particularly DNA. Features that define phyla include the organization of the body from a loose association of cells (Porifera), through tissue formation (Cnidaria), to the development of organs (Platyhelminthes). The acquisition of a fluid-filled body cavity was a defining point in evolution that allowed animals, such as Nematoda, Annelida, and many other phyla of worms, to move about by a hydraulic system driven by fluid pressure. While these phyla are soft-bodied, others are protected and supported by various types of skeletons, such as shells in Mollusca and a jointed exoskeleton in Arthropoda. The way in which embryos develop divide many advanced phyla into two lineages, one leading through the Echinodermata to the Chordata, the phylum to which vertebrates belong, the other containing the bulk of animal phyla. The continual identification of new invertebrate species indicates that the 1.3 million or so known invertebrates are nowhere near the full inventory.

Icon key
⊕ Distribution	✎ Wingspan	✪ Diet
⩕ Habitat	✄ Weight	⚡ Status
✳ Length		

PHYLUM CHORDATA
CHORDATES
53,000+ species

INVERTEBRATE CHORDATES
2,030+ SPECIES

SUBPHYLUM UROCHORDATA
SEA SQUIRTS
2,000+ species

SUBPHYLUM CEPHALOCHORDATA
LANCELETS
30 species

PHYLUM PORIFERA
SPONGES
9,000 species

PHYLUM CNIDARIA
CNIDARIANS
Sea anemones, corals, jellyfish & allies
9,000 species

Lion's mane jellyfish
Cyanea capillata
- ⊕ Arctic Ocean to northern Pacific & Atlantic oceans
- ⩕ Open ocean
- ✳ Up to 120 ft (36.5 m) including tentacles; bell diameter 7.5 ft (2.3 m)
- ✪ Zooplankton, small fish, comb jellies, moon jellies
- ⚡ Not listed

Hula skirt siphonophore
Physophora hydrostatica
- ⊕ East Pacific, West Atlantic
- ⩕ Midwater
- ✳ Up to 16 in (41 cm) including tentacles
- ✪ Phytoplankton, zooplankton
- ⚡ Not listed

PHYLUM PLATYHELMINTHES
FLATWORMS
13,000 species

PHYLUM NEMATODA
ROUNDWORMS
20,000+ species

PHYLUM MOLLUSCA
MOLLUSKS
Bivalves, snails, squid & allies
75,000 species

Giant squid
Architeuthis dux
- ⊕ All oceans but rare in tropical & polar regions
- ⩕ Deep ocean, often near continental & island slopes
- ✳ ♂ up to 33 ft (10 m) including tentacles, ♀ up to 43 ft (13 m) including tentacles
- ✄ ♂ up to 330 lb (150 kg), ♀ up to 610 lb (275 kg)
- ✪ Deep-sea fish, other squid
- ⚡ Not listed

Pacific banana slug
Ariolimax columbianus
- ⊕ Pacific coast of North America from Alaska to southern California
- ⩕ Moist forest floor, under logs & other debris
- ✳ Up to 10 in (25 cm)
- ✄ 0.7–2.6 oz (21–75 g)
- ✪ Fungus, leaves, dead plant materials, animal droppings
- ⚡ Not listed (but common)

Blue-ringed octopus
Hapalochlaena maculosa
- ⊕ Southern Australia
- ⩕ Shallow coastal waters
- ✳ Body 2.5 in (5 cm), arms 4 in (10 cm)
- ✄ 1 oz (28 g)
- ✪ Small crustaceans
- ⚡ Not listed

Caribbean reef octopus
Octopus briareus
- ⊕ Western Atlantic, Bahamas, Caribbean, coast of northern South America
- ⩕ Coral reefs, rocks, seagrass beds
- ✳ 24 in (60 cm)
- ✄ 3.3 lb (1.5 kg)
- ✪ Crabs, shrimps, lobster, fish
- ⚡ Not listed

PHYLUM ANNELIDA
SEGMENTED WORMS
12,000 species

Giant tube worm
Riftia pachyptila
- ⊕ Pacific Ocean
- ⩕ Near deep-sea volcanic vents at depths of more than 1 mile (1.6 km)
- ✳ Up to 7.9 ft (2.4 m)
- ✪ Relies on chemosynthetic symbiotic bacteria for nutrients
- ⚡ Not listed

PHYLUM ARTHROPODA
ARTHROPODS
1.1 million+ species

Caribbean reef octopus
Octopus briareus

Horseshoe crab
Limulus polyphemus

SUBPHYLUM CHELICERATA
CHELICERATES
81,000+ species

CLASS ARACHNIDA
ARACHNIDS
80,000 species

CLASS MEROSTOMATA
HORSESHOE CRABS
4 species

Horseshoe crab
Limulus polyphemus
- ⊕ East coast of North & Central America; spawns in Delaware & Chesapeake bays
- ⩕ Sandy beaches for spawning; shallow bays for juveniles; ocean for adults
- ✳ Up to 2 ft (60 cm)
- ✄ Up to 10 lb (4.5 kg)
- ✪ Sea worms, mollusks
- ⚡ Near threatened

CLASS PYCNOGONIDA
SEA SPIDERS
1,000 species

SUBPHYLUM MYRIAPODA
MYRIAPODS
Centipedes & allies
13,500 species

SUBPHYLUM CRUSTACEA
CRUSTACEANS
42,000 species

Krill, Antarctic krill
Euphausia superba
- ⊕ Southern Ocean
- ⩕ Open ocean
- ✳ 1.5–2.5 in (4–6 cm)
- ✄ 0.4 oz (1 g)
- ✪ Phytoplankton
- ⚡ Not listed (but abundant)

SUBPHYLUM HEXAPODA
HEXAPODS
1 million+ species

CLASS INSECTA
INSECTS
1 million+ species in 29 orders, including the 11 orders listed below

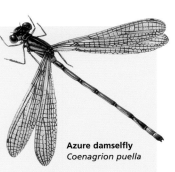

Azure damselfly
Coenagrion puella

ORDER ODONATA
DRAGONFLIES & DAMSELFLIES
5,500 species

ORDER MANTODEA
MANTIDS
2,000 species

ORDER BLATTODEA
COCKROACHES
4,000 species

ORDER ISOPTERA
TERMITES
2,750 species

ORDER ORTHOPTERA
CRICKETS & GRASSHOPPERS
20,000+ species

Cave weta, Wetapunga
Deinacrida heteracantha
- ⊕ New Zealand
- ⩕ Rain forest
- ✳ Up to 4 in (10 cm)
- ✄ Up to 2.5 oz (70 g)
- ✪ Leaves
- ⚡ Vulnerable

Migratory locust
Locusta migratoria
- ⊕ Africa, Asia, Australia
- ⩕ Widespread
- ✳ 1.5–2.5 in (4–6 cm)
- ✄ 0.07 oz (2 g)
- ✪ Vegetation
- ⚡ Not listed (but abundant)

ORDER HEMIPTERA
BUGS
80,000+ species

ORDER COLEOPTERA
BEETLES
370,000+ species

Seven-spotted ladybug/ Seven-spot ladybird
Coccinella septempunctata
- ⊕ Europe, northern Asia, introduced North America & Oceania
- ⩕ Orchards, gardens
- ✳ 0.2 in (5 mm)
- ✪ Aphids
- ⚡ Not listed

Stag beetle
Lucanus cervus
- ⊕ UK, continental Europe, Turkey, Syria
- ⩕ Oak forest, woodland, parks, gardens
- ✳ ♂ up to 3.5 in (9 cm) ♀ up to 2.5 in (6 cm)
- ✪ Larvae feed on rotting wood; adults feed on sap
- ⚡ Not listed (but legally protected in several European countries)

Fog-basking beetle
Onymacris unguicularis
- ⊕ Namib Desert
- ⩕ Sand dunes
- ✳ Up to 0.9 in (22 mm)
- ✪ Detritus
- ⚡ Not listed

Monarch butterfly
Danaus plexippus

Camberwell beauty
Nymphalis antiopa

ORDER DIPTERA
FLIES
120,000 species

ORDER LEPIDOPTERA
BUTTERFLIES & MOTHS
165,000 species

Monarch butterfly
Danaus plexippus
- ⊕ North America (Canada to Mexico), Europe, Australia
- ⋀ Forest, fields, roadsides, gardens
- ☀ 2 in (5 cm)
- ⚲ 4 in (10 cm)
- ✪ Larvae feed on milkweeds, adults feed on flower nectar
- ⚡ Not listed (abundant but wintering sites in Mexico in peril)

Julia butterfly
Dryas iulia
- ⊕ Southern Texas & Florida to Brazil
- ⋀ Tropical forest
- ☀ 2 in (5 cm)
- ⚲ 3.5 in (9 cm)
- ✪ Flower nectar
- ⚡ Not listed

Common buckeye
Junonia coenia
- ⊕ USA, Mexico
- ⋀ Open fields, beaches
- ☀ 1.1 in (2.8 cm)
- ⚲ 1.8–2.8 in (4.5–7 cm)
- ✪ Plants such as gerardias, toadflax & plantain
- ⚡ Not listed (but stable)

Red-spotted purple
Limenitis arthemis
- ⊕ Eastern USA, west to Mississippi River & south to Florida
- ⋀ Moist woodland, suburban areas
- ☀ 1.6 in (4.1 cm)
- ⚲ 2.2–4 in (5.7–10.1 cm)
- ✪ Cherry trees, other trees
- ⚡ Not listed (but stable)

Blue morpho butterfly
Morpho menelaus
- ⊕ Central & South America
- ⋀ Rain forest
- ☀ 6 in (15 cm)
- ⚲ 6 in (15 cm)
- ✪ Flowers, leaves, sap, juices
- ⚡ Not listed

Poseidon birdwing butterfly
Ornithoptera priamus poseidon
- ⊕ New Guinea
- ⋀ Rain forest
- ⚲ Up to 5 in (12.5 cm)
- ✪ Vines
- ⚡ Not listed (but locally common)

Eastern tiger swallowtail
Papilio glaucus
- ⊕ Eastern North America
- ⋀ Deciduous woodlands
- ☀ 2.2 in (5.5 cm)
- ⚲ 3.5 in (9 cm)
- ✪ Wild black cherry & tulip tree
- ⚡ Not listed (but stable)

Red Helen butterfly
Papilio helenus
- ⊕ Throughout South & Southeast Asia
- ⋀ Evergreen forest
- ⚲ 4–4.7 in (10–12 cm)
- ✪ Larvae feed on plants in the family Rutaceae, including cultivated citrus species such as lime & orange
- ⚡ Not listed (but common)

Apollo butterfly
Parnassius apollo
- ⊕ Europe
- ⋀ Mountain
- ⚲ 2.8–3.5 in (7–9 cm)
- ✪ Nectar
- ⚡ Vulnerable

Sphinx moth
(larvae = Tomato hornworm)
Protoparce quinquemaculata
- ⋀ North America
- ⋀ Croplands
- ⚲ 3 in (7.6 cm)
- ✪ Larvae are pests of corn, cotton & tomato plants
- ⚡ Not listed

Painted lady
Vanessa cardui
- ⊕ Every continent except Antarctica
- ⋀ Any open habitat
- ☀ 1.1 in (2.8 cm)
- ⚲ 2 in (5 cm)
- ✪ Larvae feed on thistles & other plants; adults feed on flower nectar
- ⚡ Not listed (but abundance varies from year to year)

ORDER HYMENOPTERA
BEES, WASPS, ANTS & SAWFLIES
198,000 species

ORDER PHASMATODEA
STICK & LEAF INSECTS
3,000 species

Lord Howe Island phasmid, Land lobster
Dryococelus australis
- ⊕ Lord Howe Island Group (Australia)
- ⋀ Shrubland, hollow trunks of living trees in forest
- ☀ Up to 5 in (12 cm)
- ✪ Leaves of *Melaleuca howea* & other trees
- ⚡ Critically endangered

Lesser purple emperor
Apatura ilia

Map butterfly
Araschnia levana

CLASS COLLEMBOLA
SPRINGTAILS
7,900 species

CLASS PROTURA
PROTURANS
500 species

CLASS DIPLURA
DIPLURANS
800 species

PHYLUM ECHINODERMATA
ECHINODERMS
Sea stars, sea urchins & allies
6,000 species

Antarctic sea urchin
Sterechinus neumayeri
- ⊕ Southern Ocean near Antarctica & subantarctic islands
- ⋀ Benthic, most abundant in shallow waters
- ☀ 2.8 in (7 cm)
- ✪ Phytoplankton, zooplankton, sponges, bristleworms, seal feces
- ⚡ Not listed

PHYLUM NEMERTEA
RIBBON WORMS
900 species

PHYLUM ENTOPROCTA
GOBLET WORMS
150 species

PHYLUM TARDIGRADA
WATER BEARS
600 species

PHYLUM CTENOPHORA
COMB JELLIES
100 species

PHYLUM ROTIFERA
ROTIFERS
Wheel animals
1,800 species

PHYLUM HEMICHORDATA
HEMICHORDATES
Acorn worms
90 species

PHYLUM CHAETOGNATHA
ARROW WORMS
90 species

PHYLUM GASTROTRICHA
GASTROTRICHS
700 species

PHYLUM KINORHYNCHA
SPINY-CROWN WORMS
150 species

PHYLUM PHORONIDA
HORSESHOE WORMS
20 species

PHYLUM ONYCHOPHORA
VELVET WORMS
100+ species

PHYLUM BRACHIOPODA
BRACHIOPODS
Lamp shells
350 species

PHYLUM BRYOZOA
BRYOZOANS
Lace animals
5,000 species

PHYLUM SIPUNCULA
PEANUT WORMS
150 species

PHYLUM ECHIURA
SPOON WORMS
160 species

PHYLUM LORICIFERA
BRUSHHEADS
22 species

PHYLUM PRIAPULIDA
PHALLUS WORMS
17 species

PHYLUM NEMATOMORPHA
HORSEHAIR WORMS
240 species

PHYLUM ACANTHOCEPHALA
SPINY-HEADED WORMS
1,000 species

PHYLUM POGONOPHORA
BEARD WORMS
80 species

PHYLUM GNATHOSTOMULIDA
SAND WORMS
80 species

PHYLUM CYCLIOPHORA
CYCLIOPHORANS
3 species

PHYLUM PLACOZOA
PLACOZOANS
2 species

PHYLUM ORTHONECTIDA
ORTHONECTIDS
20 species

PHYLUM RHOMBOZOA
RHOMBOZOANS
150 species

CORAL REEF

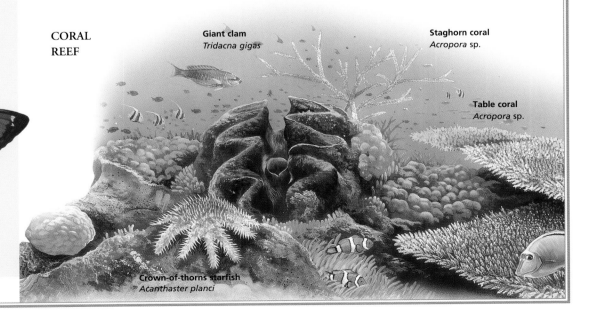

Giant clam
Tridacna gigas

Staghorn coral
Acropora sp.

Table coral
Acropora sp.

Crown-of-thorns starfish
Acanthaster planci

GLOSSARY

Adaptation

A change in an animal's behavior or body that allows it to survive and breed in new conditions.

Amphibian

A vertebrate animal, similar to a reptile, that lays its eggs in water and that spends its early life in water and its adult life on land.

Anal fin

An unpaired fin on the lower surface of a fish's abdomen. It plays an important role in swimming.

Antarctic Polar Frontal Zone

A zone, also known as the Antarctic Convergence, that surrounds Antarctica, where Antarctic waters mix with the warmer, more northerly, subantarctic waters.

Aquatic

Living all or most of the time in water; cf terrestrial.

Arboreal

Living all or most of the time in trees.

Arthropod

An animal with jointed legs and a hard exoskeleton; includes insects, spiders, crustaceans, centipedes, and millipedes.

Bacteria

Microscopic lifeforms that are usually just a single cell.

Baleen

The comblike, fibrous plates found in some whales; often referred to as whalebone.

Benthic

Relating to or occurring at the bottom of a body of water or the depths of the ocean.

Billabong

A waterhole in a branch of an Australian river that is dry during the dry season and that fills when the river is in flood.

Biodiversity

The total number of species of plants and animals in a particular location.

Biodiversity hotspot

An area where the diversity of plant and wildlife species is under threat.

Biogeography

The study of the way plants and animals are distributed.

Bioluminescence

Light produced by living organisms.

Biome

Large major habitat type that is generally identified with its dominant vegetation type. Biomes include grasslands, coniferous forests, deserts, and tundra.

Biosphere

The part of the world that can support life.

Bivalve

A mollusk, such as an oyster or a mussel, that has two shells that are joined at a hinge.

Braided watercourse

Part of a stream or river that has interlacing channels that combine and divide in irregular patterns.

Breach

The action of a whale as it springs upward from the water.

Browser

A plant-eating mammal that uses its hands or lips to pick leaves from trees and bushes.

Caecilian

A tropical, wormlike, burrowing amphibian.

Canopy

Of a forest, the upper layer composed entirely of trees.

Captive breeding

The breeding by humans of endangered animal species under controlled conditions.

Carapace

A hard outer covering, such as a turtle's shell; this provides protection for an animal's body.

Carnivore

An animal that eats mainly meat.

Carrion

The rotting flesh and other remains of dead animals.

Cartilaginous fish

A fish with a skeleton made of cartilage, such as a shark, ray, or chimaera.

Casque

A bony or horny protrusion on the head of some birds, such as cassowaries.

Cays

Small, sandy islands that form on coral reefs.

Cephalic fins

Hornlike extensions of the pectoral fins of manta rays and their relatives.

Cerebral cortex

The thin, outer layer of gray matter in the hemispheres in the brains of humans and upper mammals.

Colonial species

Species of birds and other animals that breed together in large groups.

Continental drift

The theory that the present distribution of continents is the result of the fragmentation of one or more pre-existing supercontinents that have drifted apart.

Copepod

One of a number of tiny freshwater and marine crustaceans.

Coral bleaching

The loss of color affecting coral reefs when the algae that live in them are killed or forced out.

Coteries

Groups of animals, within larger populations, that form communities and cooperate in providing food and shelter for their members.

Coverts

Small feathers that cover the base of a bird's wing and tail feathers.

Cranium

The skull of a vertebrate animal. The cranium encloses the brain.

Crepuscular

Becoming active around dusk or in the early evening.

Crop

A thin-walled, saclike pocket of the gullet, used by birds to store food before digestion or to feed chicks by regurgitation.

Cryptic

Hard to detect as a result of color, shape, or behavioral patterns.

Deciduous forest

An area dominated by woody perennial plants that shed their leaves at a particular time, season, or growth stage.

Decomposer

An organism, such as a bacterium or a fungus, that consumes dead organisms and returns them to ecological cycles.

Deep-sea hydrothermal vent

A spring of superheated, mineral-rich water found on some ridges deep in the ocean.

Deforestation

The cutting down of forest trees for timber, or to clear land for farming or building.

Dermal

To do with the skin, especially the dermis, the second layer of an animal's skin.

Diatom

One of many kinds of tiny algae in marine and freshwater environments.

Dimorphic

Having two distinct forms within a species. Sexual dimorphism is the situation in which the male and female of a species differ in size and/or appearance.

Display

Behavior used by an animal to communicate with its own species, or with other animals.

Diurnal

Active during the day. Most reptiles are diurnal because they rely on the Sun's heat to provide energy.

Diversity

The variety of plant and animal species in the natural world.

Dormant

To be in a sleeplike state, often because of environmental conditions; the body's activity slows for this period.

Echolocation

A system of navigation that relies on sound rather than sight or touch. Porpoises, dolphins, many bats, and some birds use echolocation.

Ecology

The interrelationship between organisms and the environment in which they exist, or the study of this interrelationship.

Ecosystem

A community of plants and animals and the environment to which they are adapted.

Egg tooth

A special scale on the tip of the upper lip of a hatchling lizard or snake. It is used to break a hole in the egg so that the newborn animal can escape.

Electroreceptors

Specialized organs found in some fish and mammals that detect electrical activity from the bodies of other animals.

El Niño

A warm current of equatorial water flowing southward down the northwest coast of South America. When pronounced and persistent, it results in rainfall and temperature anomalies.

Embryo

An unborn animal in the earliest stages of development. An embryo may grow inside its mother's body, or in an egg outside her body.

Emergent

A forest tree that is taller than those around it.

Emissions

Substances, such as gases and fluids, that are discharged into the environment.

Endemic

A species, or other taxon, found only in one habitat or region. For example, emus are endemic to Australia.

Ephemeral wetlands

Areas that become flooded in spring and early summer or after heavy rain.

Epiphyte

A plant that grows on a tree or other plant, but does not feed on or damage its host.

Estivate

To spend a period of time in a state of inactivity to avoid unfavorable conditions.

Evolution

Gradual change in plants and animals, over many generations, in response to their environment.

Exotic

A foreign or non-native species of animal or plant, often introduced into a habitat by humans.

Extinction

The death of a species.

Filter feeder

An animal that obtains food by straining small prey from seawater.

Fissure

A fracture in the ground. In volcanic areas, eruptions may occur as a line of vents along a fissure.

Flyway

A route regularly taken by birds when they migrate.

Food chain

A system in which one organism forms food for another, which in turn is eaten by another, and so on.

Forage

To search for and eat food.

Fossil

A remnant, impression, or trace of a plant or animal from a past geological age, usually found in rock.

Fry

Young or small fish.

Functionally extinct

Not completely extinct, but reduced to a point where extinction is inevitable.

Fungi

Lifeforms, such as mushrooms, molds, mildews, and yeasts, that contain no chlorophyll and that live parasitically on living and dead organisms.

Gastroliths

Stones swallowed by such animals as crocodilians, that stay in the stomach to help crush food.

Gelatinous

Viscous in texture, similar to the texture of jelly or gelatin.

Genera

The plural of "genus," which is the second lowest group in the scientific classification of living things.

Genetic material

The substance that stores the genetic information of a lifeform. The genetic material of almost all lifeforms is deoxyribonucleic acid (DNA).

Gestation period

The period of time during which a female animal is pregnant with her young.

Gills

Organs that collect oxygen from water and are used for breathing.

Gizzard

In birds, the equivalent of the stomach in mammals. Grit and stones inside the gizzard help to grind up food.

Glacial relics

Fossil remains of plants and animals that were originally preserved in glaciers or other bodies of ice.

Global warming

The increase in the temperature of Earth and its lower atmosphere due to human activity such as deforestation, land degradation, and the burning of fossil fuels. Global warming is also known as "the greenhouse effect."

Gullet

Found in birds, the gullet is the equivalent of the esophagus in mammals. This tube passes food from the bill to the gizzard.

Gyre

A circular motion in a body of water.

Habitat

The area in which an animal naturally lives. Many different kinds of animals live in the same environment, but each kind lives in a different habitat within that environment.

Harem

A group of female animals that mate and live with one male.

Herbivore

An animal that eats only plant material, such as leaves, bark, roots, and seeds; cf carnivore, omnivore.

Hibernate

To remain completely inactive during the cold winter months. Some animals eat as much as they can before winter, then find a sheltered spot and fall into a deep sleep.

Hierarchy

The different levels in the scientific classification of living things. "Phylum," "class," "order," "family," and "genus" are ranks in the zoological hierarchy.

Hybrid

The offspring of parents of two different species.

Hyoid bone

A single U-shaped bone or one of a number of bones at the base of an animal's tongue.

Incisors

The front teeth of an animal, located between the canines, used for cutting food.

Incubate

To keep eggs in an environment, outside the female's body, in which they can develop and hatch.

Insectivore

An animal that eats only or mainly insects or invertebrates. Some insectivores also eat small vertebrates, such as frogs, lizards, and mice.

Intertidal zone

The area of a seashore that is washed by tides. It is covered by water at high tide and exposed to the air at low tide.

Invasive species

Animal or plant species introduced by humans into areas where they do not occur naturally and which threaten species native to that area.

Invertebrate

An animal with no backbone. Many invertebrates are soft-bodied animals, such as worms, leeches, or octopuses, but most have an exoskeleton, or hard external skeleton.

Isthmus

A narrow strip of land, with water on both sides, that joins two larger landmasses.

Keratin

A protein found in horns, hair, scales, and feathers.

Keystone species

Animal or plant species that are so abundant in their environment that they make a strong impact on that environment.

La Niña

Periods of unusually cold ocean temperatures in the equatorial Pacific that occur between El Niño events.

Larva (pl. larvae)

A young animal that looks completely different from its parents. An insect larva, sometimes called a grub, maggot, or caterpillar, changes into an adult by either complete or incomplete metamorphosis.

Mammal

A warm-blooded vertebrate that suckles its young with milk and has a single bone in its lower jaw. Although most mammals have hair and give birth to live young, some, such as whales and dolphins, have little or no hair; others, the monotremes, lay eggs.

Mandible

Biting jaw of an insect.

Mangroves

Flowering shrubs and trees tolerant of saltwater, found on low-lying tropical coasts and estuaries.

Marsupial
A mammal that gives birth to young that are not fully developed. These young are usually protected in a pouch (where they feed on milk) before they can move around independently.

Mass extinction
The simultaneous extinction of an entire species or of a number of species, often as the result of a catastrophic event.

Microbial fermentation
The decomposition of foodstuffs, especially carbohydrates, by the action of microbes in an animal's large intestine.

Microhabitat
A very limited, isolated environment—such as a tree stump—in which an organism lives.

Microorganisms
Tiny lifeforms, such as bacteria, that can be seen only with a microscope.

Migration
A usually seasonal journey from one habitat to another. Many animals migrate vast distances to another location to find food, or to mate and lay eggs or give birth.

Mollusk
An animal, such as a snail or squid, with no backbone and a soft body that is often partly or fully enclosed by a shell.

Molt
To shed an outer layer of the body, such as hair, skin, scales, feathers, or the exoskeleton.

Monoculture
The use of agricultural or forest land for the cultivation of a single crop or organism.

Monotreme
A primitive mammal with many features in common with reptiles. Monotremes lay eggs and have a cloaca.

Montane forest
A forest that grows on the middle slopes of a mountain. Montane forests typically grow below higher coniferous forests.

Musth
In elephants, a time of high testosterone levels when the musth gland between the eye and ear secretes fluid.

Mutualism
An alliance between two species that is beneficial to both.

Mycorrhiza
A fungus that has a symbiotic association with the roots of a plant.

Natal burrow
The underground place where a burrowing animal gives birth to its young.

Natural selection
The process by which organisms adapt to their environment by reproducing in ways most favorable to their survival.

Nekton
Animals that swim freely in the sea and are not dependent on the action of waves or currents.

Niche
The ecological role played by a species within an animal community.

Nocturnal
Active at night. Nocturnal animals have special adaptations, such as large, sensitive eyes or ears, to help them find their way in the dark.

Omnivore
An animal that eats both plant and animal food. Omnivores have teeth and a digestive system designed to process almost any kind of food.

Opportunistic
Feeding on whatever food is available, rather than on a specific diet.

Opposable
Describing a thumb that can reach around and touch all of the other fingers on the same hand, or a toe that can similarly touch all of the other toes on the same foot.

Order
A major group used in taxonomic classification. An order forms part of a class, and is further divided into one or more families.

Organism
Any form of animal or plant life. An organism consists of separate parts that work together to support its existence.

Oviparous
Reproducing by laying eggs. Little or no development occurs within the mother's body; instead, the embryos develop inside the egg; cf ovoviviparous, viviparous.

Ovipositor
A tubelike organ through which female insects lay their eggs. The stinger of bees and wasps is a modified ovipositor.

Ovoviviparous
Reproducing by giving birth to live young that have developed from eggs within the mother's body. The eggs may hatch as they are laid or soon after; cf oviparous, viviparous.

Pair bond
A partnership maintained between a male and a female animal, particularly birds, through one or several breeding attempts. Some species maintain a pair bond for life.

Pampas
Extensive grassy plains in South America, east of the Andes.

Parallel evolution
The situation in which related groups living in isolation develop similar structures to cope with similar evolutionary pressures.

Parr
A young salmon that is able to feed independently in freshwater streams.

Passerine
Any species of bird belonging to the order Passeriformes. A passerine is often described as a songbird or a perching bird.

Patagium
A fold of skin between the forelimbs and hindlimbs of a gliding mammal or reptile, or a fold of skin on the front edge of a bird's wing.

Pelagic
Swimming freely in the open ocean; not associated with the bottom; cf benthic.

Pelvic fins
Paired fins, located on the lower part of a fish's body.

Permafrost
Ground that has remained frozen for at least two successive winters and the intervening summer.

Pheromone
A chemical released by an animal that sends a signal and affects the behavior of others of the same species.

Placental mammal
A mammal that nourishes its developing young inside its body with a blood-rich organ called a placenta.

Plankton
The plant (phytoplankton) or animal (zooplankton) organisms that float or drift in the open sea. Plankton forms an important link in the food chain.

Pleistocene
A geological epoch between about 1.8 million and 10,000 years ago, during which ice sheets advanced across northern Europe and North America. Modern humans appeared during the Pleistocene epoch.

Pneumatophores
Roots in certain marsh and swamp plants that act as respiratory organs.

Pollen
A dustlike substance produced by male flowers, or by the male organs in a flower, and used in the plant's reproduction.

Prairie
An extensive plain or undulating tract of land, covered mainly by grass, which in its natural state has deep, fertile soil.

Predator
An animal that lives mainly by killing and eating other animals.

Prehensile
Grasping or gripping. Some tree-dwelling mammals and reptiles have prehensile feet or a tail that can be used as an extra limb to help them stay safely in a tree. Elephants have a prehensile "finger" on the end of their trunk. Browsers, such as giraffes, have prehensile lips to help them grip leaves.

Prey
Animals that are hunted, killed, and eaten by other animals.

Pride
A group of lions.

Primate
A member of the mammalian order Primates. This order includes humans, apes, and lemurs.

Proboscis
In insects, a long, tubular mouthpart used for feeding. In some mammals, a proboscis is an elongated nose, snout, or trunk.

Progeny
The offspring or descendants of animals or plants.

Prokaryote
An organism, usually single-celled, in which the cell has no nucleus or membrane-bound organelles. Bacteria are prokaryotes.

Pupa (pl. pupae)
The stage during which an insect transforms from a larva to an adult.

Radiation
Energy radiated from a source as wavelengths or particles.

Rain forest
A tropical forest that receives at least 100 inches (250 cm) of rain each year. Rain forests are home to a vast number of plant and animal species.

Range
The entire geographic area across which a species is regularly found.

Raptor
A diurnal bird of prey, such as a hawk or falcon. The term is not used to describe owls.

Ratites
Flightless birds, such as emus, ostriches, cassowaries, and rheas, that lack a keel on their breastbone.

Receptors
Nerve endings through which animals receive sensory stimuli.

Red List of Threatened Species
A list of endangered animal and plant species compiled regularly by the International Union for the Conservation of Nature and Natural Resources (IUCN), which was established in 1963.

Reintroduction
The release into an area of a species that previously had lived there, but had disappeared from it.

Remnant population
A small number of surviving plants or animals in an area where they were previously abundant.

Reptile
One of about 6,000 species of animals that breathe air, are cold-blooded and have scaly bodies.

Rodent
A member of the order Rodentia. Rodents, which include mice, rats, squirrels, and beavers, are relatively small gnawing mammals.

Rudimentary
Describes a simple, undeveloped, or underdeveloped part of an animal, such as an organ or wing.

Ruminants
Hoofed animals—cattle, buffalo, bison, antelopes, gazelles, sheep, goats, and other members of the family Bovidae—with a four-chambered stomach.

Salt marsh
An area of soft, wet land periodically covered by saltwater, in temperate zones and generally treeless.

Scavenger
An animal that eats carrion—often the remains of animals killed by predators.

Seagrass
Long-leaved, grasslike marine plants that grow in coastal waters in temperate climates.

Sea ice
Ocean water that has frozen and formed ice. This occurs at temperatures of about 28.8ºF (-1.8ºC).

Seamount
An isolated submarine hill or mountain, usually of volcanic origin.

Siphonophore
One of various kinds of pelagic floating or free-swimming bell-like or disklike gelatinous invertebrates.

Smolt
A young salmon or sea trout that is ready to migrate from a freshwater stream to the sea.

Speciation
The formation of a new species by means of evolution.

Species
A group of animals with similar features that are able to breed together and produce fertile young.

Spermatophore
A container or package of sperm that is passed from male to female during mating.

Sphagnum bogs
Damp, spongy areas where decomposing mossy sphagnum plants combine with other plant materials to form deep layers of peat.

Stridulate
To make a sound by scraping objects together. Many insects communicate in this way, some by scraping their legs against their body.

Subtropical
The region that lies approximately between latitudes 35° and 40° in both hemispheres.

Symbiosis
An alliance between two species that is usually (but not always) beneficial to both.

Taxonomy
The system of classifying living things into various groups and subgroups according to similarities in features and adaptations.

Temperate
Describes an environment or region that has a warm (but not very hot) summer and a cool (but not very cold) winter. Most of the world's temperate regions are located between the tropics and the polar regions.

Terrestrial
Living all or most of the time on land; cf aquatic.

Territory
An area of land inhabited by an animal and defended against intruders. The area often contains all the living resources required by the animal, such as food and a nesting or roosting site.

Tertiary
A geological period that lasted from approximately 65.5 million years to 2.6 million years ago.

Thermal
A column of rising air, used by birds to gain height, and on which some birds soar to save energy.

Thermoregulation
The capacity of an organism to keep its temperature within a certain range.

Toothed whale
A whale that has slicing teeth and a throat that is able to swallow large pieces of prey.

Torpor
A sleeplike state in which bodily processes are greatly slowed.

Tropical forests
Forests growing in tropical regions that experience little difference in temperature throughout the year.

Tundra
A cold, barren area where much of the soil is frozen and the vegetation consists mainly of mosses, lichens, and other small plants adapted to withstand intense cold.

Turgid
Swollen or distended. The fluid content of a plant cell maintains the cell's level of turgor or turgidity.

Understory
The forest trees that form a canopy below the main canopy.

Vascular plant
A plant that has an internal system of cells that transport water, sugars, and other substances throughout the plant body.

Venom
Poison injected by animals into a predator or prey through fangs, stingers, spines, or similar structures.

Vertebrate
An animal with a backbone. All vertebrates have an internal skeleton of cartilage or bone.

Viviparous
Reproducing by means of young that develop inside the mother's body and are born live. Most mammals and some fish (such as sharks) are viviparous.

Vocalization
Vocal sounds, such as the howling of wolves, that animals use for communication.

Wadi
The Arabic name for a river channel in a desert. It is usually dry, but carries water occasionally.

Water column
The conceptual model of a body of water from the surface to the bottom.

Wetlands
Land that is covered for a part of the year with fresh or salt water. It has vegetation adapted to life in saturated soils.

INDEX

Page numbers in *italics* refer to illustrations and photographs. Numbers and letters in square brackets refer to page number and column location in the Animal Factfile.